The Poetry of Michelangelo

The Poetry of Michelangelo

An Annotated Translation by James M. Saslow

Yale University Press
New Haven and London

Published with assistance from the foundation
established in memory of Philip Hamilton
McMillan of the Class of 1894, Yale College.

Designed by Richard Hendel.
Set in Aldus type by
Keystone Typesetting Inc., Orwigsburg,
Pennsylvania.
Printed in the United States of America by
Vail-Ballou Press, Binghamton, New York.

Frontispiece:
Giovanmaria Butteri, Michelangelo
surrounded by Muses and crowned by Apollo.
Pen drawing, 1564.

10 9 8 7 6 5 4 3 2

The paper in this book meets the guidelines
for permanence and durability of the
Committee on Production Guidelines for Book
Longevity of the Council on Library
Resources.

**Library of Congress Cataloging-in-
Publication Data**

Michelangelo Buonarroti, 1475–1564.
  [Poems. English]
  The poetry of Michelangelo : an annotated
translation / James M. Saslow.
     p.   cm.
     Includes bibliographical references and
index.
  ISBN 0-300-04960-9 (cloth)
        0-300-05509-9 (pbk.)
  I. Saslow, James M.   II. Title.
PQ4615.B6A265   1991
851'.4—dc20   90-48480
                                        CIP

A catalogue record for this book is available
from the British Library.

FOR STEVE

I' mi son caro assai più ch'i' non soglio;

poi ch'i' t'ebbi nel cor più di me vaglio

Contents

List of Illustrations

Acknowledgments

This book would not have come into being without the help and encouragement of numerous individuals and institutions. In particular I wish to thank Gladys Topkis, who first suggested the project and shepherded it patiently through a lengthy and eventful gestation. A Faculty-in-Residence Award from Queens College, City University of New York, provided crucial assistance in completing the project.

I owe a great debt to my principal advisors, Professors John Ahern, Richard Howard, and William Wallace. Each contributed enthusiasm, astute comments, and helpful leads at every stage. I also appreciate the assistance and interest of Professors James Beck and David Rosand, and I wish to thank the students in my graduate courses on Michelangelo at Columbia University and Queens College, particularly Mary Vaccaro, for allowing me to try out my ideas on them and for responding with insights that enriched my own understanding.

I am grateful to Professor Joanne Glasgow of Bergen Community College for inviting me to present some preliminary findings at the University of Southern California and to the editors of *Genders* for publishing an expanded version of those remarks. I profited greatly during the time I was writing this book from the opportunity to work on a related project with Professor Martin Duberman of Lehman College, City University of New York. Among the other scholars who brought useful materials to my attention, I am thankful to Susan Zimmerman of Queens College and Gregory Lucente of the University of Michigan.

In Florence, the director of the Casa Buonarroti, Dottoressa Pina Ragionieri, and Dottoressa Morandini and the staff of the Biblioteca Laurenziana were most helpful in my efforts to inspect Michelangelo's autographs. I also thank Dr. Gino Corti for his cheerful help with problems of sixteenth-century paleography and orthography.

The publishing firm of Giuseppe Laterza e Figli graciously permitted the use of Enzo Noè Girardi's definitive Italian corpus of Michelangelo's *Rime* as the basis for the present bilingual edition.

Finally, I wish to thank my niece, Zoe Rockwood Saslow, who was born at the same time as the idea for this book. Her affection and companionship have been a delightful tonic for one who, in Plato's words, is "better equipped for offspring of the soul than for those of the body."

The Poetry of Michelangelo

1   *Introduction*

Although he was far better known as one of the most productive and influential visual artists of the Italian Renaissance, the Florentine painter, sculptor, and architect Michelangelo Buonarroti (1475–1564) also composed more than three hundred sonnets, madrigals, and other poems over the course of his long and eventful career. These verses, which treat of both grand, universal themes—love and longing, time and death, art and salvation—and very personal and particular motives (the discomfort of painting the Sistine Chapel ceiling, the physical tribulations of old age, gratitude for various gifts) were taken seriously by Michelangelo. He revised some of them six times or more, sought critical advice from learned literati of his day, and in his late sixties and early seventies, nearly completed a project to publish some 105 of them.

Although Michelangelo abandoned this scheme at the death of his principal adviser, Luigi del Riccio, his literary efforts had by that time become well known through circulation among his friends and professional acquaintances, and were highly regarded. As early as 1518 one of them (no. 12) was set to music and published by the Veronese composer Bartolommeo Tromboncino, and in 1547 Michelangelo reached the pinnacle of literary recognition during his own lifetime when Benedetto Varchi, a noted Florentine humanist, delivered two public lectures in Florence, the so-called *Lezzioni*, on artistic theory, using Michelangelo's poetic works as his highly praised examples; the lectures were published in 1550.

Michelangelo's poetic oeuvre forms one part of a corpus of biographical and autobiographical documentation that is the most extensive and revealing of any artist up to that time. His poems are among the earliest literary creations by any major visual artist, and certainly the first of such size and scope. They are matched in breadth by the more than five hundred letters by Michelangelo that survive, which chronicle his adult life in virtually month-to-month detail. Because of his great fame and "divine" reputation, his pronouncements on art and other topics were written down by (among others) his learned friend Donato Giannotti and the visiting Portuguese painter Francisco de Hollanda. The pioneering painter-art historian Giorgio Vasari culminated his extensive *Lives of the Artists* with a lengthy account of the master's life, many of whose rich details came from his long friendship with Michelangelo. Somewhat dissatisfied with the first edition of Vasari in 1550 (see no. 277), Michelangelo commissioned his disciple Ascanio Condivi to prepare a biography, published in 1553, which was all but dictated by the artist. Together, these testimonies form a unique and invaluable resource for understanding the artist's inner and outer life and the relation between them.

The poems have long proved useful to scholars, students, and interested general readers in various disciplines, including the history of art, Italian language and culture, Renaissance history and philosophy, and psychology. Art historians have mined the poems for references or significant parallels to the artist's visual creations (Panofsky, de Tolnay, Hibbard) and for statements, both explicit and symbolic, of his theory of artistic form and his views on the creative process and on the nature and value of art (de Tolnay, Summers). Psychologists and psychoanalysts have found the extensive record of Michelangelo's external life and internal emotional responses to be fertile ground for studying the creative mind and the more general workings of the unconscious (Freud, Eissler, Liebert, Leites, Oremland, Steinberg). And as a participant-observer in the cultural and political ferment of Renaissance Florence and Rome, Michelangelo periodically commented on current events, issues, and personalities of interest to historians and social scientists, from Pope Julius II to Florentine politics and the Counter-Reformation.

Notwithstanding the diverse constituencies that have found extraliterary value in the verses, in purely poetic terms the history of Michelangelo criticism has been divided over the evaluation of his poetry. The fundamental critical issues are quality and autonomy. Simply put, is the poetry on a par with Michelangelo's visual art, valuable in its own right in quality and the artist's commitment, or is it rather of interest as the virtually unmediated personal confession of an amateur who is worth our attention primarily because of his other achievements?

In exploring these issues, a survey of historical opinion is useful. Subsequent to the statements made about him by the contemporaries already mentioned, the *fortuna critica* of Michelangelo's poetry begins with his grandnephew Michelangelo the Younger, who published a first, expurgated edition of the *Rime* in 1623. The younger Buonarroti implicitly criticized his uncle in matters of both form and content by emending, sometimes extensively, what appeared to his orthodox academic taste as defects of style and by altering numerous phrases and pronouns, even whole lines, to make the poems' content conform more closely to stringent Counter-Reformation values regarding faith and passion. For him, as for many later editors troubled by the master's unorthodox emotions, the personal element of the work was something to be downplayed: when he could not eliminate embarrassing references altogether, he appended prose paraphrases that allegorized them beyond recognition.

Critical opinion through the nineteenth and early twentieth centuries tended to follow the younger Buonarroti's lead with regard to style, conceding that the verses were often awkward or obscure, although some critics admired the poetry for its intensity of personal revelation (for example, Foscolo, Croce, Clements; for a useful summary see Lucente 1983).

More recently, Enzo Girardi (editor of the standard Italian edition of the *Rime*), Walter Binni, and the poet Eugenio Montale have challenged the assessment of Michelangelo as an occasionally inspired amateur, claiming that the extensive evidence of his poems and even his letters demonstrates, in Girardi's phrase, "an authentic vocation as a writer" (1974, 3–5, 53–54). The most recent and enthusiastic reassessment is that of Glauco Cambon, whose detailed analysis of the many drafts of individual poems is intended to show the degree to which Michelangelo's unique, "rocky" literary voice was a product of serious effort and thoughtful choices.

In attempting to resolve the issues of the poetry's autonomy and quality, it is important to consider Michelangelo's own opinion of both his writing and its relation to his other work. Condivi, whose *Life* so often transcribes the artist's own opinions, frankly acknowledged that "Michelangelo has applied himself to poetry more for his own pleasure than as a profession and he has always belittled himself and asserted his ignorance in these matters" (103–5). Other examples of this self-deprecation abound in the poems themselves, especially in the postscripts and notes accompanying the forty-eight epitaphs for Cecchino Bracci (nos. 179–228) and his comment on no. 91 as "old things [fit] for the fire, not for witnesses." Also, in letters to Vasari of 1554 and 1555, Michelangelo called two enclosed sonnets "silly things" (Ramsden, no. 399) and joked that he was writing sonnets only because he was old and "many people say that I am in my second childhood" (Ramsden, no. 390); on another occasion he commented bluntly to del Riccio, "I can't write" (no. 157). Vasari himself recorded a similar comment, made in a letter from 1557, to the effect that "as writing is not my profession I find it very irksome" (Vasari: Milanesi, 7:239, trans. Bull, 401; *Carteggio*, no. MCCLVII; Ramsden, no. 434. Compare poems no. 85:48 and 267:46).

Such disclaimers should not, however, simply be taken at face value. If Michelangelo derided his literary skills, he also denigrated his abilities in painting, as in his early sonnet (no. 5) complaining about his work in the Sistine Chapel, with scant fidelity to his actual achievement: "I'm no painter." And we know from Condivi that in the period when Michelangelo developed his interest in creative literature, roughly 1504–5, he began his literary avocation with an extended period of exclusive and thorough preparation: "He remained for some time doing almost nothing in these [visual] arts, dedicating himself to the reading of poets and vernacular orators and to writing sonnets for his own pleasure" (28). Cambon's exhaustive analysis of the draft poems has gone further than any previous study toward demonstrating just how painstakingly Michelangelo reworked many of his compositions, suggesting that his complaints about lack of skill express the artist's typical frustration at being unable to make his finished product match his mental conception. In his final paragraph, Condivi mentions that he has been collecting Michelangelo's poems for publication, apparently in an effort to take up the aborted project of 1542–46, which suggests that however often he may have belittled his poetic work, Michelangelo continued to value it and still wanted it preserved and set before the public. Thus, although some measure of the praise Michelangelo received from Vasari, Varchi, and other contemporaries can be attributed to the enthusiasm of friends, there now seems little doubt that he took his poetic avocation seriously, however difficult and frustrating he found it.

All the same, this fact should not obscure a salient element of his literary endeavor that bears on the question of quality: from the outset Michelangelo was admired less for his style than for his ideas. Robert Clements began his magisterial and still largely definitive study of the poetry with the comment of Michelangelo's friend and fellow poet Francesco Berni (whose influence is apparent in Michelangelo's occasional comic verses) that "he says things, while you [orthodox Petrarchists] say words" (see no. 85). This perceptive comment is still a good starting point for evaluating Michelangelo's goals and interests as a writer.

Despite his best efforts, Michelangelo was not a polished stylist, nor indeed was he particularly interested in sophisticated matters of poetic form. His interest was first and foremost in self-expression, in itself a sign of the new, individualistic consciousness of the Renaissance era, which Michelangelo exemplified and promoted and which in turn made it possible for him to be a protomodern celebrity during his lifetime. As early as the time of his comment comparing himself to the marble David then in progress (A3, 1501–2), he projected himself into everything he did, and the poetry not only acknowledges but celebrates the subjectivity of his response to external experience. Of the inspiration lying within Cavalieri's breast, he admits that "I only draw out of it what's suitable and similar to me" (no. 84). His theoretical statements leave no doubt that all of Michelangelo's art, whether written or visual, is in some sense a self-portrait. In painting a woman, he explains (no. 173), "one portrays himself," and similarly with sculpture, "one will . . . make the image of someone else look like himself" (no. 242). This tendency to introject personal responses to outside stimuli parallels his frequent inclusion of self-images in his visual portrayals of standard subjects, such as those portraits of himself as Saint Bartholomew in the *Last Judgment* and as Nicodemus in the Florence *Pietà*.

The sometimes striking parallels between Michelangelo's visual and literary imagery and the reflection in both of the dynamics of his own psychic biography were unprecedented in modern Western culture. As the first artist to leave a large body of work in both verbal and visual media, he was consequently the first to leave both a "public" set of images and the data to illuminate the intersection between the public and interior realms. (Only Leonardo da Vinci before him left more private writings, but his thousands of notebook sheets are distinguished by their almost complete lack of personal emotion or revealing anecdote.) Ironically, although the accessibility of Michelangelo's interior life in his art is a prime reason for the scholarly and popular fascination with him, that very accessibility has contributed to the suspicion in some quarters that his poetry is therefore somehow inferior. Formalist criticism, which would banish consideration of the artist's personal associations with his subject as irrelevant to the public meaning of the work, has tended to downgrade Michelangelo's writing insofar as it cannot be understood apart from the rest of his life. More recent structuralist and poststructuralist criticism has made it difficult to sustain a rigid dichotomy between the private and public readings of a work of art, holding that any work of art demands, supports, and is indeed constituted by a multiplicity of readings. Thus the reader can accept, even celebrate, the personal component of the poetry without judging it less "autonomous" than some theoretical standard would hold.

Although it may seem like academic fence straddling, I propose that a balanced appreciation of Michelangelo's poetry could assert claims for both aesthetic autonomy and deep personal significance, though with important qualifications to each claim. In the last quarter century, Michelangelo criticism has established a convincing position that the poetry's deviations from the polished "high style" of the period reflect less the defects of a casual "Sunday" writer than a deliberate attempt to find a distinctive if idiosyncratic voice. Even the most enthusiastic revisionists, however, have acknowledged that this attempt was not uniformly successful and occasionally failed outright. In terms of content, Michelangelo tried to put into words some feelings that were then novel and even controversial, especially regarding religious doctrine and gender (see section 4). But to rank Michelangelo's personal expression as equal in importance to his limited technical sophistication is not to claim that his ideas and emotions were always carefully considered or especially compelling.

He was not a philosopher, and many of his pronouncements on love and spirituality, though heartfelt, were conventional among educated literati. But precisely because his ideas were very much of his time, his poetry has the virtue of telling more about how, for example, the philosopher Marsilio Ficino's Neoplatonic teachings were actually felt and lived than Ficino himself—who wrote primarily in the third person—ever did. Likewise, although Michelangelo's style is often exasperatingly obscure, grammatically tortuous, or unpolished (see section 4), he did contribute, at his best, significant new elements to Cinquecento literature: an openness and complexity of form that are often praised for embodying the aesthetic principles of contemporary mannerism as well as an intensity and directness of emotional expression that prefigure the baroque.

Although Michelangelo's poems are inspired by deeply personal experience, they are not mere transcriptions of experience; the relation between his life and art, while profound, is rarely direct or simple. The goal of the present translation is to provide for those who wish to explore that relationship three elements necessary to such an understanding: a clear and faithful rendering of Michelangelo's words; factual information (such as dates, recipients, and circumstances of composition); and textual commentary (including an explanation of private or learned references and sources in, or parallels with, other poems and visual creations).

Michelangelo's life and works, the poetry included, have been studied in exhaustive detail. It is my purpose here simply to provide a broad general introduction to Michelangelo's life and the functions that poetry served in it; to his principal themes and underlying ideas and concerns; to his stylistic traits and peculiarities—especially as they affect translation; and to the historiography of scholarship and criticism devoted to Michelangelo's poetic output. This overview will help situate the poems in their biographical, social, intellectual, and artistic contexts and will offer sufficient background for full appreciation and further study. Not every poem relevant to a particular point could be cited here; further examples of specific matters of iconography, style, and symbolism are noted in the annotations to individual poems.

Michelangelo's long and eventful <u>life began on 6 March 1475</u> in <u>Caprese, a small Tuscan town near Arezzo</u>, where his father was serving a temporary term as *podestà*, or visiting magistrate. This seems to have been one of the few responsible jobs held by Lodovico di Buonarrota Simone, descendant of an old Florentine family whose economic and social fortunes had declined. <u>His successful son later begrudgingly assisted him until the father's death, near age ninety, in 1531</u>. Of <u>Michelangelo's mother, Francesca</u>, we know little except that she bore four other sons; put her second infant, Michelangelo, out to wet nurse with the family of a stonemason in Settignano, just outside Florence; and <u>died when he was six</u>.

Both the amply documented father and the shadowy mother have served psychological critics to explain, whether in psychoanalytic or metaphoric terms, the fundamental character traits and tendencies in their stormy and conflicted son. Both Michelangelo's lifelong desire for, and dependence on, the emotional support of idealized, authoritative male patrons and friends as well as his frequent quarrels with those very men have been traced to the conflict and disapproval he experienced in his father, toward whom he maintained a lifelong ambivalence. The early deprivation of a maternal presence foreshadowed his lifelong sense of deprivation and scarcity in everything from family income to divine grace. We cannot know, of course, whether Michelangelo would agree with the detailed internal dynamics ascribed to him in his absence by psychoanalytic scholars; but it may be said in defense of their efforts that the artist himself did acknowledge the crucial role of childhood influences, however jocularly, when he said to Vasari of his wet nurse that "I sucked in with my mother's milk the chisels and hammer with which I make my figures" (Vasari: Milanesi, 7:137).

After some traditional elementary education, at the age of thirteen Michelangelo was apprenticed to Domenico Ghirlandaio, a leading painter in Florence; in his three years in that shop he would have learned the rudiments of fresco and panel painting. At age fifteen he terminated his brief apprenticeship, having come to the attention of Lorenzo de' Medici, the de facto leader of the city, known as "The Magnificent" for his patronage of literature, philosophy, art, and architecture. Lorenzo supported Michelangelo in his household and aided his education for two years until the Magnifico's untimely death in 1492 at age forty-three.

Condivi and Vasari record the artist's pride at being singled out for special treatment by the appreciative Lorenzo, in whose household the youth was exposed to the highest levels of Neoplatonic humanist culture. His beliefs and works show the influence of such major literary and artistic figures supported by the Medici as the poet and translator Angelo Poliziano, the philosopher Ficino, the painters Sandro Botticelli and Luca Signorelli, and Lorenzo's architect, Giuliano da Sangallo. Michelangelo's long relationship with the most powerful Florentine family continued under two Medici popes who had been his contemporaries in Lorenzo's home: the Magnifico's son Giovanni (Leo X) and his nephew Giulio (Clement VII).

Two revealing incidents from these student years center on Michelangelo's education in sculpture, probably under Bertoldo di Giovanni, a pupil of Donatello who was then in Lorenzo's household. Michelangelo's first carving was a copy after a head of an aged classical faun in the Medici collection. When Lorenzo saw it, he praised the work but joked that such an old man would not have all his teeth. The mortified student immediately knocked one of them out, a touching sign of both his eagerness to please a paternal figure and his sensitivity to criticism. Another episode reveals the quarrelsome pride that was to remain with the grown Michelangelo as long as the physical marks that resulted from it. His rivalry with a fellow pupil, Pietro Torrigiano, led to a fight in which Torrigiano broke Michelangelo's nose, permanently disfiguring it. Vasari, probably from Michelangelo's account, blames the violence on Torrigiano's jealousy, but Torrigiano's version accuses Michelangelo of picking a fight out of a habit of criticizing or mocking other pupils (Vasari: Milanesi, 7:144–45; Cellini, 31).

During these same years, Michelangelo was also exposed to the profound religious influence of the Dominican friar Girolamo Savonarola, who resumed his popular preaching in Florence in 1490 and, taking advantage of unrest and political confusion at the time of the French invasion of Italy in 1494, made himself <u>head of a religious dictatorship</u> that lasted until the friar's own excommunication and burning in 1498. The aggressive puritanism of this regime contrasted starkly with the carefree pagan antiquarianism of the Medicean Neoplatonists. Although Michelangelo had already left for his first sojourn in Rome (1496–1501) by the time Savonarola instigated the Bonfires of the Vanities in 1497 (in which citizens and artists brought lascivious and sinful books, jewelry, clothing, and art works to the Piazza della Signoria to be publicly destroyed), <u>he told Condivi more than fifty years later that he could still remember the friar's voice</u> (Condivi, 105).

For the rest of his life Michelangelo was to play out, in his art, poetry, and personal relationships, <u>the central spiritual-aesthetic conflict of his age symbolized by the successive Florentine regimes of his youth: a struggle between the ascetic, puritanical strain of his Christian culture and the more earthly, sensual ideals of classical pastorale and myth.</u> If the turmoil in Western values brought on by the rediscovery of a radically alternative yet highly revered past culture created <u>the energizing tension of the age, it provoked in this one highly susceptible individual not merely tension but agonizing conflict.</u> He was both a passionate Christian and a passionate pagan, and as the dissonance between these systems grew too loud to be silenced, <u>it was the "voice" of Savonarola—</u> heard occasionally in such earlier poems as the macabre "Whoever's born must come to death" (no. 21)—<u>that came increasingly to the fore in Michelangelo's poetry.</u>

After a brief sojourn in Bologna, where he fled after the fall of the Medici, Michelangelo moved to Rome in 1496, and during his five years there, established a reputation as the most talented sculptural prodigy of the time with such marbles as the drunken Bacchus and the renowned *Pietà* for the basilica of Saint Peter's. The Vatican *Pietà* was the only sculpture Michelangelo ever signed, and <u>the circumstances of his signature</u>—which he added to the already installed group after he overheard visitors ascribe it to another artist—<u>indicate a strong sense of identification with his work</u> (Vasari: Milanesi, 7:152). He returned to Florence in 1501 to take up a prestigious public commission, the colossal *David* placed at the door of the city hall, the Palazzo Vecchio, three years later (at which time he also received a commission for a fresco inside the building). Here again the artist seems to have felt a deeply personal identification with the work and its subject. One of his earliest poetic fragments (A3), dating from this time, reads, "<u>David with his sling and I with my bow.</u>" While the precise meaning of this parallel is open to interpretation, <u>clearly Michelangelo projected a psychological connection between himself and the biblical hero</u> (Seymour).

The first evidence for Michelangelo's interest in poetry is the series of fragments (A1–A5) written about 1501–2, when he was beginning work on the David; two are simply single lines copied from Petrarch, who along with Dante was to be Michelangelo's most important source of poetic inspiration. He often jotted such brief notes, as well as more extensive ideas for his own poems, on the same sheets of paper he used for his numerous drawings. While it has traditionally been assumed that this practice largely reflected an urge to economize on costly materials, it increased in later life (especially after no. 260), when Michelangelo had less need to save money, suggesting that the connections between adjacent visual and verbal expressions are worth further investigation. (Whenever poetic drafts are on identifiable drawings, I have noted the visual subject and referred the reader to the most recent complete catalogue of Michelangelo drawings by de Tolnay; see Concordance, 537.)

Since Condivi places Michelangelo's preparation for literary pursuits after completion of the David, it seems that he did not try writing seriously until about 1503–4, when he was already twenty-eight years old. Only a handful of his efforts survive from before 1515, when he was already forty. Such a delay in discovering or acting upon an interest in verbal expression is understandable: he had not been raised to a literary vocation and was insecure throughout his life about his limited formal education (see section 4).

Michelangelo's poetic creativity can be divided into three rough chronological phases by both the relative amount of work he produced and by shifts in theme and emphasis. To base any periodization on a numerical survey alone would require caution, for two reasons. First, it is not known how many poems have been lost or what he might have suppressed of his juvenilia or even of his later poems. Vasari tells us that Michelangelo destroyed a quantity of his drawings late in life, some of which doubtless bore written evidence. And even of those that have survived, many cannot be dated with precision. However, the borders of these periods also correspond to major events or turning points in Michelangelo's personal life and artistic career, which, if not precisely reflected in the changing quantity of his poetic output, certainly parallel and help to explain his shifting subjects and concerns.

The first period runs approximately from 1503 to 1532 and can be subdivided into two phases. From the first twenty years of poetic activity, 1503–23, only some twenty poems survive, or an average of about one a year. The subjects in this first phase range from personal chronicles and reactions to current events (nos. 5, 10) to exercises in standard Petrarchan themes of love for an idealized courtly lady—occasionally rhapsodizing over her physical charms (nos. 4, 9,

12)—to the mock-rustic no. 20, which shows Michelangelo's intermittent streak of humor.

During this period Michelangelo solidified his already established reputation, becoming the best-known and most widely admired artist in central Italy (at least after the death of his principal rival, Raphael, in 1520). He was summoned back to Rome in 1505 to work for Pope Julius II (1503–13), whose extensive program of patronage was aimed at asserting and celebrating the papacy's renewed dominance in Italian politics. (A lost bronze portrait statue of Julius was one of Michelangelo's few sculptural works *not* carved in stone.) Julius, the first of several powerful popes responsible for Michelangelo's major projects, was more than a match for him in the forceful anger Italians call *terribilità*. The artist's deep emotional investment in yet another of the father figures whom he as often deplored as admired is expressed in no. 6, which complains that "I gave myself to you like rays to the sun; but . . . the more I exert myself, the less you like me."

Julius also brought to Rome from Florence Michelangelo's slightly younger contemporary, the painter Raphael (1483–1520), and began construction of the new church of Saint Peter's, designed by Raphael's compatriot from Urbino, Donato Bramante. Michelangelo's jealous resentment toward the pope's supposed preferment of Raphael and Bramante was to recur throughout his life as a chronic suspicion of the motives and sincerity of others and a readiness to believe in conspiracies against him. It is ironic that although Michelangelo complained that an Urbino cabal was poisoning the pope against him and depriving him of work (no. 6) and railed against the hypocrisy and abuses of the Roman religious community that were soon to attract the ire of Protestant reformers (no. 10), he himself later took over Bramante's vast enterprise for the last seventeen years of his life, turning it into the crowning achievement of his career and an outlet for his final phase of devotion to the Church and its values.

Julius commissioned Michelangelo to carve a huge tomb for him, to be placed in the new Saint Peter's, but then removed him from that barely begun project, to the sculptor's frustration, to have him fresco the ceiling of the Sistine Chapel in the Vatican Palace. Michelangelo came to look upon the protracted saga of the tomb—which underwent several diminutions of scope and intermittent contract disputes before being summarily completed by assistants in the 1540s—as the single greatest tragedy of his career, which may explain why his poetry never dealt with it directly.

The ceiling project occupied the artist from 1508 to 1512; his annoyance and discomfort are chronicled in his crankily amusing *sonetto caudato* or tailed sonnet, no. 5. The ceiling was completed in the same year the Medici regained power in Florence. The following year, Michelangelo's boyhood acquaintance Giovanni de' Medici succeeded Julius as Pope Leo X. Michelangelo returned to Florence at the behest of Leo, who sought to use the resources of the papacy to aggrandize his native city. From this time until the death of Leo's cousin and successor, Clement VII, in 1534, the artist divided his time between Rome and Florence as the exigencies of papal patronage and the shifting political situation demanded.

The major Florentine projects of this period centered on the Medici family parish church of San Lorenzo. From 1516 onward, Michelangelo was commissioned to design a façade for the church (never built) as well as the library and the so-called Medici Chapel, actually the new sacristy, for which he carved the suite of sculptures that includes two early Medici dukes and the four allegorical nudes representing times of day. Many poems from this period are written on sketches for the chapel, and nos. 13 and 14 are related directly to its developing iconography. Fitful progress on the church was interrupted by political events, and the library was completed only in the 1550s, by which time Michelangelo had long since refused to return to Florence under Duke Cosimo de' Medici's domination, and inverting his earlier sculptural celebration of the family, had written no. 247 in the voice of his sleeping statue of Night, who declares that under the current political situation, she would prefer never to awaken.

It is also during this period that the first hints of Michelangelo's romantic interest in other men appear, most specifically in no. 36, a lament for a lost love who is identified as *colui*, "he"; other poems from the years 1522–24 that may refer to this unnamed figure include nos. 18, 22, and 27. It has been surmised by Tolnay and others that Michelangelo was then enamored of a young Florentine named Gherardo Perini, with whom he exchanged letters in 1522 and to whom he gave several drawings (Vasari: Milanesi, 7:276; see nos. 18, 27 nn). Nothing else is known about his feelings for Perini, though it is suggestive that some twenty years later Michelangelo's nemesis, the writer Pietro Aretino, after being refused the gift of a drawing, implied snidely that "only certain Gherardos and Tommasos [Cavalieri] can obtain them" (Aretino, no. CCCLXIV). Whether these poems allude to Perini or someone else, they indicate a subtle but important change in the artist's feelings about love, which seems due in part to a shift from a traditional female to a male object: for the first time Michelangelo links love with a sense of sin and fear of vengeance (nos. 22:50, 32:1–2), concepts more suitable to homosexual passion, which was officially and theologically proscribed (Saslow 1986, chap. 1).

The second phase of Michelangelo's early period of literary creativity runs from 1524 to 1532, when the artist was age forty-nine to fifty-six and engaged for the most part on the San Lorenzo projects, with occasional visits to Rome. This period was marked by enormous political and religious upheaval, whose repercussions were to determine the course of Michelangelo's life both in external conditions and internal conflicts. A cataclysmic breakup of Europe's still-medieval social order and relative uniformity of belief was first signaled by Martin Luther, whose challenge to Catholic orthodoxy in the Ninety-five Theses of 1517 set in motion the Protestant Reformation and a century and a half of struggle for ideological supremacy between traditional Catholicism, various Protestant offshoots, and moderate reformers within the Church. Rival powers centered around the pope and the Holy Roman Emperor Charles V did battle on Italian soil. The brutal Sack of Rome by imperial troops in 1527 was widely felt as a "split of Christendom" with a profoundly distressing impact, especially on artists. As Michelangelo's protégé, the Venetian painter and papal official Sebastiano del Piombo wrote to the sculptor several years later, "I am no longer the same Sebastiano I was before the sack" (*Carteggio*, no. DCCCXI).

Although Michelangelo did not experience the Sack directly, he was actively involved in the siege of Florence in 1529–30, which succeeded in permanently establishing the Medici family as hereditary rulers of an autocratic duchy. He served the last, doomed republic as fortifications director, and although he briefly fled in fear of reprisal, he was soon pardoned and allowed to return to work, somewhat unhappily, at the Medici Chapel. Some critics have interpreted no. 43 as an allegorized reference to events at the time of the siege, although after his early jeremiads against Rome, Michelangelo does not often discuss topical matters in his poems (but see nos. 68, 247).

During this period his surviving output rose to an average of about four poems a year, encompassing nos. 21–55. Most poems from this period are about love and when addressed to an identifiable character, that character is a woman. Michelangelo's themes embrace the delights of love and the manifold ways in which it is kindled and transmitted or the pains and trials of love, sometimes in the same poem. There is no evidence of his emotional involvement with any actual woman during this time, suggesting that the love poems are largely an exercise in standard Petrarchan forms and ideals rather than a product of lived experience.

At the same time, awareness of aging and death makes its first appearances, as in the carnival song (no. 21) and no. 22 on the theme of fading passion, written about 1524 when Michelangelo was forty-nine. He also begins the soon-familiar complaint of his own aging, describing himself as white-haired (no. 23), even though Condivi noted that his hair remained black until the end of his life. This increasing and increasingly tragic sensibility was inspired partly by the inevitable experience in middle age of the deaths of close family members: his brother Buonarroto in 1528 (see nos. 45, 46) and particularly his father in 1531, at which Michelangelo erupted in an outburst of grief and resignation in one of his longest poems, no. 86. (For the possible psychological implications of the death of his father, see Liebert, 177–80; Saslow 1986, 51–59.) The pessimism to which he now gave full literary vent had long been evident to his friends and associates: As early as 1510, Raphael included in his Vatican fresco *The School of Athens* a portrait of his fellow artist as Heraclitus, √ the "gloomy philosopher," in a pose indicating melancholy.

The major period of Michelangelo's literary creativity occupied the years 1532–48. During this time he wrote the bulk of his poems, nos. 56–279, or over two hundred in fifteen years. Even allowing that the largest single group of these poems, fifty short epitaphs for the young Cecchino Bracci, were composed in the single year 1544, Michelangelo's production had roughly quadrupled over the previous decade. Precise dating of these poems, especially of those written between 1536 and 1542, is more difficult than for other periods, largely because of their sheer number; editors can often be no more specific than this general range of dates. After 1542, when he began sending drafts of some of his poems to several learned friends for comment, it is sometimes possible to be more precise, though here too the pieces can usually be dated only between 1542 and 1546, when this exchange stopped. In any case, some of these were originally drafted somewhat earlier than when they were sent.

After 1534 Michelangelo took up permanent residence in Rome, where he could avoid the hated Medici regime. Although Cosimo I frequently entreated him to return to Florence, he never did, and poems 247–50 comment harshly on conditions there. In Rome Michelangelo found important work from his next major papal patron, Paul III (1534–49). He returned to the Sistine Chapel to provide its ultimate fresco, the *Last Judgment* (1534–41). This is perhaps the one work in his artistic career to which a great many of the poems written at that time and later can be meaningfully related, since the great fresco deals with precisely those themes that would preoccupy him henceforth: personal guilt and suffering, salvation and damnation, and the threat of Christ's rejection. Two other frescoes in the Vatican's Pauline Chapel, depicting the Conversion of Paul and the Crucifixion of Peter (1542–50)—the artist's last paintings—also treat themes of miraculous divine intervention and the suffering of the righteous. These resonate with both Michelangelo's own concerns and the rising spirit of Counter-Reformatory zeal, marked by the convening of the Council of Trent in 1545 to devise strategies against Protestant attacks.

During these years he enjoyed the most significant personal relationships of his life, with Tommaso de' Cavalieri and Vittoria Colonna. These two Roman patricians became the inspiration for his most heartfelt and intensely passionate poetry, which celebrated the moral and aesthetic uplift of their friendships and lamented, in Petrarchan fashion, his unrequited love for them. Many poems are addressed directly to them as *Donna* and *Signore*, or else to Amor, the personification of his desire for them both.

Michelangelo formed an excited passion for Tommaso de' Cavalieri (ca. 1509–87) soon after meeting the handsome and accomplished twenty-three-year-old sometime in 1532. He wrote to Cavalieri and sent him a series of highly confessional presentation drawings on Ovidian subjects—among them Ganymede, Tityos, and Phaethon—as well as numerous poems, largely concentrated between nos. 57 and 107. Cavalieri was for him what Ganymede was to Jupiter or Alcibiades to Socrates—younger, beautiful, and a spur to the most intense emotional rapture of his often solitary life. Cavalieri certainly admired the older man and may even have accepted drawing instruction from him; but just as clearly, he did not reciprocate the sculptor's passion in kind (Liebert, 270–311; Saslow 1986, chap. 1; Perrig; Frommel). Cavalieri, who was heterosexual and eventually married (his son was the noted baroque composer Emilio Cavalieri), may even have been alarmed at times by the intensity of Michelangelo's passion (see no. 58). Although their relationship grew more distant after the mid-1540s, he remained a devoted friend until Michelangelo's death thirty years later. In his capacity as one of the municipal *Conservatori*, he helped carry to completion the artist's designs for the Capitoline Hill civic complex, begun in 1538.

The sculptor's outpourings of admiration and desire for Cavalieri (and also, about 1535, for another young man named Febo di Poggio [nos. 99–101]) are couched in a nominally chaste Neoplatonic language and intellectual framework, but his customary use of overlapping language for both spiritual and earthly love leaves some ambiguity as to the nature of that desire. Beginning with the artist's grandnephew, critics uncomfortable with the specter of homosexuality have attempted to deny or minimize this possibility by allegorizing Michelangelo's obvious male references or asserting that his talk of "desire" and "sin" is simply a rhetorical flourish applied to a commonplace spiritual affection, which, as Creighton Gilbert has phrased it, by "rejecting 'the sense'

he only source for these examples, whose manuscript versions were lost or
oyed.

annotti was the author of the so-called *Dialogi*, a transcription of detailed
sophical-literary discussions on the subject of Dante's *Inferno*, which took
between him, Michelangelo, del Riccio, and two other friends in 1546 and
preserve many revealing comments by Michelangelo about his own
nality and ideas. The artist valued this professional author's opinions on
ork, sending him a number of poems and calling him a "mender of badly
things"; no. 159 went back and forth to Giannotti several times for
on (see nos. 135, 136).

gi del Riccio, like Giannotti a member of the *fuorusciti*, or community of
ntine political exiles, increasingly acted as Michelangelo's "agent," look-
ter many practical matters for him. Del Riccio first appears in the poetry
orrespondence in the spring of 1542, when Michelangelo asked him and
otti to revise nos. 130 and 131 (Ramsden, nos. 215, 223, 234). Between
and 1546, the three friends conceived a plan to publish a selection of his
s, and to that end Michelangelo transmitted his drafts to them, sometimes
l times, for corrections and suggestions. Michelangelo's marginal com-
s or attached letters to del Riccio during this process, in which he claims to
ding poems in payment of social obligations, reveal his often whimsical
lf-deprecatory attitude toward his own writing. No. 143, for example,
with the explanation, "For the melons and wine I thank you, and repay
ith a scribble" (see also no. 167). A selection of 105 poems, most dating
532 or later (see no. 62), was eventually agreed upon.

most protracted exchange with del Riccio occupied the whole of 1544. In
ry, Riccio's nephew Cecchino Bracci, of whom he was deeply fond, died
ectedly at age sixteen. The bereaved uncle, seeking a suitable memorial,
Michelangelo to carve a portrait of the youth for his tomb. Apparently
ist, who always resisted portraiture, offered to write fifty poetic remem-
s instead, which he sent in periodic batches accompanied by further
ical or pleading notes. The full Bracci series, consisting of forty-eight
ne epitaphs, one sonnet, and one madrigal, constitutes the only large,
group of poems by Michelangelo (nos. 179–228). Their sheer number
rrow range of mourning subjects led to much repetition and, to judge
he author's notes, periodic tedium and lack of inspiration: "Clumsy
! The spring is dry" (no. 211). Nonetheless, they offer a concentrated
tion on his favorite themes of earthly transience and the preservative
of art.

. . . does not involve homosexuality" (Gilbert, xvi; Ramsden, 2:237, with
earlier references).

This approach to Michelangelo's sexuality does not do justice to either his
intensity or his ambivalence. As other poems and letters make clear, he was
well aware of both historical and contemporary homosexuality, was thought to
be homosexual by others, and was at some pains to deny such rumors and
accusations (nos. 83, 197; Condivi, 105). And, by the terms of the day, he was
probably justified in that denial. There is no evidence of sexual activity on
Michelangelo's part with either men or women, and as long as he refrained
from physical acts he was not, legally or theologically, a sodomite (Saslow 1986,
28–32, 48–51).

Nevertheless, Michelangelo's statements about love and desire leave little
doubt that he conceived of intimate relationships in what would now be consid-
ered fundamentally homosexual terms. Where Renaissance society drew a
sharp divide between chaste feeling and forbidden sexual acts, modern psycho-
sexual theory since Freud grades various degrees of male-male attraction along
a single continuum of homoeroticism from simple affection to genital expres-
sion. What controls psychological definition today is more the object of one's
attraction than the manner in which one expresses that feeling. Thus it is
revealing that Donato Giannotti, in his *Dialogi* (see below), records the master's
calling himself "of all men, the most inclined to love persons," but in the next
phrase Michelangelo adds that whenever he meets someone of great worth "I
am compelled to fall in love with him," pointedly using the masculine pronoun
whereas his first phrase spoke of *persone*, a feminine noun (Giannotti, 68).
Similarly, though in poem no. 276 he declares himself equally susceptible to
love persons "of all ages and all sexes," in no. 260 he bluntly ranks the love of
men above that of women.

Moreover, while evidence for the orientation of desire may prove nothing
about the physical expression of it, the artist's protestations are too much and
his elliptically described but agonizing sense of lustful guilt too pervasive to
suppose that his longings were exclusively for sacred and not profane forms of
love. For him to speak in later life of regretting great "sin" and "wicked,
depraved desires" (nos. 254, 291, 293, 302) suggests that there must have been
some component of physical desire in his earlier loves, since it was physical
lust, not friendship, that was considered sinful.

The crux of Michelangelo's erotic dilemma was that he was both excep-
tionally loving and passionate toward men and exceptionally endowed with
moral scruples, a combination whose unending internal conflict bred a mixture

of touchiness about others' opinions of him and a deepening self-disgust. At that embryonic point in the evolution of modern homosexual awareness, Michelangelo could never have articulated his internal distress as a personal conflict with unjust or limiting external constraints. Nevertheless, interpretation would do well to heed John Addington Symonds's perceptive suggestion that "the tragic accent discernible throughout Michelangelo's love poetry may be due to his sense of discrepancy between his own deepest emotions and the customs of Christian society" (Symonds, 2:385; Saslow 1988).

The most important, indeed virtually the only woman in Michelangelo's adult emotional life was the serious and learned Vittoria Colonna (1490–1547), whom he met some time in 1536 and with whom he maintained a close and adoring friendship until her rather early death at age fifty-seven. Like Cavalieri, she too was a member of an ancient and important Roman family—the line from Petrarch that Michelangelo copied early in life, "Rotta è l'alta colonna" ("Broken is the high column," A4), referred to an ancestor—and the widow of Ferrante Francesco d'Avalos, Marchese of Pescara. After his death she devoted herself largely to spiritual concerns, residing in convents for extended periods between visits to Rome, consorting with the circle of internal Catholic reformists. She composed a great deal of religious verse, some of which she sent to Michelangelo in exchange for his poems; their literary influence on Michelangelo's later work is clear (see section 4; Gibaldi, 22–46; Ramsden, 2:237–43).

Michelangelo was attracted by her intellectual and spiritual sympathy and credited her with the "great favor" of "bringing [him] back from death to life" (no. 160). She was for him both an actual friend with whom he shared his increasing religious piety and a traditional muse who inspired scores of love poems, beginning with no. 111. If Cavalieri was Michelangelo's Ganymede or Alcibiades, Colonna was for him what Beatrice was to Dante or Laura to Petrarch, with the differences that she was alive and in communication with him for more than a decade (albeit often at a distance) and physically unattractive. While she clearly admired him and enjoyed his company, it seems that, like Cavalieri, she played a more central role in his life than he did in hers.

Simultaneously with the many laudatory poems clearly intended for Colonna, Michelangelo addressed many others to a female persona who, though equally desirable by virtue of her beauty and charms, was much less admirable, being disinclined to yield to his desires and thus relieve his suffering (see nos. 112–74 passim.). Because these poems in a "minor key" seem to describe a woman quite unlike Colonna (who was far from conventionally beautiful and

not emotionally distant), critics have long speculated a[bout] another woman in Michelangelo's life at this time. Th[is] independent existence (analogous to Shakespeare's sl[ightly] call her, in a traditional *stil nuovo* formula, the "donna and cruel lady.

Although such scholars as Frey tried ingeniously t[o] her from those for Colonna, her existence seems unlik[e] of any such person or relationship in all of the letters [of] Michelangelo's desire to refute persistent rumors of such proof of normality would certainly have been [of] others, as a defense. It seems most probable rathe[r] reversion to the conventions of the courtly-love tra[dition] replaced Michelangelo's more unorthodox male poem[s to] Cavalieri cooled. It is as if Michelangelo was inspire[d by] Colonna to once again explore the entire gamut of women, as independently of actual experience as he poems before 1530. Thus, just as he praises Colonna' beautiful (except in a spiritual sense), so he also "pay[s]" describing her, or someone based on her, as capabl[e] negative, emotional effects prescribed for the distant though Colonna herself did not, so far as we know, [any] feelings toward him.

Besides Colonna and Cavalieri, Michelangelo fre[quented] circles in Rome, and although he was reclusive whe[n] defensive about his lack of formal classical educati[on] stimulus of conversation and debate with a variety of (Ramsden, no. 70, n. 2; Giannotti, 65; no. 192). Th[e] and literary-artistic acquaintances of this period for [him] the poems include Francisco de Hollanda, a Portug[uese] conversations with Michelangelo and Colonna in Benedetto Varchi, Donato Giannotti, and Luigi del

The Florentine humanist Benedetto Varchi, as [he] most important public discussion of Michelangelo'[s] the *Lezzioni* of 1547, before the Florentine Academ[y] deliver Michelangelo's funeral oration. (No. 263 is to Varchi for sending him the manuscript of the L seen a good deal of Michelangelo's poetic output, a[s] example, no. 105), his transcriptions of those poe[ms]

The year 1546/47 marked a crucial transition in Michelangelo's life and writing from his most productive middle period to a final stage of diminished output and deepening gloom. Having just reached the age of seventy (in 1545), Michelangelo was on the threshold of his exceptionally protracted old age, and his spiritual life changed focus (or, better, intensified what it was already tending toward) as his earthly existence underwent a series of brutal shocks. Between 1544 and 1546, the artist had fallen very ill twice and was nursed back to health by del Riccio (see no. 206). Thoughts of death and his sense of the fragility of existence naturally intensified, not surprisingly in view of the catalogue of physical infirmities, from kidney stones to ear trouble, graphically described with black humor in no. 267.

Then del Riccio himself died in 1546, and the publication project was suspended, never to be revived. Next and hardest of all to bear, Vittoria Colonna died in February 1547, prompting further spiritual despair and an increased sense of having outlived his own times and vitality. Poems lamenting this loss continued long after her death (for example, nos. 265, 266). In no. 272 he begs Love repeatedly to "bring back to me the time" of youth and ardor, now vanished forever. Death also intervened in his professional life: the architect Antonio da Sangallo died, and Michelangelo was appointed superintendent of Saint Peter's, the professional task to which he devoted the seventeen years that remained to him.

From his final period, 1548–60, a scant twenty-three poems survive, or about two a year, almost all of them on themes of impending death, renunciation of past pleasures and achievements, personal guilt, and hope for salvation symbolized by the sufferings and intercession of Christ. He was, in fact, no longer actively engaged in many of his former activities: no painting, little sculpture, and no mention of a current love relationship after about no. 270. One of the few exceptions is his unfinished sculptural group, the Florence *Pietà*, which he began in 1547 and originally intended for his own tomb. Art was no longer to represent earthly beauty in the present, but a spiritual perfection that was possible in the future. This resolve to withdraw was once again intensified by the death of his devoted servant and assistant Urbino in December 1555 (nos. 300 and A41, the last fragment).

Whereas in his middle period many poems were addressed to specific mortal loved ones, mainly Cavalieri and Colonna, or to the personified Amor, the late verses are most often addressed directly to Christ. The renowned sonnet *Giunto è già* (no. 285), written in 1552–54, is in many ways Michelangelo's touching valedictory to his most deeply felt lifelong pursuits, both visual arts and poetry, as he declares his exclusive concern for spiritual goals: "Neither painting nor sculpture will be able any longer to calm my soul."

No poems are known from Michelangelo's final four years. Although he continued to work on Saint Peter's, his increasingly frail health often kept him from the construction site, with the unfortunate result that some parts of the building were not erected according to his intentions and had to be torn down and rebuilt. He continued working on a final sculptural project, the Rondanini *Pietà*, until a few days before his death, but left it an incomplete testimony to frustration. Of particular importance to his writing, which is such a solitary and self-expressive act, was the fact that Michelangelo's eyesight was deteriorating. Some of his later letters were dictated and merely signed by the artist, indicating that he may no longer have been able to draft poems by himself.

When at last he died, on 18 February 1564, at his bedside were his artist-disciple Daniele da Volterra and Tommaso de' Cavalieri. Although Cosimo I had been unable to cajole the artist into returning to Florence during his lifetime, Michelangelo's body was finally brought back from Rome. The procession transferring the coffin to the Buonarroti parish church of Santa Croce, the pantheon of great Italian citizens, attracted such a huge crowd that officials were forced to open the church to the public. Plans were laid, under the direction of the fledgling Florentine Academy of Design, for a splendid state funeral, which took place on 14 July and featured a two-hour eulogy by Varchi that paid homage to the master's unprecedented achievements in all three visual arts and in poetry. A surviving drawing for one of the temporary decorations at the ceremony (see frontispiece) depicts Michelangelo crowned by Apollo; since the god and his attendant Muses presided over the literary and lyric arts, not the visual, this painting was clearly a tribute to Michelangelo's poetic gifts.

3   *Themes and Content*

ince Michelangelo's poetic oeuvre is, in terms of subject matter, restricted to several principal and interrelated themes, it may be helpful to begin with a discussion of what he does not write about. He is only intermittently concerned with humor (for example, nos. 20, 54; see Cambon, chap. 1) or with historical or topical events (nos. 10, 247–50). He is not a lyric poet: as in his painting, there is very little celebration of nature, landscape, or physical objects and not much description of his beloveds' appearances beyond stock Petrarchan praise of their eyes or brows. Nor does he invent narratives about either historical or fictional personages. Only one poem, the lengthy no. 67 in praise of country life, personifies a series of allegorical abstractions (Wealth, Doubt, and the like). Instead, the mode Michelangelo favors almost exclusively is the discursive over the symbolic or dramatic. His writing takes the form of philosophical discourse prompted by the particulars of his experience. The characteristic poem seeks to outline an argument or a chain of ideas and to develop these conceits through complex verbal play.

The central themes of this discourse are: love, both earthly and divine, and the bodily and spiritual attributes that inspire it; time and death, the enemies of worldly fulfillment; art, which can counteract the transience of physical beauty; and God, whose eternal realm and laws hold out hope for the spirit's salvation from the sinful tragedy of earthly life. Neither the uplifting rapture of love for an idealized, angelic beloved nor the profound yearning for God's love is unique to Michelangelo. These twin themes had been the staples of Italian vernacular literary tradition since his models, Dante and Petrarch, turned their longings for Beatrice and Laura into a pathway to divine grace.

The grand protagonists of Michelangelo's psychic and moral universe are interlocked in a series of complex and polyvalent relations. At times his emotional attitudes toward different spheres run parallel: Neoplatonic love and religious fervor are similarly enraptured states, and Michelangelo's language to describe them is much the same. At bottom, however, the components of his world are characterized by their sharp polarization. His world is profoundly dualistic in the sense—central to Christian culture in the medieval and Renaissance eras—of a great division in the universe between opposing forces of good and evil, flesh and spirit, earth and heaven. As he says, "within my soul I feel both death and life, though opposites, together" (no. 124).

Notwithstanding his susceptibility to physical beauty and his incomparable skill in representing and recording it, Michelangelo is even more susceptible to spiritual imperatives. Thus, although love is an ecstatic delight, he experiences it simultaneously as a source of conflict. A central ambivalence of his life and career is the conviction that beauty is a *threat* to the soul: "terror, closely linked to beauty, feeds my great desire with a strange food" (no. 241). Especially in his most prolific period, from about 1536 to 1546, his poems work endless variations on the theme of love in conflict with death, God, and spirit; no. 92 explicitly makes Time and Love into allegorical protagonists.

If Michelangelo sees the larger world as a battleground of titanic moral and spiritual forces, he sees that same combat played out most often within himself. In line with the Neoplatonic doctrine that the microcosm reflects the macrocosm, his every action embodies universal principles. He often employs military images, such as *arme* (weapons), *segno* (battle standard, flag, nos. 10, 66), and the verb *vincere* (to conquer), to characterize the relations between himself and his beloved, as well as between art and nature or love and death.

Concomitant with the metaphor of battle is a powerful sense of loss, which derives from the Judeo-Christian doctrine of original sin. Adam and Eve's loss of the state of innocent purity that once prevailed in Eden is the archetype of moral failure and exile into eternal struggle and damnation in the afterlife, from which only the merciful intervention of God can save us. Michelangelo is acutely conscious, as a devout Christian, of the world's, and his own, postlapsarian state. Invoking the very image used in Genesis for the expulsion, the fiery sword, he laments that his soul has "been struggling in vain to get back on its earlier road" (no. 18). Hence the world appears to him as a long, tragic series of losses, failures, and deprivations.

A literary prototype that may have helped Michelangelo to conceptualize the characters and hierarchical values of this large-scale conflict is Petrarch's poem *I trionfi*. This long vernacular allegory provides a paradigm for the morally striving Christian's "pilgrimage through the world" that, while not exactly parallel to Michelangelo's worldview, expresses the same basic values and general concerns and dramatizes much the same idea of successive conflicts and yieldings. Petrarch's epic outlines six successive *all'antica* triumphal processions, each celebrating a personification of a fundamental human ideal or divine principle, which in turn is superseded by a higher or more powerful principle. The six stages are: Love, which is overcome by Chastity, which yields to Death, which is outlived by Fame, which is subdued by the pernicious gnawing of Time, which is annihilated by the cosmic scale of Divine Eternity, whose triumph is complete and ultimate. Vestiges of this hierarchical succession are evident throughout Michelangelo's poems, as for example in no. 50, which answers the question, "What will be left of her [body] . . . if time destroys all beauty?" with the reply "Fame," followed by the caution that "even this is fleeting" (compare poems no. 85:28–30 and 188).

While this schema helps us to understand the underlying dramatics of Michelangelo's poetry, it would be misleading to specify a single body of consistent, stable beliefs within his writing. Some of his statements are contradictory. In no. 239 he yearns for the images of himself and Vittoria Colonna to last "a thousand years" as a memorial to his love. Yet some years before, when reproached because his sculptures of the Medici dukes for the Chapel at San Lorenzo did not accurately depict their subjects, Michelangelo had shot back contemptuously that "a thousand years from now no one would be able to know that they looked otherwise" (see no. 239).

Many such inconsistencies are the result of passing time. While Michelangelo remained concerned with the same *issues* for most of his life, his convictions about those issues are dynamic, not static. For example, before 1536, he most often emphasizes the power of love to overcome death and "make it sweet" (no. 83); between 1536 and 1546, his emphasis shifts to how impending death makes love seem paltry and deceptive: "What once tasted sweet now seems bitter to me" (no. 158). Even later, in the final years after the crucial period 1546–47, love is spoken of as a remnant from long ago that has lost its power. His perception of art similarly changes, from regarding art as a powerful way to preserve and celebrate the beauty of one's beloved to seeing it as an oppressive form of idolatry.

Love, in its many guises and ramifications, is the animating and uplifting force of Michelangelo's life and art. It is his most powerful impulse and joy, at least in his early poetry. As mentioned, he described himself to Giannotti as "most inclined to love persons." His poems to Cavalieri are of special interest as the first large body of love poetry in any modern European vernacular directed by one man to another. There did exist a rather discontinuous tradition of male-male love literature in late medieval France and Moorish Spain. But most of this legacy was doubtless unknown to Michelangelo, who thus occupies a key position—after his mentor Poliziano, who wrote a series of impassioned poetic epistles to beautiful young men—in the emergence of modern homoerotic poetry (see section 4; Boswell). At the same time, his two great loves, Cavalieri and Vittoria Colonna, are praised for such similar attributes and in such parallel language that in some poems it is not clear which of the two he is writing about. Although he explicitly says that love for men is more able to lead to spiritual uplift than love for women (no. 260), his theoretical distinction is not so sharp in practice: he writes of Colonna that "her beautiful features call me upward, so that I see death in all other beauty" (no. 235).

This passage implies that love is inspired, on its first level, by physical beauty. Michelangelo was extremely susceptible to such attractiveness, as Condivi noted: "He has loved not only human beauty but everything beautiful in general" (105). Physical perfection is apprehended through the sense of sight, and the eye is the critical organ of the body in the Petrarchan language of love that Michelangelo uses. The act of seeing is central to both lovers and artists; hence its images are doubly important to Michelangelo, and he alludes to the eye or its glances constantly throughout the poems. Three times he points out that one cannot love what cannot be seen (nos. 163, 258, A26), and in speaking of his desire to enjoy Colonna he prays, "Make my whole body nothing but an eye" (no. 166). This interest seems to lie behind the cryptic no. 35, a description of the structure and function of the eye perhaps meant to instruct artists. Although much of Michelangelo's imagery of vision is conventional, with so much critical interest attached to "the gaze" by contemporary critics, his attitude toward sight is ripe for further study.

Besides the eye, Michelangelo's principal images to express the force of love and its effect on him are such Petrarchan-Dantesque standards as fire and flame or arrows and darts, which create wounds (no. 22:23). He often describes himself as wood, especially dry wood, which is kindled by love's heat, with the concomitant danger that the flames may destroy him, turning him to ashes (no. 96). Many times he employs the phoenix, the mythical bird that was destroyed by fire only to be resurrected, as a symbol of the transformative power of love, which both obliterates and renews (nos. 43, 52, 61, 62, 100, 108, 217).

Later, when his evolving priorities lead him to attempt to concentrate solely on divine love, earthly love's continuing power over him is attested by the vehemence of his denial of and struggle against it. His imagery changes dramatically to reflect his sense (or desire) of being exhausted by love and beyond its power. Whereas in his early poems love easily kindles his "dry wood" (nos. 92, 97), later he describes himself as "charred wood" or "wood already burned" by the flame of love, so diminished or destroyed as to be incapable of further earthly passion (no. 176).

Inextricable from the excitement and inspiration of love is the strongly felt danger of losing himself in it: a favorite phrase recurring in many variations is "I am no longer my own" (nos. 8, 108, 235). He repeatedly calls himself a slave or prisoner of love (nos. 12, 25, 32, 52, 54, 176). Images of being bound and tied by love, which recur frequently, express his belief that, however joyful, it causes loss of control over one's inner self or higher impulses (nos. 23:5, 41). Hence he conceives of himself as "fragile" (no. 285; Leites, 30) and often speaks of being "tortured" and "martyred" by conflicting desires or by either an excess or lack of love. This sense of threatened fragility is present from the very beginning of his poetic career, embracing contexts other than love. In no. 1, written about 1503–6, he speaks of how good fortune can be undone "in a moment"; four decades later he accuses even his best friend, Luigi del Riccio, of stabbing him in the back, noting cynically that one such bad deed (unspecified) can cancel a thousand kindnesses (no. 251).

Such wariness of other people's love bespeaks, in the psychoanalytic phrase of Robert Liebert, Michelangelo's sense of "the fragility of his ego boundaries." In a revealing episode chronicled by Giannotti, the artist declined a dinner invitation out of fear that the excitement of social interaction with the eminent guests "would take from me a portion of myself" (Giannotti, 68; Liebert, 172–76; Saslow 1986, 51–59). While this resistance to close relationships and suspicion of others owe their origins to intrapsychic dynamics, their intensity was in part a logical, even a sociological, response to the real threat of other people's suspicions. He was assumed to be actively homosexual by the father of a prospective apprentice and accused of the same by Aretino and the unnamed "cruel and stupid rabble" he attacks in no. 83 in an attempt to allay Cavalieri's fear of his intentions (*Carteggio*, no. cxiv; Saslow 1986, 48–50).

Time and its inevitable companion, Death, ultimately triumph, in the Petrarchan sense, over earthly beauty and love. Death is a prominent theme in Michelangelo's visual art, which is often based on such central Christian scenes of suffering and redemption as the Crucifixion, the Pietà, and the condemned souls at the Last Judgment. The poems express in more personal terms the same obsessive concern over death and the belief that its imminence is a constant reminder of higher goals and values. Michelangelo's sensitivity could reach the macabre: he painted a fresco in his house in Rome that depicted a skeleton holding a coffin and inscribed on it a terza rima caption that is preserved as no. 110, reminding himself that "within this dark coffin is your resting place." Elegiac regret that life is fleeting and beauty transient is explored in exhaustive variation in the fifty poems for Cecchino Bracci (nos. 179–228). Here and elsewhere, however, Michelangelo tempers his lament with the belief that death can also be a gift: it is better for the soul's salvation that we die young, before our evil nature can cause us to go astray (nos. 127, 128, 132, 226).

Notwithstanding his fear lest too much time on earth encourage sin, Michelangelo most often describes time and its passage as *breve e corto*, "short and fleeting," and feels he is being robbed or unjustly deprived: "Have you not so used up all my time within your realm that not one hour of my years is left for me?" (no. 22:40; see also no. 232). "Nothing is worse than lost time," he writes (no. 51), as a result of which he sees himself as *vecchio e tardi*, "old and slow." His most heartfelt outburst against the inexorable passage of time, occasioned by the death of Colonna, begs Love to "Bring back to me the time when bridle and bit were slack" (no. 272; compare no. 95).

This lament is part of a broader psychological sense of shortage and scarcity, which reinforces his sense of fragility. Many diverse elements of life—beauty, love, grace, artistic inspiration—are conceived of as being in limited supply. In his postscripts to del Riccio, he jokes wryly about poetic inspiration, claiming that "the spring is dry," although he says with achingly pathetic religious humility that "my meager grace is sweet . . . to me" (nos. 116, 211; compare no. 150). Even beauty, he implies, exists in a fixed quantity, so that one person's possession of it deprives others (nos. 186, 285). Happiness, when found, cannot endure, for "joy in old age lasts but a short time" (no. 261).

Some psychoanalytically inclined biographers trace this attitude to childhood deprivation, symbolized by the death of his mother and a lack of fatherly approval. As with his sense of fragility, however, the roots of this deprivation may have been sociological as well as psychological. The Buonarroti family's diminished circumstances during Michelangelo's childhood, compared to what his proud (but not very hardworking or ambitious) father claimed the family had once had, gave him an individual parallel for the Christian scenario of the postlapsarian fall from Edenic plenitude and ease, which reinforced his sense of diminution and distance from a better time.

RELIGION

As a deeply devout man, Michelangelo sought one goal even higher than the love of earthly individuals: the love of God. His paramount concern is the salvation that God alone can provide, and his ultimate desire is to free his soul from the restraints and failings of the body so that it may in time ascend to heaven (nos. 99, 107).

The single greatest obstacle to this transcendent goal is the conflict between earthly love and the call to heavenly piety—an opposition that, Michelangelo laments, "keeps me split in two halves" (no. 168). Beauty, which can tempt us into lustful distraction, is a painful reminder of the constant threat to salvation. Hence "there comes over me, while I am close to sweetness, a strong, harsh thought of shamefulness and death" (no. 131). Thus he writes of "terror, closely linked to beauty" (no. 241), and more emphatically, of "my enemy, beauty" (no. 82).

The poems speak constantly of Michelangelo's deeply ingrained sense of his own sinfulness, an outgrowth of both the doctrine of universal original sin and a nearly insuperable guilt over his own personal transgressions, even when these are not clearly understood or admitted by him. His internalization of the most ascetic, self-critical "Savonarolan" aspects of Christian doctrine is clear in his reference to "my predestined state of wickedness" (nos. 34, 66). He refers frequently to the consequence of this predisposition in his own life: a chronic guilt over "my bad habits" and "my longstanding fault [which], the older I get, keeps on growing stronger" (no. 92; also 130, 131, 143, 293, 301). This spiritual yearning, which intensified as he grew older, may be traced to both a natural individual process and the broad changes in Catholic society as the Counter-Reformation took hold in the years after the Council of Trent convened in 1545.

Although at times he seems unable or unwilling to specify just what these habits are—"some grave sin, scarcely known to me" (no. 280)—he is elsewhere painfully aware that his actual or potential transgression is erotic. He begins early to lament his "slavery" to love and to analyze the inexorable links between love, death, and sin (no. 22, 1524). Religious themes appear with increasing frequency beginning about 1532 (no. 66)—significantly, about the same time as his passion for Cavalieri—and toward the end of his life he confesses, with rueful retrospection, that "my senses and their own burning have deprived / my heart of peace and my desire of all hope" (no. 291). As with other themes, Michelangelo explores several contradictory aspects of this problem as he grows older: in no. 167 he expresses confidence that thoughts of death drive away earthly love in old age, but later he fears that passion may return and tempt him anew (no. 263). His pervasive sense of *distance* from virtue and his corresponding sense of impending doom are summed up in one of his most frequently quoted lines, "so near to death and so far from God" (no. 66). His basic metaphors for his own progress through the moral battlefield that is earthly life are images of distance, pathways, and movement. His is a "pilgrim soul" (nos. 244, 258), wandering a long, hard earthly road, exiled from heaven at birth and trying to get back "home." But, like Ulysses, he is beset by long years of temptations and obstacles. Several times he figures life as a sea voyage with its attendant dangers and tempests (nos. 264, 285). Toward the end, exhausted by struggle and unsure of his ability to prevail, he begs God to "shorten by half the road that leads to heaven" (nos. 288, 293).

NEOPLATONISM AND THE BODY

For a time—especially during the 1530s, the period of his most intense infatuation with Cavalieri—Michelangelo found the answer to his conflicted double awareness in the theory of love initially advanced by the Neoplatonists of his Florentine youth. This philosophy, with roots in late antiquity, attempted to resolve the central tension of the Renaissance between traditional Christian values and the newly rediscovered and greatly respected ideas and images of antiquity, particularly their divergent attitudes toward eros. Its method was allegory, reinterpreting ancient mythical characters as occult repositories of an ancient, universal wisdom that was held to be—beneath an often frivolous or lascivious surface narrative—harmonious with Christianity. The goal of this wisdom, as in all religions, was for mortals to apprehend the higher harmony of divine order. Hence, for example, Ganymede (whom Michelangelo illustrated for Cavalieri), who was carried off by Jupiter to serve him as cupbearer and sexual companion, was interpreted as a symbol of the innocent soul being lifted heavenward by divine love, at once de-eroticizing the story and transferring its overpowering rapture to an acceptable religious object.

Marsilio Ficino, the reigning philosopher in the circle of Lorenzo de' Medici, wrote a commentary on Plato's *Symposium* outlining this theory of love, taking as his key mythological symbol Venus, the goddess of love and passion. He wrote, allegorizing the two variant myths of Venus's birth, "Let there be two Venuses in the soul, the one heavenly, the other earthly." That is, there are two forms of love, in hierarchical relation to one another: the worldly and the spiritual. The key to Christianizing the lower term was the principle of *anagogy*. Derived from the Greek for "leading upward," this doctrine held that earthly goodness and beauty are reflections of the greater beauty and perfection of their heavenly creator, and that enraptured contemplation of such perfection can lead the observer upward to a perception of divine love.

Whereas his juvenilia praise physical attraction for its own sake (nos. 4, 7), already at no. 9 Michelangelo introduces in embryo the Ficinian idea that earthly beauty is a proof of divine creative power. In no. 15 he describes the anagogical function of love, as a force that can lead the lover to transcend the physical and ennoble the soul. He continually contrasts the kind of love that "descends from heaven" with the more earthly sort, again using Ficinian terms (no. 276), and frequently figures the ecstatic force that draws him upward as wings or winged flight, an image earlier used by Ficino. Several poems treat in detail the principle that the highest value of love is what it points to above itself. In no. 259 Michelangelo asks,

> What better reason for my loving you
> can there be, than to glorify that eternal peace
> from which descends the divine I love through you. . . ?

a sentiment developed further in no. 260:

> A violent burning for prodigious beauty
> is not always a source of harsh and deadly sin . . .
>   Far from hindering empty passion from flying higher,
> love stirs and wakes us, and feathers our wings;
> and from that first step, with which it's not satisfied,
> the soul can mount up and rise to its creator.

In the scheme of spiritual salvation, then, bodily beauty may be said to be necessary but not sufficient.

Recent critical theory has exposed the ways in which the cultural construction of the body reflects broader values (Foucault, Weeks, Ferguson). Michelangelo hews closely to Neoplatonic and Christian principles in his often stark or negative presentation of the body—the source of passionate yearning—as a mere transitory shell for its spiritual content, a prison (nos. 99, 107) of scant value in its own right. He often metaphorizes the body as a veil, a fragile and temporary wrapper for the soul (nos. 106, 209, 215, 227, 265). This may be one reason why he so seldom specifically describes any part of his beloved's body, except the face and eyes (the "windows to the soul"). Elsewhere, he imagines his own body made of sulfur or oakum, ready to burst into flame (no. 97). Other metaphors for the body are coarse and vegetal (images of rind or bark) or, when drawn from the animal kingdom, bespeak a desire to slough off the outer skin, as snakes do, in acts of self-destruction that parallel the sacrifice of Christ (nos. 12, 32, 51, 94, 105, 152, 161; Leites 72–74). With such an attitude of physical disgust and abnegation, it is not surprising to learn from Condivi that the artist kept his boots on for such extended periods that when he removed them his flesh peeled off like a snake molting.

The disjunction between literary and visual attitudes is ironic. In his visual art, the nude human form, usually male—David, Adam, the Christ of Santa Maria sopra Minerva—was Michelangelo's lifelong "signature" subject, representing the perfection and dignity of humanity. But the visual arts, which must reveal the abstract through concrete forms, necessarily compromise with hostile attitudes toward the body. In his poetry, Michelangelo can reveal more fully how much he denies the body out of fear. The fantasy of bodily satisfaction carries with it, for Michelangelo and his culture, the fear of bodily destruction. In no. 94, a fantasy for Cavalieri in which Michelangelo wishes he were a silkworm that could offer himself up ("strip off its own skin") to clothe his beloved, his tactile desire to "clothe another's hand" is instantly associated with the result of such desire on himself, "to be born only for death."

Ultimately, however, neither this insistent denial of the body nor the strategy of confining it within a highly idealized and officially nonerotic behavioral schema could withstand the artist's growing religious concern and self-doubt. After the pivotal tragedies of 1546–47, he became gradually less and less hopeful of resolving the dilemma of earthly attraction—of being able to "have it all"—and increasingly concerned about divine aid to ensure his own safety in what remained of this life and in *quest'altro,* the next one. His personal evolution paralleled, and internalized, the resurgent religious orthodoxy of his time: He abandoned earthly love, even in its most spiritualized form, as he also abandoned art and poetry, during the same years the Council of Trent was preparing to condemn allegorized images of classical myth as potentially misleading temptations. Where once he had thought to find an earthly foretaste of paradise in the eyes of his beloved, in the end he came to look back over this period of his life as a tragic detour:

> On you and with you, Love, for many years
> I fed my soul . . .
> But now, weary, I raise my thoughts on wings, and spur
> myself toward a more secure and noble place. (no. 271)

ART

Since Michelangelo was, unlike most other poets of his time, also consummately skilled in another art form, his comments on the visual arts and the connections he drew between visual and verbal art are of particular importance. His poems address the visual arts in several complementary ways: through direct discussion of artistic theory or specific works of art, the use in more general contexts of metaphors and images drawn from the arts, and comments on the function of art in the context of his Neoplatonic concerns.

Art is an essential weapon in his universal vision of the conflict between love and death. He extends the topos of the rivalry between art and nature, familiar since antiquity, beyond the simple reproduction of natural appearances to a metaphysical function. To be sure, art can, first and most simply, celebrate the beauty of one's present beloved. But because the artistic image then freezes the appearance of the loved one while he or she inevitably changes and decays, art plays an important role in the task of defeating the destructive power of time over all things. Throughout the Bracci epitaphs runs the theme that the image of the deceased can preserve his memory, which is stated most eloquently in no. 277, written in thanks to Giorgio Vasari for the first edition of his life of the artist. Through your works, Michelangelo graciously claims,

> by rekindling memories of others,
> long extinguished, you make both them and yourself
> live for eternity.

This power confers on art the crucial function of vindicating the judgment of the artist-lover in the absence of the beloved,

so that a thousand years after our departure
may be seen how . . .
in loving you, I was no fool. (no. 239)

It is significant that the sonnet for Vasari praises its recipient's skills with pen as well as brush. Both the visual and the verbal arts can perform the preservative function, in different modalities. In fact, on a few occasions when Michelangelo refused a request to make a funerary portrait of someone, he obliged instead with a written portrait, which, he said, will also preserve the memory of the deceased. He turned aside Gandolfo Porrini's request for a portrait of his late beloved, "La Mancina," with verses (nos. 177–78), and throughout the epitaphs for Cecchino—offered as a group in place of the desired sculpture— the memorial functions of visual art and poetry are interchangeable.

In no. 277, however, Michelangelo makes it clear that ultimately, in the hierarchy of the arts, he ranks writing "the worthier task." In this judgment he follows the current theoretical convention, based on humanist values, that accorded highest value to activities of the mind and to literary content. Michelangelo may thus seem to be denigrating his own major calling, but in fact his assertion of the ability to write about such issues at all constitutes a high-water mark in Renaissance artists' ongoing attempt to insinuate themselves into the enhanced status of a liberal art.

Michelangelo discusses art theory, a key component of the upgrading of art's status, in a number of poems, particularly in the series 236–42. His theory has a strong Neoplatonic basis, not surprisingly since metaphors of sculpting or painting one's beloved are commonplace in Neoplatonic writing on love and in Petrarch and Benivieni (Girardi 1974, 65). The central term in this theory of artistic creativity is the Platonic idea of *concetto*, which I have generally translated as "conception" to preserve its double connotation of both *ideation* and *gestation*.

To describe briefly a subtle term to which much scholarly exposition has been devoted (Summers, 203–33), Michelangelo means by *concetto* the ideal, preexisting image of an artistic project, which is formulated in the mind of the artist by a process of inspiration that is quasi-divine and which the artist then attempts to "real-ize" in the less than perfectly tractable medium of the physical world (nos. 62, 84, 236, 241, 279). Just as the individual mortal body is a pale reflection of the ideal spiritual Maker who conceived its soul, so too the individual work of art, imprisoned alike in earthly matter, can be but an imperfect embodiment of the pure idea behind its creation. The most explicit formulation of this idea is in no. 151, which is among Michelangelo's best-known poems, the one to which Varchi devoted special attention in his *Lezzioni*:

> Not even the best of artists has any conception
> that a single marble block does not contain
> within its excess, and *that* is only attained
> by the hand that obeys the intellect.

Following logically from this notion of the creative process is Michelangelo's insistence that the essential sculptural act is "taking away" (*levare*)—that is, a subtractive process of carving away parts of a stone block to reveal the "preexisting" form within—rather than "adding on" (*porre*), the kind of cumulative process used in making the clay or wax models for metal casting (nos. 152, 275).

It is because of this theoretical basis that art historians have long been so interested in Michelangelo's many unfinished sculptures, which reveal his subtractive working method and mark the beginnings of an aesthetic appreciation for the incomplete, the *non-finito*. These works, often abandoned when little more than a torso had "emerged" (such as the various slaves for the Julius tomb), exemplify the sense of frustration and disappointment that inevitably afflicts an artist with Neoplatonic beliefs, since it is virtually impossible for any mere physical example of the artist's craft to live up to the perfection of its *concetto*. As Michelangelo lamented, "the wise artist only attains a living image / faithful to his fine conception" at the very end of life, if at all (no. 241). And Vasari suggested that so many of Michelangelo's sculptures remained unfinished "because his judgment was so severe that he was never content with anything he did" (Vasari: Milanesi, 7:243, trans. Bull, 404). Thus Michelangelo has come to exemplify the prototype of the modern artist, tortured by the difficulty of the creative quest. About half of his surviving poems are also *non-finito*; through these visual and verbal miscarriages runs the same sense of frustrated longing for an unattainable ideal that pervades his discussion of human love (see no. 144).

In poems such as no. 241, which concludes with a meditation on "my great pleasure," Michelangelo's comments on the visual arts, like so many of his pronouncements, tend to ripple out beyond philosophical generalization to encompass the more personal meanings of his art. His strong sense of artistic vocation, for example, is revealed in his reference to sculpture as "that esteemed art" (no. 267:52). He suggests more than once that his acute susceptibility to beauty was ordained at his birth (no. 164), an important step in the growing idealization of creative genius by Renaissance culture. While the phraseology is quasi-astrological, the intent is Neoplatonic: this innate ideal of beauty would inspire him toward higher ideals. All the same, as noted earlier, he remained ambivalent toward his actual abilities as a painter and draftsman. He had complained while working on the Sistine chapel, "I'm no painter" (no. 5), and in a poem to Cavalieri (no. 79), he apologizes for his "most awful pictures," probably the series of allegorical presentation drawings that accompanied his poems in 1532–33. And his statements about his own artistic process offer strong support for those who would read his work as a psychological self-portrait, for he says, "one will at times / make the image of someone else look like himself" (no. 242).

Even in poems that are not overtly about art, Michelangelo's metaphors are often drawn from artistic processes, materials, and customs. Not surprisingly, the man who signed himself "Michelangelo the sculptor" often speaks of actual rocks and stone and of stoniness of character (nos. 63, 152, 170, 239–242). He uses images of carving, such as the sculptor's file reducing bodily form, and at one point he even compares God to a sculptor, whose handiwork is individual humans (nos. 161, 236, 275). Although he seldom worked in metal himself, he drew on the smithy and on metalworking as metaphors for creativity (nos. 46, 62, 64, 77, 122), as well as on the imagery of metalcasting and molds to suggest how he was open to inspiring influence from Colonna (see section 4). Less frequently and rather indirectly, he drew on metaphors from architectural trades such as the limekiln (nos. 63, 143, 170), and once on the terminology of printmaking, an art he himself never practiced (no. 264).

The poems can shed light on the meanings of specific art works by Michelangelo, although for the most part the connections between his two forms of expression lie in implicit parallels rather than in direct verbal commentary on specific works. Except for no. 5, describing the discomfort of painting the Sistine ceiling, or nos. 13 and 14, which appear to epitomize the *concetto* underlying the Medici Chapel, only one poem attempts to create a verbal equivalent of a named work. No. 247, a speech written for his statue of Night in the Medici Chapel, makes the figure a literal mouthpiece for Michelangelo's disgust at the political situation in Florence under Duke Cosimo de' Medici, a subject alluded to further in his sonnets on Dante and Florence, nos. 248–250. But these late poems postdate the actual creation of the chapel (under a more benign Medici, Clement VII) by several decades, and are less a gloss on the sculpture's original meaning than a reinterpretation of it to suit a much-changed context.

The links between poems and paintings or sculptures lie most often at the level of shared images and references. For example, the anti-Medicean sentiments of nos. 247–50 are close enough in time to the unfinished bust of Brutus, the heroic Roman tyrannicide, to allow us to read that statue as a visual condemnation of the same regime. More generally, such images as arrows occur so often in the *Rime* that their symbolism of love's violence and painfulness helps us to interpret a drawing like *Archers Shooting at a Herm* (about 1530), while the repeated images of winged flight recall the Neoplatonic rapture of the Ganymede drawing for Cavalieri (for example, no. 89). Similarly, the companion drawing of *The Punishment of Tityos* for Cavalieri, with its contrasting message about the danger of enslavement to sensuality, is paralleled by the many lines that speak of love's slavery and bondage, most notably no. 98, which declares that "to be happy, I must be conquered and chained . . . naked and alone" by "an armed cavalier," an obvious pun on the name of his beloved (compare no. 41). And, although Michelangelo never wrote of Bartholomew by name, the famous self-portrait that he painted into that saint's flayed skin in the *Last Judgment* is surely a reflection of the poet's obsession with bodily destruction and martyrdom in all forms.

Even when images appear in the poetry at some chronological distance from their evocation in the artist's visual work (as much as several decades), the parallels are too striking not to be meaningful. The imagery of a group of religious drawings made for Colonna in 1545–47—on one of which, a *Pietà*, Michelangelo wrote a line of Dante's complaining that "no one thinks of how much blood it costs" (A40)—is evoked by such contemporaneous poems as nos. 159 and 161. But the series' concern for Christ's life and the Cross is even more explicitly paralleled by the final group of poems, written a decade later, in which images of Christ's sacrifice and blood become paramount as the artist sees himself near death and more in need of salvation than ever (nos. 280–302). Though there is little evidence about this process, contemplation of his own earlier images could have suggested to Michelangelo such later lines as his plea to Christ in the 1550s, "may your stern arm not stretch out to [my sinful past]" (no. 290), which so strongly echoes the action of Christ in his *Last Judgment* of the 1530s.

In tandem with his attitudes about beauty, the body, and love, Michelangelo's feelings about his artistic vocation altered dramatically over time. As Nathan Leites has succinctly written, after the Cavalieri period "all in man that is not oriented toward God became for Michelangelo associated with evil" (70). Hence art, insofar as it too serves to keep our attention fixed on the mere surface of the material realm, came to seem idolatrous. This idea is introduced in no. 267, then starkly and compellingly developed in the late series, nos. 282–85 and 288, from the early 1550s. "Art and death do not go well together," he laments (283), since the thought of death makes aesthetic goals pall and fade (284). While he retains some nostalgic sympathy for the artistic dedication he once had, he is firm in his new-found conviction that those pursuits were ultimately a delusion; he refers to his lifelong concerns as "fables" (288) and regrets the "affectionate fantasy / that made art an idol and sovereign to me" (285). This ultimate rejection of art in favor of religion is most powerfully and sadly expressed in no. 285, which concludes:

> Neither painting nor sculpture will be able any longer
> to calm my soul, now turned toward that divine love
> that opened his arms on the cross to take us in.

Although Michelangelo lived another decade after writing no. 285, it can be seen as his valedictory to love, to art, to life itself, and to all the forces and activities that had once made it meaningful for him. From being "the most inclined to love persons" and the most divinely skilled at figuring the beauty of the body in artistic form, he had become the most inclined to love God. The *signor* he addresses in his final poems is no longer the personified Eros or a mortal beloved who is "lord" of Michelangelo's passions, but the Lord God, to whom he cries out in a tone alternately confident of divine aid and anguished with doubt. His associations with arms shift from his earlier yearning to have Cavalieri, "my sweet and longed-for lord / in my unworthy yet ready arms forever" (no. 72), to a focus on the body of the avenging God and his yearning to be embraced by the crucified Christ who "opened his arms on the cross to take us in" (nos. 285, 290).

As Michelangelo's poetic conception of the male body turned from celebration of ideal beauty to the image of Christ's suffering and threatening form, so his visual representations of the male figure evolved from the ideal heroic nudes of the early *David* or *Battle of Cascina* to the overwhelmingly massive and looming figures of the *Last Judgment*. Similarly, where he had once prayed, in the throes of his love for Colonna, "make my whole body nothing but an eye" for gazing on her beauty (no. 166), toward the end he wanted his intense visual acuity to be put at the service only of the divine: "God, make me see you everywhere!" (no. 276).

4 *Form, Style, and Literary Sources*

Numerous critics have traced in detail Michelangelo's formal qualities, stylistic predilections, and sources and influences. This essay can do no more than introduce some of the broad issues studied by Robert Clements, Enzo Girardi, Walter Binni, Glauco Cambon, and others, and raise the question of stylistic parallels between Michelangelo's visual and verbal art. One's attitude toward these stylistic tendencies is affected by how willing one is to grant that the poet's choices were fully deliberate products of sufficient skill to merit analysis (see section 1). His irregularities and deviations from the polished standards of more orthodox poets like Pietro Bembo may either be read as unresolved "imperfections" or claimed as a stylistic liberalization, a "breaking loose" from worn Petrarchan stereotypes.

In comparison to Michelangelo's artistic genius, his literary talent was genuine but modest. He worked hard to develop his gifts, in part because it was an important outlet for his pressing emotional life and in part because of Cinquecento cultural expectations that a visual artist had to prove literary eligibility for the liberal arts. Poetry meant more to him—and occupied him more intensely and far longer—than it did such artistic contemporaries and sometime writers as Benvenuto Cellini, Agnolo Bronzino, and Raphael. Indeed, he was the most deeply committed to verbal expression of any artist before William Blake. All the same, Michelangelo himself never advanced great claims for his literary output and responded with touched gratitude to anyone who complimented it.

The resultant poetry is, by common consent, inconsistent, and thus both rewarding and exasperating: Although often labored or incomplete and sometimes ungrammatical to the point of obscurity, it can also be deeply personal, sincere, and directly expressed. Most of the successful poems have the virtues of Michelangelo himself, a moving combination of the blunt, plain-speaking artisan with the passionate artistic intellect. Nos. 59, 72, 83, and 261, to cite but a few favorite examples, are clear, direct, heartfelt, and avoid the pitfalls of grammatical confusion or conceptual overelaboration. Many of the best are datable, at least in their final versions, to the period 1542–46, when Michelangelo was culling and revising the cream of his last decade's production under the guidance of del Riccio and Giannotti.

On occasion, the intensity of feeling and effort produced by especially important events in his life brought forth a particularly eloquent and impassioned cry that represents Michelangelo at his inspired best. Many of the Cavalieri sonnets are in this category (nos. 72, 83), as are some of his most heartfelt paeans to Colonna and, toward the end, his laments over passing time and life's vanity that were occasioned by her death (nos. 272, 285). As noted earlier, Varchi spoke of no. 166, in which Michelangelo yearns for the sight of her, as "one of his weightiest sonnets." Especially when these outbursts speak passionately of spiritual ecstasy, they have been claimed by such critics as Clements as part of that trend of intensified piety and mystical vision, exemplified by Michelangelo's near-contemporary, Saint Teresa of Avila, that paved the way for the theatrical emotionalism of the Counter-Reformation and the baroque.

Even Michelangelo's most ardent admirers, however, admit that he only seldom reached such heights of literary quality or of novel and powerful content. Cambon, who demonstrated carefully and at length that Michelangelo took much more time and care over his poetic form than was previously believed, conceded that great effort does not guarantee consistently great achievement. Michelangelo often made unsuccessful attempts at sophisticated verbal artifice, chose labored or artificial conceits, and could not resolve problems of syntax, rhyme, or imagery. No. 91 for Cavalieri twists its way through the conceit of becoming one with his beloved's heart with what Cambon characterizes (in another poem) as "labyrinthine complexity." In an accompanying note to del Riccio, Michelangelo himself later disparaged two parts of this poem as "old things for the fire, not for witnesses." Nos. 123 and 255 offer other examples of the tendency toward artificial metaphors and hairsplitting distinctions that lose their emotive power in intellectual refinement.

Michelangelo essayed most of the conventional poetic forms of his day, but the bulk of his poems are either sonnets (or unfinished parts of sonnets) and madrigals. In the middle period, roughly from 1536 to 1546, madrigals predominated (beginning about no. 100), whereas earlier and later (after no. 159), the sonnet was his preferred form. Occasionally, at least in Michelangelo the

Younger's opinion, a poetic idea that could not be precisely fitted into the planned sonnet ended up as a madrigal, a form whose flexible line lengths make it less constricting. It is suggestive that the looser, relatively "open" madrigal form predominated in the years around the painting of the *Last Judgment* and the Pauline Chapel, the works of Michelangelo's late period of painting in which he developed a similarly "open" visual style, characterized by larger and cruder forms, greater instability and movement, and an increasing deviation from the aesthetic canons of ideal proportions and simple symmetries that prevailed in the earlier, High Renaissance phase of his career.

Other poetic forms were used less frequently, for specific occasions or as intermittent formal experiments. He attempted the intricate sestina form (in which the same end words are repeated throughout several stanzas in a fixed pattern), but only twice, and one of them was unfinished (nos. 33, 70). More congenial to his desire for a freer discursive form was the *capitolo*, or open-ended series of short stanzas in terza rima (*a b a, b c b,* and so forth), which he used for several of his long and very personal meditations on such topics as the death of his father (no. 86) and his own aging and physical decay (no. 267). Nos. 67 and 68 are long sequences using the slightly more restricted ottava rima, or eight-line stanza, much used by Poliziano, which still allows for indefinite extension.

LANGUAGE

Michelangelo's poetic language is ambitious: he employs a great variety of figures of speech and grammatical structures in an attempt to create a style that is formally complex, intellectually sophisticated, and aphoristically condensed. When he is at his best, this "high style," heavily indebted to Petrarch and Lorenzo de' Medici, poignantly captures the bliss or frustration of love and the melancholy of earthly decay. However, many lesser efforts betray the self-consciousness of this approach and his occasional willingness to sacrifice clarity of thought for a bravura display of formal inventiveness.

Michelangelo structures much of his poetry around various tropes long since developed by the vernacular Petrarchan tradition (Lucente 1983). These devices serve two functions in his art, one purely aesthetic, the other a means of expressing his view of the underlying structure of reality. His most commonly used figures of speech are antithesis, paradox, and oxymoron. All these tropes, based on a degree of dramatic contrast or contradiction between two opposite terms or ideas, embody Michelangelo's strongly dualistic view of the world: the presence of one pole precludes the other or, at least, portends a struggle or some problematic symbiosis. Hence his penchant for verbal structures that yoke disparate concepts or facts in ways that emphasize mutual incompatibility.

Antithesis, or the juxtaposition of opposites, was frequent in Renaissance literature from Dante onward and was richly exploited by Petrarch and Lorenzo de' Medici. Such traditional oppositions as burning–freezing, sun–shade, fire–ice, life–death, and pleasure–pain thread continuously throughout Michelangelo's imagery. In paradox and oxymoron, these antitheses are pitted in more dynamic relation to one another. The first would include such seemingly illogical but philosophically dense statements as "one who lives on death never dies" (no. 74) or "being sick is healthy" (no. 244, which is overloaded with such forced conceits; compare nos. 73, 89). The oxymoron, in which the two terms are incongruously joined to emphasize their internal contradiction, is exemplified by such pairings as "cruel mercy" (no. 265) to refer to God, who relieved Vittoria Colonna's suffering by allowing her to die.

Michelangelo was particularly fond of one formulation of this type—what might be called the "comparative paradox," usually indicated by the Italian sequence *tanto . . . quanto*: for example, "You kill more quickly the later you arrive" (no. 232) or "as more time passes, it provides less space" (no. 233), or [happiness] "harms us the more, the more that it delights us" (no. 296). This structure is a verbal equivalent of the sense of scarcity that, as noted earlier, Michelangelo voiced explicitly in many poems. It presupposes (to use a modern term) the "zero-sum" universe, in which an increase in one quality is necessarily offset by a decrease in some other, whether for good or ill. Less frequently, he also made use of puns, especially on proper names: those of Cecchino Bracci (whose surname means "arms," no. 184 and other epitaphs), La Mancina (177–78), and of course his beloved Tommaso, the "armed cavalier" of no. 98.

In formal terms, these literary devices, which place a premium on the invention and manipulation of clever verbal conceits, are the equivalent of the characteristically mannerist trait that the art critic Lodovico Dolce, in his dialogue *L'Aretino* (1557), found in the sculptor's visual art: "Michelangelo has always sought difficulty in all his works." That is, he sought the challenge of setting and overcoming progressive problems of pure formal complexity in order to demonstrate his bravura facility with the manipulation of the medium itself (Barocchi, 1:196). Philosophically, these linguistic structures embody certain of his underlying assumptions about the nature of reality (see section

3): that the temporal universe is unstable and mutable and that consequently truth resides only in universal abstractions.

Two other favorite devices of Michelangelo's bespeak the same beliefs: his frequent use of the word *se* and his tendency to alternate or conflate statements in the first and third person. Forty-six, or nearly one in six, of the poems begin with *se*—usually meaning "if"—and one poem, no. 59, uses the term to introduce no fewer than ten clauses. This structure expresses his prevailing sense of conditionality. Unsure of all moral, amatory, and spiritual principles, he must pose them not as givens but as hypotheses to be tested against experience or as propositions whose potential ramifications he explores mentally in each discursive poem. This device is the stylistic equivalent of his inner conviction that the world is full of doubtful contingencies that threaten his fragile, insecure self. Similarly, twenty-six poems begin with *non*—"no" or "not"—and six with *mentre*, often connoting "although."

All the same, after such speculative beginnings, Michelangelo often concludes with an affirmative statement arrived at through his development of the initial premise. No. 296, for example, opens with the possibility, "If my great desire often gives false hope . . . of many more years to come." This premise leads to the final thought that such hope is undesirable, since "the longer the time [before death], the less good intentions last."

Here, as often, the train of thought is paralleled by movement from an introductory section of personal experience, recounted in the first person, to some aphoristic principle, stated in the third person or in a vaguely inclusive plural "we," as an impersonal rule of behavior or consequence. This deliberate blurring of the boundaries between "I" and "one" can be seen in no. 263, which shifts abruptly from "I, who had come to terms with my white head" to "One who fears less loses more." This meaningful ambiguity is facilitated by the general disuse in Italian of possessive pronouns to refer to parts of the body, so that *il cuore* may mean either "*my* heart" or "*the* heart."

Michelangelo's desire to proceed from the specific to the general can sometimes lend his ratiocinations an abstract, overly theoretical quality. He is a moral analyst: he aims to draw broadly applicable truths from his own or others' specific experience and, conversely, to write the events of his own, individual life as instances of transcendent, archetypal paradigms. In line with the metaphoric discourse of Renaissance culture as a whole, his interest is ultimately in the universal behind or within the particular.

Certain of Michelangelo's grammatical structures also exhibit the desire for both formal complexity and dualistic contradiction, particularly the frequent use of litotes, double and even triple negatives (nos. 114, 239). This rhetorical element is a verbal equivalent of the mannerist visual device of the *figura serpentinata*: the "snakelike figure"—either of speech or of body—turned back against itself, twisted into a series of opposing movements that create a dynamic tension. At best, such devices energize the figure with contrary lines of force, whether visual or verbal. When pushed to extremes, however, as in nos. 121 and 182: "death did not want not to kill without," they strain for effect to the point of confusing or diminishing the force of the thought.

Similarly, Michelangelo often seeks a heightened verbal drama by joining two pairs of linked terms in one compound group rather than expressing them independently (schematically, this device speaks of "the A and B of C and D" rather than "the A of C and the B of D"). When all four terms are compatible, as in no. 45, "death and grief, which I long for and seek," the device can be effective. When they are not so simply interchangeable, however, the resultant hybrid can be confusing. In no. 135 he complains of "the fear and deceits of love and death," thus obscuring two very different ideas, fear of death and deceits of love.

Whether through a lack of literary sensitivity or misguided aesthetic aims, Michelangelo is occasionally prone to other formal weaknesses that result in infelicitous or murky passages. His use of enjambment, the overflow of a phrase from one line to the next, has been interpreted as a loosening of formal rules that can lend a propulsive intensity to groups of lines or thoughts. But when it occurs three lines in a row in one poem (no. 61:1–3), he has all but crossed the boundaries of verse into prose. Similarly, it is permissible in Italian to rhyme a word with itself, as Michelangelo sometimes does (no. 107), but his repetitions seem at times motivated less by any expressive goal than by an inability to think of another word. In no. 117(line 9), however, the repetition of the same internal rhyme, *amo-bramo-chiamo*, does seem to be aiming at a sense of obsessive yearning, but veers close to comical excess.

LITERARY SOURCES

Although Michelangelo is not, as a rule, concerned with proving his erudition by extended or obvious quotes or adaptations, a broad range of sources and influences is evident in his verses, ranging from classical authors to his immediate forebears and contemporaries.

Michelangelo could not read Latin (see no. 192) and hence had no direct access to original sources for classical imagery, though his correspondence with del Riccio reveals that his friends must have offered him some help in this regard (see section 1). He seems to have been somewhat sensitive about his lack of classical learning and occasionally—perhaps with an eye to impressing his literary friends—used a Latin phrase (no. 192) or a term associated with Roman history (*lustro*, no. 195); and no. 29 includes a variant of Virgil's well-known line from Eclogue 4, "omnia vincit amor."

However, allusion to classical authors was the common coin of Renaissance culture, and Michelangelo's use of antique myth and symbols is quite limited in comparison to that of, for example, his admired Petrarch. His knowledge of ancient literature was sufficient to inform such important visual works as his mythological drawings for Cavalieri, based on Ovid's *Metamorphoses,* but he did not make extensive use of such references in his poems. The sole classical deity regularly invoked is Amor, or Cupid, who is more a generalized person-ification of love than a figure based specifically on the Greco-Roman god. A few other classical figures appear sporadically: Medusa in no. 10, Echo in no. 95, Arachne in no. 267, and Daedalus in no. A24. He also uses Phoebus, a Roman epithet for Apollo, in a number of poems, especially around the time of his friendship with Febo di Poggio, where he puns on the young man's name (nos. 99–101). Occasional passing references allude to mythic commonplaces, but are not presented as such: the "cup of beauty" in no. 20 (line 21) may refer to the heavenly nectar cup that kept the gods young.

Among the authors whom Michelangelo knew personally during his youth in the Neoplatonic circles of Florence, Lorenzo de' Medici (no. 266) and Poliziano (nos. 27, 120) have often been noted as important influences, especially regard-ing the comic or light-hearted vein of, for example, no. 20, a poem clearly inspired by Lorenzo's *Nencia di Barberino* in praise of rustic love (Girardi 1974, 72–4). The slightly younger burlesque poet Francesco Berni, who so percep-tively praised Michelangelo's preference for "things" over "words," is also cited often as an inspiration for the satirical and even grotesque compositions, such as nos. 20 and 267 (ibid.). Ficino and the other Neoplatonist philosophers influ-enced Michelangelo more on the level of fundamental concepts and themes than on the level of specific language, particularly since they tended to express their beliefs in prose, usually in Latin. Ficino's ideas, though not his lexicon, lie behind the hierarchy of loves and the phenomenology of passion expressed in, among other poems, nos. 39, 62, 83, and 260 (see section 3).

By far the two most important influences on Michelangelo's verse are, as Condivi said (p. 103), the fountainheads of Italian poetry, Dante and Petrarch. He depended on these two giants (as did so many writers in the fifteenth and sixteenth centuries) for basic themes, both amorous and spiritual; for repeated images and figures of speech; and for a number of actual lines and phrases that he copied or adapted. His many borrowings and adaptations, both conceptual and verbal, themselves form the subject of full studies. In the notes to individual poems I have marked only those correspondences that are particularly extended or specific.

Michelangelo's admiration for Dante is well attested by Condivi and Vasari, and Giannotti's *Dialogi* records a learned series of conversations about Dante's *Inferno* in which the artist shows himself to be thoroughly acquainted with the content of Dante's vast poem. His letters show that as late as the 1540s he was keeping up with newly published Dante commentary (*Carteggio*, MXLII; Ramsden, no. 254). At widespread times he transcribed specific lines from the *Divine Comedy* onto his worksheets (A11, A40), and no. 299 reverses the opening lines of *Purgatorio*. The revered poet influenced Michelangelo's visual art as well: he based the iconography of the lower tier of his *Last Judgment* fresco on Dante's description of Charon, the angry boatman, ferrying damned souls across the Styx to the mouth of Hell.

While he obviously was drawn to Dante as the great poet of both religious faith and uplifting earthly love, Michelangelo seems also to have felt a personal kinship with the earlier writer on the basis of social or political parallels. In his two sonnets dedicated to Dante himself (nos. 248, 250), he stresses the unjust political exile that Dante suffered at the hands of the fickle Florentines and makes the earlier author a symbol of heroic opposition to his times and his native city, an image that strongly parallels Michelangelo's own situation at the time as a voluntary exile from Medici rule in Florence.

Michelangelo also knew Petrarch's oeuvre intimately. He refers to the earlier poet in a letter to Vittoria Colonna (*Carteggio*, no. CMLXVII; Ramsden, no. 202), and he copied or adapted even more lines and phrases of Petrarch than of Dante in his own notes and poems. One-sixth of the fragments in the Appendix, ranging from the very first to the very last of his career, copy lines from Petrarch (nos. A1, 4, 13, 14, 22, 31, 41). The most extensive of these, the eight lines of no. 31, was apparently written from memory, since it contains some minor changes probably attributable to forgetfulness. Many poems take entire conceits, situations, or quotations directly from specific poems by Petrarch (for example, nos. 36, 135, 251, 253).

Petrarch was of less utility than Dante as a source of religious imagery, but he offered abundant models for analyzing nearly every aspect of spiritualized earthly love. Michelangelo's images and sentiments follow closely on Petrarch's, from the bodily mechanisms by which desire is transmitted and kindled to the renewal of passion in old age (Petrarch's no. 55 inspired no. 136 and many others), to the proper sentiments for mourning (one of the dirges for Vittoria Colonna, no. 266, is closely modeled on the topoi Petrarch developed for mourning Laura). And, though the parallels with Michelangelo's theoretical statements are merely generic, Petrarch's poems praising his friend the great Trecento Sienese painter Simone Martini and the portrait Martini made of Laura raised issues that interested Michelangelo, issues pertaining to the nature and role of art.

For the large proportion of Michelangelo's output that is devoted to spiritual concerns, he seems to have found a model, at least for his generally urgent and anguished tone, in the sermons of Savonarola and in a few other religious authors. No. 110, for example, the caption to the grisly image of a skeleton that Michelangelo painted in his stairwell, recalls the grim carnival songs—with their reminders of the omnipresence of death and decay—that were popular in Florence from before Savonarola's time to the sixteenth century.

For a person as deeply religious as Michelangelo, however, there are surprisingly few specific references to characters from the Bible or religious history, other than Christ and God. Late in life he alludes to the archangel Michael and his scales of divine judgment (no. 299), and he refers to such elemental symbols as the cross or the instruments of the passion (no. 290), but he never invokes any other saints by name or any historical figures except Cain (no. 71). A few phrases suggest familiarity with biblical or liturgical texts and formulations— for example, the last line of no. 254, which adapts a phrase spoken by Christ, or the Edenic "fire and sword" alluded to in no. 18. As with his treatment of classical myth, however, the references are often indirect and show little desire to draw overt analogies with religious traditions. No. 267 draws on popular customs around the feast of the Epiphany, but the tone is folksy and humorous rather than theological (line 30).

The Florentine Girolamo Benivieni, who in a long career moved from passionate Neoplatonism to Christian pietism, provided an occasional image: In the crucial late poem no. 285, the image of God stretching out his arms to welcome the speaker seems derived from Benivieni's work (compare no. 263). So too did his beloved Vittoria Colonna, who acted as his muse in both the metaphorical and more literal senses: no. 162 is his homage to the powerful inspiration of her "sacred ink." His no. 298 is an adaptation of one of her poems, and in several other cases a line or an image is drawn from roughly contemporary works by her.

One formally innovative and socially radical aspect of Michelangelo's poetics that has not yet received focused critical attention is his flexibility and ambiguity regarding gender. The novelty and interchangeability in his poetry of terms and images dealing with such traditionally dichotomized categories as man and woman, masculine and feminine, active and passive, suggest a strikingly "protomodern" awareness of the arbitrariness of gender constructs and can be read as a embryonic attempt to subvert the heterosexual conventions of the courtly-love tradition to the exaltation of a male beloved—or, in the case of his adored Vittoria Colonna, of traditionally "masculine" qualities within the female.

The tradition of spiritualized love poetry, descended from the medieval chivalry of the *dolce stil nuovo*, Dante, and Petrarch, was uniformly directed at a woman by a male writer. No one, with a few pioneering but isolated exceptions such as the ribald verse of Beccadelli and Poliziano's lyrical Greek epistles, had yet written of similar sentiments directed by one man to another man. Michelangelo can hardly have been unaware of the potentially shocking subversion in his alteration of long-sacred prototypes. As seen earlier, his letters and poetry reveal that he knew people had suspicions about his professions of chastity toward unorthodox love objects (section 2), and in many cases his successive drafts shift the gender of a poem's addressee back and forth depending on the intended audience.

Although Michelangelo's predecessors could never have foreseen such a parallel, their poetic tradition was well suited to embody the emotional dynamics of homosexual love. Three of its constitutive elements paralleled, in strikingly apt ways, the moral strictures and social conditions within which homosexual love also had to operate in Michelangelo's culture. Chivalric love was focused on a semilicit love object—another man's wife (or, as with Beatrice and Laura, on a woman who was unavailable for reasons of absence or death). Hence, courtly convention prescribed resistance on the part of the beloved, who keeps her distance and does not respond. The tradition therefore celebrated a passionate yearning that must remain eternally chaste and unfulfilled.

All of these structures and values could be translated almost without alteration, except for the pronouns, into the service of describing and justifying homosexual love as it was constructed by Michelangelo and his culture. Given the strong official condemnation of, and legal restraints on, homosexual acts, a beloved male like Cavalieri was equally, if differently, illicit as a love object. Especially in the case of a Cavalieri, himself seemingly without homosexual desire, resistance was inevitable and is in fact alluded to by Michelangelo more than once (no. 58). Coupling this social scenario with the Neoplatonic idea that chaste yearning for a beloved's beauty is anagogic to the spiritual love of God, and with the prevailing misogyny that held men to be more intellectually and spiritually inspiring than women (no. 260), Michelangelo was able to construct a legitimizing framework for his male passions that assimilated them to Christian values by declaring that they would never be consummated. So his writing of homosexual love—the only expression of such feelings that could be imagined and openly made at the time—is poignantly (as Anne Freadman has written of Petrarch's writing) a "poetry of desire, and of desire repeated and maintained, not of satisfaction" (Freadman, 157; Saslow 1988).

The practice of gender inversion seems to have first occurred to Michelangelo in the early 1530s, when he was seeking a language to express his passion for Cavalieri. In this project of intertextuality—adapting the inherited heterosexual text of courtly love for a changed purpose—Michelangelo is both radical and cautious. On one hand, his language treats male and female as virtually interchangeable, thus problematizing established conventions. On the other, however, he seems to step back from full exposition of these potentially troublesome concepts, employing several strategies to obscure his "deviant" object-choice.

Two aspects of this ambivalent strategy stand out. Many poems underwent one or more shifts in the gender of their addressee, and some of these versions are pointedly ambiguous about who is being addressed. In their final versions for Cavalieri, nos. 76 and 81 make use of earlier drafts originally addressed to a woman, simply altering the addressee from *donna* to *signore* without changing the sentiment or images. No. 76, which was inspired by a specific Petrarchan model addressed to Laura, shows even more clearly Michelangelo's conscious reworking of the heterosexual tradition, while in no. 72 Petrarch's cry of happiness at seeing "my Lord and my lady" (God and Laura) in heaven is compressed by Michelangelo into the single sight of his "lord," who serves the purposes of both the male and female members of Petrarch's spiritually inspiring dyad. Similarly, no. 246 began as an address to a woman but was altered in a later draft, probably intended for Febo di Poggio, to address a man.

The subsequent evolution of this poem reveals the artist's awareness of the novelty of his practice and his ambivalence and fear about expressing his male desires too openly. The final version of no. 246, as prepared by Michelangelo for publication, reverts to female pronouns and references, suppressing the intermediate male stage and making the poem more comprehensible and acceptable to a public audience in traditional terms, both social and literary. No. 230 underwent a similar transposition from masculine to feminine pronouns, again with an eye to publication; Michelangelo here pointedly went so far as to spell out the feminine pronoun *quella* in the final version (line 11), whereas in the male version he had obscured the masculine ending of the equivalent term *questo* by eliding it to *quest'*.

The second method by which he softened or obscured intended references is ambiguity: the avoidance of any term or pronoun that would indicate gender. Numerous poems address the beloved as "you" in the second person and avoid any adjectives that would directly describe this person and require a commitment as to gender. These poems describe instead only the beloved's attributes (physical or spiritual), so that any adjectives agree with the gender of that part, not of the person as a whole (though Lucente [1987] cautions against over-interpreting Michelangelo's adjectives). Second-person address was not, of course, uncommon in traditional poetry, and such early exercises as nos. 15 and 28, clearly written to a female "you," are innocent of any intent to obfuscate. But during the mid-1530s, when Michelangelo was writing more or less simultaneously about both Colonna and Cavalieri, many poems are addressed to an ambiguous "you," and commentators are reduced to guessing who is meant (for example, nos. 113, 114). In the case of no. 259, which went through several drafts addressed to *signor mio*, a male beloved, the change in the publication version to *tu* again suggests some conscious degree of self-censorship.

Moving beyond grammar to vocabulary and imagery, Michelangelo displays a similar flexibility in his characterizations of himself and others and of the emotional relations between them. His sense of inherent androgyny—the capacity of either sex to exhibit traits and emotions normatively restricted to the other—coincides meaningfully with the hermaphrodite or androgyne symbolism common throughout the Renaissance. These mythographic and occult images embodied ideas about spiritual wholeness and complementarity that were closely linked to prevailing theories of homosexuality as a psychic hybrid or "third sex" (Saslow 1986, chaps. 2 and 3). Michelangelo's awareness of this tradition can be inferred from his early statue of the tipsy Bacchus, described in antique literary sources as androgynous and bisexual. Vasari lauded this youthful sculpture as offering "a marvelous harmony of various elements, notably in giving it the slenderness of a youth combined with the fulness and roundness of the female form" (Vasari: Milanesi, 7:150, trans. Bull, 335).

In praising Vittoria Colonna, Michelangelo describes her in terms that stress her similarity to a man. He symbolizes her intellect and valor—qualities that both he and his culture generally associated more with the other sex—as "a man within a woman" (no. 235), going on to declare that it is because of this inherent masculinity that he is beside himself with love. He also refers to her as his "lord" (*signore*) and, in a related letter, as *amico*, using the masculine form of the word for "friend" (no. 160). This implicit praise of her androgyny is deeply informed by the prevailing misogyny of Renaissance culture, with its twin principles that men are superior to women (see no. 260) and that a woman is improved to the degree she models herself on masculine norms and forms. Such ideas and images form a suggestive parallel to Michelangelo's painting practice (not infrequent at the time) of basing female figures on drawings made from male models, as in his Doni Madonna or the Sibyls of the Sistine Ceiling.

Conversely, while Michelangelo uses masculine images to describe Colonna, he often embodies himself in metaphors that are feminine and passive in essence, metaphors that then imply the beloved's "masculine" identity and activity toward him, whether that individual be male or female. In no. 73, speaking through the persona of his soul (*anima*, feminine) enables him to use feminine adjectives to refer to himself. More substantially, he calls himself a "bride" in relation to his "lord," who in context is both God and Cavalieri (no. 87)—the term "bride of Christ" being, significantly, a phrase applied to nuns— and then calls upon his lord to "rend that veil" that separates them, in a powerfully multivalent image that conflates sexual and spiritual penetration in terms not unlike the mystical visions of Saint Teresa.

His metaphors of relationship with Vittoria Colonna similarly cast her as the "masculine" partner who is invited to transform his inert body and soul in ways that diverge widely from customary images of female behavior. Drawing many images from the creative arts, he describes himself as unformed matter await- ing the inspired hand of the creator to bring him to life or improve him. He envisions himself as a rough sculptural model who is to be filed down and polished by Colonna (no. 236), and as an archetypally feminine "mold" waiting to be filled and then ruptured by the inflow of her seminal beauty (nos. 152, 153). Similar metaphors are taken from the two-dimensional arts: he is a "blank sheet" waiting for her to "draw within me" (no. 111), and from poetry: "I offer my blank page to your sacred ink" (no. 162).

The language in these examples is indeed revolutionary in its ambiguity and inversion, sufficiently so to make Michelangelo the Younger alter just such usages; but the degree to which it represents a self-conscious rejection of con- temporary norms of masculine and feminine behavior or sexual categories needs more sophisticated scrutiny. Although Michelangelo was clearly aware of the novelty and unorthodoxy of his gender devices, one should beware of reading into them a sociopolitical agenda more characteristic of today. On a deeper structural level, his characterization of himself as feminine and Vittoria Colonna as masculine does not fundamentally challenge the established gender conventions of that time, which required a dichotomy between active and passive attributes that was to be embodied in two polarized partners. This inability to break completely with his society's constructions of sex and gender may be read in terms of what Jonathan Dollimore and others have labeled "transgressive reinscription": the kind of apparent violation or denial of an established conceptual framework that in fact, by continuing to employ the same terms set by that order, albeit in an alternative manner, ultimately continues to accept and reinforce existing categories of thought (Dollimore, 53–81).

It is pertinent here that other writers, not too distant in time from Michelangelo, who attempted to forge similarly alternative language for gender-variant behavior also tended to transpose existing terms rather than to dispense with old categories altogether. In the fifteenth century, the humanist educator Guarino Veronese had urged the renowned religious scholar Isotta Nogarola (1418–66), one of the first highly educated women in Verona, to "create a man within the woman" (Margaret King, in LaBalme, 66–90). Perhaps the most revealing case is England's bisexual King James I (1566–1625). In his letters to his beloved favorite, the Duke of Buckingham, James calls Buckingham his "wife" and characterizes himself as a prospective widow, whereas in public utterances as the monarch he called himself, more traditionally, the "father" and "husband" of his realm (Akrigg, no. 218; Ferguson, xxiv; Jonathan Goldberg, in Ferguson, 3–32).

Like Michelangelo's, these examples of alternative language remain fixed in what Michel Foucault termed the *episteme* of polarized opposites: even when they reject, either implicitly or explicitly, the specific role assigned to a particular individual or sex, the speakers cannot altogether break out of their habitual binary frame of reference. Perhaps the most poignant example of this dilemma of transitional consciousness is from the pen of an author far more flamboyantly outspoken about sexuality than Michelangelo. The Englishman Richard Barnfield, writing later in the sixteenth century, asserted frankly that "if it be sin to love a lovely lad, O then sin I," a boldly heterodox statement that nevertheless does not overtly challenge, any more than Michelangelo did, the notion that such behavior should be assigned to the category of sin.

5 *Editions and Translations*

Since changes in the presentation and explanation of Michelangelo's texts have influenced the historiography of larger issues in Michelangelo scholarship and in Renaissance art and literary history, it is necessary for a complete understanding of the present book to outline the long history of publishing, translation, and scholarship on Michelangelo's poetry, and to clarify the editorial ideals and policies underlying this translation.

The projected first edition of the poetry, on which Michelangelo worked with Giannotti and del Riccio between 1542 and 1546, remains a "phantom" edition, since it was never actually published. However, before del Riccio's death put a stop to the plan, preparations had been nearly completed, and fair copies had been made of those 105 poems that had been selected and given a final revision, with a sequential numbering by del Riccio. This abortive edition survives conceptually in the group numbering used by Carl Frey (see below).

The first printed selection of the *Rime* was edited by the author's grand-nephew, Michelangelo the Younger, in 1623. The basis for his edition was the manuscripts then in the family's possession (the nucleus of the Buonarroti Archive now preserved in the Biblioteca Laurenziana in Florence), including the fair copies from 1542–46. As noted earlier, in the name of protecting his forebear from literary or doctrinal criticism, Michelangelo the Younger took many liberties with the manuscripts, both completing unfinished poems and silently altering completed ones.

These bowdlerized versions, though of no interest in revealing what Michelangelo himself meant, are of historical importance for two reasons. First, they were the only form in which the poetry was known to readers throughout the seventeenth, eighteenth, and early nineteenth centuries, and thus greatly influenced the scholarly perception of Michelangelo. Second, the changes his nephew made identified precisely those aspects of his uncle's work that would continue to cause scholarly disagreement and discomfort down to the present day. As Girardi succinctly phrased it, Michelangelo the Younger's alterations tended in two opposite directions: in terms of form, he tried to increase the variety and sophistication of his uncle's language, while in terms of content he aimed at pruning any diversity that could be construed as unorthodox, especially in the areas of sexuality and religious doctrine (Girardi 1974, 78–95, especially 91).

Modern scholarship on the poems began with the Italian Cesare Guasti, who prepared his critical edition of 1863 by returning, for the first time, to the manuscripts themselves. Where Michelangelo's original text differed from the 1623 published version, Guasti printed both, along with the nephew's commentary and his own prose paraphrase. He thus brought to light Michelangelo's actual sentiments and images and made available for study the nature of the nephew's critical and ideological biases. Guasti grouped the poems by formal type—sonnet, madrigal, fragment, and so forth—rather than trying to establish a unified chronology.

The English critic and historian John Addington Symonds (1840–93) had a great and personal interest in Michelangelo. He wrote a full biography (*The Life of Michelangelo*, London, 1893) after having translated into English for the first time all of the artist's completed sonnets (1878). His corpus, based on Guasti's edition, comprised some seventy-seven poems, or approximately a quarter of the total oeuvre known today. Symonds, whose interest in Michelangelo was stimulated in part by his own homosexuality, was an early pioneer in what is now termed gay studies. In the course of his search for historical records of homosexual life and consciousness, he issued a stinging denunciation of earlier editors who had falsified or reinterpreted the poet's manifest love of men as an allegory for love of women or of God (Symonds 1899, 2:132–40, 166n1, 381–85; Saslow 1986, Introduction). Unfortunately his renditions, while faithful to the content and passion of the originals, are couched in a high-flown, semi-archaic language that is far from Michelangelo's own diction and are tightly rhymed, which often necessitates significant alteration of the actual phrasing. Another translation of the sonnets was prepared by S. Elizabeth Hall (London, 1905). Like Symonds's, Hall's versions are fully rhymed and persist in the use of archaic language, though they are somewhat less "Victorian" in tone and stay closer to the original meaning.

The critical edition prepared by the German scholar Carl Frey (1897) remained for most of this century the standard scholarly edition of the *Rime*.

Frey's corpus was more complete than Guasti's and, in place of Guasti's organization by poetic forms, was the first to attempt a chronological ordering of the poems based on handwriting, paper, watermarks, and the collation of internal evidence with biography. His only exception to this scheme was to group the 105 poems that Michelangelo and del Riccio had once intended for publication into a unit of their own, his no. 109.1–109.105. Although useful for scholars who want to study those poems Michelangelo considered his best or in some way most representative up to 1546, this decision unfortunately pulls them out of chronological order. Frey's massive critical apparatus detailed the location of every manuscript then available, including drafts and variants. For those texts written on sheets of paper that contained drawings, he identified and briefly described the accompanying visual material.

Frey's numbering and chronology were the basis of many later editions in Italian, such as that of G. R. Ceriello (1954), and in other languages. Ceriello, like Ausonio Dobelli (1933), was dependent on Frey, Valentino Piccoli, and other scholars. Both editors tended to overemphasize in their interpretations a traditional Christian orthodoxy, reading a spiritual cast into works even when other levels of meaning are implied. Dobelli is very useful on Michelangelo's literary sources but tends to cite a "source" in Dante, Petrarch, or other writers for any passage where there is a general similarity of thought, especially an orthodox religious thought as Dobelli interprets it, even when the language or imagery of the two passages is not meaningfully related.

The Frey edition was at last superseded by the now-standard edition of the poetry in Italian, published by Enzo Girardi in the uniform *Scrittori d'Italia* series (1960). The numbering and Italian texts used in the present edition are those established by Girardi. Like Frey, Girardi collated and annotated all the manuscript variants in a more precise chronological order, adding a number of poems that had come to light since the nineteenth century as well as numerous brief fragments found on various drawings (Appendix, 1–41, in his edition, numbered A1–41 in the present volume). Girardi's subsequent book of philology and criticism, *Studi su Michelangiolo scrittore* (1974), updated and extended his thoughts on the *Rime*, providing many useful insights. A condensed version of the Girardi corpus, providing simply the preferred final text for each poem and a few notes of textual explication and dating, was prepared by Ettore Barelli (1975) and issued as an inexpensive paperback (first edition Bari, 1967).

There have been two English translations of Michelangelo's corpus in the twentieth century, one by Joseph Tusiani (1964) and one by Creighton Gilbert (1963). Tusiani's work, unfortunately, was out of date by the time of its publication, since he used the numbering, texts, dates, and many annotations of the Frey edition. Moreover, his renderings fall short of accurate transcription on two counts: they are carefully rhymed, often veering far from Michelangelo's imagery to complete a rhyme or fill out a line, and they tend to "improve" his metaphors and images in the direction of more vividness and specificity than the originals.

The only previous English translation based on Girardi's texts and chronology is that by Creighton Gilbert. However, Gilbert refused to admit two of Girardi's poems to his corpus (nos. 13 and 14; also many from the Appendix), with the result that comparing his translations to any Girardi example is slightly confusing to the uninitiated (after his no. 12, Gilbert's numbering is always two less than Girardi's), and his explanatory notes are minimal. Gilbert's translation is often excessively literal in its rendering of Michelangelo's phrasing and word order and is thus at times obscure. At other times he tends, like Tusiani, toward enriching the poet's own, rather restricted, vocabulary, with the result that he fails to capture the plainspoken tone of the original. Another factor that works against fidelity to the originals is Gilbert's decision to aim, if not for rhyme, for a loose scheme of assonance or consonance. This device has the advantage of preserving some sense of Michelangelo's formal diction while widening the translator's choice of words, but it still leads to some selections having been made more for sound than sense.

A few recent works in English, mainly concerned with literary criticism, are also useful for their translation of selected poems. Robert Clements's *Poetry of Michelangelo* (1965), still the basic and most complete study of the artist's meanings and style, takes an eclectic approach to translation. Sometimes he gives the original Italian, sometimes older English versions by Henry Wadsworth Longfellow, Symonds, or Hall, and elsewhere he provides reliable new translations of his own. David Summers's study of *Michelangelo and the Language of Art* (1981), an invaluable and intellectually sophisticated analysis of Michelangelo's theories of artistic creativity and meaning as revealed in his poems, letters, and other recorded statements, provides prose translations of the poems most important for this purpose. Most recently, the late Glauco Cambon, in his study of Michelangelo's processes of literary creativity (1986), provided idiomatically satisfying translations of the numerous poems he considered most revealing of the struggle for expressive complexity and autonomy.

A concordance to the principal scholarly editions and translations consulted in the preparation of the present edition is provided at the end of this volume (p. 527). To avoid cluttering the notes to individual poems, references there to specific information provided in the earlier literature have been kept to a minimum. It is hoped that the acknowledgment that all such sources have been consulted and collated, together with a collective and sequential cross-reference to these editions for the convenience of readers who may wish to inspect the earlier literature, will suffice as scholarly acknowledgment. To the extent that one goal of the present edition is to collate and summarize previous critical opinion, it could not exist at all without these often encyclopedic and detailed contributions to Michelangelo scholarship.

I have attempted to note whenever a poem is written on a sheet of drawings, correspondence, or personal notes that has been published. Drawings are cited by their numbers in the uniform catalogue of Charles de Tolnay (1975–80); see also the Concordance to Drawings (p. 537). Michelangelo's letters are cited from the authoritative Italian edition, *Il carteggio di Michelangelo* (1965–79) and the standard English translation by Ramsden (1963). His personal memoranda are cited from the standard edition of his *Ricordi* (1970). For the location of manuscript poems that have not been published, the reader is referred to the extensive archival information supplied in the critical apparatus to Girardi (1960).

TRANSLATION

Several issues face every translator and editor of Michelangelo's words and unavoidably introduce an element of judgment into the task of rendering him into either modern Italian or another tongue. His poetic language is so often archaic, obscure, or elliptical that many editors from Guasti to Girardi have felt it necessary to provide prose paraphrases as well as line-by-line annotations. Previous English translators have tended to clarify the probable intent of difficult passages by paraphrasing Michelangelo's usage. Except in cases where the original text was hopelessly ambiguous, I have generally preferred to leave his phrases and images as he wrote them and to explore their probable meaning in the notes, rather than to adjust the text itself. Where necessary, I have provided a general summary of the argument of a poem, along with line-by-line annotations of unclear phrases, symbols, and allusions, supplying cross-references to related usages elsewhere in the corpus.

In two matters of language the difficulties posed by Michelangelo's practice are attributable to prevailing literary norms shared with other writers of his time: his punctuation is often irregular or nonexistent, and his grammatical structure and word order are, by modern conventions, obscure or incorrect. Even allowing for the greater flexibility generally permitted to word order in Italian than in English and the generally greater degree of formal complexity sought by both languages in the sixteenth century than today, Michelangelo's verse straddles the line between expressive complexity and convoluted artificiality.

Where his word order, though unorthodox, is comprehensible in English and where alteration would destroy the structure of the lines and the flow of ideas, I have generally kept it (for example, nos. 78:1–3, 295:1–2). Where it violates standard modern norms to the point that a reasonably direct English transcription would be unintelligible, I have rewritten it. Doubtless, in these cases, some appreciation of the dramatic effects Michelangelo achieved by orchestrating the development of a thought has been lost. Since, however, the original Italian is available in this edition, I have opted for clarity of meaning rather than precise re-creation of form. Sometimes the inherent ambiguity of sentence structure requires a choice between multiple possible interpretations of a sentence. In these cases, I have chosen the reading that seems most appropriate in context, though this necessarily rules out other readings (some of which, when equally plausible, I have indicated in the notes). Similarly, I have altered random punctuation wherever necessary to clarify Michelangelo's overall meaning and the placement and significance of his many overlapping subordinate clauses.

Michelangelo's gender ambiguity, as outlined earlier, is in part deliberate, but it is also a natural consequence of the pronoun structures of Italian, whose lesser degree of specificity compared to English poses a problem for the contemporary translator. In general, Italian verbs do not require a subject pronoun, so that a third-person verb standing alone need not betray who is performing the action. This can, however, prove awkward to render into English, which usually requires a defining pronoun (he/she/it; for example, no. 57:4).

One term can provide a specific, and particularly problematic, example: the pronoun *chi,* which can be used to mean not simply "who" but also "the one who." Unlike its most common English equivalents (he who, she who), *chi,* when used alone to mean "the agent who," does not specify the gender of that agent. I have tried wherever possible to translate it as "one who" or "the one who" (occasionally "those who," although *chi* is always singular), in order to preserve the ambiguity inherent in the original structure. To reduce it to that formerly standard English form, the generic masculine ("he who"), would impose a male bias not enforced by the original. However, in those instances where it proved impossible to maintain the impersonality without awkward circumlocutions, I have settled for "he who," with the justification that, given Michelangelo's own male-oriented psyche and milieu, he himself would have most often understood a masculine referent where the context does not specify otherwise.

Other translation problems posed by Michelangelo's texts are more distinctively his own, such as his level of poetic language, particularly in the use of conjunctions. Notwithstanding his frequent efforts at formal complexity, his natural writing voice is very plain, almost blunt, with relatively little variety. Although he exploited several specialized vocabularies at times, especially those of the arts and religious ideas, and although his Bernesque strain found an outlet in an occasional humorous or grotesque use of terms drawn from agriculture, rural life, and bodily anatomy and physiology, the bulk of his work uses a limited repertory of fairly common and undifferentiated words. For example, Michelangelo uses *cose*, "things," to refer not only to objects but also to emotions, character traits, and virtues (for example, no. 41).

I have for the most part resisted the urge that has tempted editors and translators since Michelangelo the Younger to "upgrade" the language in variety or sophistication. In no. 4, for example—an exercise in Petrarchan longing for a beautiful woman—he writes of a flowery garland that desires to "kiss her head," rather than the conventionally poetic "brow." While some previous translators have silently emended this to "brow," I have kept to what he actually said in order to preserve his unadorned, everyday diction: the equivalent in words of his virtually vegetation-free Eden on the Sistine Chapel ceiling or the barren hillsides of the Pauline Chapel narratives.

Michelangelo's use of conjunctions can pose a similar problem for translators. Whereas more literary contemporaries like Giannotti explored the niceties of such elaborate compound conjunctions as *conciossiachè* ("inasmuch as"), Michelangelo makes a few common words serve many different functions in relating one thought to another, often deviating widely from their standard connotations. Here, in contrast to the general policy of not "improving" his language, I have often opted to increase the number and specificity of these connectors to make the train of thought more manifest than it sometimes is in his abrupt or implicit transitions and vague or generic logical connectors.

The word *e*, for example, does not (in his usage) always carry its customary meaning of "and." In the context of various poems it is used to signify "but" (nos. 15:10, 134:14, 139:7), "yet," or "even so" (no. 7:3). The term *ma*, usually meaning "but," at times means something closer to "anyway" or "besides which" (no. 178:7). Conversely, in no. 280:3, *onde*, normally implying causality ("thus"), seems to imply "but." Similarly, *se*, which normally means "if," is often best translated as "although" or "since" (nos. 9, 228, 261, 297; see section 4).

Finally, in contrast to previous English translators, I have not tried to make my translations rhyme or otherwise convey the formalized sound patterns of the original, since this practice, even when followed as loosely as Gilbert's assonance, inevitably forces word choices and structures that deviate too much from the original phrasing. (The format of a bilingual edition permits those interested in Michelangelo's use of this important formal device to examine it in the original text.) I have, however, maintained the length of line and, to the extent possible, the lineation of separate phrases within a sentence. The rhythmic basis of my English lines, as in standard Italian, is the iambic foot, almost exclusively trimeter or pentameter. Where necessary in order to include the whole of a thought, however, I have not shied from adding hypermetric syllables (as Michelangelo himself not infrequently did), at times approximating a Hopkinslike "sprung rhythm."

In conclusion, in this era of structuralist and poststructuralist criticism, a further level of personal preferences needs to be made explicit. Every generation of translators inevitably creates a new reading of an original text, inflected by the values and concerns of its own culture. So too my versions of Michelangelo's poetry, since they must bear the stamp of this particular time and temperament, are inflected by a preference above all for clarity, directness, and passionate sincerity over arbitrary complexity and impersonal formalism.

Hence I have often found Michelangelo's ambiguities exasperating, and in striving to unravel his knotted train of thought, I may at times have eliminated alternative possibilities not so sharply ruled out by his multivalent text. On the level of language, it was partly a personal sympathy for his blunt, no-nonsense style that made it impossible for me to put into his mouth a word more conventionally "poetic" than he chose ("brow" for head), even though some canons of literary modesty might wish to euphemize his occasional graphic use of such scatological terms as *shit* and *snot* (no. 267) and such vulgarities as *ass* (no. 5).

As for his passion, I have responded with a pang of sympathetic sadness only slightly mollified by a consciousness of the historical discontinuity between his world and mine. However difficult it is for a postmodern atheist to empathize with the moral conflicts of a Counter-Reformation Catholic, a man of the polymorphously perverse twentieth century—especially if he shares Michelangelo's passionate orientation toward other men—cannot but be pained by the spectacle of a profound love that could not be fully understood, much less accepted, by the lover himself as anything more than either chaste longing or "concealed sin."

After living for five years with Michelangelo's immense and stormy personal legacy, I have come (as biographers often complain) to speak to him like an ever present companion. Inevitably, my construction of this imaginary friend, irritant, adversary, and tragic hero is only one version of the man and his work. Ultimately, my sole aim and greatest satisfaction in undertaking to present his literary testimony to the modern English reader is the hope that, in Michelangelo's words (no. 237), "the beauty that once existed is remembered."

Bibliographical Abbreviations
Used in Notes to Poems

C.   *Il carteggio di Michelangelo,* ed. Giovanni Poggi, Paola Barocchi, and Renzo Ristori. Citations are to item numbers, in Roman numerals.

CR   Vittoria Colonna, *Le Rime di Vittoria Colonna.*

CW   Ascanio Condivi, *Life of Michelangelo,* trans. Alice Sedgwick Wohl and ed. Hellmut Wohl.

DC   Dante Alighieri, *Vita nuova; Rime,* ed. Fredi Chiappelli. Citations are by poem number, in Roman numerals; poems included in the *Vita nuova* are preceded by that title.

FJ   Marsilio Ficino, *Commentarium in Convivio Platonis,* trans. and ed. Sears R. Jayne.

Frey   *Die Dichtungen des Michelagniolo Buonarroti,* ed. Carl Frey. Citations are to poem numbers, in Roman numerals.

GD   Donato Giannotti, *Dialogi di Donato Giannotti,* ed. Dioclecio Redig de Campos.

Girardi   *Michelangelo Buonarroti: Rime,* ed. Enzo Noè Girardi.

H   Francisco de Hollanda, *Dialogues in Rome,* trans. Charles Holroyd, in his *Michael Angelo Buonarroti.*

LM   Lorenzo de' Medici, *Canzoniere,* ed. Paolo Orvieto. Citations are to poem numbers, in Roman numerals.

PD   Petrarch, *Petrarch's Lyric Poems: The "Rime Sparse" and Other Lyrics,* trans. and ed. Robert M. Durling. Citations are to poem numbers (Arabic), which follow the standard sequence for Petrarch's oeuvre.

PO	Angelo Poliziano, *Poesie italiane*, ed. Saverio Orlando.
R.	*The Letters of Michelangelo*, trans. and ed. E. H. Ramsden. Citations are to the numbers of individual letters, in Arabic numerals, or to the detailed appendixes.
Ricordi	*I ricordi di Michelangelo*, ed. Lucilla Bardeschi Ciulich and Paola Barocchi. Citations are to individual *ricordo* numbers, in Roman numerals.
TC	Charles de Tolnay, *Corpus dei disegni di Michelangelo*. Citations are to drawing numbers.
VB	Giorgio Vasari, *Lives of the Artists*, trans. George Bull.
VM	———, *Le vite de' più eccellenti pittori scultori ed architettori*, ed. Gaetano Milanesi.

Citations and quotes from Dante, *The Divine Comedy*, are from the edition translated and edited by Charles Singleton.

Sheet of sketches with text of poem no. 1 (TC no. 36v)

1

Molti anni fassi qual felice, in una
brevissima ora si lamenta e dole;
o per famosa o per antica prole
altri s'inlustra, e 'n un momento s'imbruna.
Cosa mobil non è che sotto el sole   5
non vinca morte e cangi la fortuna.

One who lives happily for many years
in one brief hour suffers and laments;
another, through famous or ancient lineage
shines brightly, and in a moment grows dark.

There isn't a moving thing under the sun   5
that death does not defeat and fortune change.

Beginning of a sonnet, written ca. 1503–6 on the verso of a sheet of studies for such early
projects as the Battle of Cascina (1504) and an apostle for the Florence Duomo (TC no. 36v);
next to the verses are early architectural sketches for the tomb of Julius II, ca. 1505–6. For
three further fragments on the same sheet, see A7–9. Even in this earliest literary attempt,
written before the age of thirty, M displays his lifelong pessimism about passing time and the
vagaries of fortune.

   3. *lineage:* M was greatly concerned with his family pedigree; cf. no. 21.

2

Sol io ardendo all'ombra mi rimango,
quand'el sol de' suo razzi el mondo spoglia:
ogni altro per piacere, e io per doglia,
prostrato in terra, mi lamento e piango.

I alone keep burning in the shadows
when the sun strips the earth of its rays;
everyone else from pleasure, and I from pain,
prostrate upon the ground, lament and weep.

Quatrain, perhaps the beginning of a sonnet, ca. 1503–5, on a sheet of various sketches (TC no. 46). On the recto are nudes and a Madonna; on the verso, a leg and other subjects, and, partly crossed out, a written fragment (A10) using the same antithesis of light and shadow. The topos of people or animals lying down to rest at the end of day, which dates back to Virgil, occurs in Dante (*Inferno* 2:1–6); and in several poems by Petrarch, the evening brings rest to all but the lovesick poet (PD nos. 50, 164, 216; M's thought most closely parallels no. 22, "A qualunque animale").

3–4. The sense, unclearly expressed, is: Everyone lies down on the ground after sunset, but while others do so to enjoy the cool evening, M, still aflame with suffering, lies down to cry. *Prostrato*, like English *prostrate*, means both "lying horizontally" and "emotionally exhausted," but the latter meaning would apply here only to M himself.

3

Grato e felice, a' tuo feroci mali
ostare e vincer mi fu già concesso;
or lasso, il petto vo bagnando spesso
contr'a mie voglia, e so quante tu vali.

E se i dannosi e preteriti strali   5
al segno del mie cor non fur ma' presso,
or puoi a colpi vendicar te stesso
di que' begli occhi, e fien tutti mortali.

Da quanti lacci ancor, da quante rete
vago uccelletto per maligna sorte   10
campa molt'anni per morir po' peggio,

tal di me, donne, Amor, come vedete,
per darmi in questa età più crudel morte,
campato m'ha gran tempo, come veggio.

Grateful and happy, I was once allowed
to resist and defeat your evil cruelties;
now, alas, I often bathe my breast with tears
against my will, and realize how strong you are.

And if your previous damaging arrows   5
never came near the target of my heart,
now you can take your vengeance in the blows
of those fair eyes, and all of them are deadly.

From so many snares, even from so many nets
a pretty little bird, by evil fate,   10
escapes for many years, to die worse later;

So with me, ladies, Love, as you can see,
to give me at this age a crueler death,
let me escape for a long time, as I can see.

M's earliest known complete sonnet, written some time after 1504, on the verso of a sheet of drawings of horses and mounted combat (TC no. 102v); the same sheet also contains nos. 6–9. The theme is a Dantesque/Petrarchan standard; the imagery of Love's arrows (lines 5–8) reappears frequently in M's poems (e.g., nos. 22–24, 27, 77, 131, 137, 142), as does the eye (see no. 8). The poet addresses first Love, then "ladies" (lines 12–14); the shift is more evident in the Italian verbs, which change from singular (tu) to plural (voi) forms.

5. *damaging arrows:* cf. nos. 3, 23, etc.

4

Quanto si gode, lieta e ben contesta
di fior sopra ' crin d'or d'una, grillanda,
che l'altro inanzi l'uno all'altro manda,
come ch'il primo sia a baciar la testa!

Contenta è tutto il giorno quella vesta   5
che serra 'l petto e poi par che si spanda,
e quel c'oro filato si domanda
le guanci' e 'l collo di toccar non resta.

Ma più lieto quel nastro par che goda,
dorato in punta, con sì fatte tempre   10
che preme e tocca il petto ch'egli allaccia.

E la schietta cintura che s'annoda
mi par dir seco: qui vo' stringer sempre.
Or che farebbon dunche le mie braccia?

How joyful is the garland on her golden locks,
so happy and well fashioned out of flowers
each one of which thrusts forward past the others
that it might be the first to kiss her head.

Throughout the day, that dress is gratified   5
which locks her breast and then seems to stream down;
and what they call a spun-gold thread
never ceases to touch her cheeks and neck.

But even more delighted seems that ribbon,
gilded at the tips, and made in such a way   10
that it presses and touches the breast it laces up.

And her simple belt that's tied up in a knot
seems to say to itself, "Here would I clasp forever!"
What, then, would my arms do?

Sonnet, written on the verso of a letter dated 24 December 1507, which M received while working in Bologna. Much speculation has centered on whether this poem, one of the very few in which M praises specific details of the female form, was inspired by some particular woman he had met there (the putative "bella bolognese"). But there is no evidence linking him romantically to anyone at this time, and the sonnet seems essentially an exercise in a traditional Petrarchan conceit (cf. PD no. 160: "Qual dolcezza . . . vederla . . . tessendo un cerchio a l'oro"). The sensuous cataloguing of the woman's clothing may also derive from Poliziano (*Stanze* I:43, 46, 102). A17, written on the same sheet, expresses the same note of physical desire. Cf. no. 94 for a similar fantasy involving clothing.

5

I' ho già fatto un gozzo in questo stento,
come fa l'acqua a' gatti in Lombardia
o ver d'altro paese che si sia,
c'a forza 'l ventre appicca sotto 'l mento.
    La barba al cielo, e la memoria sento   5
in sullo scrigno, e 'l petto fo d'arpia,
e 'l pennel sopra 'l viso tuttavia
mel fa, gocciando, un ricco pavimento.
    E' lombi entrati mi son nella peccia,
e fo del cul per contrapeso groppa,   10
e' passi senza gli occhi muovo invano.
    Dinanzi mi s'allunga la corteccia,
e per piegarsi adietro si ragroppa,
e tendomi com'arco soriano.
    Però fallace e strano   15
surge il iudizio che la mente porta,
ché mal si tra' per cerbottana torta.
    La mia pittura morta
difendi orma', Giovanni, e 'l mio onore,
non sendo in loco bon, né io pittore.   20

    I've already grown a goiter at this drudgery—
as the water gives the cats in Lombardy,
or else it may be in some other country—
which sticks my stomach by force beneath my chin.
    With my beard toward heaven, I feel my memory-box   5
atop my hump; I'm getting a harpy's breast;
and the brush that is always above my face,
by dribbling down, makes it an ornate pavement.
    My loins have entered my belly, and I make
my ass into a crupper as counterweight;   10
without my eyes, my feet move aimlessly.
    In front of me my hide is stretching out
and, to wrinkle up behind, it forms a knot,
and I am bent like a Syrian bow.

I o gia fatto ngozo isoneçto steto
chome fa lacq̄a agacti ilonbardia
o uer daltro paese chessisia
cha forza luetre apicha sottolmeto

L abarba alcielo ellamemoria seto
isullo scrignio espeeto fo darpia
elpennel sopraluiso tuctania
melfa gocciando u richo pauimeto

E lobi entrati miso nella peccia
efo delcul ꝑ chotrapeso groppa
epassi seza gliochi muouo inuano

D imāzi misalluga lachoraccia
eꝑ piegarsi adietro siragroppa
e tedomi comarcho soriano

ꝑo fallace esrano
surgie iludicio ꝓ lamēte porta
ꝓ mal sipra ꝑ cerbottana torta

lamia pictura morta

di fe di orma giouanni elmio onore
nō sedo iloͤg bo ne io pictore

Manuscript of poem no. 5 with self-portrait (TC no. 174r)

71

Therefore the reasoning that my mind produces   15
comes out unsound and strange,
for one shoots badly through a crooked barrel.
   Giovanni, from now on
defend my dead painting, and my honor,
since I'm not in a good position, nor a painter.   20

Written ca. 1509–10, while M was frescoing the Sistine Chapel (1508–12). Next to the autograph is a sketch illustrating the artist standing and craning his neck upward while painting a cartoonlike figure on the ceiling (TC no. 174r). The tone is facetious yet bitter. M wrote numerous complaints to his family about being "worn out with this stupendous labor" and "enduring the utmost discomfort and weariness" (C. LXX, C, CIII, CVII; R. 51, 77, 81, 82); Vasari reported the same experience. The *sonetto caudato*, with its additional three-line "tail" (here doubled), was employed in the sixteenth century by the burlesque poet Francesco Berni; cf. nos. 25, 71. For another example of Bernesque humor, see no. 54.

   2. *cats: gatti* might also refer to human residents of the area; the word was used by Burchiello to mean peasants or country people.

   5. *memory-box:* i.e., the lower rear part of the skull. In his *Lezzioni*, Benedetto Varchi explained that the Florentines used *memoria* to mean both "memory" and the area of the brain where that faculty was believed located.

   6. *hump:* here, a jocular reference to the spinal column, implying its deformation into something animal-like. *Harpies*, in Greek mythology, were hideous female creatures with a human head and the body of a bird.

   10. *crupper* (*groppa*) refers to the rump of four-legged animals, again implying inhuman distention.

   12. *hide: corteccia*, more literally "rind" or "bark," meaning an external covering, usually refers to grain or fruit.

   14. a *Syrian bow* was shaped into a single semicircular arc. The image, found in Berni, recurs in no. 20.

   17. *barrel: cerbottana*, originally a tubular blowpipe for bird hunting, was later applied to a small firearm of similar shape.

   18. *Giovanni:* the autograph is addressed "A Giovanni, a quel propio da Pistoia"—probably the humanist and academician Giovanni di Benedetto da Pistoia, who wrote several sonnets to M. For later poems sent to him, see nos. 10, 71.

   20. Vasari and Condivi record M's resentment at being removed from work on Julius II's tomb to fresco the ceiling. When one section of the painting was attacked by mold, the artist told the pope that painting "is not my art" (CW 57). Similarly, in 1509 he wrote to his father that painting "is not my profession" (C. LXII; R. 45).

6

Signor, se vero è alcun proverbio antico,
questo è ben quel, che chi può mai non vuole.
Tu hai creduto a favole e parole
e premiato chi è del ver nimico.

I' sono e fui già tuo buon servo antico,   5
a te son dato come e' raggi al sole,
e del mie tempo non ti incresce o dole,
e men ti piaccio se più m'affatico.

Già sperai ascender per la tua altezza,
e 'l giusto peso e la potente spada   10
fussi al bisogno, e non la voce d'eco.

Ma 'l cielo è quel c'ogni virtù disprezza
locarla al mondo, se vuol c'altri vada
a prender frutto d'un arbor ch'è secco.

My lord, if any ancient proverb is true,
it's surely this one, that one who can never wants to.
You have believed fantastic stories and talk
and rewarded one who is truth's enemy.

I am and long have been your faithful servant,   5
I gave myself to you like rays to the sun;
but you don't suffer or care about my time,
and the more I exert myself, the less you like me.

Once, I hoped to rise up through your eminence,
and the just scales and the powerful sword   10
were what was needed, and not an echoing voice.

But heaven is the one that scorns all virtue
if it puts it in the world, and then wants us
to go and pluck fruit from a tree that's dry.

Sonnet, an angry denunciation of the ingratitude of some important patron who had given
commissions to rivals and rewarded M insufficiently for his labors; written on the same sheet
as nos. 5, 7–9 (TC no. 102v). Probably written ca. 1511 and thus most likely referring to Pope
Julius II. M fled from Rome in April 1506, and his letters of 1506–7 complain of the pope's
inconstant patronage, threats, and delay in payment (C. viii–xv; R. 8–12). He later com-

plained that about 1507 Raphael and Bramante were trying to convince Julius to transfer M from the tomb to the Sistine Ceiling (VM 7:172; VB 349; CW 39), and in 1542 he wrote at length about the envy felt by Raphael and Bramante, though no other source confirms his view (C. MI; R. 227). Line 7, implying that much of M's time has been unproductive, may refer to the way that Julius often abruptly shifted the artist from one unfinished project to another. Two phrases are usually taken as references to the pope. *The powerful sword* recalls Julius's military prowess; when M, planning the bronze portrait of Julius cast in 1507, asked if he would like to be portrayed holding a book, Julius replied, "Put a sword there. I know nothing about reading" (VM 7:171; VB 349). The *tree that's dry* suggests a veiled pun on Julius's family name, *Rovere* = oak.

9. *altezza*, more properly "height," is rendered as *eminence* to preserve its dual meaning of "highness," as used in royal titles.

10. *giusto peso*, i.e., the scales of justice.

14. *secco*, "dry" has also been read as *seco*, "with him/with one," i.e., someone M is associated with. Cf. the same image in nos. 22:37, 199.

7

Chi è quel che per forza a te mi mena,
oilmè, oilmè, oilmè,
legato e stretto, e son libero e sciolto?
Se tu incateni altrui senza catena,
e senza mane o braccia m'hai raccolto, 5
chi mi difenderà dal tuo bel volto?

Who's this who leads me to you against my will,
alas, alas, alas,
bound and confined, though I'm still free and loose?
If you can chain others without a chain,
and without hands or arms you've drawn me in, 5
who will defend me from your beautiful face?

Madrigal, written ca. 1511, on the same sheet as nos. 3, 6, 8, 9 (TC no. 102v). For the theme of love binding (*legare*) the lover, cf. nos. 23, 36, 41, 70. The antithesis of chains and liberty derives from poems by Benivieni and Lorenzo de' Medici.

1. *Who's this*, presumably Amor (Cupid).

8

Come può esser ch'io non sia più mio?
O Dio, o Dio, o Dio,
chi m'ha tolto a me stesso,
c'a me fusse più presso
o più di me potessi che poss'io?   5
O Dio, o Dio, o Dio,
come mi passa el core
chi non par che mi tocchi?
Che cosa è questo, Amore,
c'al core entra per gli occhi,   10
per poco spazio dentro par che cresca?
E s'avvien che trabocchi?

How can it be that I'm no longer mine?
O God, O God, O God!
Who's snatched me from myself
so that he might be closer to me
or have more power over me than I have?   5
O God, O God, O God!
How can someone pierce my heart
who doesn't seem to touch me?
What is this thing, O Love,
that enters the heart through the eyes,   10
and in the small space inside it, seems to expand?
And what if it should overflow?

Written ca. 1511, on the same sheet as nos. 3, 6, 7, 9. A madrigal, apparently not fully polished in form (line 11 has no corresponding rhyme), though expressing a complete thought.

   1. *I'm no longer mine:* cf. no. 235:4.

   3. For similar images of being taken away from himself, cf. nos. 108, 161, 235.

   2, 6. The repeated *O Dio,* doubtless intended to evoke pathetic fervor, veers close to the cadences of maudlin sentimentality (cf. *oilmè,* no. 7). The lines were omitted by Michelangelo the Younger, whether out of literary or religious nicety we cannot say.

   4. *he:* the Italian is gender-neutral; *closer to me* than myself: M's thought is incomplete.

   9. *this thing,* i.e., love itself, inspired by the sight of beauty. Other editors read *questo amore,* "this love"—identifying the god more exactly as subject as well as addressee.

   10. Cf. Petrarch, PD no. 3: "Love found . . . the way open through my eyes to my heart." A frequent metaphor in Neoplatonism for love's entrance, also found in Ficino. Some years later (1533), M wrote of his passionate feelings for Cavalieri (then in Rome), adding, "Imagine, if the eye were also playing its part, the state in which I should find myself" (C. CMXVI; R. 193).

9

Colui che 'l tutto fe', fece ogni parte
e poi del tutto la più bella scelse,
per mostrar quivi le suo cose eccelse,
com'ha fatto or colla sua divin'arte.

He who made everything, first made each part
and then from all chose the most beautiful
to demonstrate here his sublime creations,
as he has now done with his divine art.

A quatrain, perhaps the beginning of a sonnet. Written ca. 1511, on the same sheet as nos. 3, 6, 7, 8. *The most beautiful* may allude either to a person or to some work of nature, etc. The theme of God as the source of all beauty, and hence of art as a creation of divine forces, dates back to Petrarch's praise of Laura (nos. 4, 72, 154). Francisco de Hollanda's *Dialogues* record several parallel remarks by M: "Good painting is nothing else but a copy of the perfections of God and a reminder of His painting," and "the painting which I so much vaunt and praise will be the imitation of some single thing amongst those which immortal God made with great care and knowledge and which He invented and painted, like to a Master" (H 240, 276).

    3. *here*: on earth.

Qua si fa elmi di calici e spade
e 'l sangue di Cristo si vend'a giumelle,
e croce e spine son lance e rotelle,
e pur da Cristo pazïenzia cade.

    Ma non ci arrivi più 'n queste contrade,   5
ché n'andre' 'l sangue suo 'nsin alle stelle,
poscia c'a Roma gli vendon la pelle,
e ècci d'ogni ben chiuso le strade.

    S'i' ebbi ma' voglia a perder tesauro,
per ciò che qua opra da me è partita,   10
può quel nel manto che Medusa in Mauro;

    ma se alto in cielo è povertà gradita,
qual fia di nostro stato il gran restauro,
s'un altro segno ammorza l'altra vita?

Here they make helmets and swords from chalices
and by the handful sell the blood of Christ;
his cross and thorns are made into lances and shields;
yet even so Christ's patience still rains down.

    But let him come no more into these parts: 5
his blood would rise up as far as the stars,
since now in Rome his flesh is being sold,
and every road to virtue here is closed.

    If ever I wished to shed my worldly treasures,
since no work is left me here, the man in the cope   10
can do as Medusa did in Mauretania.

    But even if poverty's welcomed up in heaven,
how can we earn the great reward of our state
if another banner weakens that other life?

Sonnet, a bitter attack on the bellicosity and materialism of Rome under Julius II, reminiscent of Petrarch's invectives against the Avignon popes (*Rime* nos. 113, 114, etc.). *No work is left me here* (line 10) suggests a date shortly after M's completion of the Sistine Chapel ceiling in 1512.

    9–11. The thought is incomplete: If ever I wished to become poor, now is the time, since my work is no longer appreciated here.

10. *the man in the cope*, the pope.

11. *Medusa,* the hideous Gorgon whose stare could turn living creatures to stone, was said to have created Mount Atlas in northern Africa (Roman *Mauretania,* hence M's *Mauro*) by petrifying the ancient Titan Atlas, who supported the heavens on his shoulders. The pope, implicitly, can annihilate the artist by anger or neglect.

13. In the Italian as in English, *state* (*stato*) may refer either to a spiritual state (salvation through poverty) or the temporal state (purification of the papal domains); cf. no. 248:14. *Il gran restauro* echoes Dante (*Inferno* 3:58–61), who writes of *il gran rifiuto* of Pope Celestine V; he resigned the papacy in 1294, giving way to Boniface VIII, on whom Dante blamed many of the failures of the church.

14. *another banner:* that of war rather than the banner of Christ, i.e., eternal life. M ended his ms. (a letter to Giovanni di Benedetto da Pistoia; see no. 5) with the phrase, "Your Michelangelo, in Turkey"—presumably an ironic comparison of the Romans to the Turkish infidels, whose proverbial violence then menaced the Mediterranean.

Quanto sare' men doglia il morir presto
che provar mille morte ad ora ad ora,
da ch'in cambio d'amarla, vuol ch'io mora!
Ahi, che doglia 'nfinita
sente 'l mio cor, quando li torna a mente   5
che quella ch'io tant'amo amor non sente!
Come resterò 'n vita?
Anzi mi dice, per più doglia darmi,
che se stessa non ama: e vero parmi.
Come posso sperar di me le dolga,   10
se se stessa non ama? Ahi trista sorte!
che fia pur ver, ch'io ne trarrò la morte?

How much less painful a quick death would be
than to suffer a thousand deaths, hour after hour,
since in return for loving her she wishes me dead.
Oh, what infinite pain
my heart feels, when it is reminded   5
that she whom I love so much feels no love!
How can I go on living?
She even tells me, to cause me greater pain,
that she does not love herself—and that seems true.
How can I hope that she'll take pity on me   10
if she does not love herself? Ah, wretched fate!
Might it yet be true, that my death shall come of it?

Madrigal, variously dated 1505–11 or 1513–18. M's autograph is lost, but the copy by
Michelangelo the Younger records that the original was written on a sheet of unspecified
sketches, and refers to this poem as a *ballata*, though there is no evidence that it was set to
music (but see further no. 12). M expands the courtly tradition of the resistant beloved with
the idea that her own psychological state makes her incapable of love and that she herself is
aware of this.

Com'arò dunche ardire
senza vo' ma', mio ben, tenermi 'n vita,
s'io non posso al partir chiedervi aita?
Que' singulti e que' pianti e que' sospiri
che 'l miser core voi accompagnorno,   5
madonna, duramente dimostrorno
la mia propinqua morte e' miei martiri.
Ma se ver è che per assenzia mai
mia fedel servitù vadia in oblio,
il cor lasso con voi, che non è mio.   10

How will I ever have the nerve
without you, my beloved, to stay alive,
if I dare not ask your help when leaving you?
Those sobs and those tears and those sighs
that came to you with my unhappy heart,   5
my lady, testified distressingly
to my impending death and to my torments.
But if it is true that through my absence
my faithful servitude may be forgotten,
I leave with you my heart, which is not mine.   10

Madrigal, probably dated 1513–18. In slightly altered and extended form, the text was set to music and published in Naples as part of a song collection by Bartolommeo Tromboncino of Verona (*Fioretti di frottole, barzellette, capitoli, strambotti e sonetti*, bk. 2). The edition appeared in 1518, which suggests that this poem was already known somewhat earlier. Line 8 lacks a corresponding rhyme.

8–10. For the conceit of leaving one's heart with a beloved, cf. Petrarch, no. 242.

10. In an alternative draft, M makes explicit that the heart is left as a pledge (*pegno*) of love.

13

La fama tiene gli epitaffi a giacere; non va né inanzi né indietro, perché son morti, e el loro operare è fermo.

Fame holds the epitaphs in place; she goes neither forward nor backward, for they are dead, and their work is stilled.

Inscribed on a sheet of sketches for the tombs of Giuliano and Lorenzo de' Medici in the Medici Chapel of San Lorenzo, Florence, which M worked on from 1519 to 1534 (TC no. 189r). The fragment, which some editors transcribe as lines of free verse, dates from the initial phase of the project, ca. 1520. It probably records a rejected conception in which a kneeling allegorical figure of Fame (faintly sketched in the drawing with arms outstretched toward two rectangular plaques) would have supported inscriptions over each of the sarcophagi.

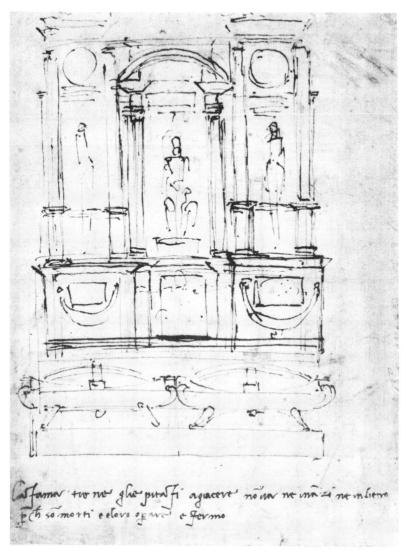

Drawing for the Medici Chapel (TC no. 189r)

El Dì e la Notte parlano, e dicono: —Noi abbiàno col nostro veloce corso condotto alla morte el duca Giuliano; è ben giusto che e' ne facci vendetta come fa. E la vendetta è questa: che avendo noi morto lui, lui così morto ha tolto la luce a noi e cogli occhi chiusi ha serrato e' nostri, che non risplendon più sopra la terra. Che arrebbe di noi dunche fatto, mentre vivea?—

Day and Night speak and say: "We, in our swift course, have led Duke Giuliano to his death; it is only fair that he should take revenge on us as he does. And his revenge is this: Having been killed by us, he, being dead, has deprived us of light, and by closing his eyes has shut ours, which no longer shine upon the earth. What might he have done with us, then, if he had lived?"

Like no. 13, related to the Medici chapel tombs (TC no. 201r). M imagines an oration by his paired statues of Night and Day (ca. 1521–24), which recline on the sarcophagus beneath the effigy of Giuliano de' Medici, duke of Nemours (d. 1519). It is uncertain whether this passage was meant to stand on its own as a kind of free verse, or was rather a conceptual "argument" later to be rendered into more formal rhyme. The conceit of a world darkened by the death of a heroic figure had been used by Dante in reference to the tradition surrounding the death of Christ (*Paradiso* 27:35–36), and Petrarch wrote of his eyes finding the sun darkened by the death of Laura (no. 275). For M's later poem personifying his statue of Night, see no. 247.

15

Di te me veggo e di lontan mi chiamo
per appressarm'al ciel dond'io derivo,
e per le spezie all'esca a te arrivo,
come pesce per fil tirato all'amo.

   E perc'un cor fra dua fa picciol segno   5
di vita, a te s'è dato ambo le parti;
ond'io resto, tu 'l sai, quant'io son, poco.
E perc'un'alma infra duo va 'l più degno,
m'è forza, s'i' voglio esser, sempre amarti;
ch'i' son sol legno, e tu se' legno e foco.   10

I see I'm yours, and from afar I'm called
to draw nearer to that heaven whence I come,
and, with your beauties as bait, I reach you
like a fish on a hook pulled in by the line.

   And since a heart split in two shows little sign   5
of life, it gave both of its halves to you;
which leaves me (as you know I am) not much.
And since a soul tends, between two things, toward the worthier,
I'm forced, if I want to live, to love you forever—
For I'm only wood, but you are wood and fire.   10

Though often described as a madrigal, this poem is structured like the last ten lines of a sonnet. It was written on the verso of a sheet of sketches for the Medici tombs (ca. 1521–24) along with nos. 16 and A21 (TC no. 185v). Here for the first time M goes beyond simply describing his passionate feelings and introduces the Neoplatonic idea that the love of beauty can draw the lover upward to a sense of the divine origin of all love. Several commentators have assumed M is addressing a woman, but as so often occurs, the gender of the addressee is not specified.

   3. *beauties:* the Italian *spezie* connotes singular or exceptional traits.

16

D'un oggetto leggiadro e pellegrino,
d'un fonte di pietà nasce 'l mie male.

From a thing of graceful and exotic beauty,
from a fountain of mercy my suffering is born.

Written on the same sheet as nos. 15 and A21 (TC no. 185v). The common rhyme with no. A21 (*male, tale*) suggests that these two fragments were part of one abandoned idea; A21 might follow the two lines of no. 16. The use of antithesis in the second line recalls Petrarch and Lorenzo de' Medici and is ironic in tone: one who *ought* to be a source of kindness, and perhaps even considers himself or herself to be, unwittingly causes M pain.

17

Crudele, acerbo e dispietato core,
vestito di dolcezza e d'amar pieno,
tuo fede al tempo nasce, e dura meno
c'al dolce verno non fa ciascun fiore.

    Muovesi 'l tempo, e compartisce l'ore   5
al viver nostr'un pessimo veneno;
lu' come falce e no' siàn come fieno,

.   .   .   .

    La fede è corta e la beltà non dura,
ma di par seco par che si consumi,   10
come 'l peccato tuo vuol de' mie danni.

    .   .   .   .

.   .   .   .

sempre fra noi fare' con tutti gli anni.

Cruel, harsh, and pitiless heart,
cloaked with sweetness and filled with bitterness,
your fidelity, born into time, lasts less
than any flower does in the sweet spring.

    Time moves on, and portions out the hours,   5
the very worst of poisons to our life;
he is like a scythe and we are like the hay,

.   .   .   .

    Fidelity is brief and beauty does not last,
but, like the former, seems to waste away,   10
just as your sin would like my woes to do.

    .   .   .   .

.   .   .   .

would always do to us through all the years.

Incomplete draft of a sonnet, written on the back of a letter to M in Carrara from Stefano di Tommaso in Florence, dated 20 April 1521. M unites the complaint of the spurned lover (in the Petrarchan antithesis of sweet–bitter; cf. nos. 76, 158) with a lament for the destructive power of time over all love.

3. *into time:* subject to change.

7. Alluding to the traditional image of Father Time as "the grim reaper," whose attribute is a scythe or sickle.

14. The unstated subject of the abbreviated verb *fare'* (would do) might be either singular (e.g., Time) or plural (love, beauty, etc.).

Mille rimedi invan l'anima tenta:
poi ch'i' fu' preso alla prestina strada,
di ritornare endarno s'argomenta.
Il mare e 'l monte e 'l foco colla spada:
in mezzo a questi tutti insieme vivo.   5
Al monte non mi lascia chi m'ha privo
dell'intelletto e tolto la ragione.

The soul tries a thousand remedies in vain;
since I was captured, it's been struggling
in vain to get back on its earlier road.
The sea, and the mountain, and the fire with the sword:
I live in the midst of all of these together.   5
The one who's deprived me of my mind, and taken
away my reason, won't let me up the mountain.

Written on the back of a letter from the artist Giovanni da Udine in Venice to M in Florence, dated Eastertide, 1522 (27 April). The form is irregular and perhaps incomplete.

1. *remedies in vain:* cf. no. 54:100.

2. Recalls the opening line of Dante's *Inferno*, in which the author loses his way "in the middle of life's road" (*cammin*).

4. *the fire with the sword* recalls the flaming sword that God placed at the gates of the Garden of Eden to bar Adam and Eve from returning after their expulsion (Genesis 3:23–24). M implies that he has lost some Edenic, early state of faith or innocence.

6. *the one who:* It is tempting to relate the "depriver" to M's affection for the young Gherardo Perini, with whom he was in correspondence in January and February 1522 (C. MLI; R. 151), but clear evidence is lacking (on Perini, see also VM 7:276 and nos. 22, 27, 32, 36).

7. *the mountain:* an example of M's infrequent use of allegory. This image of the spiritual life, mounting up toward God, recalls Dante's *dilettoso monte*.

Natura ogni valore
di donna o di donzella
fatto ha per imparare, insino a quella
c'oggi in un punto m'arde e ghiaccia el core.
Dunche nel mie dolore 5
non fu tristo uom più mai;
l'angoscia e 'l pianto e ' guai,
a più forte cagion maggiore effetto.
Così po' nel diletto
non fu né fie di me nessun più lieto. 10

Nature made every virtue
in a woman or a girl
only as training, up until this one
who today, in one moment, burns and freezes my heart.
Therefore, as to my grief, 5
no man was ever more wretched:
with anguish and weeping and woes,
the stronger the cause, the greater the effect.
So too, as to my joy,
No one has been, or can be, happier than I. 10

An incomplete madrigal, written on a sheet bearing the date 25 November 1522 and containing various expense records and architectural sketches, probably for the Medici Chapel (*Ricordi* cx).

4. *burns and freezes:* a commonplace Petrarchan antithesis, also used by Poliziano, Lorenzo de' Medici, and Girolamo Benivieni; cf. nos. 87, 89, 257, 261, 281, etc. *in one moment: in un punto* may mean either "simultaneously" or "suddenly."

Tu ha' 'l viso più dolce che la sapa,
e passato vi par sù la lumaca,
tanto ben lustra, e più bel c'una rapa;
e' denti bianchi come pastinaca,
in modo tal che invaghiresti 'l papa;   5
e gli occhi del color dell'utriaca;
e' cape' bianchi e biondi più che porri:
ond'io morrò, se tu non mi soccorri.

   La tua bellezza par molto più bella
che uomo che dipinto in chiesa sia: 10
la bocca tua mi par una scarsella
di fagiuo' piena, sì com'è la mia;
le ciglia paion tinte alla padella
e torte più c'un arco di Sorìa;
le gote ha' rosse e bianche, quando stacci,   15
come fra cacio fresco e' rosolacci.

   Quand'io ti veggo, in su ciascuna poppa
mi paion duo cocomer in un sacco,
ond'io m'accendo tutto come stoppa,
bench'io sia dalla zappa rotto e stracco.   20
Pensa: s'avessi ancor la bella coppa,
ti seguirrei fra l'altre me' c'un bracco:
di che s'i massi [?] aver fussi possibile,
io fare' oggi qui cose incredibile.

   You have a face sweeter than boiled grape juice—
it looks as if a snail had walked across it,
it shines so much—and prettier than a turnip;
and teeth as white as parsnips,
so much so that you could entice the Pope;   5
and eyes the color of a medicinal brew;
and hair whiter and blonder than a leek;
so that I'll die, if you give me no relief.
   Your beauty seems much more beautiful to me
than any man that's painted in the church;   10
your mouth, it seems to me, is like a sack

Drawing of a woman and child with text of poem no. 20 (TC no. 25v)

filled up with beans, just like my own is;
your eyebrows seem tinted from the frying pan,
and curved more sharply than a Syrian bow;
your cheeks, when you sift flour, get red and white 15
like poppies in fresh cheese.

  When I look down upon each of your breasts
they look like two watermelons in a bag,
so that I'm set on fire just like tow
even though I'm worn and broken by the hoe. 20
Just think: if I still had the cup of beauty,
I'd follow you through the other girls like a hound;
so too, if getting blocks of stone were possible,
I would make incredible things here today.

Three ottava stanzas written on a sketch of a woman standing with a child at her feet (TC no. 25v). Although the drawing is dated 1503–5, the verses were clearly added later, perhaps ca. 1523. An example of M's burlesque mode, with language full of comically incongruous adjectives and references to unusual vegetable products; cf. nos. 5, 54, 267. There are close precedents in Poliziano ("Una vecchia mi vagheggia," PO p. 157) and especially Lorenzo de' Medici's comic poem, "La Nencia di Barberino," in which an excited peasant youth praises his rustic beloved. The general influence of Francesco Berni's "Alla sua innamorata" is also discernible.

  1. *boiled grape juice: sapa* is a condiment made by boiling and condensing newly pressed grape juice.

  6. *medicinal brew: utriaca* (English "theriac"), a mixture of various herbal drugs and honey, held to have medicinal properties.

  9–10. i.e., more beautiful than the paintings seen in churches.

  11–12. The speaker seems to be trying to impress the girl with his prosperity.

  13. *tinted from the frying pan:* i.e., with soot or grease.

  14. *Syrian bow:* the analogy, derived from Berni, also appears in no. 5.

  17–18. The description is similar to a humorous sketch by M of a bust-length female with grotesquely large and sagging breasts (see nos. 47, 68:25–28).

  21. That is, if I were still young and attractive. The Olympian cupbearers, Hebe and Ganymede, served from their *bella coppa* the ambrosial nectar that retained the gods' eternal youth.

21

Chiunche nasce a morte arriva
nel fuggir del tempo; e 'l sole
niuna cosa lascia viva.
Manca il dolce e quel che dole
e gl'ingegni e le parole;   5
e le nostre antiche prole
al sole ombre, al vento un fummo.
Come voi uomini fummo,
lieti e tristi, come siete;
e or siàn, come vedete,   10
terra al sol, di vita priva.
Ogni cosa a morte arriva.
Già fur gli occhi nostri interi
con la luce in ogni speco;
or son voti, orrendi e neri,   15
e ciò porta il tempo seco.

Whoever's born must come to death
in the course of time, and the sun
doesn't leave a thing alive.
Gone are joy and cause of sadness,
and all thinking and all speech,   5
and our ancient pedigrees,
shadows in the sun, smoke in the wind.
Once, we too were men like you,
sad and joyful, just as you are;
now we are, as you can see,   10
dust in the sun, deprived of life.
Everything must come to death.
Once our eyes were fully whole,
with a light within each cavern;
now they're empty, black, and frightful: 15
that's what time brings in its wake.

Now considered to date from 1524 or earlier, this songlike *barzelletta* or *frottola* uses the same
trochaic meter and macabre imagery as the songs written for carnival processions, which were

popular in the late fifteenth and early sixteenth centuries, particularly during the rule of Savonarola. M's text most closely recalls the song "Dolor, pianto e penitenza" by Antonio Alamanni, which Vasari tells us (in his *Vita* of Piero di Cosimo) was chanted around the chariot bearing the figure of Death in the Florentine Carnival of 1511:

> Morti siam come vedete,
>
> così morti vedrem voi:
>
> fummo già come voi siete,
>
> voi sarete come noi.

M's stress on the relentless flow of time, expressed through the repeated image of the sun, accords with the symbolism of his four sculptures of the times of day for the Medici Chapel, then in progress (see nos. 13, 14). Cf. no. 110.

6. *antiche prole:* cf. the same expression in no. 1, used also as an image of declining fortunes over time. M was acutely conscious of changes in dynastic status, later claiming to have discovered his own descent from the Countess Matilda of Canossa (CW pp. 5–6). His letters show great concern that his brothers live up to the family's social position (C. CDLXXIII, MLXX; R. 272).

14. *a light within each cavern,* with a pupil in each eye socket.

22

Che fie di me? che vo' tu far di nuovo
d'un arso legno e d'un afflitto core?
Dimmelo un poco, Amore,
acciò che io sappi in che stato io mi truovo.

Gli anni del corso mio al segno sono, 5
come saetta c'al berzaglio è giunta,
onde si de' quetar l'ardente foco.
E' mie passati danni a te perdono,
cagion che 'l cor l'arme tu' spezza e spunta,
c'amor per pruova in me non ha più loco; 10
e s'e' tuo colpi fussin nuovo gioco
agli occhi mei, al cor timido e molle,
vorria quel che già volle?
Ond'or ti vince e sprezza, e tu tel sai,
sol per aver men forza oggi che mai. 15

Tu speri forse per nuova beltate
tornarmi 'ndietro al periglioso impaccio,
ove 'l più saggio assai men si difende:
più corto è 'l mal nella più lunga etate,
ond'io sarò come nel foco el ghiaccio, 20
che si distrugge e parte e non s'accende.
La morte in questa età sol ne difende
dal fiero braccio e da' pungenti strali,
cagion di tanti mali,
che non perdona a condizion nessuna, 25
né a loco, né tempo, né fortuna.

L'anima mia, che con la morte parla,
e seco di se stessa si consiglia,
e di nuovi sospetti ognor s'attrista,
el corpo di dì in dì spera lasciarla: 30
onde l'immaginato cammin piglia,
di speranza e timor confusa e mista.
Ahi, Amor, come se' pronto in vista,
temerario, audace, armato e forte!
che e' pensier della morte 35
nel tempo suo di me discacci fori,

per trar d'un arbor secco fronde e fiori.

   Che poss'io più? che debb'io? Nel tuo regno
non ha' tu tutto el tempo mio passato,
che de' mia anni un'ora non m'è tocca?   40
Qual inganno, qual forza o qual ingegno
tornar mi puote a te, signore ingrato,
c'al cuor la morte e pietà porti in bocca?
Ben sare' ingrata e sciocca
l'alma risuscitata, e senza stima,   45
tornare a quel che gli diè morte prima.

   Ogni nato la terra in breve aspetta;
d'ora in ora manca ogni mortal bellezza:
chi ama, il vedo, e' non si può po' sciorre.
Col gran peccato la crudel vendetta   50
insieme vanno; e quel che men s'apprezza,
colui è sol c'a più suo mal più corre.
A che mi vuo' tu porre,
che 'l dì ultimo buon, che mi bisogna,
sie quel del danno e quel della vergogna?   55

   What's to become of me? What would you do once more
to this charred wood and to this burdened heart?
Tell me a little, Love,
so I'll know what my situation is.
   My years in their flow have hit their mark   5
like an arrow that has reached its target,
and so my burning flame ought to die down.
Now I forgive you your past wrongs toward me;
thanks to them, my heart can blunt and shatter your weapons,
for there's no more room in me for love's ordeals.   10
And even if your blows were some new game
to my eyes, and to my timid and tender heart,
would it want what it once wanted?
So now it defeats and scorns you—and you know it—
only by having less strength today than ever.   15
   Perhaps you're hoping, by some fresh loveliness,
to draw me back into that dangerous snare
where the wiser a man, the less he defends himself.

But the longer one's lived, the shorter his suffering lasts;
and so I will be like ice in the fire,   20
which dwindles and vanishes, but does not ignite.
At this age, only death can defend us
from the fierce arm and from the piercing darts,
cause of so many pains—
Love, who does not spare any rank whatever,   25
nor any place, nor time, nor any fortune.
    My soul is in conversation with Death,
and is consulting with him about itself,
saddened by new anxieties constantly,
the body hoping to leave it from day to day;   30
so it sets off down the road it's had in mind,
confused by its compounded hope and fear.
Ah, Love, how quickly you come into view,
so reckless and daring, armed and powerful
that you drive out of me   35
the thought of death, even though it is time,
to draw new leaves and flowers from a dry tree.
    What more can I do? What should I? Have you not
so used up all my time within your realm
that not one hour of my years is left for me?   40
What trickery, what power or mental skill
could bring me back to you, ungrateful lord,
with compassion in your mouth, death in your heart?
The revived soul would be
foolish, ungrateful, unworthy of respect   45
to return to the one who earlier gave it death.
    The earth awaits shortly everyone who's born;
hour by hour, every mortal beauty fades,
yet he who loves, I see, can't free himself.
Great sin and cruel vengeance go together;   50
and it's only he who values himself the least
who runs most quickly to be hurt the most.
What would you put me through:
that my last day, which must needs be good,
should become one of injury and shame?   55

Written on a letter from M to Giovanni Francesco Fattucci dated January 1524 (C. DCII; R. 159), this is M's first surviving attempt at a long, linked sequence. The stanzas, in *canzone* form, are of irregular length. M asks for relief from a new infatuation on the ground of being too old; given the date, he perhaps refers again to Gherardo Perini (see nos. 18, 27, 32, 36).

23. Love's piercing darts or arrows are a recurrent image; cf. nos. 3, 23, 27, 77, 131, 137, 142, etc.

25. *Love* is not specified as the subject of this last phrase, which could, less probably, refer to Death.

37. *arbor secco:* cf. the same image in nos. 6, 199.

38. This line recalls Petrarch, no. 268, "Che debb'io far . . . Amore?"

40. For the complaint of being robbed of time, see also no. 51:14.

54. I need the end of my life to be virtuous (in order to assure salvation).

23

I' fu', già son molt'anni, mille volte
ferito e morto, non che vinto e stanco
da te, mie colpa; e or col capo bianco
riprenderò le tuo promesse stolte?

Quante volte ha legate e quante sciolte   5
le triste membra, e sì spronato il fianco,
c'appena posso ritornar meco, anco
bagnando il petto con lacrime molte!

Di te mi dolgo, Amor, con teco parlo,
sciolto da' tuo lusinghi: a che bisogna   10
prender l'arco crudel, tirare a voto?

Al legno incenerato sega o tarlo,
o dietro a un correndo, è gran vergogna
c'ha perso e ferma ogni destrezza e moto.

Many years ago, I was not merely beaten
and wearied, but wounded and killed a thousand times
by you—my own fault—and now, with my head white,
should I be taken in again by your foolish promises?

How many times you bound, and how many untied   5
my sad limbs, and so spurred my flanks
that I can scarcely get back to myself
even after bathing my breast with many tears!

I feel sorry for you, Love, and speak to you
released from your delusions: what good is it   10
to take up your cruel bow and shoot in vain?

Like a saw or a worm on wood that's burned to ashes,
it's a great waste to run after someone
who's lost all agility and ceased all motion.

A sonnet written on the same sheet as nos. 24 and 25 and datable about 1524–25. The page contains the beginning of a letter to M's sometime friend Giovanbattista Figiovanni, a cleric at San Lorenzo in Florence, seemingly referring to Pope Clement VII's plans for M's work there. This complaint against love is couched in an ironic solicitousness that contrasts with M's other angry denunciations.

3. *my own fault:* the Italian *mie colpa* closely resembles the Latin phrase of penitence, *mea culpa* (my guilt); cf. no. 289. *with my head white:* now that I am old. Condivi recorded that M's hair in fact remained dark all his life.

5. For images of love's binding, cf. nos. 7, 36, 41, 70, etc.

24

I' fe' degli occhi porta al mie veneno,
quand' el passo dier libero a' fier dardi;
nido e ricetto fe' de' dolci sguardi
della memoria che ma' verrà meno.
    Ancudine fe' 'l cor, mantaco 'l seno   5
da fabricar sospir, con che tu m'ardi.

I made my eyes a gateway for my poison
when they left the way open for your savage darts;
I made my memory, which will never fade,
into a nest and shelter for sweet glances.
    My heart I made an anvil, my breast a bellows,   5
for forging sighs with the flame you kindle in me.

Incomplete beginning of a sonnet, on the same sheet as nos. 23 and 25. Love's entrance through the eyes is a common theme dating back to Dante's description of Beatrice (*Paradiso* 26:13–15); Dante also wrote of a bellows creating sighs (*Purgatorio* 15:51).

    2. *savage darts:* cf. nos. 22, 27, 77, 131, 137, 142, etc.

    6. *the flame you kindle in me,* i.e., the heat of love; M's construction is presumably elliptical.

25

Quand'il servo il signor d'aspra catena
senz'altra speme in carcer tien legato,
volge in tal uso el suo misero stato,
che libertà domanderebbe appena.

E el tigre e 'l serpe ancor l'uso raffrena, 5
e 'l fier leon ne' folti boschi nato;
e 'l nuovo artista, all'opre affaticato,
coll'uso del sudor doppia suo lena.

Ma 'l foco a tal figura non s'unisce;
ché se l'umor d'un verde legno estinge, 10
il freddo vecchio scalda e po' 'l nutrisce,

e tanto il torna in verde etate e spinge,
rinnuova e 'nfiamma, allegra e 'ngiovanisce,
c'amor col fiato l'alma e 'l cor gli cinge.

E se motteggia o finge, 15
chi dice in vecchia etate esser vergogna
amar cosa divina, è gran menzogna.

L'anima che non sogna,
non pecca amar le cose di natura,
usando peso, termine e misura. 20

When the master keeps the slave in prison, bound
by a harsh chain, with hope of nothing else,
he grows so accustomed to his wretched state
that he would scarcely ask for liberty.

Habit tames even the tiger and the serpent, 5
and the fierce lion, born in the dense forest;
and the novice artist, exhausted by his work,
in growing used to sweat doubles his wind.

But fire is not bound by such an image;
for while it sears the sap out of green wood, 10
it warms the chilled old man, then nourishes him,

propels him back so close to his green years,
renews and kindles, cheers and rejuvenates him,
that love's breath twines around his heart and soul.

And if anyone pretends 15
or teases that in old age it is shameful
to love something divine, it's a great lie.
    The soul that does not dream
commits no sin in loving natural things
if it respects balance, limits, and moderation. 20

A double *sonetto caudato*, on the same sheet as nos. 23 and 24, ca. 1524–25; for other examples of this form, see nos. 5 and 71.

1–4. The imagery of perpetual bondage recalls M's self-description as "tied" to the project for the tomb of Julius II, which was still unfinished at this time. He frequently refers to himself as a slave or prisoner of love, e.g., nos. 12, 52, 54, 176.

9. *fire*, i.e., of love.

15–17. These lines read almost as if a reply to the sentiment expressed by Ludovico Ariosto in the second edition of his *Orlando furioso* (1522): "I would say to you that he who, though old, still loves, deserves the penalty that he be bound and chained" (24:2). The first edition of *Orlando* (1516) mentions M by name, though there is no evidence M ever read it.

18. *The soul that does not dream:* one with no illusions, aware of the realities of one's stage in life.

20. *peso,* "weight," is at times used by M to mean a balance or a scale (cf. no. 6). Here it may also refer to weighing one's actions, that is, careful mental consideration.

26

Quand'avvien c'alcun legno non difenda
il propio umor fuor del terrestre loco,
non può far c'al gran caldo assai o poco
non si secchi o non s'arda o non s'accenda.
    Così 'l cor, tolto da chi mai mel renda,   5
vissuto in pianto e nutrito di foco,
or ch'è fuor del suo propio albergo e loco,
qual mal fie che per morte non l'offenda?

Since it happens that no wood can retain
its own moisture out of its place in the earth,
it cannot help it, in more or less great heat,
if it dries out and ignites and burns.
    So my heart, seized by one who may never return it,   5
spending its life in tears and nourished by fire,
now that it's out of its proper place of shelter,
what injury would not wound it mortally?

Two quatrains, perhaps the beginning of a sonnet, datable to the 1520s.
    5. *one who may never return it:* alternatively, "one who I hope never returns it."
    7. *out of its proper place,* out of my own body.

27

Fuggite, amanti, Amor, fuggite 'l foco;
l'incendio è aspro e la piaga è mortale,
c'oltr'a l'impeto primo più non vale
né forza né ragion né mutar loco.

Fuggite, or che l'esemplo non è poco   5
d'un fiero braccio e d'un acuto strale;
leggete in me, qual sarà 'l vostro male,
qual sarà l'impio e dispietato gioco.

Fuggite, e non tardate, al primo sguardo:
ch'i' pensa' d'ogni tempo avere accordo;   10
or sento, e voi vedete, com'io ardo.

Flee, lovers, from Love, flee from his fire;
its flame is cruel and its wound is deadly.
For after its first assault, nothing avails—
neither force nor reason nor changing location.

Flee, now that an example is not lacking   5
of the power of a fierce arm and a sharp arrow:
read in me what your own misfortune will be,
what his merciless, ungodly sport will be.

Flee at the first glance, and do not linger:
for I thought we could come to terms at any time;   10
now I feel, and you can see, how much I'm burning.

Incomplete sonnet, ca. 1524, written on the back of a sheet of architectural sketches for the Medici tombs (TC no. 181v). It seems inspired by an ottava of Poliziano (PO p. 226), "Pigliate esemplo, voi ch'Amor seguite," which ends with the advice "Fuggite Amor." The exhortation of line 9, "do not linger," also echoes Petrarch's sonnet 88, "voi ch'Amore avampa, non v'indugiate." What Clements reads in this poem as M's "mistrust of love's militant power" may be reflected in the drawing of a screaming head, the so-called Damned Soul (TC no. 306r). This drawing, among M's gifts to Gherardo Perini, was interpreted by Goldscheider as an expression of M's sense of the madness inspired by his feelings for the young man, though some scholars date the drawing later, to 1529–31. On Perini, see also nos. 18, 22, 32, 36.

6. *sharp arrow:* cf. nos. 22, 24, 77, 131, 137, 142, etc.

28

Perché pur d'ora in ora mi lusinga
la memoria degli occhi e la speranza,
per cui non sol son vivo, ma beato;
la forza e la ragion par che ne stringa,
Amor, natura e la mie 'ntica usanza,   5
mirarvi tutto il tempo che m'è dato.
E s'i' cangiassi stato,
vivendo in questo, in quell'altro morrei;
né pietà troverei
ove non fussin quegli.   10
O Dio, e' son pur begli!
Chi non ne vive non è nato ancora;
e se verrà dipoi,
a dirlo qui tra noi,
forz'è che, nato, di subito mora;   15
ché chi non s'innamora
de' begli occhi, non vive.

Since hour after hour I'm still beguiled
by the memory of your eyes and by hope,
through which I am not merely alive, but blissful,
I seem compelled by power and by reason,
by love, and nature, and my own old habits   5
to gaze at you for all the time I'm granted.
If I changed my situation,
being alive in this one, in another I'd die,
and would find no mercy
wherever they were absent.   10
Oh God, how beautiful they are!
He who doesn't live on them is as if unborn,
and if he should come later
(I say so just between us),
he would, once born, instantly have to die;   15
for one who does not fall in love
with those fair eyes can't live.

Incomplete madrigal, written ca. 1524–26. Together with nos. 29 and A26, it is written on the back of a version of no. 81; all four share the Petrarchan theme of desire for the sight of the beloved and the power of the love it induces.

2. *hope* of seeing those eyes again, or of obtaining the favor of their return glance.

12. *as if unborn:* cf. M's first letter to Tommaso de' Cavalieri (1533), where he says that if Cavalieri had not consented to receive the gift of some drawings, "I should deem myself unborn, or rather stillborn" (C. DCCCXCVII; R. 191).

13. *come later,* i.e., be born too late to see those eyes.

Ogn'ira, ogni miseria e ogni forza,
chi d'amor s'arma vince ogni fortuna.

Every anger, every misery, every force—
one who's armed with love can defeat any misfortune.

Probably a fragment of a projected poem, since the rhymes are incomplete; for other writings on the same sheet, see no. 28. These present a contrasting mood to the complaint of no. 27; here M works a variation on Virgil's *Omnia vincit amor* (*Eclogues* 10:69); cf. no. 128.

30

Dagli occhi del mie ben si parte e vola
un raggio ardente e di sì chiara luce
che da' mie, chiusi ancor, trapassa 'l core.
Onde va zoppo Amore,
tant'è dispar la soma che conduce,   5
dando a me luce, e tenebre m'invola.

From my beloved's eyes there issues and flies
a ray that burns with a light so bright
that through mine, even when shut, it pierces my heart.
Hence love walks with a limp,
so unbalanced is the burden he transports,   5
bringing me light, and carrying away my darkness.

Madrigal, ca. 1524–26. The comparison of the beloved's glance to a piercing arrow or beam is common in Dante, Petrarch, and Poliziano. The last line has been interpreted to mean that Love brings to the speaker the beloved's beauty but takes back in return only his melancholy or ugliness. On the surface, however, the image refers only to M's reactions to love, not to those of the recipient.

4. For a repeated use of *zoppo Amore,* see no. 113:11.

31

Amor non già, ma gli occhi mei son quegli
che ne' tuo soli e begli
e vita e morte intera trovato hanno.
Tante meno m'offende e preme 'l danno,
più mi distrugge e cuoce;   5
dall'altra ancor mi nuoce
tante amor più quante più grazia truovo.
Mentre ch'io penso e pruovo
il male, el ben mi cresce in un momento.
O nuovo e stran tormento!   10
Però non mi sgomento:
s'aver miseria e stento
è dolce qua dove non è ma' bene,
vo cercando 'l dolor con maggior pene.

My eyes are the ones that have found, not only love,
but life and death together
in yours, which alone are beautiful.
The less their harm besets and weighs on me
the more it sears and destroys me;   5
yet on the other hand,
love hurts me more the more grace I receive.
While I ponder and experience
evil, my good increases in an instant.
O new and strange anguish!   10
But I am not daunted;
if poverty and toil
are sweet here, where there's never any good,
then I'll seek suffering with even worse punishments.

Madrigal, written on a sheet containing a sketch of a putto and various personal memoranda, one dating from 1525 (TC no. 267v). The left edge of the page is cut; Girardi's reconstruction of the first word of each line is tentative. See also A27, on the same sheet.

32

Vivo al peccato, a me morendo vivo;
vita già mia non son, ma del peccato:
mie ben dal ciel, mie mal da me m'è dato,
dal mie sciolto voler, di ch'io son privo.

Serva mie libertà, mortal mie divo   5
a me s'è fatto. O infelice stato!
a che miseria, a che viver son nato!

I live in sin, and dying to myself I live;
my life no longer belongs to me, but to sin.
My good comes from heaven, my evil from myself,
from my own free will, of which I've been deprived.

My freedom's been made a slave, my godly part   5
made mortal for me. O unhappy condition!
To what misery, to what a life I was born!

Part of a sonnet, written on the back of a letter from Sandro, a stonecutter in Carrara, dated 8 October 1525, the period of quarrying for the Medici tombs (*Carteggio*, DCCXVI). For the first time, M introduces his acute sense of sin as a concomitant of love; the repentant urgency recalls Savonarola. The staple image of a lover "dying" for love is transformed into a sense that "living death" comes from that emotion. Since love was not considered sinful in itself, but illicit sexual passion was, M would seem here to be contemplating a more carnal "slavery" than the emotional yearning described in the earlier poems. If he is still thinking of his feelings for Gherardo Perini (see nos. 18, 22, 27, 36), the official condemnation of homosexuality might be the source of M's sense of guilt; his previous poems about women do not mention sinfulness.

5. *godly part*, i.e., the soul, debased and deprived of eternal life. For similar images of slavery to love, cf. no. 70, etc.

.

Sie pur, fuor di mie propie, c'ogni altr'arme
difender par ogni mie cara cosa;
altra spada, altra lancia e altro scudo
fuor delle propie forze non son nulla,
tant'è la trista usanza, che m'ha tolta 5
la grazia che 'l ciel piove in ogni loco.

Qual vecchio serpe per istretto loco
passar poss'io, lasciando le vecchie arme,
e dal costume rinnovata e tolta
sie l'alma in vita e d'ogni umana cosa, 10
coprendo sé con più sicuro scudo,
ché tutto el mondo a morte è men che nulla.

Amore, i' sento già di me far nulla;
natura del peccat' è 'n ogni loco.
Spoglia di me me stesso, e col tuo scudo, 15
colla pietra e tuo vere e dolci arme,
difendimi da me, c'ogni altra cosa
è come non istata, in brieve tolta.

Mentre c'al corpo l'alma non è tolta,
Signor, che l'universo puo' far nulla, 20
fattor, governator, re d'ogni cosa,
poco ti fie aver dentr'a me loco;

. . . .

. . . .

. . . . 25

. . . .

che d'ogn'uomo veril son le vere arme,
senza le quali ogn'uom diventa nulla.

. . . .

. . . . . : . . 30

Even if every weapon but my own
seems to defend everything dear to me,
any other sword, or lance, or shield
but my own powers is of no avail,

so wicked is my habit that has robbed me   5
of the grace that heaven rains down everywhere.
    Like an old serpent through a narrow space
may I pass, shedding my old armor,
and may my soul, stripped of its old habit
and of everything human, be restored to life,   10
covering itself with a more trusty shield;
for the whole world, faced with death, is less than nothing.
    Love, I already feel reduced to nothing:
the nature of sin is in every part of me.
Strip me of myself, and with your shield,   15
your rock, and your true and kindly weapons,
defend me from myself, for everything else,
if quickly removed, is as if it had never been.
    While my soul is not yet taken from my body,
Lord, who can reduce the universe to nothing,   20
maker, governor, king of everything,
it would be a small thing for you to lodge in me;

.   .   .   .
.   .   .   .
      25
.   .   .   .
which are the true weapons of every virile man,
without which every man turns into nothing.

.   .   .   .
.   .   .   .   30

An incomplete sestina, written on the verso of a drawing of the Madonna and Child (TC no. 390); the poem was probably written between 1524 and 1529, though the drawing may be dated much later. A28 is on the recto of the same sheet. The sestina form, used by Dante, Petrarch, and Lorenzo de' Medici, consists of interlinked six-line stanzas. The six words that end the lines of the first stanza are repeated in each succeeding stanza in a fixed pattern of variation. In the interest of clarity, this rigid scheme is not maintained in the translation. For M's later use of the form, see no. 70.

7–8. For related images of sloughing one's skin, see nos. 51, 94, 161.

16. *rock:* a symbol of God's protectiveness in the Old Testament; here, perhaps, also recalling the rock and sling with which David killed Goliath.

34

La vita del mie amor non è 'l cor mio,
c'amor di quel ch'i' t'amo è senza core;
dov'è cosa mortal, piena d'errore,
esser non può già ma', né pensier rio.

Amor del dipartir l'alma da Dio   5
me fe' san occhio e te luc' e splendore;
né può non rivederlo in quel che more
di te, per nostro mal, mie gran desio.

Come dal foco el caldo, esser diviso
non può dal bell'etterno ogni mie stima,   10
ch'exalta, ond'ella vien, chi più 'l somiglia.

Poi che negli occhi hai tutto 'l paradiso,
per ritornar là dov'i' t'ama' prima,
ricorro ardendo sott'alle tuo ciglia.

The life of my love is not in my heart,
for the love I love you with is not of the heart;
it could never be found where there is anything
earthly and full of error, or wicked thoughts.

Love, when our souls took their leave of God,   5
made me a sound eye and you light and splendor;
so my great desire can't help but see Him again
in that part of you that, to our grief, is mortal.

Like heat from fire, one cannot separate
eternal beauty from my regard, which exalts   10
whoever most resembles Him from whom it came.

Since your eyes have in them all of paradise,
to return to that place where I loved you before
I run back, burning, underneath your brows.

Sonnet, ca. 1526, on the same sheet as no. 35.

2. *not of the heart,* i.e., devoid of physical passion. M's phrase *senza core,* literally "without heart," unfortunately takes on in English the unwanted overtone of "heartless."

6. *sound eye,* able to discern your beauty. *light and splendor:* cf. Petrarch, no. 59, "da' begli occhi . . . mi passò nel core . . . un subito splendore."

10. *regard,* in the dual sense of "esteem" and "looking upon."

12. This line recalls Beatrice's words to Dante, "non pur ne' miei occhi è paradiso" (*Paradiso* 18:21).

13. *before:* before birth (cf. line 5).

El ciglio col color non fere el volto
col suo contrar, che l'occhio non ha pena
da l'uno all'altro stremo ov'egli è volto.

L'occhio, che sotto intorno adagio mena,
picciola parte di gran palla scuopre,   5
che men rilieva suo vista serena,

e manco sale e scende quand'el copre;
onde più corte son le suo palpebre,
che manco grinze fan quando l'aopre.

El bianco bianco, el ner più che funebre,   10
s'esser può, el giallo po' più leonino,
che scala fa dall'una all'altra vebre.

Pur tocchi sotto e sopra el suo confino,
e 'l giallo e 'l nero e 'l bianco non circundi.

The eyelid, when it contracts, doesn't limit sight
with its shadow, for the eye has no constraint
from one end of its turning-place to the other.

But the eye, which moves around slowly underneath,
can reveal just a small part of its full ball,   5
which shows but little of its serene gaze,

and it moves up and down less when it's covered;
therefore its eyelids seem of shorter length,
since they wrinkle less when they are being used.

The white's white, the black more so than funeral drapes   10
(if that can be), and more than a lion the yellow
that makes a path from one fiber to the next.

Even if you touch its top and bottom edges,
you can't surround the yellow, black, and white.

An incomplete *capitolo*, or sequence in terza rima, written on the same sheet as no. 34, ca. 1526. This particularly obscure and elliptical description of the human eye has been interpreted as M's practical advice for artists wishing to draw and understand that organ; he made drawings of the eye for his pupils Antonio Mini and Andrea Quaratesi to copy (TC no. 96v).

    1. *contracts:* begins to close. *limit sight:* literally, "harm the face."

3. *its turning-place*: the eye socket, in which the eyeball is free to rotate.

4. *underneath*: below the eyelid.

8–9. The sense is unclear, but seems to refer to the apparent size of the eyelid when it is stretched taut over the eyeball.

10–11. *white*, the white of the eye; *black*, the pupil; *yellow*, perhaps markings or blood vessels in the eye.

Oltre qui fu, dove 'l mie amor mi tolse,
suo mercè, il core e vie più là la vita;
qui co' begli occhi mi promisse aita,
e co' medesmi qui tor me la volse.

    Quinci oltre mi legò, quivi mi sciolse;   5
per me qui piansi, e con doglia infinita
da questo sasso vidi far partita
colui c'a me mi tolse e non mi volse.

It was over here that my love, in his mercy,
took my heart from me and, farther on there, my life;
here with his beautiful eyes he promised me solace,
and here, with the same, he turned to take it from me.
    Over here he bound me, there he set me loose;   5
here I wept for myself, and from this rock,
with infinite pain, I saw him go away,
he who took me from myself and didn't turn back to me.

Two quatrains, probably the beginning of a sonnet though expressing a complete thought. Written on a sheet of accounts, the verso of which bears various architectural profiles, perhaps for the Laurentian Library, ca. 1524–25 (TC no. 531r). Petrarch, no. 112, used the same conceit of pointing out specific places where events in his love for Laura occurred; M expands the idea into an allegorical "highway robbery" (*togliere* can imply "rob" as well as "take away"). This poem may also have been inspired by Poliziano's "Una donna el cor m'ha tolto" (*Canzoni a ballo*, no. 10), though the gender of M's love is clearly male (*colui*, line 8). The reference may be to Gherardo Perini, though their correspondence dates from slightly earlier, in 1522 (see nos. 18, 22, 27, 32).

    5. *he bound me:* for images of love's binding, cf. nos. 7, 23, 41, 70, etc.

In me la morte, in te la vita mia;
tu distingui e concedi e parti el tempo;
quante vuo', breve e lungo è 'l viver mio.
    Felice son nella tuo cortesia.
Beata l'alma, ove non corre tempo,   5
per te s'è fatta a contemplare Dio.

In me is my death, in you is my life:
you determine, grant, and parcel out my time;
as you wish, my life is short or long,
    and I am happy at your kind discretion.
Blessed is the soul where time does not flow: 5
it has been brought by you to contemplate God.

Fragment, perhaps the concluding sestina of a sonnet, from the 1520s, on an undated sheet bearing an address to M in Florence (*Ricordi* cxi). The unnamed addressee of the poem could be Amor, or the abstraction of divine love, or perhaps Christ himself; the actions of line 2 also suggest the three Parcae, or Fates, who were believed in antiquity to spin, measure, and cut the thread of each life. On the same sheet as no. 38, whose similarity in theme has led to speculation that the two fragments were to have been combined in some way.

    5. *where time does not flow,* in heaven.

Quanta dolcezza al cor per gli occhi porta
quel che 'n un punto el tempo e morte fura!
Che è questo però che mi conforta
e negli affanni cresce e sempre dura.
   Amor, come virtù viva e accorta,   5
desta gli spirti ed è più degna cura.
Risponde a me: —Come persona morta
mena suo vita chi è da me sicura.—
   Amore è un concetto di bellezza
immaginata o vista dentro al core,   10
amica di virtute e gentilezza.

How much sweetness he brings to my heart through my eyes,
he who takes away time and death at the same time!
That's why he is the one who comforts me,
and amidst my anguish grows and lasts forever.
   Love, being a force for liveliness and wisdom,   5
rouses my spirits and is most worth my concern.
He answers me: "He who is proof against me
leads his life like a person who is dead."
   Love is a conception born of beauty
(that friend of virtue and of graciousness)   10
that is imagined or seen within the heart.

Incomplete sonnet, 1520s, on the same sheet as no. 37. An exposition of the Platonic theory of love; cf. Dante, *Purgatorio* 18:22–27: "Your faculty of apprehension draws an image from a real existence and displays it within you, so that it makes the mind turn to it; and if, thus turned, the mind inclines toward it, that inclination is love." The same imagery of sweetness entering the heart through the eyes was developed more lyrically by Lorenzo de' Medici (e.g., LM no. cxxii). Cf. the related theme of no. 42.

   9. *conception:* the Italian *concetto*, most precisely "concept" in the sense of "idea," may here also connote conception in the sense of physical generation; see further no. 151.

39

Del fiero colpo e del pungente strale
la medicina era passarmi 'l core;
ma questo è propio sol del mie signore,
crescer la vita dove cresce 'l male.

   E se 'l primo suo colpo fu mortale,   5
seco un messo di par venne d'Amore
che mi disse: —Ama, anz'ardi; chè chi muore
non ha da gire al ciel nel mondo altr'ale.

   I' son colui che ne' prim'anni tuoi
gli occhi tuo infermi volsi alla beltate   10
che dalla terra al ciel vivo conduce.—

The cure for his fierce blow and stinging arrow
would be for it to pierce me through the heart;
but only my lord has this ability
to increase my life while increasing my suffering.

   And while the first blow of his was fatal,   5
a messenger from Love also came with it,
who said to me, "Love—nay, burn; for one who's mortal
has no other wings on earth for going to heaven.

   I am the one who, in your early years,
turned your feeble eyes toward that beauty   10
that leads the living from earth up to heaven."

Incomplete sonnet from the 1520s; on the back of the autograph is a sketch, probably by a student, depicting Christ rising from the tomb. The Petrarchan paradox of the delightful wound of love was used similarly by Lorenzo de' Medici (LM no. 1): "So cruel was the first wound, so fierce and vehement the first dart."

   7. *Love—nay, burn:* cf. no. 279:7.

40

Quand'Amor lieto al ciel levarmi è volto
cogli occhi di costei, anzi col sole,
con breve riso ciò che preme e dole
del cor mi caccia, e mettevi 'l suo volto;
    e s'i' durassi in tale stato molto,   5
l'alma, che sol di me lagnar si vole,
avendo seco là dove star suole,

.   .   .   .

When merry Love's set on raising me to heaven
with that woman's eyes, or better, with her sun,
with a quick smile he chases from my heart
all that crushes and grieves it, and puts her face in there.
    And if I stayed for long in such a state,   5
my soul, which, when alone, wants to groan against me,
having with it, where it's used to living,

.   .   .   .

Beginning of a sonnet, 1520s. The incomplete thought of the second stanza is unclear.
  1–2. Cf. Lorenzo de' Medici (LM no. LXI), "If Love shows to my eyes their beautiful Sun."
  3. *with a quick smile:* whether by Love or the lady is ambiguous.

Spirto ben nato, in cu' si specchia e vede
nelle tuo belle membra oneste e care
quante natura e 'l ciel tra no' può fare,
quand'a null'altra suo bell'opra cede:
spirto leggiadro, in cu' si spera e crede   5
dentro, come di fuor nel viso appare,
amor, pietà, mercè, cose sì rare,
che ma' furn'in beltà con tanta fede:
l'amor mi prende e la beltà mi lega;
la pietà, la mercè con dolci sguardi   10
ferma speranz'al cor par che ne doni.
Qual uso o qual governo al mondo niega,
qual crudeltà per tempo o qual più tardi,
c'a sì bell'opra morte non perdoni?

High-born spirit, in whose pure and precious limbs
there can be seen, as if within a mirror,
how heaven and nature can create among us
a work which yields in beauty to no other;
fair spirit, within whom one has hope and faith   5
of finding, as there appears on your outward face,
love and pity and kindness, things so rare
that they've never been found with beauty to such degree:
Love takes me captive and beauty binds me fast,
while pity and kindness, with your sweet glances,   10
seem to give some firm hope to my heart.
What custom or earthly law, what cruelty
either now or later, could wish to prevent
death from sparing such a beautiful piece of work?

Sonnet, ca. 1530 or after, written on the recto of a sheet whose verso bears no. 42. Michelangelo the Younger's note on the verso indicates that this sheet once bore "a *ricordo* from 1529" [N.S. 1530], which suggests that it might originally have been part of the sheet now containing nos. 43 and 44, which carries a dated note of 6 January 1529/30 (see no. 43). There are many Petrarchan echoes in both theme and structure, e.g., his nos. 53:1–4, 248.

3. *among us:* here on earth.

9. This image anticipates M's drawing for Tommaso de' Cavalieri of *The Punishment of Tityos* (1532–33), who was bound to a rock in Hades for the sin of lustfully attacking the Titaness Latona (TC no. 345). For other images of binding, cf. nos. 7, 23, 36, 70, etc.

Dimmi di grazia, Amor, se gli occhi mei
veggono 'l ver della beltà c'aspiro
o s'io l'ho dentro allor che, dov'io miro,
veggio scolpito el viso di costei.

Tu 'l de' saper, po' che tu vien con lei   5
a torm'ogni mie pace, ond'io m'adiro;
né vorre' manco un minimo sospiro,
né men ardente foco chiederei.

—La beltà che tu vedi è ben da quella,
ma cresce poi c'a miglior loco sale,   10
se per gli occhi mortali all'alma corre.

Quivi si fa divina, onesta e bella,
com'a sé simil vuol cosa immortale:
questa e non quella agli occhi tuo precorre.—

Kindly tell me, Love, whether my eyes
really see the beauty that I long for,
or if it's just in me when, looking around,
I see that woman's face carved everywhere.

You must know, since you come along with her   5
to rob me of all peace, which makes me angry;
yet I wouldn't want to lose even the smallest sigh,
nor would I ask for a less burning fire.

"The beauty that you see does come from her,
but it grows when it rises to a better place,   10
if through the mortal eyes it reaches the heart.

There it is made divine and pure and beautiful,
since what's immortal wants things to be like itself:
it's this, not that, that first leaps to your eyes."

Sonnet, ca. 1530 or after, on the same sheet as no. 41. A dialogue between M and Love over whether beauty is inherent in the person perceived or is, using the modern phrase, "in the eye of the beholder"; cf. the similar theme in no. 38.

10–13. The soul (*what's immortal*) spiritualizes and elevates whatever it absorbs into itself. The theme dates back to Dante, e.g., DC no. XC, *Paradiso* 3:45.

14. *this, not that:* the spiritual beauty of the soul, rather than the physical beauty of the body, is what you are apprehending.

43

La ragion meco si lamenta e dole,
parte ch'i' spero amando esser felice;
con forti esempli e con vere parole
la mie vergogna mi rammenta e dice:
—Che ne riportera' dal vivo sole   5
altro che morte? e non come fenice.—
Ma poco giova, ché chi cader vuole,
non basta l'altru' man pront' e vittrice.

I' conosco e' mie danni, e 'l vero intendo;
dall'altra banda albergo un altro core,   10
che più m'uccide dove più m'arrendo.

In mezzo di duo mort' è 'l mie signore:
questa non voglio e questa non comprendo:
così sospeso, el corpo e l'alma muore.

Reason complains about me and laments
because I hope for happiness through loving;
with strong examples and with truthful words
it reminds me of my shame, and says,
"What will you get back from the living sun   5
other than death?—and not the phoenix' kind."
But it's little use, since for one who wants to fall
someone else's quick, strong hand is not enough.

I recognize my danger, and know the truth;
yet on my other side dwells another heart   10
that slays me more the more I yield to it.

My lord is thus poised in between two deaths:
one I don't want, the other I don't understand;
left hanging like this, both soul and body are dying.

Sonnet, on the verso of a sheet whose recto bears no. 44 and some earlier personal notes dated 6 January 1530 (*Ricordi* CCXXXVII; TC no. 207bis; see also no 41). Beneath the writing is a sketch of a female figure. Given a date close to the siege of Florence, some critics have seen in this poem's allegorical language of struggle an allusion to M's role in the siege, but the text seems a straightforward meditation on love itself. Its sentiment is similar to Petrarch, no. 264, where he laments his internal conflict between divine and earthly love and expresses an urgency to choose between them in the face of impending death.

5. *the living sun:* the poet's beloved, otherwise unidentified, but allegorized in standard Petrarchan fashion.

6. *the phoenix' kind:* the phoenix was a legendary Arabian bird believed to be reborn every five hundred years from the ashes of its own funeral pyre. The metaphor is common in poetry, used by Boccaccio and Petrarch, e.g., PD nos. 135, 185, 321. Here, however, reason warns that M's death will be final. M used the phoenix image several times, e.g., nos. 52, 61, 62, 108, 217.

8. No one outside myself, no matter how willing to help, can prevent my folly in love, since I wish to yield to it.

12. *my lord:* this term may refer here to God, to Cupid-Amor, to M's own overmastering feelings, or to the object of his affections.

12–13. *between two deaths:* I am faced with a dilemma—If I subdue my passion, my body will die of frustration, which I do not want; but if I overcome reason's objections to my passion, my soul will die (in damnation), which as yet I cannot even imagine. For the image of twin deaths, cf. nos. 285:10, 293:13.

44

Mentre c'alla beltà ch'i' vidi in prima
appresso l'alma, che per gli occhi vede,
l'immagin dentro cresce, e quella cede
quasi vilmente e senza alcuna stima.
    Amor, c'adopra ogni suo ingegno e lima,   5
perch'io non tronchi 'l fil ritorna e riede.

While I draw my soul, which sees through the eyes,
closer to the beauty that I saw at first,
the image within it grows, and it gives way,
almost cowardly and with no self-esteem.
    Love, who sharpens his wits and uses all of them   5
so I won't cut the thread, keeps coming back.

Unfinished sonnet, 1530 or after, on the recto of the sheet containing no. 43. The density of M's language is ambiguous. The sense seems to be that his attempt to direct his soul back to a higher spiritual ideal fails before the vivid impression of a more earthly beauty, which is presented by Love (Amor, the pagan, worldly Cupid), who wishes to keep M bound to the lower life.

2. *at first:* before birth, i.e., spiritual beauty.

3. *the image within it:* an alternative image of earthly beauty that has lodged in the soul (through the senses). *it gives way:* the soul yields to more earthly powers.

5. *wits:* for the various meanings of *ingegno,* cf. nos. 84, 149, 151, 159, 284.

6. *cut the thread* either of life (i.e., to die into the spirit) or of love (the ties of earthly passion).

Ben doverrieno al sospirar mie tanto
esser secco oramai le fonti e ' fiumi,
s'i' non gli rinfrescassi col mie pianto.
  Così talvolta i nostri etterni lumi,
l'un caldo e l'altro freddo ne ristora,   5
acciò che 'l mondo più non si consumi.
  E similmente il cor che s'innamora,
quand'el superchio ardor troppo l'accende,
l'umor degli occhi il tempra, che non mora.
  La morte e 'l duol, ch'i' bramo e cerco, rende   10
un contento avenir, che non mi lassa
morir; ché chi diletta non offende.
  Onde la navicella mie non passa,
com'io vorrei, a vederti a quella riva
che 'l corpo per a tempo di qua lassa.   15
  Troppo dolor vuol pur ch'i' campi e viva,
qual più c'altri veloce andando vede,
che dopo gli altri al fin del giorno arriva.
  Crudel pietate e spietata mercede
me lasciò vivo, e te da me disciolse,   20
rompendo, e non mancando nostra fede
  e la memoria a me non sol me tolse,

.   .   .   .

By now the springs and streams would certainly
have had to dry up from my sighing so much,
if I did not replenish them with my weeping.
  In this way, by turns, our eternal lamps,
the one hot and the other cold, revive us   5
so that the world will not be worn out further.
  And similarly, the heart that falls in love:
when excess ardor heats it up too much,
the eyes' moisture tempers it, so it will not die.
  Death and grief, which I long for and seek,   10
make for a happy future that will not let
me die, for those who give pleasure do no harm.

Therefore my little boat will not cross over
to see you, as I would like, to that shore
that leaves my body on this side yet a while.   15
  Excess of pain still makes me survive and live,
like one who, going faster than all others,
sees himself reaching the end of his days after them.
  Cruel mercy and merciless grace
left me alive and cut you off from me,   20
breaking but not extinguishing our bond;
  and not only did they deprive me of your memory,

.   .   .   .

Incomplete stanzas in terza rima in which M expresses his grief over the death of a loved one through a series of Petrarchan antitheses and paradoxes (TC no. 225r). The poem can be dated to ca. 1528 by the handwriting and may thus refer to the death of M's brother Buonarroto in that year (see also no. 46).

  4. *eternal lamps:* the sun and the moon, alternating their effect on the earth.

  7–9. An allusion to Renaissance physiological theories of the four bodily humors and their mutual effects.

  13. *my little boat:* the soul, not yet able to separate from the body in death; Dante wrote of "la navicella del mio ingegno," *Purgatorio* 1:2. For the repeated image of life's journey as a sea voyage, cf. nos. 285, 299.

Se 'l mie rozzo martello i duri sassi
forma d'uman aspetto or questo or quello,
dal ministro che 'l guida, iscorge e tiello,
prendendo il moto, va con gli altrui passi.

Ma quel divin che in cielo alberga e stassi,   5
altri, e sé più, col propio andar fa bello;
e se nessun martel senza martello
si può far, da quel vivo ogni altro fassi.

E perché 'l colpo è di valor più pieno
quant'alza più se stesso alla fucina,   10
sopra 'l mie questo al ciel n'è gito a volo.

Onde a me non finito verrà meno,
s'or non gli dà la fabbrica divina
aiuto a farlo, c'al mondo era solo.

If my crude hammer shapes the hard stones
into one human appearance or another,
deriving its motion from the master who guides it,
watches and holds it, it moves at another's pace.

But that divine one, which lodges and dwells in heaven,   5
beautifies self and others by its own action;
and if no hammer can be made without a hammer,
by that living one every other one is made.

And since a blow becomes more powerful
the higher it's raised up over the forge,   10
that one's flown up to heaven above my own.

So now my own will fail to be completed
unless the divine smithy, to help make it,
gives it that aid which was unique on earth.

Sonnet, ca. 1528. The theme of losing someone who has served as the artist's earthly inspiration ("flown up to heaven") may refer to the death of M's brother Buonarroto (see no. 45), whose son Leonardo may be the person addressed in an accompanying prose passage, which continues the theme of the poem:

"Lionardo. Era solo a exaltar al mondo con gran virtù le virtù; non avea chi menassi e' mantaci. Ora nel cielo arà molti compagni, perché non v'è se non a chi è piaciuto le virtù; ond'io spero che di lassù finirà quaggiù el mio m[artello?]. . . . Arà ora in cielo chi almeno merrà i mantaci; ché quaggiù non aveva nessun compagnio alla fucina do' si exaltano le virtù.

"Lionardo. He was alone on earth in exalting virtues with his great virtue; he had no one who would work the bellows. Now in heaven he will have many companions, since there is no one there but those who loved the virtues; so I hope that, from up there, he will complete my [hammer?] down here. At least in heaven he will have someone to work the bellows, for down here he had no companion at the forge where virtues are exalted."

The metaphor of poem and postscript derives from Dante, *Paradiso* 2:127–32: "The motion and virtue of the holy spheres / should be inspired by the blessed movers / as is the hammer's art by the smith," an image dating back to Plato's *Cratylus*.

3. *the master:* the hand of the divine sculptor, God.

5. *divine one:* heavenly hammer.

9–11. The force (person) that inspired my work has risen to heaven in death.

12. *my own* hammer, which needs forming and guidance by another, will necessarily fail.

Quand'el ministro de' sospir mie tanti
al mondo, agli occhi mei, a sé si tolse,
natura, che fra noi degnar lo volse,
restò in vergogna, e chi lo vide in pianti.

Ma non come degli altri oggi si vanti   5
del sol del sol, c'allor ci spense e tolse,
morte, c'amor ne vinse, e farlo il tolse
in terra vivo e 'n ciel fra gli altri santi.

Così credette morte iniqua e rea
finir il suon delle virtute sparte,   10
e l'alma, che men bella esser potea.

Contrari effetti alluminan le carte
di vita più che 'n vita non solea,
e morto ha 'l ciel, c'allor non avea parte.

When the commander of my abundant sighs
was taken from the world, from my eyes, from himself,
nature, who willingly bestowed him on us,
was left in shame, and all who'd seen him in tears.

But let not death now boast, as it does of others,   5
of using up and taking from us the sun of suns,
for love has triumphed, taking him to make him live
on earth and in heaven among the other saints.

Thus did unjust and evil death think it would
put an end to the widespread report of his virtues,   10
and that it could make his soul less beautiful.

But the opposite effect brightens his pages
with more life than he was used to in his life;
and, dead, he has heaven, which he had no share in then.

Sonnet, probably dating from the late 1520s like nos. 45 and 46. Written on the recto of a
sheet whose verso contains various sketches, including an old, bearded man facing a woman
with exposed, pendulous breasts, probably by a student and dating from 1506–12 (TC no.
312; see also poem no. 20). The reference to "pages" (line 12) and to "lovers" and "songs" in
one early draft suggests allusion to a literary personage of greater emotional intimacy with M

than his brother Buonarroto, who died in 1528. The metaphors of an earth darkened and saddened by the loss of a loved one are Petrarchan staples (cf. his no. 275).

7. *love:* divine love, God.

10. *widespread report:* the Italian *suono,* sound, carries the association of the sound of a trumpet, symbol of fame.

11. *make his soul less beautiful:* by depriving it of the body.

12. *opposite effect:* cf. nos. 141:7, 145:8. *pages:* of the book of his life.

48

Come fiamma più cresce più contesa
dal vento, ogni virtù che 'l cielo esalta
tanto più splende quant'è più offesa.

As a flame grows more, the more it's buffeted
by the wind, every virtue that heaven extols
shines the more, the more it is assaulted.

A single terzina, dating ca. 1528. Similar metaphors of moral resilience appear twice in Dante's *Paradiso*: "For the will, if it be not willing, is not weakened, but does as nature does in fire" (4:76–78); "as the bough that bends its tip in the passing wind, and then lifts itself by its own virtue" (26:85–89).

49

Amor, la tuo beltà non è mortale:
nessun volto fra noi è che pareggi
l'immagine del cor, che 'nfiammi e reggi
con altro foco e muovi con altr'ale.

Love, your beauty is not a mortal thing:
there is no face among us that can equal
the image in the heart, which you kindle and sustain
with another fire and stir with other wings.

Quatrain, ca. 1530, on a sheet of notes (*Ricordi* CCCXV).

3. *the image in the heart:* Neoplatonic philosophy held that the inner image of the beloved expands beyond physical appearance to include all that is known of the individual's personality.

4. *another fire:* other than physical beauty or passion.

50

Che fie doppo molt'anni di costei,
Amor, se 'l tempo ogni beltà distrugge?
Fama di lei; e anche questa fugge
e vola e manca più ch'i' non vorrei.
   Più e men . . .   5

What will be left of her after many years,
O Love, if time destroys all beauty?
Her fame; yet even this is fleeting, and flies
and fades away more quickly than I'd wish.
   More and less . . .   5

Beginning of a sonnet, of uncertain date, perhaps ca. 1530 (TC no. 536r). The successive triumphs of time over earthly beauty and fame over time recall the sequence in Petrarch's poem *I trionfi* (see Introduction).

51

Oilmè, oilmè, ch'i' son tradito
da' giorni mie fugaci e dallo specchio
che 'l ver dice a ciascun che fiso 'l guarda!
Così n'avvien, chi troppo al fin ritarda,
com'ho fatt'io, che 'l tempo m'è fuggito: 5
si trova come me 'n un giorno vecchio.
Né mi posso pentir, né m'apparecchio,
né mi consiglio con la morte appresso.
Nemico di me stesso,
inutilmente i pianti e ' sospir verso,   10
ché non è danno pari al tempo perso.
   Oilmè, oilmè, pur riterando
vo 'l mio passato tempo e non ritruovo
in tutto un giorno che sie stato mio!
Le fallace speranze e 'l van desio,   15
piangendo, amando, ardendo e sospirando
(c'affetto alcun mortal non m'è più nuovo)
m'hanno tenuto, ond'il conosco e pruovo,
lontan certo dal vero.
Or con periglio pèro;   20
ché 'l breve tempo m'è venuto manco,
né sarie ancor, se s'allungassi, stanco.
   I' vo lasso, oilmè, né so ben dove;
anzi temo, ch'il veggio, e 'l tempo andato
mel mostra, né mi val che gli occhi chiuda.   25
Or che 'l tempo la scorza cangia e muda,
la morte e l'alma insieme ognor fan pruove,
la prima e la seconda, del mie stato.
E s'io non sono errato,·
(che Dio 'l voglia ch'io sia),   30
l'etterna pena mia
nel mal libero inteso oprato vero
veggio, Signor, né so quel ch'io mi spero.

   Alas, alas, for I have been betrayed
by my fleeting days and by the mirror

that speaks the truth to all who look hard at it!
That's what happens when one delays too long at the end,
as I have done, while time has fled from me: 5
he finds himself in one day, as I have, old.
And I can neither repent, nor prepare myself,
nor ask for guidance, with death so near to me.
Enemy of myself,
in vain do I pour out my sighs and tears, 10
for there's no hurt that's equal to time lost.

   Alas, alas, though I keep going back
over my past, I can't find in all of it
even one single day that was my own!
False hopes and empty desire 15
—weeping, loving, burning, and sighing
(no earthly feeling is new to me any more)—
have surely kept me, as I know from experience,
far away from the truth.
Now I'm dying, in great danger, 20
for my short span of time has gotten less,
and even if it grew longer, I wouldn't be tired.

   So, alas, I go wearily on, but hardly know where;
or rather, fear to know—for I see it, my past
shows it to me, and closing my eyes can't help. 25
Now that time is changing and sloughing off my hide,
death and my soul are still battling,
one against the other, for my final state.
And if I'm not mistaken
(God grant that I may be), 30
I see, Lord, my eternal penalty
for having, though free, poorly grasped or practiced truth,
and I don't know what I can hope for.

Canzone, ca. 1528–30, on a sheet of drawings of Hercules and Antaeus and other subjects (TC no. 237v).

   2. *mirror*: a symbol of conscience, self-reflection; cf. no. 172.

   4. *delays too long at the end*: puts off repenting and preparing for imminent death.

   11. Cf. Dante, *Purgatorio* 3:78.

12–14. For the complaint of time's theft, cf. no. 22:40.

20–22. As I head toward death, my soul is in great danger of damnation: It lacks the time needed to repent for the sins I've already committed, and even if I were to gain longer life, my evil energies, which are still unabated, would continue piling up further sins.

24–25. *it*: the future prospects toward which I am heading, and which I cannot avoid by ignoring them.

26. This image of the artist's outer skin (literally "bark") being removed anticipates M's portrayal of his own face in the flayed skin of Saint Bartholomew in the *Last Judgment* (begun 1534); cf. nos. 33, 94, 161.

31–32. I envision the damnation I will suffer for not having recognized and acted on true principles of morality, despite possessing free will, and I cannot imagine any alternative.

52

S'alcun se stesso al mondo ancider lice,
po' che per morte al ciel tornar si crede,
sarie ben giusto a chi con tanta fede
vive servendo miser e 'nfelice.

Ma perché l'uom non è come fenice,   5
c'alla luce del sol resurge e riede,
la man fo pigra e muovo tardi el piede.

If anyone's allowed to kill himself in this world,
thinking to return to heaven through death,
it would surely be justified for one who lives
in such loyal service, wretched and unhappy.

But, because man is not like the phoenix,   5
which rises again and returns to the sun's light,
I keep my hand slack and move my foot slowly.

Unfinished sonnet; written, along with no. 53, on the back of a letter from Battista Figiovanni datable to 1531 (C. DCCCXXVII). Since the date is soon after the siege of Florence of 1529–30, "service" could refer to M's work for the city as military architect and the troubles it caused him; cf. his letter to his brother Giovan Simone, 1531: "I . . . had endured many hardships, in order that you might not endure any" (C. CMXXXVIII; R. 185). Alternatively, "loyal service" might refer ironically to his having to return to work for the Medici following the collapse of the Republic. More conventionally, he may mean simply servitude to a beloved, as Petrarch referred to in a poem that similarly contemplates suicide (his no. 36).

    5. *phoenix*: cf. the same image in nos. 43, 61, 62, 108, 217.

    7. That is, I do nothing to hasten toward death.

53

Chi di notte cavalca, el dì conviene
c'alcuna volta si riposi e dorma:
così sper'io, che dopo tante pene
ristori 'l mie signor mie vita e forma.
Non dura 'l mal dove non dura 'l bene,   5
ma spesso l'un nell'altro si trasforma.

For one who rides at night, it's necessary
to lie down and sleep a while during the day:
and so I hope that, after so many troubles,
my master will refresh my life and form.
Evil does not last where good does not last,   5
but one is often turned into the other.

Fragment of a sonnet, 1531, on the same sheet as no. 52. The declaration of weariness "after so many troubles" and the sense of alternation of fortune may reflect M's state of mind after the privations and shifting political situation of the siege of Florence (1529–30), during and after which he and his family suffered along with the entire citizenry.

4. *life and form*: soul and body.
6. Cf. the similar conceit in nos. 193, 194.

54

Io crederrei, se tu fussi di sasso,
amarti con tal fede, ch'i' potrei
farti meco venir più che di passo;
se fussi morto, parlar ti farei,
se fussi in ciel, ti tirerei a basso   5
co' pianti, co' sospir, co' prieghi miei.
Sendo vivo e di carne, e qui tra noi,
chi t'ama e serve che de' creder poi?

I' non posso altro far che seguitarti,
e della grande impresa non mi pento.   10
Tu non se' fatta com'un uom da sarti,
che si muove di fuor, si muove drento;
e se dalla ragion tu non ti parti,
spero c'un dì tu mi fara' contento:
ché 'l morso il ben servir togli' a' serpenti,   15
come l'agresto quand'allega i denti.

E' non è forza contr'a l'umiltate,
né crudeltà può star contr'a l'amore;
ogni durezza suol vincer pietate,
sì come l'allegrezza fa 'l dolore;   20
una nuova nel mondo alta beltate
come la tuo non ha 'ltrimenti il core;
c'una vagina, ch'è dritta a vedella,
non può dentro tener torte coltella.

E non può esser pur che qualche poco   25
la mie gran servitù non ti sie cara;
pensa che non si truova in ogni loco
la fede negli amici, che è sì rara;

.   .   .   .
.   .   .   .   30
.   .   .   .
.   .   .   .

Quando un dì sto che veder non ti posso,
non posso trovar pace in luogo ignuno;
se po' ti veggo, mi s'appicca addosso,   35
come suole il mangiar far al digiuno;

com'altri il ventre di votar si muore,
ch'è più 'l conforto, po' che pri' è 'l dolore.   40

    E non mi passa tra le mani un giorno
ch'i' non la vegga o senta con la mente;
né scaldar ma' si può fornace o forno
c'a' mie sospir non fussi più rovente;
e quando avvien ch'i' l'abbi un po' dintorno,   45
sfavillo come ferro in foco ardente;
e tanto vorre' dir, s'ella m'aspetta,
ch'i' dico men che quand'i' non ho fretta.

    S'avvien che la mi rida pure un poco
o mi saluti in mezzo della via,   50
mi levo come polvere dal foco
o di bombarda o d'altra artiglieria;
se mi domanda, subito m'affioco,
perdo la voce e la risposta mia,
e subito s'arrende il gran desio,   55
e la speranza cede al poter mio.

    I' sento in me non so che grand'amore,
che quasi arrivere' 'nsino alle stelle;
e quando alcuna volta il vo trar fore,
non ho buco sì grande nella pelle   60
che nol faccia, a uscirne, assa' minore
parere, e le mie cose assai men belle:
c'amore o forza el dirne è grazia sola;
e men ne dice chi più alto vola.

    I' vo pensando al mie viver di prima,   65
inanzi ch'i' t'amassi, com'egli era:
di me non fu ma' chi facesse stima,
perdendo ogni dì il tempo insino a sera;
forse pensavo di cantare in rima
o di ritrarmi da ogni altra schiera?   70
Or si fa 'l nome, o per tristo o per buono,
e sassi pure almen chi i' ci sono.

    Tu m'entrasti per gli occhi, ond'io mi spargo,
come grappol d'agresto in un'ampolla,

che dopo 'l collo cresce ov'è più largo; 75
così l'immagin tua, che fuor m'immolla,
dentro per gli occhi cresce, ond'io m'allargo
come pelle ove gonfia la midolla;
entrando in me per sì stretto vïaggio,
che tu mai n'esca ardir creder non aggio. 80

Come quand'entra in una palla il vento,
che col medesmo fiato l'animella,
come l'apre di fuor, la serra drento,
così l'immagin del tuo volto bella
per gli occhi dentro all'alma venir sento; 85
e come gli apre, poi si serra in quella;
e come palla pugno al primo balzo,
percosso da' tu' occhi al ciel po' m'alzo.

Perché non basta a una donna bella
goder le lode d'un amante solo, 90
ché suo beltà potre' morir con ella;
dunche, s'i' t'amo, reverisco e colo,
al merito 'l poter poco favella;
c'un zoppo non pareggia un lento volo,
né gira 'l sol per un sol suo mercede, 95
ma per ogni occhio san c'al mondo vede.

I' non posso pensar come 'l cor m'ardi,
passando a quel per gli occhi sempre molli,
che 'l foco spegnerien non ch'e' tuo sguardi.
Tutti e' ripari mie son corti e folli: 100
se l'acqua il foco accende, ogni altro è tardi
a camparmi dal mal ch'i' bramo e volli,
salvo il foco medesmo. O cosa strana,
se 'l mal del foco spesso il foco sana!

I believe I could, even were you made of stone,
love you so faithfully that I'd be able
to make you come with me at more than a walk;
if you were dead, I could make you speak,
and if you were in heaven, I could pull you down 5
with my tears, with my sighs, and with my prayers.
But since you're alive, made of flesh, and here among us,

what then can one who loves and serves you hope for?
  I can do nothing else but follow you,
and I do not regret this great endeavor.   10
You are not made like a tailor's mannequin,
which can be moved from outside or within;
and if you do not take leave of your wits,
I hope that someday you will make me happy:
for good treatment takes away the serpent's bite,   15
as sour fruit does by setting the teeth on edge.
  Nothing has power against humility,
neither can cruelty withstand love;
mercy always conquers every hardness,
just the way that happiness does sorrow;   20
a lofty beauty like yours, novel on earth,
cannot have any other kind of heart;
for a scabbard that looks straight to the eye
cannot hold a crooked knife inside.
  And it cannot be true that my great service   25
is not dear to you, at least a little;
consider that one does not find everywhere
faithfulness among friends, which is so rare;

.   .   .   .

.   .   .   .   30

.   .   .   .

.   .   .   .

  When there's a day on which I cannot see you,
then I can find no peace anywhere;
and when I do see you, it sticks fast to me   35
as food will do to one who has been fasting;

.   .   .   .

.   .   .   .

like someone who is dying to empty his belly,
for the more one suffered before, the more the relief.   40
  Not a single day slips through my fingers
that I don't see or feel her in my mind;
nor can any furnace or oven ever get so warm
that it wouldn't grow even more red-hot with my sighs.
Then when I get to have her near me a little,   45

I give off sparks like iron glowing in a fire;
and I want to say so much, if she'll attend me,
that I say less than when I am not hurried.

    If she should smile at me, even a little,
or greet me in the middle of the street,   50
I am uplifted as gunpowder is
from a cannon or some other artillery;
if she asks me a question, I instantly grow hoarse
and lose my voice and ability to answer,
and instantly my great desire gives out,   55
and my hope surrenders to my meager strength.

    I feel a love of such unknown size within me
that it could almost take me to the stars;
but when at times I want to get it out,
I have no opening in my skin big enough   60
not to make it seem, issuing from there,
much smaller, and the things I say much less fine:
for to speak of love or its power comes only through grace,
and one who flies higher can say less about them.

    I keep on thinking about my former life,   65
about what it was like before I loved you:
no one ever had any regard for me,
as I wasted my time every day from morning to night;
was I likely then to think of singing in verse,
or of making myself stand out from the rest of the crowd?   70
But now my name's made known, for good or ill,
and at least people are aware that I exist.

    You entered me through my eyes (whence I spill tears)
as a cluster of unripe fruit goes into a bottle
and, once past the neck, grows where it is wider;   75
so does your image, which when outside soaks me,
grow once it's inside the eyes, so that I stretch
like a skin inside of which the pulp is swelling;
having entered me by such a narrow route,
I can hardly dare to believe you'll ever get out.   80

    Just as, when air is blown into a ball,
the same breath that opens up the valve
from the outside, keeps it shut from the inside,

so do I feel the image of your lovely face
come into my soul through my eyes, 85
open them, and then get shut in there.
And like a ball hit by a fist on the first bounce,
when struck by your eyes, I'm lifted up to heaven.
   To a beautiful woman, it is not enough
to enjoy praise from only a single lover, 90
since her beauty could die along with it;
so even though I love, honor, and adore you,
I've power to utter but little of what you deserve:
for a cripple cannot match even a slow flight,
nor does the sun turn its blessings only toward one, 95
but toward every sound eye on earth that can see.
   I can't understand how you can burn my heart,
passing into it through my eyes, which are always so wet
that they could extinguish not only your glances, but fire.
All my remedies are inadequate and pointless: 100
if fire kindles water, it's too late for anything
to save me from the pain I've wanted and still yearn for,
except for fire itself. What a strange thing,
that the pain of fire is often cured by fire!

A series of stanzas in ottava rima, two of them incomplete; lines 73–80 are written on a sheet
of accounts dating from 1531–32 (*Ricordi* CCXLV). Their exaggerated praise of a beautiful be-
loved and of her effects on him has the facetiously comic tone, similar to the verses of Lorenzo
de' Medici and Francesco Berni, that M occasionally adopts (cf. no. 20); the quasi-scatological
image of line 39 recalls similar vulgarisms in nos. 5 and 267. In its last two stanzas, the poem
turns from mocking overstatement to a more serious and sincere mood. There seems to have
been some initial ambiguity regarding the gender of M's beloved: although she is later re-
ferred to clearly as a woman, in the first stanza the adjectives are all masculine.
   3. *at more than a walk:* at a brisk pace, i.e., enthusiastically.
   11–12. That is, you possess reason and thus cannot be swayed by the opinions of others.
   15–16. My faithful service to you should have the power to remove your antipathy toward
me, to prevent your "biting" me in the same way that eating sour fruit (i.e., unripe; the term
agresto is used in both senses, cf. line 74) puckers the mouth and prevents it from opening.
   22. *cannot have any other kind of heart:* you, too, must have a heart that is capable of being
moved by my efforts.
   23–24. Cf. the same image in no. 216.
   25–28. My attentions must be somewhat welcome to you, if you realize how rare it is to
find such loyalty anywhere, even among your friends.

35. *it:* peace, a feeling of satisfaction.

39. *dying to empty his belly:* constipated.

47–48. When she has the patience to listen to me, I talk so excitedly that I end up saying less than I could if I were speaking at a normal pace.

51–52. *uplifted as gunpowder is:* ignited, i.e., I explode into the air like a cannonball.

55–56. I lose all hope of being able to get what I want from her, because my powers of speech are so limited by my faint-heartedness in her presence.

57. *a love of such unknown size:* a love whose power is so mysteriously great and unfamiliar.

59. *get it out:* express the depth and strength of my love verbally.

60–62. My power to express my thoughts is so limited that what is inside me inevitably comes out sounding unimportant.

61. *it:* my verbal expression of love. *there:* any orifice (the mouth).

63–64. The ability to communicate the intensity of one's love is a gift only rarely given; for most people, the more one is carried away by emotion, the harder it is to express one's feelings, since one loses one's rational faculties.

65. Cf. Petrarch, no. 264:1, "I' vo pensando."

73–80. The absurdly overstated imagery of this stanza parodies the Neoplatonic convention of love entering the soul through the eyes, which M elsewhere develops more seriously (e.g., nos. 8, 44).

73–75. You entered my soul with difficulty, through the narrow opening of my eyes, just as unripe fruits are forced into jars through their narrow necks and then expand and ripen in the lower part of the jar (an agricultural practice for protecting tender fruit).

76–78. When I see your beautiful image outside of me, it makes me cry; once it has penetrated me, it grows so large that it makes my body swell up like the outer husk of a fruit or vegetable as its pulp grows within it.

81–83. The air that is blown into a ball exerts pressure on the flap from outside and thus opens it, but once inside, the same air exerts pressure from the other side of the flap and keeps it closed.

86. *in there:* in the soul (where it then shuts out any other sensations or feelings).

87–88. That is, once filled with your divine influence, I am so buoyant that the shock of seeing you can levitate me to heavenly ecstasy; cf. the similar image of being "uplifted" in line 51.

91. *it:* praise from him; i.e., if he ceased to speak about her beauty, no one would hear about it any more (or: if he lost interest in her, there would be no one else to appreciate it).

92–96. My verbal gifts are insufficient to do justice to your beauty; my best efforts are halting and earthbound in comparison to your angelic perfection. In any case I can never hope to become your sole admirer, since the sun, in its endless rotation through the sky, does not shed its light (your beauty) only on me but on all who are prepared to see it (i.e., appreciate you).

100–3. If the fire of your beauty is not quenched by the tears of my pain but in fact makes them flow more copiously, then the only thing that can still heal my lovesickness, which I have deliberately sought out, is to receive your love in return; cf. no. 18:1.

55

I' t'ho comprato, ancor che molto caro,
un po' di non so che, che sa di buono,
perc'a l'odor la strada spesso imparo.
Ovunche tu ti sia, dovunch'i' sono,
senz'alcun dubbio ne so certo e chiaro. 5
Se da me ti nascondi, i' tel perdono:
portandol dove vai sempre con teco,
ti troverrei, quand'io fussi ben cieco.

I've bought you, even though it's quite expensive,
a little something that smells very sweet;
since I often manage to find my way by scent,
wherever you may be, wherever I am,
I'll be clear and sure about it, there's no doubt. 5
If you hide from me, I will forgive you for it:
for wherever you go, as long as you carry this with you
I'd find you, even if I were quite blind.

Octave of an incomplete sonnet, ca. 1531–32. On the same sheet, probably written after the poem, is a draft of M's letter to Cavalieri from the summer of 1533 (*Ricordi* CCXLVII; C. CMXVII; R. 193 and draft 5), but the jocular style of the poem bears little resemblance to the impassioned gravity with which M usually addresses Tommaso. Whether the poem served as a letter accompanying an actual gift, and to whom, is conjectural.

  5. *about it:* i.e., of your whereabouts.

56

Vivo della mie morte e, se ben guardo,
felice vivo d'infelice sorte;
e chi viver non sa d'angoscia e morte,
nel foco venga, ov'io mi struggo e ardo.

I live on my death and, if I see rightly,
I live happily on my unhappy fate;
one who doesn't know how to live on death and anguish
should enter the fire where I'm burned and destroyed.

Beginning of a sonnet inviting those who have not felt the pleasurable pain of love to join M in the flames. Written, along with no. 57, on the back of a letter from Sebastiano del Piombo dated 8 June 1532 (C. DCCCLXXI). The series of antitheses is common in Petrarch and Poliziano.

1. *my death:* the love that makes me suffer.

57

S'i' vivo più di chi più m'arde e cuoce,
quante più legne o vento il foco accende,
tanto più chi m'uccide mi difende,
e più mi giova dove più mi nuoce.

Since I gain more life from one who burns and sears me,
just as more fuel or wind makes a fire flare up,
so too he who slays me protects me more,
and does more good for me the more he harms me.

Quatrain, 1532, written on the same sheet as no. 56 and similar in imagery; the two are perhaps alternative openings for the same projected poem. This may be an early example of the poems inspired by Tommaso de' Cavalieri, whom M met in spring or summer of 1532 (though the Italian does not specify the gender of the "slayer"); see no. 58.

58

Se l'immortal desio, c'alza e corregge
gli altrui pensier, traessi e' mie di fore,
forse c'ancor nella casa d'Amore
farie pietoso chi spietato regge.

Ma perché l'alma per divina legge 5
ha lunga vita, e 'l corpo in breve muore,
non può 'l senso suo lode o suo valore
appien descriver quel c'appien non legge.

Dunche, oilmè! come sarà udita
la casta voglia che 'l cor dentro incende 10
da chi sempre se stesso in altrui vede?

La mie cara giornata m'è impedita
col mie signor c'alle menzogne attende,
c'a dire il ver, bugiardo è chi nol crede.

If the wish for what's immortal, which uplifts
the thoughts of other men, would bring out mine,
perhaps that could again make merciful the one
who rules mercilessly in the house of Love.

But since the soul, by divine decree, 5
has a long life, while the body swiftly dies,
the senses can't fully describe or celebrate
its worth, which they cannot fully perceive.

Therefore—alas!—how can the chaste desire
that burns my heart inside make itself heard 10
by those who always see themselves in others?

So I am deprived of my precious time
with my lord, who pays heed to falsehoods,
for in truth, the liar's the one who doesn't believe.

Sonnet, 1532; although this is the first poem to Tommaso de' Cavalieri in Girardi's chronology, it would seem to follow an initial period of acquaintance (alluded to in line 12) during which M had already tried to make his strong feelings clear (perhaps in some of the more lyrical poems below; cf. no. 57). Here M strikes for the first time a note of frustration and fear that his passion, inadequately expressed, may be misunderstood as carnal rather than purely spiritual, at least by those unnamed individuals who impute their own base motivations to others (line 11), who have apparently already planted similar suspicions in Cavalieri's mind (cf. nos. 60, 83).

2. *would bring out mine:* if it were capable of making clear that my feeling is the same.

8. *its worth:* the praiseworthy aspects of the soul.

14. *doesn't believe:* the truth about me, and about my feelings.

59

S'un casto amor, s'una pietà superna,
s'una fortuna infra dua amanti equale,
s'un'aspra sorte all'un dell'altro cale,
s'un spirto, s'un voler duo cor governa;

s'un'anima in duo corpi è fatta etterna,   5
ambo levando al cielo e con pari ale;
s'Amor d'un colpo e d'un dorato strale
le viscer di duo petti arda e discerna;

s'aman l'un l'altro e nessun se medesmo,
d'un gusto e d'un diletto, a tal mercede   10
c'a un fin voglia l'uno e l'altro porre:

se mille e mille, non sarien centesmo
a tal nodo d'amore, a tanta fede;
e sol l'isdegno il può rompere e sciorre.

If one chaste love, if one sublime compassion,
if one fate are equally shared between two lovers;
if the hard lot of one troubles the other;
if one spirit, if one will governs two hearts;

if one soul in two bodies is made eternal,   5
raising both to heaven with similar wings;
if Love with one blow and one gilded dart
can burn and rend the vitals in two breasts;

if neither loves himself, and they love each other
with one joy and one zeal, to such a degree   10
that both might wish to come to a single end:

Thousands and thousands would not make a fraction
of such a love-knot, such fidelity,
and only anger could untie and break it.

Sonnet written for Cavalieri, along with nos. 60 and 61, all of them on a letter sent to M in Rome and dated 5 August [?] 1532 (C. DCCCXCI). The theme and the repeated "if" phrases recall Petrarch, no. 224, "S'una fede amorosa"; while forty-six of M's poems begin with *se* (if), this one uses the word ten times, more than any other single poem.

5. Marsilio Ficino had written of his young beloved, Giovanni Cavalcanti, in similar terms, saying that the two "have only one soul" (see de Tolnay, *Medici Chapel*, p. 114).

6. The image of the winged soul rising to heaven parallels M's drawing of Ganymede swooning ecstatically in the pinions of a rising eagle-Jupiter, composed as a gift for Cavalieri in 1532–33 (TC no. 344). Cf. the similar image in no. 99.

12. *Thousands and thousands:* of similar sympathies, if they were found elsewhere, could not compare to the intensity of feeling in this relationship. *fraction (centesmo,* lit. "hundredth"): cf. Dante, *Paradiso* 24:107–8.

14. Earlier editors inserted a question mark at the end of this line, but M's autograph variant makes clear that this is a statement rather than a question. Read in conjunction with no. 58, he seems to imply that Cavalieri, having believed the falsehoods about M's intentions toward him, has become angry and that this feeling threatens their relationship; cf. nos. 60, 83.

60

Tu sa' ch'i' so, signor mie, che tu sai
ch'i' vengo per goderti più da presso,
e sai ch'i' so che tu sa' ch'i' son desso:
a che più indugio a salutarci omai?

Se vera è la speranza che mi dai,   5
se vero è 'l gran desio che m'è concesso,
rompasi il mur fra l'uno e l'altra messo,
ché doppia forza hann' i celati guai.

S'i' amo sol di te, signor mie caro,
quel che di te più ami, non ti sdegni,   10
ché l'un dell'altro spirto s'innamora.

Quel che nel tuo bel volto bramo e 'mparo,
e mal compres' è dagli umani ingegni,
che 'l vuol saper convien che prima mora.

You know that I know, my lord, that you know
that I come closer to take delight in you,
and you know I know you know just who I am:
why then delay our meeting any longer?

If the hope that you give to me is real,   5
if the great desire I've been granted is real,
let the wall raised between them be broken down,
for troubles left concealed have double strength.

If I love in you, my dear lord, only what
you love most in yourself, do not be angry,   10
for it's one spirit falling in love with the other.

What I yearn for and learn from your fair face
is poorly understood by mortal minds;
whoever wants to know it must die first.

Sonnet, 1532, on the same sheet as nos. 59 and 61, also for Cavalieri and treating related themes of spiritual attraction and complaint of some reticence or anger on Cavalieri's part (cf. also no. 58). The structure of elaborately encoded yet unspoken meanings and the allusion to "troubles left concealed" suggests the awkwardness of speaking directly about feelings of a passionate nature and M's desire to insist that, despite any surface misunderstanding, his chaste intentions are at bottom self-evident (line 11). Cf. also his letter to Cavalieri remarking that "though it would be permissible for the giver to name what he is giving to the recipient, for obvious reasons it is not being done in this case" (C. DCCCXCIX, CM; R. 191 [my translation]; see Saslow 1986, 50).

1, 3. Cf. Dante, *Inferno* 13:25: "I believe that he believed that I believed."

1–2. In the margin, M wrote "Donna gentil a chi vengo per vederti" (gentle lady whom I come to see), an example of his familiarity with standard female topoi and his flexibility in altering them to suit his male addressees.

2, 6. Cf. the sonnet by Gasparo Visconti, *Ancor mi son nel cor:*

> Felice dì nel qual mi fu concesso . . .
>
> intender contemplando più dappresso

(cf. also no. 72).

4. Though *salutare* means "to greet," it derives from *salute* (health, salvation); M may thus also mean to imply a healing or reconciliation (cf. no. 61:11).

14. *die:* either literally or in the sense of losing concern for earthly matters.

61

S'i' avessi creduto al primo sguardo
di quest'alma fenice al caldo sole
rinnovarmi per foco, come suole
nell'ultima vecchiezza, ond'io tutt'ardo,

    qual più veloce cervio o lince o pardo   5
segue 'l suo bene e fugge quel che dole,
agli atti, al riso, all'oneste parole
sarie cors'anzi, ond'or son presto e tardo.

    Ma perché più dolermi, po' ch'i' veggio
negli occhi di quest'angel lieto e solo   10
mie pace, mie riposo e mie salute?

    Forse che prima sarie stato il peggio
vederlo, udirlo, s'or di pari a volo
seco m'impenna a seguir suo virtute.

If I'd believed at the first glance that I could,
in the warm sun of this blessed phoenix,
renew myself by fire, with which I'm burning,
as is its custom in extreme old age,

    then, as the swiftest stag or lynx or leopard   5
pursues its good and flees from what is painful,
toward his actions, his laughter, and his virtuous words
I'd have run before, while now I'm eager but slow.

    But why complain any more, now that I see
in the eyes of this unique and joyous angel   10
my peace, my repose and my salvation?

    Perhaps to see or hear him earlier
would have been worse, since now, in flight with him,
he gives me equal wings to follow his power.

Another sonnet for Tommaso de' Cavalieri, on the same sheet as nos. 59 and 60, more celebratory and less conflicted in tone. Cavalieri's power to ignite and restore him is compared to the legendary self-immolating phoenix (cf. nos. 43, 52, 62, 108, 217).

    2. *sun*, the passionate warmth radiated (or caused) by the youth.

    7. *his:* the beloved man.

    9. *complain*, of the delay in meeting him.

    11. *salvation:* cf. no. 60:4.

Sol pur col foco il fabbro il ferro stende
al concetto suo caro e bel lavoro,
né senza foco alcun artista l'oro
al sommo grado suo raffina e rende;
   né l'unica fenice sé riprende   5
se non prim'arsa; ond'io, s'ardendo moro,
spero più chiar resurger tra coloro
che morte accresce e 'l tempo non offende.
   Del foco, di ch'i' parlo, ho gran ventura
c'ancor per rinnovarmi abbi in me loco,   10
sendo già quasi nel numer de' morti.
   O ver, s'al cielo ascende per natura,
al suo elemento, e ch'io converso in foco
sie, come fie che seco non mi porti?

Only with fire can the smith shape iron
from his conception into fine, dear work;
neither, without fire, can any artist
refine and bring gold to its highest state,
   nor can the unique phoenix be revived   5
unless first burned. And so, if I die burning,
I hope to rise again brighter among those
whom death augments and time no longer hurts.
   I'm fortunate that the fire of which I speak
still finds a place within me, to renew me,   10
since already I'm almost numbered among the dead;
   or, since by its nature it ascends to heaven,
to its own element, if I should be transformed
into fire, how could it not bear me up with it?

Sonnet, ca. 1532, probably for Tommaso de' Cavalieri. Among the earliest of the poems that M prepared for publication in 1546.

2. *conception:* the Italian term *concetto* is central to the language of artistic theory and practice, referring to the original creative *idea* whose abstract (platonic) perfection must be realized in the artist's physical material; see no. 151.

11. *I'm almost numbered among the dead:* M used the same phrase in a letter to Benedetto Varchi in 1547 (C. MLXXXII; R. 280); cf. no. 263.

12–13. Dante speaks of the "instinct" that "bears fire upwards towards the moon," *Paradiso* 1:14–15; so too does Ficino, *Sopra lo amore,* oration 3, chap. 4.

Sì amico al freddo sasso è 'l foco interno
che, di quel tratto, se lo circumscrive,
che l'arda e spezzi, in qualche modo vive,
legando con sé gli altri in loco etterno.

E se 'n fornace dura, istate e verno   5
vince, e 'n più pregio che prima s'ascrive,
come purgata infra l'altre alte e dive
alma nel ciel tornasse da l'inferno.

Così tratto di me, se mi dissolve
il foco, che m'è dentro occulto gioco,   10
arso e po' spento aver più vita posso.

Dunche, s'i' vivo, fatto fummo e polve,
etterno ben sarò, s'induro al foco;
da tale oro e non ferro son percosso.

So kindly to the cold stone is the fire within it
that if, drawn out from it, the flame surrounds it
so it's burnt and shattered, it lives in another form,
itself binding others eternally in place.

Thus, if it survives the kiln, it can defeat   5
summer and winter, and claim a higher price than before,
as a soul, purified, returns from hell
to be among the high, worthy others in heaven.

If, drawn out from me in this way, the fire
that plays within me secretly, dissolves me,   10
burnt and extinguished I can have further life.

For, if I live, turned into smoke and dust,
once hardened by the fire I'll be immortal;
by such gold, not by iron, am I struck.

Sonnet of uncertain date, placed here by Girardi for its thematic affinity to the Cavalieri series
(cf. nos. 62, 64). M's note at the end indicates that he sent it to Luigi del Riccio for comments
and arranged for its return by way of one Raffaello; this might refer to M's assistant, Raffaello
da Montelupo, who worked with him in 1542–45, in which case the object of his flame of love
would more likely be Vittoria Colonna. The two central metaphors derive from properties of

stone: flint (lines 1–2, 14) and marble, which is burned to make the lime used in mortar to bind other stones together (lines 3–6); cf. nos. 143, 170.

1–2. *the fire within . . . drawn out from it:* the potential of stone (flint) to make a spark when struck by metal.

5–6. *defeat summer and winter:* transformed into mortar, its building can withstand the elements.

7/8. *hell:* more correctly, purgatory; elsewhere, M refers to this intermediate place of purification as *l'inferno pio* (no. 248).

14. That is, the person who has produced the spark of love in me is of such a superior spiritual character that the results will be ennobling.

64

Se 'l foco il sasso rompe e 'l ferro squaglia,
figlio del lor medesmo e duro interno,
che farà 'l più ardente dell'inferno
d'un nimico covon secco di paglia?

If fire shatters stone and melts down iron,
though the child of their shared hard inner substance,
what will the even more blazing fire of hell
do to a hated bundle of dry straw?

Quatrain—probably autonomous, since M copied it out in full—using the same image of flint and iron as no. 63. The "bundle of dry straw" is presumably the artist, already thinking of himself as withered by age and worthless or morally deficient.

Archers shooting at a herm (TC no. 336)

65

In quel medesmo tempo ch'io v'adoro,
la memoria del mie stato infelice
nel pensier mi ritorna, e piange e dice:
ben ama chi ben arde, ov'io dimoro.
   Però che scudo fo di tutti loro . . .   5

At the very moment that I'm worshipping you,
the memory of my unhappiness
comes back into my thoughts, and weeps, and says:
"One truly loves who truly burns—the state I'm in."
   And yet I make a shield from all of them . . .   5

Sonnet fragment, on the back of a draft of a letter to Andrea Quaratesi, datable May–June
1532 (C. DCCCLXXVI; R. 190); perhaps for Tommaso de' Cavalieri. The image of a shield,
though incomplete and obscure, is suggestive of the shield in M's drawing of *Archers shooting
at a herm* (TC no. 336, with a date on the verso of April 1530), which alludes to the violence of
passion.

Forse perché d'altrui pietà mi vegna,
perchè dell'altrui colpe più non rida,
nel mie propio valor, senz'altra guida,
caduta è l'alma che fu già si degna.

Né so qual militar sott'altra insegna   5
non che da vincer, da campar più fida,
sie che 'l tumulto dell'avverse strida
non pèra, ove 'l poter tuo non sostegna.

O carne, o sangue, o legno, o doglia strema,
giusto per vo' si facci el mie peccato,   10
di ch'i' pur nacqui, e tal fu 'l padre mio.

Tu sol se' buon; la tuo pietà suprema
soccorra al mie preditto iniquo stato,
sì presso a morte e sì lontan da Dio.

Perhaps so pity for others will come over me,
so I'll no longer laugh at others' faults,
trusting my own power, and no other guide,
my soul, which was so worthy once, has fallen.

Nor know I what soldier under another banner   5
could trust, let alone to win, even to escape,
so that in the tumult of the hostile cries
he would not perish, where your power did not support him.

O flesh, O blood, O wood, O ultimate pain!
through you may be justified all of my sin,   10
in which I was born, just as my father was.

You alone are good; may your infinite mercy
relieve my predestined state of wickedness,
so near to death and so far from God.

Sonnet, written on the back of a letter from Battista Figiovanni dated 23 November 1532 (C. DCCCXCV). Much different in its religious tone from the contemporaneous sonnets for Cavalieri, this introduces themes that predominate in M's later poetry, anticipating the emotions and iconography of the *Last Judgment*, begun in 1534.

5. *another banner:* cf. no. 10:14. For the same image of two contrasting military "camps," cf. Petrarch, no. 80:23, "le 'nsegne di quell'altra vita."

9. *wood:* the cross. *ultimate pain:* of the crucifixion.

10. *justified:* a theological term (purified, redeemed).

12. *you:* Christ.

14. This line is among M's most quoted phrases.

Nuovo piacere e di maggiore stima
veder l'ardite capre sopr'un sasso
montar, pascendo or questa or quella cima,
e 'l mastro lor, con aspre note, al basso,
sfogare el cor colla sua rozza rima,   5
sonando or fermo, e or con lento passo,
e la suo vaga, che ha 'l cor di ferro,
star co' porci, in contegno, sott'un cerro;
    quant'è veder 'n un eminente loco
e di pagli' e di terra el loro ospizio: 10
chi ingombra 'l desco e chi fa fora 'l foco,
sott'a quel faggio ch'è più lor propizio;
chi ingrassa e gratta 'l porco, e prende gioco,
chi doma 'l ciuco col basto primizio;
el vecchio gode e fa poche parole,   15
fuor dell'uscio a sedere, e stassi al sole.
    Di fuor dentro si vede quel che hanno:
pace sanza oro e sanza sete alcuna.
El giorno c'a solcare i colli vanno,
contar puo' lor ricchezze ad una ad una.   20
Non han serrami e non temon di danno;
lascion la casa aperta alla fortuna;
po', doppo l'opra, lieti el sonno tentano;
sazi di ghiande, in sul fien s'adormentano.
    L'invidia non ha loco in questo stato;   25
la superbia se stessa si divora.
Avide son di qualche verde prato,
o di quell'erba che più bella infiora.
Il lor sommo tesoro è uno arato,
e 'l bomero è la gemma che gli onora;   30
un paio di ceste è la credenza loro,
e le pale e le zappe e' vasi d'oro.
    O avarizia cieca, o bassi ingegni,
che disusate 'l ben della natura!
Cercando l'or, le terre e ' ricchi regni,   35
vostre imprese superbia ha forte e dura.

L'accidia, la lussuria par v'insegni;
l'invidia 'l mal d'altrui provvede e cura:
non vi scorgete, in insaziabil foco,
che 'l tempo è breve e 'l necessario è poco.   40

    Color c'anticamente, al secol vecchio,
si trasser fame e sete d'acqua e ghiande
vi sieno esemplo, scorta, lume e specchio,
e freno alle delizie, alle vivande.
Porgete al mie parlare un po' l'orecchio: 45
colui che 'l mondo impera, e ch'è sì grande,
ancor disidra, e non ha pace poi;
e 'l villanel la gode co' suo buoi.

    D'oro e di gemme, e spaventata in vista,
adorna, la Ricchezza va pensando;   50
ogni vento, ogni pioggia la contrista,
e gli agùri e ' prodigi va notando.
La lieta Povertà, fuggendo, acquista
ogni tesor, né pensa come o quando;
secur ne' boschi, in panni rozzi e bigi,   55
fuor d'obrighi, di cure e di letigi.

    L'avere e 'l dar, l'usanze streme e strane,
el meglio e 'l peggio, e le cime dell'arte
al villanel son tutte cose piane,
e l'erba e l'acqua e 'l latte è la sua parte;   60
e 'l cantar rozzo, e ' calli delle mane,
è 'l dieci e 'l cento e ' conti e le suo carte
dell'usura che 'n terra surger vede;
e senza affanno alla fortuna cede.

    Onora e ama e teme e prega Dio   65
pe' pascol, per l'armento e pel lavoro,
con fede, con ispeme e con desio,
per la gravida vacca e pel bel toro.
El Dubbio, el Forse, el Come, el Perché rio
no 'l può ma' far, ché non istà fra loro: 70
se con semplice fede adora e prega
Iddio e 'l ciel, l'un lega e l'altro piega.

    El Dubbio armato e zoppo si figura,
e va saltando come la locuste,

tremando d'ogni tempo per natura,   75
qual suole al vento far canna paluste.
El Perché è magro, e 'ntorn'alla cintura
ha molte chiave, e non son tanto giuste,
c'agugina gl'ingegni della porta,
e va di notte, e 'l buio è la suo scorta.   80

   El Come e 'l Forse son parenti stretti,
e son giganti di sì grande altezza,
c'al sol andar ciascun par si diletti,
e ciechi fur per mirar suo chiarezza;
e quello alle città co' fieri petti   85
tengon, per tutto adombran lor bellezza;
e van per vie fra sassi erte e distorte,
tentando colle man qual istà forte.

   Povero e nudo e sol se ne va 'l Vero,
che fra la gente umìle ha gran valore: 90
un occhio ha sol, qual è lucente e mero,
e 'l corpo ha d'oro, e d'adamante 'l core;
e negli affanni cresce e fassi altero,
e 'n mille luoghi nasce, se 'n un muore;
di fuor verdeggia sì come smeraldo,   95
e sta co' suo fedel costante e saldo.

   Cogli occhi onesti e bassi in ver' la terra,
vestito d'oro e di vari ricami,
il Falso va, c'a' iusti sol fa guerra;
ipocrito, di fuor par c'ognuno ami;   100
perch'è di ghiaccio, al sol si cuopre e serra;
sempre sta 'n corte, e par che l'ombra brami;
e ha per suo sostegno e compagnia
la Fraude, la Discordia e la Bugia.

   L'Adulazion v'è poi, ch'è pien d'affanni,   105
giovane destra e di bella persona;
di più color coperta di più panni,
che 'l cielo a primavera a' fior non dona:
ottien ciò che la vuol con dolci inganni,
e sol di quel che piace altrui ragiona;   110
ha 'l pianto e 'l riso in una voglia sola;
cogli occhi adora, e con le mani invola.

Non è sol madre in corte all'opre orrende,
ma è lor balia ancora, e col suo latte
le cresce, l'aümenta e le difende.   115

What a new and more worthwhile pleasure
to see the daring goats climbing atop a rock,
grazing now on this peak, now on another;
and their master, down below, pouring out his heart
in his crude verses sung with a rough voice,   5
now playing motionless, now at a slow pace;
and his fair lady, who has a heart of stone,
standing demurely with the pigs beneath an oak.
   So, too, is it to see, on a high spot,
their abode made out of earth and straw: 10
one sets the table, one lights an outdoor fire
beneath the beech tree most favorable to them;
one fattens and prods the pig, making sport of it,
one breaks the donkey in with its first load;
and the old man says few words, and takes delight   15
in sitting outside the doorway in the sun.
   From outside, one can see what they have within:
peace without gold and with no thirst for it.
By day, when they go out to plow the hills,
you can count up their riches, one by one.   20
They have no locks and they fear no harm,
and they leave their house open to fortune;
then, after work, they merrily go to bed
and, filled up with acorns, fall asleep on the hay.
   In such conditions there is no room for envy,   25
and pride is devoured by itself.
They are greedy only for some green meadow
or for some grass that flowers more beautifully.
The greatest of their treasures is a plow,
and its blade is the jewel that brings them honor;   30
a pair of baskets serve them as their cupboard,
and hoes and shovels are their golden vessels.
   O blind avarice, O base intellects,
you who make ill use of nature's goods!

Seeking gold, and land, and wealthy realms,   35
your ventures are ruled by powerful, cruel pride.
Sloth and lust seem to be your teachers,
and envy supplies your desire for others' harm;
you do not notice, in your unquenchable fire,
that time is short and little is necessary.   40
   Let those who formerly, in olden days,
relieved their hunger and thirst with water and acorns
be your example, guide, lamp, and mirror,
and a curb on your pleasures and your victuals.
Lend your ear for a little while to my words: 45
He who rules the world, and is so great,
still longs for more, and never has any peace,
while the country fellow with his oxen enjoys it.
   Wealth goes about lost in thought, adorned with gold
and jewels, yet with a face that's filled with terror;   50
every wind and every rain makes her grieve,
and she goes around observing omens and marvels.
Yet merry Poverty, by fleeing them, acquires
every treasure, and does not think of how or when,
safe in the woods, clad in coarse gray cloth,   55
free of obligations, cares, and quarrels.
   Credits and debits, those strange and excessive customs,
and better and worse, and the pinnacles of art
are all things that seem flat to the peasant;
grass and water and milk are his concerns,   60
and his rough song and the calluses on his hands
are for him the tens and hundreds, the accounts and papers
of the moneylenders seen springing up around the world;
and he gives himself up to fortune without concern.
   He honors and loves and fears God, and prays to Him   65
for his pastures, for his herds, and for his work;
he prays with faith, and with hope, and with yearning
for the pregnant cow and for the handsome bull.
Doubt and Perhaps and How and Why can never
spoil him, for he is not involved with them: 70
if he adores and prays to God and heaven
with simple faith, he'll bind one and bend the other.

Doubt is depicted armed and crippled,
and moves around by jumping, like the locust,
quivering all the time by his very nature,   75
just as a marsh reed will do in the wind.
And Why is thin, and all around his belt
has many keys, but they don't fit at all;
so he must pick the lock of every door,
and travel by night, with darkness as his escort.   80
    How and Perhaps are close relatives,
and they are giants of so great a height
that both seem to delight in reaching the sun,
but have been blinded by gazing at its brightness.
With their fierce breasts they keep it away from the cities,   85
overshadowing its beauty everywhere;
they travel steep and winding roads through the rocks,
testing with their hands which ones are stable.
    Poor and naked and alone goes Truth,
who is greatly valued among humble people.   90
He has only one eye, which is pure and shining,
and has a body of gold, and a heart of adamant;
in suffering he grows and is exalted,
and he's born in a thousand places if he dies in one;
outwardly, he is as green as an emerald,   95
and is firm and constant to his faithful followers.
    With eyes modestly lowered toward the ground,
dressed in gold and varicolored embroideries,
goes Falsehood, who only makes war on the righteous;
a hypocrite, he pretends to love everyone;   100
being made of ice, he covers and hides from the sun,
is always in the court, and seems to yearn for shadow;
and he has for his support and company
Fraud, and Discord, and Mendacity.
    Then there is Adulation, who's full of troubles,   105
a clever young maiden of lovely appearance,
covered with more fabrics, of more colors,
than heaven gives to the flowers in springtime;
she gets what she wants with sweet deceptions,
and only says what pleases other people;   110

she has tears and laughter in one single will,
and adores with her eyes, while with her hands she robs.

    At court, she's not only mother to horrible deeds,
but is their wet nurse too, and with her milk
she feeds them, and builds them up, and defends them.   115

This long sequence of stanzas in ottava rima, written shortly before 1534, is M's sole contribution to the ancient tradition of praise for rural life, descended from such classical sources as Virgil's *Georgics* and *Eclogues*. Similar "stanze in lode della vita rusticale" abound in earlier Italian literature. Petrarch, no. 50, praises the peaceful simplicity of the peasant life in similar phrases, as does Lorenzo de' Medici in various poems, notably his *La Nencia di Barberino*. Much of M's imagery and phrasing in his first two stanzas more explicitly recalls his teacher Angelo Poliziano's *Stanze per la Giostra*, book 1, cantos 17–21, and the rustic shepherds of his *Orfeo*, esp. lines 54–84; the personified allegories of M's later stanzas resemble those in canto 45 of Poliziano's *Stanze*. Some literary parallels have also been suggested with the works of such younger Cinquecento poets as Luigi Alamanni (*Coltivazione dei campi*) and Luigi Tansillo (*Il podere*). The second half of the poem turns from description to moral allegory, personifying various virtues of rural life and contrasting them with the vices associated with cities or courts. Here M draws on, but at times varies, the emblem-book symbols first published by Andrea Alciati (*Emblemata*, 1531) and the similar iconographical traditions later codified in Cesare Ripa's *Iconologia* (1593) and other mythographies. No. 67 shares both its allegorical structure and specific images with no. 68 (e.g., the giants of lines 81–88), and early editors printed them as one unit, though their thematic concerns are in fact different.

6. Sometimes playing and singing while standing still, at other times while slowly walking about.

12. *most favorable:* that provides the most shade.

13. One feeds the pig and, while doing so, makes a game of teasing it.

25–38. Envy, pride, greed or avarice, sloth, and luxury or lust are among the proverbial seven deadly sins.

26. Pride must eat itself because it finds no other nourishment (encouragement) there.

33. Many years earlier, in 1512, M had written to his brother Buonarroto that "avarice is a deadly sin and nothing sinful can succeed" (C. xci; R. 66).

39. *unquenchable fire:* trapped as you are in the fever of covetousness, distracted by earthly desires.

40. That is, life is brief and very little of material goods is truly needed for earthly happiness.

41–42. *in olden days* (literally "the old century"): in the Golden Age. In the classical literary tradition, the Golden Age was the first and most idyllic of four "Ages of Man" (gold, silver, bronze, iron) of declining glory and increasing strife and unhappiness. Cf. Dante, *Purgatorio* 22:148–51.

43. *mirror:* a pattern for imitation.

52. That is, her fear of losing her wealth makes her superstitious.

54. *how or when* it may acquire or lose wealth.

55. Cf. M's letter to Giorgio Vasari in 1556, during a stay in the mountains near Spoleto, in which he declares that "peace is not really to be found except in the woods" (C. MCCXXXVII; R. 426). *coarse gray cloth* may refer to the traditional costume of the Franciscan order.

57. *Credits and debits:* the verbs *avere* and *dare* are used in this sense in accounting terminology.

58–59. Developing a refined discrimination of quality or an appreciation of aesthetic achievement is of no interest to the peasant.

60–63. In the peasant's mind, his physical labors and simple pleasures occupy the same place of occupational importance as do financial manipulations to usurers, whose numbers seem to be growing everywhere.

71. (Understood): On the contrary, he believes that . . .

72. *he'll bind one and bend the other:* bind heaven to himself in love, and influence God to grant his wishes.

73. *is depicted:* in paintings and prints, a reference to iconographical traditions.

78. *keys . . . don't fit:* i.e., a doubting mind cannot unlock the secrets of truth.

79. *pick the lock:* literally, "apply a sharp object to the mechanism." M seems to have coined the verb *aguginare*, related to *aguzzo* (pointed, sharp, etc.), to express the idea of forcing or picking a lock with a pointed tool.

80. *darkness:* ignorance.

81–86. Cf. the description and actions of the giant in no. 68, esp. lines 1–8.

85–86. *it . . . its:* the sun and its beauty.

89–96. M follows the iconographic tradition which specified that Truth was depicted nude ("the naked truth"), but in that tradition the figure was female. His name for this allegory, *Il Vero*, is more properly "The True" than "Truth" (*La Verità*); cf. lines 97–104.

92. *adamant:* as in English, a poetic term for "diamond"; i.e., Truth can resist all temptation to falsehood and error.

97–104. As with Truth in the preceding stanza, M personifies Untruth as masculine, *Il Falso*, which means "The False" rather than "Falsehood" (*La Falsità*, the more customary feminine form). The description of this figure is similar to Dante's hypocrites in *Inferno* 23, who wear cloaks that are dazzlingly decorated on the outside but are so heavy that they bend the wearers' heads downward, keeping their gaze fixed on the ground.

99. *makes war on the righteous:* cf. no. 68:43.

101. *covers and hides from the sun:* so as not to be melted by the light of Truth.

102. *the court,* as in English, may refer either to the courtyard of a building (that is, a shadowed area) or to the court of people surrounding a powerful ruler, where Falsehood may be presumed to flourish for political reasons; cf. line 113.

111. That is, she is prepared to express any emotion at will, as required by the wish to please others.

113. *at court:* here referring, less ambiguously than in line 102, to a political setting.

114–15. *wet nurse:* cf. the similar image of a hideous hag who nurses the giant of evil in no. 68:25–28.

68

Un gigante v'è ancor, d'altezza tanta
che da' sua occhi noi qua giù non vede,
e molte volte ha ricoperta e franta
una città colla pianta del piede;
al sole aspira e l'alte torre pianta   5
per aggiunger al cielo, e non lo vede,
ché 'l corpo suo, così robusto e magno,
un occhio ha solo e quell'ha 'n un calcagno.

Vede per terra le cose passate,
e 'l capo ha fermo e prossim'a le stelle;   10
di qua giù se ne vede dua giornate
delle gran gambe, e irsut' ha la pelle;
da indi in su non ha verno né state,
ché le stagion gli sono equali e belle;
e come 'l ciel fa pari alla suo fronte,   15
in terra al pian col piè fa ogni monte.

Com'a noi è 'l minuzzol dell'arena,
sotto la pianta a lui son le montagne;
fra ' folti pel delle suo gambe mena
diverse forme mostruose e magne: 20
per mosca vi sarebbe una balena;
e sol si turba e sol s'attrista e piagne
quando in quell'occhio il vento seco tira
fummo o festuca o polvere che gira.

Una gran vecchia pigra e lenta ha seco,   25
che latta e mamma l'orribil figura,
e 'l suo arrogante, temerario e cieco
ardir conforta e sempre rassicura.
Fuor di lui stassi in un serrato speco,
nelle gran rocche e dentro all'alte mura;   30
quand'è lui in ozio, e le' in tenebre vive,
e sol inopia nel popol prescrive.

Palida e gialla, e nel suo grave seno
il segno porta sol del suo signore:
cresce del mal d'altrui, del ben vien meno,   35
né s'empie per cibarsi a tutte l'ore;

il corso suo non ha termin né freno,
e odia altrui e sé non porta amore;
di pietra ha 'l core e di ferro le braccia,
e nel suo ventre il mare e ' monti caccia. 40
   Sette lor nati van sopra la terra,
che cercan tutto l'uno e l'altro polo,
e solo a' iusti fanno insidie e guerra,
e mille capi ha ciascun per sé solo.
L'etterno abisso per lor s'apre e serra, 45
tal preda fan nell'universo stuolo;
e lor membra ci prendon passo passo,
come edera fa el mur fra sasso e sasso.

   And then there is a giant of such a height
that he can't see us down here from where his eyes are,
and many times he has covered and crushed
an entire city with the sole of his foot.
He aspires to the sun, and he erects 5
high towers to reach heaven, yet cannot see it,
for his body, although so powerful and huge,
has only one eye, and that one's on his heel.
   So he sees only things he's passed by on the ground,
while he holds his head up firmly near the stars; 10
from down here we can see a two-day journey
of his great legs, which have a hairy skin;
from there on up he feels neither winter nor summer,
for the seasons are all equally fine to him;
and just as his forehead is on a level with heaven, 15
on earth he levels every mountain with his foot.
   As a tiny grain of sand seems to us,
so do the mountains beneath his heel to him;
within the thick hair of his legs he carries
various huge and monstrous forms of life; 20
a whale would seem like a mere fly to him,
and he only becomes troubled and sad and weeps
when the wind brings along into that eye
some smoke or whirling wisp of straw or dust.
   He has with him a large old woman, slow and lazy, 25

who nurses and suckles his horrifying figure,
and who always gives support and encouragement
to his arrogant, daring, and blind recklessness.
When not with him, she stays in a closed cave,
within great rocks and behind high walls;   30
while he rests, she lives in the shadows, and on her own
she ordains destitution among the people.

    She is pallid and yellow, and the only sign she carries
in her weighty breast is that of her lord;
she grows strong from others' ills, weak from their good fortune,   35
and is never full, though feeding all the time;
in her course she has neither rein nor finish,
and she hates others yet does not love herself;
she has a heart of stone and arms of iron,
and she thrusts mountains and seas into her belly.   40

    Their seven offspring go all over the earth,
searching from one pole to the other,
and only set snares or make war against the righteous;
and each of them by himself has a thousand heads.
They take such prey from the universal throng   45
that the eternal abyss opens and shuts for them;
and their limbs take hold of us little by little,
as ivy does a wall between the stones.

A series of stanzas in ottava rima related in form and imagery to no. 67, and probably dating
from about the same time, prior to 1534. The first stanzas of M's draft are written on the recto
of a sheet whose verso contains no. 71 (TC no. 627r), the later stanzas on the same sheet as
nos. 69 and 70. The grotesque characterization of the pair of giants and their children recalls
the giantess in Lorenzo de' Medici, *Selva* 2, stanzas 39, 67, and, more generally, the giants of
Dante, *Purgatorio* 32:142–60. M was fascinated by colossal figures from at least 1501–4,
when he carved his David, popularly called "Il Gigante"; Condivi reports that in 1505 M
dreamed of sculpting a giant figure into the hills of Carrara that would be visible at sea (CW
29–30). The family of giants here seems allegorical in intent, like the two named How and
Perhaps in no. 67, but there are few clues to a reading more specific than gross sinfulness.
(The poem's obscurity may be due in part to its being incomplete: the opening "and then"
implies some prior action, and the narrative breaks off without a conclusion.) Michelangelo
the Younger thought that the two giants represented Fury and Pride, their children the seven
deadly sins. The male giant has also been interpreted in political terms, as a veiled critique of
Alessandro de Medici's recently established tyranny in Florence; in a letter of 1525, M had

ridiculed a colossal figure that Clement VII proposed to erect at the Medici palace in Florence (C. DCCXXX; R. 176; Seymour 68–72).

1–8. Cf. the same imagery in no. 67:81–86; *and then:* alternatively, "still" or "also."

9. That is, he has only hindsight.

11. *a two-day journey:* i.e., as much of the length of his legs as could be covered in a two-day walk. In painting, the term *giornata* refers to the division of a large fresco into daily work areas, the size of which is determined by the amount of wet plaster that can be painted before it dries.

25–28. Cf. the wet nurse in no. 67:114–15. The description of the giantess recalls the drawing, probably by a student of M's, showing a withered hag with exposed, pendulous breasts, on which is written no. 47 (TC no. 312); see also no. 20.

31–32. *she lives in the shadows:* cf. no. 67:101–2. *she ordains destitution:* condemns humanity to abject poverty, by spells or other supernatural means.

33–34. Possibly meaning that she is pregnant, though the passage is unclear; *grave seno,* literally "grave [or heavy] breast," may mean figuratively "gravid womb."

37. In her constant activity she moves like a racehorse, never slowing down or coming to an end.

38. Cf. no. 11:11.

41–48. The seven offspring have often been interpreted as the seven deadly sins, who insidiously seek out, lure, and grasp the righteous. M depicted these seven major sins in his *Last Judgment* for the Sistine Chapel "in the form of devils, assailing and striving to drag down to hell the souls that are flying towards heaven" (VM 7:213; VB 381) and in his drawing *The Dream of Human Life* (TC no. 333r).

43. *only . . . the righteous:* cf. no. 67:99.

45–46. The giants' children kill so many human victims throughout the world that the gates of hell must continually open to receive the souls of the dead.

47–48. If the seven giants represent the seven deadly sins, this passage would imply that sinfulness insinuates itself into our being slowly and imperceptibly, as tentacles of ivy penetrate slowly into the chinks of a wall.

69

Ben provvide natura, né conviene
a tanta crudeltà minor bellezza,
ché l'un contrario l'altro ha temperato.
* Così può 'l viso vostro le mie pene*
tante temprar con piccola dolcezza,   5
e lieve fare quelle e me beato.

Nature arranged things well, for no less beauty
should have been given to such great cruelty,
so one opposite could moderate the other.
  In this way, your face can moderate
my great sufferings with a little of its sweetness,   5
and, by making them lighter, make me happy.

Two tercets, perhaps the conclusion of a sonnet, written on the same sheet as no. 70 and part
of no. 68, in 1534.
  1–2. It was wise of nature to unite in you qualities of equally great beauty and cruelty. Cf.
Petrarch, no. 128:33.

70

Crudele stella, anzi crudele arbitrio
che 'l potere e 'l voler mi stringe e lega;
né si travaglia chiara stella in cielo
dal giorno [in qua?] che mie vela disciolse,
ond'io errando e vagabondo andai,   5
qual vano legno gira a tutti e' venti.

Or son qui, lasso, e all'incesi venti
convien varar mie legno, e senza arbitrio
solcar l'alte onde ove mai sempre andai.
Così quagiù si prende, preme e lega   10
quel che lassù già 'll'alber si disciolse,
ond'a me tolsi la dote del cielo.

Qui non mi regge e non mi spinge il cielo,
ma potenti e terrestri e duri venti,
ché sopra me non so qual si disciolse   15
per [darli mano?] e tormi del mio arbitrio.
Così fuor di mie rete altri mi lega.
Mie colpa è, ch'ignorando a quello andai?

Maladetto [sie] 'l dì che ïo andai
col segno che correva su nel cielo!   20
Se non ch'i' so che 'l giorno el cor non lega,
né sforza l'alma, ne' contrari venti,
contra al nostro largito e sciolto arbitrio,
perché [. . .] e pruove ci disciolse.

Dunche, se mai dolor del cor disciolse   25
sospiri ardenti, o se orando andai
fra caldi venti a quel ch'è fuor d'arbitrio,
[. . .], pietoso de' mie caldi venti,
vede, ode e sente e non m'è contra 'l cielo;
ché scior non si può chi se stesso lega.   30

Così l'atti suo perde chi si lega,
e salvo sé nessun ma' si disciolse.
E come arbor va retto verso il cielo,
ti prego, Signor mio, se mai andai,
ritorni, come quel che non ha venti,   35
sotto el tüo grande el mïo arbitrio.

Colui che sciolse e lega 'l mio arbitrio,
ov'io andai agl'importuni venti,
fa' mie vendetta, s' tu mel desti, o cielo.

O cruel star, or rather, cruel will
that constrains and binds my power and my volition!
There's been no bright star working for me in heaven
since the day on which my sail was unfurled,
and so I have wandered about and gone astray   5
like an empty ship turning in every wind.
    Now here I am, weary, and in those enflamed winds
I must launch my boat, and without any will
plow those same high waves over which I've always gone.
Thus down here is seized (and it crushes and binds)   10
what earlier was plucked from the tree up there,
and by which I've deprived myself of the gift of heaven.
    Here it's not heaven that controls and moves me,
but rather the harsh and powerful earthly winds,
for I don't know what's been unleashed on me   15
to give them a hand in taking my free will from me.
Thus, another net besides my own now binds me;
is it my fault if I went toward it unawares?
    Accursed be the day when I first moved
beneath the sign that was passing over in heaven!   20
Although I know that the day does not bind the heart
nor compel the soul, in unfavorable winds,
against the free will liberally granted to us,
since . . . and ordeals set us free.
    Therefore, if pain ever let loose burning sighs   25
from my heart, or if I moved through hot winds
praying to him who is beyond our will,
. . . heaven, taking pity on my hot winds,
sees, hears and feels me, and is not against me;
for one who binds himself can't untie himself.   30
    One who binds himself loses control of his own actions,
and no one has ever untied himself by himself.
And, as a tree grows straight up toward heaven,
I pray you, my Lord, though I strayed so long,

that my will may, like one that has no winds, 35
come back underneath your greater will.

    On him who let loose and now binds my will,
toward whom I was moved by the troublesome winds,
take revenge for me, O heaven, since you gave him to me.

Nearly complete sestina, written on the verso of the sheet containing no. 69, ca. 1534; the "him" who has overpowered the artist's free will (line 37) might refer to Tommaso de' Cavalieri, whom M met in late 1532. For M's only other attempt at this intricate stanza form, see no. 33 (the sestina's pattern of repeated end words has not been consistently translated here, for the sake of clarity). The handwriting is obscured by retracing; editors before Girardi transcribed only the opening lines, and his reconstruction is conjectural and incomplete. The theme of losing one's free will in the slavery of love is explored through numerous Petrarchan images; cf. the similar theme in, e.g., no. 32 above.

    4. *the day on which my sail was unfurled:* when I was born.

    7. *enflamed winds:* the heat of passion.

    10–12. Here on earth I have fallen prey to the same temptation that once defeated Adam and Eve in Eden—that is, I have "seized" the same fruit that they once plucked from the Tree of Knowledge "up there" (in the earthly paradise)—and my slavery to base desires now denies me salvation.

    15. *what's been unleashed:* what unknown, powerful force (or person).

    17. For images of binding, cf. nos. 7, 23, 36, 41, etc.

    19–20. Accursed be the day on which I was stirred to life (born) under the influence of an adverse star.

    21. *the day does not bind the heart:* the day of birth, i.e., the influence of one's astrological horoscope, does not control one's emotions.

    25. *pain:* of repentance.

    27. *beyond our will:* superior to human judgment or control.

    29. *sees, hears, and feels me:* is aware of my sufferings.

    31. *one who binds himself:* in sinful desire.

    35. *one that has no winds:* like a soul freed from buffeting by the winds of passion.

    39. *you gave him to me:* you imposed him on me, placed his temptation in my path. Cf. Petrarch, no. 121, "fa di te e di me, signor, vendetta."

71

I' l'ho, vostra mercè, per ricevuto
e hollo letto delle volte venti.
Tal pro vi facci alla natura i denti,
co' 'l cibo al corpo quand'egli è pasciuto.
I' ho pur, poi ch'i' vi lasciai, saputo 5
che Cain fu de' vostri anticedenti,
né voi da quel tralignate altrimenti;
ché, s'altri ha ben, vel pare aver perduto.
Invidiosi, superbi, al ciel nimici,
la carità del prossimo v'è a noia, 10
e sol del vostro danno siete amici.
Se ben dice il Poeta, di Pistoia,
istieti a mente, e basta; e se tu dici
ben di Fiorenza, tu mi dai la soia.
Qual prezïosa gioia 15
è certo ma per te già non si intende,
perché poca virtù non la comprende.

I have received it, thanks to your courtesy,
and have read it over about twenty times:
Teeth would do as much good for your nature
as food does for the body when it's been fed.
Since I last saw you, I have also learned 5
that Cain was one of your ancestors,
and you have not forsaken his legacy:
for when others gain something, you think you've lost it.
Envious, arrogant, enemies of heaven,
you find your neighbor's charity annoying, 10
and you are friends only with your own ruin.
Since what the Poet says of Pistoia is true,
bear it in mind, and that's enough; and if you
speak well of Florence, you're trying to fool me.
It is a precious jewel, 15
surely, but that's not understood by you,
since meager wisdom cannot comprehend it.

A *sonetto caudato*, ca. 1532–34, on the verso of a sheet bearing part of no. 68 (TC no. 627). Given the poem's attack on the citizens of Pistoia, and the reference in line 1 to having received an earlier communication from the addressee, it has long been assumed that this poem was sent to Giovanni di Benedetto da Pistoia, who exchanged poems with M (he also received one of M's earlier exercises in this extended "tailed sonnet" form, no. 5; cf. no. 25). The precise tone of the poem is unclear—is it, like no. 5, a Bernesque, mock-grumpy joke, or does it refer to some real falling out?—and interpretation is complicated by the shift from the plural *voi* (lines 1–11) to the singular *tu* (12–17).

3–4. Presumably a sarcastic reaction to a sharp, biting tone in the text M has just read, further alluded to in lines 9–11.

6–8. Cain killed his brother Abel out of jealous anger that God had accepted Abel's sacrifice and rejected his own (Genesis 4).

9. Cf. Dante's attacks on Florentines as filled with arrogance, envy, and greed, *Inferno* 6:74, 15:67–69.

12. *the Poet:* Dante, who inveighs against the morals of the city and individual residents in *Inferno* 24:126, 25:10–15.

15. *it:* Florence.

72

Se nel volto per gli occhi il cor si vede,
altro segno non ho più manifesto
della mie fiamma; addunche basti or questo,
signor mie caro, a domandar mercede.

Forse lo spirto tuo, con maggior fede   5
ch'i' non credo, che sguarda il foco onesto
che m'arde, fie di me pietoso e presto,
come grazia c'abbonda a chi ben chiede.

O felice quel dì, se questo è certo!
Fermisi in un momento il tempo e l'ore,   10
il giorno e 'l sol nella su' antica traccia;

acciò ch'i' abbi, e non già per mie merto,
il desïato mie dolce signore
per sempre nell'indegne e pronte braccia.

If the heart can be seen in the face through the eyes,
I have no other, more apparent sign
of my flame; so let these be enough,
my dear lord, to petition for your mercy.

Perhaps your spirit, which sees, with greater credence   5
than I dare to believe, the virtuous fire
that burns me, will be quick to pity me,
like the grace that abounds for one who truly asks.

O happy that day, when this be sure to happen!
Let time and its hours stand still all at once,   10
and the day, and the sun in its ancient circuit,

so that I might have, even if it's not
on my own merits, my sweet and longed-for lord
in my unworthy yet ready arms forever.

Sonnet for Tommaso de' Cavalieri, whom M refers to as "signor mie caro" in several poems and letters. As often in the Cavalieri series, the language conflates earthly passion and the terms used to define the love of God. Eight autograph drafts survive; in one (Girardi IIIb), M wrote more specifically of his desire to embrace "the breast and neck of my lord" (*il petto e 'l collo al mie signiore*).

3. *these:* eyes.

9. Cf. Petrarch, no. 349, "O felice quel dì . . . ch'i' veggia il mio Signore et la mia donna," and Gasparo Visconti (as in poem no. 60).

9–11. M echoes the traditional belief that the sun and moon would stand still and time stop on Judgment Day.

73

Mentre del foco son scacciata e priva,
morir m'è forza, ove si vive e campa;
e 'l mie cibo è sol quel c'arde e avvampa,
e di quel c'altri muor, convien ch'i' viva.

When I'm driven away from and deprived of fire,
I'm compelled to die, where others survive and live;
for my only food is what flares up and burns,
and that which others die from, I need to live.

Quatrain from 1533; this and the following fragment are written on a copy of no. 72, and are probably also addressed to Cavalieri. Here M personifies himself as feminine, speaking presumably as his own soul (*l'anima*), deprived of the passion of love. His image derives from a Petrarchan oxymoron, "I feed on my death and live in flames: strange food and a wondrous salamander!" (PD no. 207:40–41); cf. no. 122. The image of nourishment parallels M's letter to Cavalieri of July 1533, in which he calls the young man "the food on which I live" (C. CMXVI; R. 193). For similar claims of M's difference from other people, cf. nos. 122, 136.

74

I' piango, i' ardo, i' mi consumo, e 'l core
di questo si nutrisce. O dolce sorte!
chi è che viva sol della sua morte,
come fo io d'affanni e di dolore?
Ahi! crudele arcier, tu sai ben l'ore   5
da far tranquille l'angosciose e corte
miserie nostre con la tuo man forte;
ché chi vive di morte mai non muore.

I weep, I burn, I waste away, and my heart
is fed by all this. O sweet destiny!
Who else is there who lives only on his death,
as I do, on suffering and pain?
Oh, cruel archer, you know just the moment   5
in which to put to rest, with your powerful hand,
our brief and anguished misery;
for one who lives on death never dies.

On the same sheet as no. 73 and continuing its paradoxical theme.

5. *archer:* Cupid, a common image in the *Rime*. Here it recalls M's drawing, *Archers shooting at a herm* of ca. 1530 (TC no. 336), in which he depicts a crowd of nudes raining arrows on a sculptured male figure, an apparent allegory of the invasive power of passion.

75

Egli è pur troppo a rimirarsi intorno
chi con la vista ancide i circustanti
sol per mostrarsi andar diporto attorno.
    Egli è pur troppo a chi fa notte il giorno,
scurando il sol co' vaghi e be' sembianti,   5
aprirgli spesso, e chi con risi e canti
ammuta altrui non esser meno adorno.

It's really too much that he who with his glance
slays every bystander, should look around
and saunter about just to show himself.
    It's really too much that he who makes night of day,
eclipsing the sun with his fair and charming features,   5
should open them often, that he who strikes others dumb
with smiles and song, is not less adorned.

A fragment from 1533. Transcriptions of the text differ; the present version seems to suggest a jocular irony unusual in M's tone toward Cavalieri.
    5. *features:* the eyes, a Petrarchan metaphor.

Rape of Ganymede, pencil drawing (TC no. 344)

76

Non so se s'è la desïata luce
del suo primo fattor, che l'alma sente,
o se dalla memoria della gente
alcun'altra beltà nel cor traluce;
    o se fama o se sogno alcun produce   5
agli occhi manifesto, al cor presente,
di sé lasciando un non so che cocente
ch'è forse or quel c'a pianger mi conduce.
    Quel ch'i' sento e ch'i' cerco e chi mi guidi
meco non è; né so ben veder dove   10
trovar mel possa, e par c'altri mel mostri.
    Questo, signor, m'avvien, po' ch'i' vi vidi,
c'un dolce amaro, un sì e no mi muove:
certo saranno stati gli occhi vostri.

I don't know if it is the longed-for light
of its first maker, which my soul feels;
or whether, from my memories of people,
some other beauty shines forth in my heart;
    or whether reports or dreams bring someone   5
before my eyes and present to my heart,
leaving behind something unknown and smarting
that is, perhaps, what now leads me to weep.
    What I feel and seek, and who might guide me to it,
are not within me; nor can I see clearly   10
where I might find them, though others seem to show me.
    This, lord, has happened to me since I saw you:
a bitter sweetness, a yes-and-no feeling moves me;
certainly it must have been your eyes.

A complete sonnet from summer, 1533, for Tommaso de' Cavalieri (TC no. 538r).

    3. *my memories:* M was in Florence at this time and thinking of Cavalieri. He wrote to Sebastiano del Piombo in Rome during August 1533 asking for news of Tommaso, adding that "if he were to fade from my memory I think I should instantly fall dead" (C. CMXXIII; R. 194)."

Punishment of Tityos (TC no. 345)

12. *lord:* In several draft versions, the poem is addressed to an unnamed woman (*donna*), finally changed to *signor*.

13. *bitter sweetness:* a familiar Petrarchan oxymoron (e.g., *Rime* no. 173); cf. nos. 17, 158.

14. That is, your eyes are the cause of this feeling.

77

Se 'l foco fusse alla bellezza equale
degli occhi vostri, che da que' si parte,
non avrie 'l mondo sì gelata parte
che non ardessi com'acceso strale.

Ma 'l ciel, pietoso d'ogni nostro male, 5
a noi d'ogni beltà, che 'n voi comparte,
la visiva virtù toglie e diparte
per tranquillar la vita aspr'e mortale.

Non è par dunche il foco alla beltate,
ché sol di quel s'infiamma e s'innamora 10
altri del bel del ciel, ch'è da lui inteso.

Così n'avvien, signore, in questa etate:
se non vi par per voi ch'i' arda e mora,
poca capacità m'ha poco acceso.

If the fire that radiates from them
were equal to the beauty of your eyes,
there would be no part of the world so frozen
that it would not burn like a flaming dart.

But heaven, merciful toward all our troubles, 5
takes and removes from us the power to see
all the beauty that it has allotted to you,
in order to calm our harsh earthly life.

So my fire is not equal to your beauty,
for one only catches fire and falls in love 10
with that part of heaven's beauty he can take in.

Thus it happens to us, my lord, at this age:
if it doesn't seem that I burn and die for you,
my slight capacity has but slightly ignited me.

Sonnet for Tommaso de' Cavalieri, probably written between June and October 1533, while
M was in Florence. The attempt to explain why his feelings may not seem as intense as
Cavalieri's qualities deserve echoes M's letter of 28 July 1533, in which he refers to "the grave
apprehension shown by your [Cavalieri's] letter that I might have forgotten you" and
suggests that Cavalieri complained "in order to kindle anew a greater flame, if a greater were
possible" (C. CMXVI; R. 193).

4. *flaming dart:* the attribute of Cupid/Eros, and a common Petrarchan image.

14. Understood: *it is because* my slight capacity. . . .

78

Dal dolce pianto al doloroso riso,
da una etterna a una corta pace
caduto son; là dove 'l ver si tace,
soprasta 'l senso a quel da lui diviso.

Né so se dal mie core o dal tuo viso   5
la colpa vien del mal, che men dispiace
quante più cresce, o dall'ardente face
de gli occhi tuo rubati al paradiso.

La tuo beltà non è cosa mortale,
ma fatta su dal ciel fra noi divina;   10
ond'io perdendo ardendo mi conforto,

c'appresso a te non esser posso tale.
Se l'arme il ciel del mie morir destina,
chi può, s'i' muoio, dir c'abbiate il torto?

From sweet weeping to a painful smile,
from an eternal to a briefer peace
have I fallen; for, where truth keeps silent,
the senses take over whoever's cut off from it.

And I don't know whether my heart or your face   5
deserves the blame for this pain, which hurts less
the more it grows, or if it's the burning torch
of your eyes, which are stolen from paradise.

Your beauty is not an earthly thing,
but made up in heaven as something divine among us;   10
thus, though deprived, I'm comforted by burning,

for near to you I cannot be otherwise.
Since heaven has ordained these weapons of my death,
who, if I die, could say you both were wrong?

Sonnet from 1533, probably for Tommaso de' Cavalieri; nos. 79 and 81 are on the verso of this poem in M's autograph. Here M acknowledges that his love is passionately physical as well as spiritual and tries to rationalize the sensual component.

4. *it:* truth, that is, spiritual concerns.

11. *deprived:* of peace of mind or spiritual well-being.

14. *you both:* the final Italian verb is plural, presumably referring both to the addressee (otherwise addressed in the singular) and to God.

79

Felice spirto, che con zelo ardente,
vecchio alla morte, in vita il mio cor tieni,
e fra mill'altri tuo diletti e beni
me sol saluti fra più nobil gente;
  come mi fusti agli occhi, or alla mente,   5
per l'altru' fiate a consolar mi vieni,
onde la speme il duol par che raffreni,
che non men che 'l disio l'anima sente.
  Dunche, trovando in te chi per me parla
grazia di te per me fra tante cure,   10
tal grazia ne ringrazia chi ti scrive.
  Che sconcia e grande usur saria a farla,
donandoti turpissime pitture
per rïaver persone belle e vive.

O joyful spirit, who with eager burning
keep alive my old heart, near to death,
and, among your thousand other delights and blessings,
greet only me out of more noble people!
  As you once did to my eyes, now to my mind   5
you come to console me for loss of others' time,
so that hope now seems to hold in check that sadness
which the soul feels no less than it feels desire.
  Therefore, since he who speaks for me has found
grace for me from you amidst all your concerns,   10
he who writes to you thanks you for your grace.
  What great, unseemly usury it would be,
presenting you with the most awful pictures
to get in return beautiful, living people.

Sonnet for Tommaso de' Cavalieri, from summer 1533 (see note to no. 78), apparently written in response to some news or letter from the young man.

   3. *your . . . blessings:* i.e., that I receive from you. Quoted and discussed by Benedetto Varchi in his *Lezzioni.*

   5–8. Cf. M's letter (C. CMXVI; R. 193) telling Cavalieri that memories of him render M "insensible to sorrow or fear of death" and noting the absence of Cavalieri from M's eyes.

9. *he who speaks for me:* perhaps Bartolomeo Angiolini or Sebastiano del Piombo, who acted as intermediaries between the two men while M was in Florence (cf. C. CMXXIII; R. 194).

10–11. The triple use of *grazia* is a manneristic play on words difficult to reproduce in English.

13. *awful pictures:* M had given Cavalieri several drawings on mythological and other themes (VM 7:271; C. DCCCXCIX: R. 191). He seems here to express his surprised gratitude that such meager gifts have earned him Cavalieri's affection; perhaps also (given the conditional "would be") to be responding to some request from Cavalieri for more such gifts. M expressed some reserve about naming the subjects of the drawings, which included the erotic myths of Ganymede and Tityos (TC nos. 344, 345); thus the term *turpissime,* which can mean either "of low quality" or "shameful," may also indicate some ambivalence about the drawings' moral content.

80

I' mi credetti, il primo giorno ch'io
mira' tante bellezze uniche e sole,
fermar gli occhi com'aquila nel sole
nella minor di tante ch'i' desio.

Po' conosciut'ho il fallo e l'erro mio: 5
ché chi senz'ale un angel seguir vole,
il seme a' sassi, al vento le parole
indarno isparge, e l'intelletto a Dio.

Dunche, s'appresso il cor non mi sopporta
l'infinita beltà che gli occhi abbaglia,   10
né di lontan par m'assicuri o fidi,

*   che fie di me? qual guida o qual scorta*
fie che con teco ma' mi giovi o vaglia,
s'appresso m'ardi e nel partir m'uccidi?

I thought, on the first day that I gazed upon
so many charms, unique and singular,
that I'd fix my eyes, as the eagle on the sun,
on the smallest of the many that I desire.

Then I recognized my mistake and error: 5
for one who, lacking wings, would pursue an angel
flings seed on stones, and words into the wind,
and the intellect at God, all in vain.

So, if the infinite beauty that dazzles my eyes
cannot bear for my heart to come close to it,   10
nor seems to trust or assure me at a distance,

   what will become of me? What guide or escort
might be of use or value to me with you,
if, near, you burn me and, by leaving, you slay me?

Sonnet for Tommaso de' Cavalieri, ca. 1533, written on the back of the final version of no. 79. The blinding light of the beloved is a Petrarchan image (e.g., no. 221).

3. *fix my eyes:* Dante uses the same simile regarding Beatrice, *Paradiso* 1:46–48, and similarly at 20:31–33. Vittoria Colonna also writes of "nel mio bel sol la vostra aquila altera / fermando gli occhi" (CR, p. 12).

5. Cf. M's first letter to Cavalieri, "afterwards I recognized my error" (C. DCCCXCIX; R. 191).

8–9. Dante, too, casts down his eyes at the brightness of the angel of God (*Purgatorio* 2:37–40).

12. *guida, scorta:* Dante's terms for Virgil, e.g., *Purgatorio* 16:8–10.

81

Ogni cosa ch'i' veggio mi consiglia
e priega e forza ch'i' vi segua e ami;
ché quel che non è voi non è 'l mie bene.
Amor, che sprezza ogni altra maraviglia,
per mie salute vuol ch'i' cerchi e brami 5
voi, sole, solo; e così l'alma tiene
d'ogni alta spene e d'ogni valor priva;
e vuol ch'i' arda e viva
non sol di voi, ma chi di voi somiglia
degli occhi e delle ciglia alcuna parte. 10
E chi da voi si parte,
occhi, mie vita, non ha luce poi;
ché 'l ciel non è dove non siate voi.

Everything that I see advises me,
begs and compels me to love and follow you,
for whatever is not you is not my good.
Love, who despises every other marvel,
for my well-being wants me to seek and yearn 5
for you, O sun, alone; and so he deprives
my soul of any high hopes and of all powers.
And he wants me to live and burn
not just for you, but for anyone whose eyes
and brows resemble yours to some degree. 10
Whoever goes away from you,
O eyes, my life, then lacks any light,
for heaven does not exist where you do not.

M rewrote this madrigal extensively in twelve versions between the early 1520s and 1534. Some of the earlier drafts are addressed to a woman; in the final text the addressee's gender is unspecified (probably Cavalieri). A29 is written on one of the drafts; nos. 28, 29, and A26 on another; another is on a sheet of sketches (TC no. 557r).

1–2. Cf. Petrarch no. 280, "tutti insieme pregando ch'i' sempre ami."

6–7. To force me to preoccupy myself with you, love has taken away my mental faculties and spiritual concerns.

82

Non posso altra figura immaginarmi
o di nud'ombra o di terrestre spoglia,
col più alto pensier, tal che mie voglia
contra la tuo beltà di quella s'armi.

    Ché da te mosso, tanto scender parmi,   5
c'Amor d'ogni valor mi priva e spoglia,
ond'a pensar di minuir mie doglia
duplicando, la morte viene a darmi.

    Però non val che più sproni mie fuga,
doppiando 'l corso alla beltà nemica,   10
che 'l men dal più veloce non si scosta.

    Amor con le sue man gli occhi m'asciuga,
promettendomi cara ogni fatica;
ché vile esser non può chi tanto costa.

I can't imagine in my highest thoughts
any other figure, either of naked shade
or clothed in earthly carcass, such that my will
could arm itself with it against your beauty.

    For, removed from you, I seem to sink so low   5
that Love deprives and strips me of all powers;
so while I think of lessening my pain,
he, doubling it, comes to bring me death.

    Therefore it's useless to spur on my flight,
doubling my speed from my enemy, beauty,   10
for the less swift can't escape from one who's more so.

    Love with his own hands dries my eyes,
promising me my troubles will be sweet:
for that which costs so much cannot be worthless.

Sonnet for Tommaso de' Cavalieri, ca. 1534.

    2–3. *naked shade . . . earthly carcass:* either dead or alive.

    4. Cf. Dante's *canzone,* "Così nel mio parlar" (DR no. ciii), lines 14–15.

83

Veggio nel tuo bel viso, signor mio,
quel che narrar mal puossi in questa vita:
l'anima, della carne ancor vestita,
con esso è già più volte ascesa a Dio.

E se 'l vulgo malvagio, isciocco e rio,   5
di quel che sente, altrui segna e addita,
non è l'intensa voglia men gradita,
l'amor, la fede e l'onesto desio.

A quel pietoso fonte, onde siàn tutti,
s'assembra ogni beltà che qua si vede   10
più c'altra cosa alle persone accorte;

né altro saggio abbiàn né altri frutti
del cielo in terra; e chi v'ama con fede
trascende a Dio e fa dolce la morte.

I see in your beautiful face, my lord,
what can scarcely be related in this life:
my soul, although still clothed in its flesh,
has already risen often with it to God.

And if the evil, cruel, and stupid rabble   5
point the finger at others for what they feel themselves,
my intense longing is no less welcome to me,
nor my love, my faith, and my virtuous desire.

To people of good judgment, every beauty
seen here resembles, more than anything else does,   10
that merciful fountain from which we all derive;

nor have we another sample or other fruit
of heaven on earth; so he who loves you in faith
rises up to God and holds death sweet.

One of M's best-known sonnets, for Tommaso de' Cavalieri, ca. 1534; written on the other side of a sheet of diagrams for architectural blocks (TC no. 485r). The language and metaphor are thoroughly Neoplatonic, praising the transport of the soul, through the medium of physical beauty, to knowledge of the divine source of all beauty; cf. nos. 89, 107, etc. Ficino had written in his *Commentary* how "the splendor of heavenly light can be admired and astound one through the body" (FJ 2:6).

3. *my soul:* the possessor is unspecified; some editors suggest "your soul," but "my" accords better with the final couplet.

4. *with it:* with your face.

5–6. M seems to hint that rumors are circulating about the "impure" nature of his love for Cavalieri and turns the accusation back on the moral character of the accusers; cf. nos. 58, 60.

11. *merciful fountain:* God, the origin of all Being.

14. *death sweet:* cf. no. 99:4.

84

Sì come nella penna e nell'inchiostro
è l'alto e 'l basso e 'l medïocre stile,
e ne' marmi l'immagin ricca e vile,
secondo che 'l sa trar l'ingegno nostro;

   così, signor mie car, nel petto vostro,   5
quante l'orgoglio è forse ogni atto umile;
ma io sol quel c'a me propio è e simile
ne traggo, come fuor nel viso mostro.

   Chi semina sospir, lacrime e doglie,
(l'umor dal ciel terreste, schietto e solo,   10
a vari semi vario si converte),

   però pianto e dolor ne miete e coglie;
chi mira alta beltà con sì gran duolo,
ne ritra' doglie e pene acerbe e certe.

Just as within pen and ink there exist
the lofty and the low and the middling style,
and within marbles are images rich or worthless,
depending on what our talents can draw out of them,

   thus, my dear lord, there may be in your breast   5
as much pride as acts of humility;
but I only draw out of it what's suitable
and similar to me, as my face shows.

   As earthly rain from heaven, single and pure,
is turned into various forms by various seeds,   10
one who sows sighs and tears and pains

   harvests and reaps from them sorrow and weeping;
and one who looks on high beauty from great sadness
is sure to draw from it harsh pain and suffering.

Sonnet for Tommaso de' Cavalieri, ca. 1534 (TC no. 366r). The theme is similar to no. 151, written for Vittoria Colonna: that the individual or artist can draw out either of two contrasting lessons from the experience of another person, according to his own disposition. M also implies here the aesthetic theory more overtly stated in no. 151: that the raw material of art already contains within it the artist's *concetto* (idea), which merely awaits the artist's action to uncover or reveal it.

4. *talents:* there is no precise English equivalent for *ingegno,* which connotes both mental intelligence and practical skill. The term is common in art theory; cf. nos. 44, 149, 151, 159, 284.

7–8. M admits here what art historians have long observed, that his art is intensely subjective and is all, in some sense, a "self-portrait."

9. *earthly rain from heaven:* the metaphor is drawn from astrology, in which Aquarius, the constellation of the Waterbearer, pours down heavenly liquid to the earth. Aquarius was understood as the figure into which Ganymede (the subject of one of M's drawings for Cavalieri, TC no. 344) was metamorphosed after his death.

with this letter of yours; and whoever's not satisfied
can be drowned at the executioner's hand.

    The Meat who is dried and cured in salt,
and would be excellent as a grilled cutlet,   20
seems to think of you more than of himself.

    And our Buonarroti, who adores you,
having seen your letter—if my eyes judge rightly—
seems lifted to heaven a thousand times an hour;

    and he says that there is insufficient life   25
within his marbles to make your name eternal
in the same way your divine odes do for his.

    Neither summer nor winter can do harm to them,
exempt from time and from cruel death, which holds
no power over fame that's based on merit.   30

    And as that faithful friend of yours and mine
said, after having seen your lovely verses,
"People light candles to pictures and hang prayers on them.

    Therefore I, too, am numbered among those things
brought forth by a clumsy, worthless painter   35
with his brushes and his pots of paint.

    For my sake, then, please give my thanks to Berni,
who alone among many knows the truth about me;
for one who regards me well is greatly mistaken.

    But his teaching could well provide for me   40
full light, and it will be a great miracle
to make a painted man into a real one."

    Thus he spoke to me; and I, from courtesy,
commend him to you as much as I know how,
since he himself will bring this reply of mine.   45

    And as I write it, line by line, I'm turning
very red, thinking of whom I'm sending it to,
since it's clumsy and crude, and not my own profession.

    Even so, I commend myself to you
along with him, and there's nothing else to say;   50
I'm yours at all times and on all occasions.

    To you, who are numbered among the rarest things,
I offer myself completely; do not think
that I will fail you, unless my hood falls off.

Thus I say and swear to you, and rest assured
that I'd do more for you than for myself;
so don't despise me because I am a friar.
   Command me, and then do whatever you like.

Capitolo, written in thankful reply to a poem in praise of M by the burlesque author Francesco
Berni, sent from Venice to M's friend in Rome, Sebastiano del Piombo; M's reply dates from
late 1533 or early 1534 (before the death of Pope Clement VII, who is mentioned in line 4). In
his ironic and light-hearted poem, Berni wrote of M that "he says things, and you [Petrarch-
ists] say words" (see Introduction). One ms. of M's equally facetious poem is headed "Reply
of Buonarroti in the name of Brother Sebastiano"; the poem's speaker is Sebastiano, not M
himself (see lines 22, 45).

   3. Berni's poem had requested Sebastiano to convey these greetings (for complete text see
his *Poesie e prose,* ed. E. Chiorboli [Florence, 1968], 167; Girardi, *Rime,* 261).

   4. *the greatest Medic:* a pun on the name of Giulio de' Medici, then Pope Clement VII
(whose name means "doctors" in Italian). Clement and the other men M mentions were all
referred to in Berni's poem.

   7–12. *the man who's served by you:* Cardinal Ippolito de' Medici (called *the lesser Medic,*
line 11), a cousin of Pope Clement and patron of Michelangelo. Berni's poem had written of
him, "I will serve him near and far; tell him that his grace keeps me alive." *both here and
there:* in Rome and Florence. *him who keeps the greatest secrets:* Ippolito's secretary, the
humanist Francesco Maria Molza. *it would do the same to him:* would make Molza laugh, too.

   18. *executioner:* Raphael had given M this nickname, in response to M's often surly
behavior, which he also alluded to by portraying M as Heraclitus, the "gloomy philosopher,"
in his fresco *The School of Athens.*

   19. *The Meat:* a pun on the papal official, Monsignor Pietro Carnesecchi, whose name
means "dried meat."

   25–27. For similar ideas about art's power, cf. nos. 265, 277.

   27. *his:* his name (reputation).

   28. *them:* your poems.

   31–42. *faithful friend:* Michelangelo, whose own sentiments are then expressed in the first
person as if being quoted by Sebastiano. M echoes Berni, who had written that when he sees
Michelangelo "I have a mind to burn incense to him and attach prayers [or "votive offerings"]
to him," as one would do in tribute to a sacred picture or statue. Berni was making fun of M's
reputation as "divine," and M demurs humbly that if he is in any way like a picture, he is but
a badly made and worthless one, adding that Berni's desire to "decorate" him the way one
honors crude religious images shows that Berni does not overvalue M's worth.

   42–48. A playful conceit on M's part, claiming that when he himself gives the poem to
Berni, he will merely be acting as a messenger for words written by Sebastiano; the disclaimer
by "Sebastiano" of any training in writing echoes, of course, M's frequently stated opinion of
his own literary skill (see Introduction).

   54. *my hood:* a friar's hood; Sebastiano had taken minor orders in 1531 and gradually
abandoned painting for a career in ecclesiastical service.

   57. *don't despise me:* Berni had written an anticlerical sonnet, "Contra li preti."

86

Ancor che 'l cor già mi premesse tanto,
per mie scampo credendo il gran dolore
n'uscissi con le lacrime e col pianto,

fortuna al fonte di cotale umore
le radice e le vene ingrassa e 'mpingua
per morte, e non per pena o duol minore,

col tuo partire; onde convien destingua
dal figlio prima e tu morto dipoi,
del quale or parlo, pianto, penna e lingua.

L'un m'era frate, e tu padre di noi;
l'amore a quello, a te l'obrigo strigne:
non so qual pena più mi stringa o nòi.

La memoria 'l fratel pur mi dipigne,
e te sculpisce vivo in mezzo il core,
che 'l core e 'l volto più m'affligge e tigne.

Pur mi quieta che il debito, c'all'ore
pagò 'l mio frate acerbo, e tu maturo;
ché manco duole altrui chi vecchio muore.

Tanto all'increscitor men aspro e duro
esser dié 'l caso quant'è più necesse,
là dove 'l ver dal senso è più sicuro.

Ma chi è quel che morto non piangesse
suo caro padre, c'ha veder non mai
quel che vedea infinite volte o spesse?

Nostri intensi dolori e nostri guai
son come più e men ciascun gli sente:
quant'in me posson tu, Signor, tel sai.

E se ben l'alma alla ragion consente,
tien tanto in collo, che vie più abbondo
po' dopo quella in esser più dolente.

E se 'l pensier, nel quale i' mi profondo
non fussi che 'l ben morto in ciel si ridi
del timor della morte in questo mondo,

crescere' 'l duol; ma ' dolorosi stridi
temprati son d'una credenza ferma
che 'l ben vissuto a morte me' s'annidi.

5

10

15

20

25

30

35

Nostro intelletto dalla carne inferma
è tanto oppresso, che 'l morir più spiace
quanto più 'l falso persuaso afferma.

Novanta volte el sol suo chiara face   40
prim'ha nell'oceàn bagnata e molle,
che tu sie giunto alla divina pace.

Or che nostra miseria el ciel ti tolle,
increscati di me, che morto vivo,
come tuo mezzo qui nascer mi volle.   45

Tu se' del morir morto e fatto divo,
né tem'or più cangiar vita né voglia,
che quasi senza invidia non lo scrivo.

Fortuna e 'l tempo dentro a vostra soglia
non tenta trapassar, per cui s'adduce   50
fra no' dubbia letizia e certa doglia.

Nube non è che scuri vostra luce,
l'ore distinte a voi non fanno forza,
caso o necessità non vi conduce.

Vostro splendor per notte non s'ammorza,   55
né cresce mai per giorno, benché chiaro,
sie quand'el sol fra no' il caldo rinforza.

Nel tuo morire el mie morire imparo,
padre mie caro, e nel pensier ti veggio
dove 'l mondo passar ne fa di raro.   60

Non è, com'alcun crede, morte il peggio
a chi l'ultimo dì trascende al primo,
per grazia, etterno appresso al divin seggio

dove, Die grazia, ti prosumo e stimo
e spero di veder, se 'l freddo core   65
mie ragion tragge dal terrestre limo.

E se tra 'l padre e 'l figlio ottimo amore
cresce nel ciel, crescendo ogni virtute,

. . . .

Although my heart was already so weighed down,
I still believed that I could make my escape
from my great pain through my tears and weeping;
 but Fortune has enriched and fattened the roots

and the veins of such moisture at their source 5
—and by no less a pain or grief than death—
   with your departure; so now I must separate
the tears, pen, and speech for the son who died first,
from those for you who died later, of whom I'm speaking.
   One was brother to me, and you father of us both; 10
I'm bound to him by love, to you by duty;
I don't know which pain grips or upsets me more.
   Memory still paints my brother for me,
but it sculpts you within my heart as if alive,
which afflicts my heart and stains my face even more. 15
   Yet it calms me that the debt my brother paid
to the hours when still unripe, you paid full-grown;
for one who dies old saddens others less.
   For, to the sufferer, the event must be
less hard and bitter the more it seems necessary 20
to that place where truth is safest from the senses.
   But who is there who would not weep for his dear,
dead father, since he'll never see again
him whom he saw so many, countless times?
   Our griefs and troubles seem more or less intense 25
depending on how each person feels them—
and you know, Lord, how much they can affect me.
   So, even though the soul gives in to reason,
its neck must bear so much that afterward
my abundance of sadness keeps increasing. 30
   Were it not for the thought into which I plunge myself—
that one who died well is in heaven, laughing
at the fear of death in this world down here—
   my pain would grow even more; but my sorrowful cries
are tempered by a firm faith that one 35
who lived well will settle better into death.
   Our mind is so overwhelmed by our feeble flesh
that death displeases us more, the more the falsehood
of which we are persuaded asserts itself.
   Ninety times did the sun plunge and soak 40
its bright torch in the ocean, before
you attained to divine peace.

Now that heaven has taken you from our misery,
have pity on me, who am living as if dead
here where it willed me to be born through you.   45

Now you are dead to death and made divine,
and no longer fear a change of life or desire,
which I can scarcely write without envy.

Fortune and Time, who produce among us
doubtful merriment and certain pain,   50
no longer try to cross beyond your doorstep.

There is no cloud that can obscure your light,
the successive hours have no power over you,
neither chance nor necessity controls you.

Your brilliance is not damped down by the night,   55
nor ever increased by the day, however bright,
even when the sun intensifies the heat among us.

In your death I am learning how to die,
O my dear father, and in my thoughts I see you
up there where the world only rarely lets us pass.   60

Death is not, as some believe, the worst for one
who, through grace, rises up on his final day
to his first eternal one near the divine throne,

where, God willing, I presume and believe you are,
and where I hope to see you, if my reason   65
can draw my cold heart out of the earthly mud.

And if even the highest love between father and son
increases in heaven, where every virtue grows

.   .   .   .

An unfinished *capitolo*, or sequence of terza rima stanzas, mourning the death of M's father,
Lodovico. Lodovico was born in 1444 and died in 1531. Although the reference to ninety time
periods (line 40) led early editors to date this poem to 1534, M seems merely to have rounded
off the actual age at death, 87, to a more poetically satisfying number (Ramsden, appendix
22). *The son who died first* (line 8) refers to the death in 1528 of M's brother Buonarroto, about
which he had written a few years earlier; lines 8–18 compare the impact on M of the deaths of
father and son.

5. *moisture:* the tears I was already shedding, which are now made even more copious.

8–9. Now I must distinguish between two mournings, both of which I express in writing
(*pen*) and orally (*speech,* literally "tongue"). *pen . . . for the son* probably refers to the poems
for Buonarroto, nos. 45–46.

13–15. Although I recall my brother fondly, my recollections of you are even more vivid (in part because they are more recent). M's choice of metaphors reveals the higher value he placed on sculpture; for the intimate connection between art and memory, see also nos. 177–79, 239–42. Line 15 reads literally, "which afflicts and stains my heart and my face," an example of M's habit of conflating two separate phrases (see chapter 4).

17. *to the hours:* to time; *unripe . . . full-grown:* although Buonarroto died prematurely, you at least died when fully ripe, i.e., mature.

18. Cf. the similar line in an epitaph for Cecchino Bracci, no. 205.

19. *the event:* death.

21. That is, in the mind, to reason. Cf. the similar phrase in no. 78:3–4.

23–24. *he:* Michelangelo . . . *him:* Lodovico.

25–26. One's reaction to misfortune depends not on a rational, objective assessment of its severity (cf. line 21), but on each individual's subjective degree of susceptibility to events.

27. *how much they can affect me:* how sensitive I am to emotional stimuli.

29–30. It costs my soul so much effort (literally "holds so much on the neck," like an animal's yoke) to accept and bear this pain that after acceptance I am sadder than ever.

32. *one who died well:* in a state of grace, hence able to ascend to heaven.

36. One whose life has been virtuous may go easily to a better place, that is, heaven; *annidarsi* connotes "nesting" or "nestling" into a place of comfort and safety.

37–39. Because our spiritual faculties are deceived by their physical shell, our senses encourage a false attachment to earthly life and persuade us, wrongly, that death is bad.

40. Although this image has been read as referring to ninety years, the metaphor is unclear, since the sun sets into the ocean every day.

45. *it:* heaven; *through you:* by means of your physical paternity.

46. *dead to death:* liberated from the fear of dying (alternatively, "Now you are slain and made divine by death").

47. *fear a change of life or desire:* fear death or the consequent loss of earthly passions and delights.

57. *even when . . . :* in summer, when the sun warms the earth most strongly.

58. M later used a similar phrase in a letter on the death of his servant and assistant Urbino in 1556: "In dying he taught me how to die" ("morendo m'à insegniato morire"; C. MCCXIX; R. 410; VM 7:240; VB 403).

60. That is, in paradise.

61–63. The last day on earth is not a tragedy, since it is also the first of an eternity of days in God's presence.

66. *earthly mud:* the entrapping swamp of worldly passions.

87

Vorrei voler, Signor, quel ch'io non voglio:
tra 'l foco e 'l cor di ghiaccia un vel s'asconde
che 'l foco ammorza, onde non corrisponde
la penna all'opre, e fa bugiardo 'l foglio.

I' t'amo con la lingua, e poi mi doglio   5
c'amor non giunge al cor; né so ben onde
apra l'uscio alla grazia che s'infonde
nel cor, che scacci ogni spietato orgoglio.

Squarcia 'l vel tu, Signor, rompi quel muro
che con la suo durezza ne ritarda   10
il sol della tuo luce, al mondo spenta!

Manda 'l preditto lume a noi venturo,
alla tuo bella sposa, acciò ch'io arda
il cor senz'alcun dubbio, e te sol senta.

I wish I wanted, Lord, what I don't want:
between my heart and the fire hides a veil of ice
which moderates the fire, so that my deeds
don't match my pen, and makes my page a liar.

I love you with my tongue, and then regret   5
that love doesn't reach my heart; yet I don't know where
I might open a door to grace, so it can spread
within my heart, and chase out all pitiless pride.

Rend that veil, you, O Lord, break down that wall
which with its hardness keeps delayed from us   10
the sun of your light, extinguished in this world.

Send that promised light, which we will see someday,
to your beautiful bride, so that my heart
may burn free from any doubt, and feel only you.

A sonnet from the Cavalieri period, notable for its conflation of the languages of divine and earthly love.

2. *the fire*: of love. *ice*: egotism and pride (cf. line 8). A common Petrarchan antithesis; cf. nos. 19, 89, 257, 261, 281, etc.

4. *my pen*: my words, my written protestations of devotion.

9. The emotional directness and intensity conveyed by the use of the pronoun *tu* (you), normally omitted in Italian, has no counterpart in English. This very line and similar images occur in the poetry of Vittoria Colonna, e.g., "spezza dell'ignoranza il grosso muro," "squarcia omai la man piagata il velo" (CR pp. 214, 347). Earlier editors dated this poem during M's friendship with her, though the question of their mutual influence is unresolved.

11. Cf. no. 295:7.

13. *bride:* the soul, which yearns to be united with the beloved. The formula "bride of Christ" was used to characterize nuns and by male and female mystics.

88

Sento d'un foco un freddo aspetto acceso
che lontan m'arde e sé con seco agghiaccia;
pruovo una forza in due leggiadre braccia
che muove senza moto ogni altro peso.

Unico spirto e da me solo inteso,   5
che non ha morte e morte altrui procaccia,
veggio e truovo chi, sciolto, 'l cor m'allaccia,
e da chi giova sol mi sento offeso.

Com'esser può, signor, che d'un bel volto
ne porti 'l mio così contrari effetti,   10
se mal può chi non gli ha donar altrui?

Onde al mio viver lieto, che m'ha tolto,
fa forse come 'l sol, se nol permetti,
che scalda 'l mondo e non è caldo lui.

I feel my cold face kindled by a fire
that burns me from afar, yet itself is icy;
I sense within two lovely arms a force
that can move any weight without itself being moved.

I see a unique spirit, known only to me,   5
that does not die yet causes death to others;
find one who, although free, shackles my heart;
and feel hurt by him who does nothing but good.

How can it be, lord, that from a fair face
my own should draw such opposite effects,   10
if one can't give others what one does not have?

Perhaps, then, by taking away my joy in life
(if you don't stop it), it is acting like the sun,
which heats the world yet is not hot itself.

Sonnet for Tommaso de' Cavalieri, ca. 1532–34, structured as a series of Petrarchan antitheses or paradoxes. An early draft is written on a sheet of notes and accounts, ca. 1530 (*Ricordi* CCXLIX).

13. *it is acting:* the face of his beloved.

Veggio co' be' vostr'occhi un dolce lume
che co' mie ciechi già veder non posso;
porto co' vostri piedi un pondo addosso,
che de' mie zoppi non è già costume.

Volo con le vostr'ale senza piume;   5
col vostro ingegno al ciel sempre son mosso;
dal vostro arbitrio son pallido e rosso,
freddo al sol, caldo alle più fredde brume.

Nel voler vostro è sol la voglia mia,
i miei pensier nel vostro cor si fanno,.   10
nel vostro fiato son le mie parole.

Come luna da sé sol par ch'io sia,
ché gli occhi nostri in ciel veder non sanno
se non quel tanto che n'accende il sole.

I see, with your beautiful eyes, a sweet light
that with my blind ones I could never see;
I bear, with your feet, a burden upon me
to which my lame ones are no longer accustomed.

I fly, though lacking feathers, with your wings;   5
with your mind I'm constantly impelled toward heaven;
depending on your whim, I'm pale or red,
cold in the sun, hot in winter's coldest depths.

Within your will alone is my desire,
my thoughts are created in your heart,   10
and within your breath are my own words.

Alone, I seem as the moon is by itself:
for our eyes are only able to see in heaven
as much of it as the sun illuminates.

Sonnet for Tommaso de' Cavalieri, ca. 1534. This poem was discussed by Benedetto Varchi in his *Lezzioni* on M's poetry, with slight textual differences. The theme and the succession of antitheses are inspired by Petrarch, e.g., *Rime* no. 72. Cf. nos. 83, 107.

5. The Ficinian imagery of winged flight parallels M's drawing for Cavalieri of Ganymede borne heavenward in the pinions of a giant feathery eagle (1532–33; TC no. 344).

8. For other examples of the antithesis of freezing and burning, cf. nos. 19, 87, 257, 261, 281, etc.

I' mi son caro assai più ch'i' non soglio;
poi ch'i' t'ebbi nel cor più di me vaglio,
come pietra c'aggiuntovi l'intaglio
è di più pregio che 'l suo primo scoglio.

O come scritta o pinta carta o foglio   5
più si riguarda d'ogni straccio o taglio,
tal di me fo, da po' ch'i' fu' berzaglio
segnato dal tuo viso, e non mi doglio.

Sicur con tale stampa in ogni loco
vo, come quel c'ha incanti o arme seco,   10
c'ogni periglio gli fan venir meno.

I' vaglio contr'a l'acqua e contr'al foco,
col segno tuo rallumino ogni cieco,
e col mie sputo sano ogni veleno.

I'm much dearer to myself than I used to be;
since I've gotten you in my heart, I value myself more,
as a stone to which carving has been added
is worth more than its original rock.

Or, as a written or painted page or sheet   5
is better thought of than any scrap or shred,
so do I of myself, since I became
a target marked by your face, which does not hurt me.

Secure with such a mark, I go anywhere
like one who has with him amulets or weapons   10
that make every danger fade away from him.

I prevail against water and against fire,
with your mark I restore light to all the blind,
and with my spittle I can cure every poison.

Sonnet, probably for Tommaso de' Cavalieri, ca. 1534. One of M's most exultant poems, in which he expresses the feeling that with the power of love he can do anything, even perform miracles. He feels almost like another Christ, or more precisely, like a saint who has been invested with special powers by his direct infusion of divinity. The "mark" of lines 5–13 recalls both the mark of Cain, which God placed on him as a protection from harm (Genesis

4:15) and the stigmata or Christ-like wounds indicating divine favor received by Saint Francis and Saint Catherine of Siena, among others. The Italian word, *segno*, is reminiscent of the Emperor Constantine's dream in which an angel shows him the sign (Latin *signo*) of the cross and declares, "In this sign you will conquer" (cf. the depiction by Piero della Francesca in San Francesco, Arezzo, and no. 264).

6. *scrap or shred:* i.e., a sheet that is blank.

8. *marked by your face:* by a glance from your eyes. The target image recalls M's drawing of the early 1530s, *Archers shooting at a herm,* an allegory of the attack of love's arrows (TC no. 336). A similar image recurs in no. 264, for Colonna.

13–14. *restore light to all the blind . . . spittle:* as Jesus did; cf. Mark 7:32–35, 8:22–23, and John 9.

Perc'all'estremo ardore
che toglie e rende poi
il chiuder e l'aprir degli occhi tuoi
duri più la mie vita,
fatti son calamita 5
di me, de l'alma e d'ogni mie valore;
tal c'anciderm' Amore,
forse perch'è pur cieco,
indugia, triema e teme.
C'a passarmi nel core, 10
sendo nel tuo con teco,
pungere' prima le tuo parte streme;
e perché meco insieme
non mora, non m'ancide. O gran martire,
c'una doglia mortal, senza morire, 15
raddoppia quel languire
del qual, s'i' fussi meco, sare' fora.
Deh rendim' a me stesso, acciò ch'i' mora.

So that my life may better
resist the extreme heat
that the closing and the opening of your eyes
takes away and then gives back,
those eyes have become such magnets 5
for me, for my soul, and for all my powers,
that Love, perhaps because
he's blind, hesitates and trembles
and is afraid to kill me.
For to penetrate my heart, 10
since I'm in yours with you,
he first would have to pierce your outer parts;
thus, so that you won't die
along with me, he won't kill me. Oh, what great martyrdom
that a deadly pain from which I do not die. 15
should double that slow aching

of which, if my heart were with me, I'd be free.
Oh, give me back to myself, that I may die!

A somewhat labored madrigal, ca. 1534–36, probably for Tommaso de' Cavalieri. In 1542, M sent two parts of this poem to Luigi del Riccio with a note disparaging them as "old things for the fire, not for witnesses" (C. CMXCIX; R. 224).

Quantunche 'l tempo ne constringa e sproni
ognor con maggior guerra
a rendere alla terra
le membra afflitte, stanche e pellegrine,
non ha però 'ncor fine   5
chi l'alma attrista e me fa così lieto.
Né par che men perdoni
a chi 'l cor m'apre e serra,
nell'ore più vicine
e più dubiose d'altro viver quieto;   10
ché l'error consueto,
com più m'attempo, ognor più si fa forte.
O dura mia più c'altra crudel sorte!
Tardi orama' puo' tormi tanti affanni;
c'un cor che arde e arso è già molt'anni   15
torna, se ben l'ammorza la ragione,
non più già cor, ma cenere e carbone.

Although time compels us and spurs us along
with ever-increasing battle
to give back to the earth
our afflicted, tired, and wandering limbs,
yet there is still no end   5
to him who makes my soul sad and me so happy.
And he who opens and locks my heart
does not think to release me
in these hours ever closer to
the other life, but more uncertain of its calm,   10
since my longstanding fault,
the older I get, keeps on growing stronger.
O my harsh fate, crueler than any other!
Now it's too late for you to remove all my woes;
for a heart that's burning and has burned for many years   15
will turn into, even if reason finally damps it,
no longer a heart, but ashes and charred wood.

Madrigal, ca. 1534–6, for Tommaso de' Cavalieri.

6. *him:* Love.

11. *longstanding fault:* his susceptibility to love.

12. Cf. Dante, *Inferno* 26:12: "for it will burden me more, the older I get."

17. *ashes and charred wood:* cf. nos. 266, 272.

93

Spargendo il senso il troppo ardor cocente
fuor del tuo bello, in alcun altro volto,
men forza ha, signor, molto
qual per più rami alpestro e fier torrente.
Il cor, che del più ardente   5
foco più vive, mal s'accorda allora
co' rari pianti e men caldi sospiri.
L'alma all'error presente
gode c'un di lor mora
per gire al ciel, là dove par c'aspiri.   10
La ragione i martiri
fra lor comparte; e fra più salde tempre
s'accordan tutt'a quattro amarti sempre.

When sense spreads its excessive, searing heat
beyond your beautiful face to some other one,
it loses strength, lord, much like
a wild alpine torrent in many branches.
Then the heart, which is more alive   5
the hotter the fire, hardly finds agreeable
the more infrequent tears and less heated sighs.
The soul, faced with such error,
is glad that one of them dies,
so it can go to heaven, where it seems to aspire.   10
Reason distributes the torments
among them, and all four tempers, made more steady,
agree among themselves to love you always.

Madrigal, ca. 1534–6, for Tommaso de' Cavalieri. The "four tempers" or conflicting tempera-
ments of the poem's metaphor—senses, heart, soul, reason—loosely echo the Renaissance
theory of four bodily humors (fluids) governing personality and emotions. This poem as well
as no. 147 were set to music before 1531 by the French or Flemish composer Jacques Arcadelt
(1505?–1568), who served in the papal musical establishment from 1540–51, and were
published in his *Primo libro de' madrigali* (1539). In 1542, M wrote to Luigi del Riccio how
much he appreciated the musical settings and inquiring about a suitable gift for Arcadelt (C.
CMLXIV; R. 217).

    1–2. That is, when the passionate eye looks at other people.

    9. *one of them:* either sense or heart, with whom soul is in conflict.

    12. *among them:* sense, heart, and soul.

D'altrui pietoso e sol di sé spietato
nasce un vil bruto, che con pena e doglia
l'altrui man veste e la suo scorza spoglia
e sol per morte si può dir ben nato.

    Così volesse al mie signor mie fato   5
vestir suo viva di mie morta spoglia,
che, come serpe al sasso si discoglia,
pur per morte potria cangiar mie stato.

    O fussi sol la mie l'irsuta pelle
che, del suo pel contesta, fa tal gonna   10
che con ventura stringe sì bel seno,

    ch'i' l'are' pure il giorno; o le pianelle
che fanno a quel di lor basa e colonna,
ch'i' pur ne porterei duo nevi almeno.

Merciful to others and merciless only to itself,
a lowly creature's born, who with pain and sorrow
clothes another's hand and strips off its own skin,
and only through death might be called truly born.

    I wish it were my own fate thus to clothe   5
my lord's living body with my dead hide,
so that, as a snake sheds its skin on a rock,
likewise through death could I change my condition.

    Oh, if only the furry pelt were mine
which, with its woven hair, makes such a robe   10
that has the luck to bind so fair a breast,

    so I'd have him in the daytime; or the slippers
that make themselves a base and support for him,
so I might carry him for at least two snows.

Sonnet, probably for Tommaso de' Cavalieri, written on the back of a letter to M in Rome, ca. spring 1535. The metaphor, somewhat obscurely elaborated, is drawn from the silkworm, whose cocoon is destroyed to use its silken wrapping (cf. nos. 33, 51, 161). The motif of being skinned can be traced back to the myth of Marsyas, flayed for challenging Apollo, and to Saint Bartholomew, whom M portrayed in the Sistine *Last Judgment* holding his flayed skin, whose face is M's self-portrait. Ideas for the *Last Judgment,* commissioned in 1534, were taking shape at the time of this poem.

3. *clothes another's hand:* with silken gloves.

9–10. *furry pelt . . . hair:* the silkworm's cocoon, woven into silk.

10. *robe:* the Italian *gonna,* usually but not exclusively "dress," is somewhat ambiguous when referring to Cavalieri. Cf. no. 4 for a similar fantasy of becoming a dress in order to embrace the beloved, there a woman.

12. *the slippers:* also made from the silk of the speaker's imagined pelt (understood).

14. *two snows:* two winters, i.e., for two years.

Rendete agli occhi mei, o fonte o fiume,
l'onde della non vostra e salda vena,
che più v'innalza e cresce, e con più lena
che non è 'l vostro natural costume.

E tu, folt'aïr, che 'l celeste lume   5
tempri a' trist'occhi, de' sospir mie piena,
rendigli al cor mie lasso e rasserena
tua scura faccia al mie visivo acume.

Renda la terra i passi alle mie piante,
c'ancor l'erba germugli che gli è tolta,   10
e 'l suono eco, già sorda a' mie lamenti;

gli sguardi agli occhi mie tuo luce sante,
ch'i' possa altra bellezza un'altra volta
amar, po' che di me non ti contenti.

Give back to my eyes, O fountain and stream,
the waves from that spring, perpetual but not yours,
which swells and lifts you higher, with stronger flow
than you possess in your natural course.

And you, dense air, who shade the heavenly light   5
from my sad eyes, and are full of my sighs,
give them back to my weary heart, and clear
your darkened face for my penetrating sight.

Let the earth give back to my feet their footsteps,
so the grass taken from it may sprout again;   10
and Echo, now deaf to my plaints, return my sound,

and your blessed lights the glances to my eyes,
so I may love another beauty once again
now that you are not satisfied with me.

Sonnet for Tommaso de' Cavalieri, ca. 1534–8. An example of M's relatively infrequent use of extended nature imagery, in which he calls on various woodland forces as well as his unresponsive beloved to return all the marks of his unsatisfied desire.

7. *them*: my sighs.

11. *Echo*: according to classical mythology, she was a wood nymph whom Juno, angered by

her role in concealing Jupiter's infidelities, condemned to utter only repetitions of others' words. She pined away for unrequited love of Narcissus until nothing was left of her but her voice.

12. *lights:* your eyes, a common Petrarchan metaphor.

13. *another beauty:* although the reference is vague and formulaic, it might refer to the handsome young Febo di Poggio, whom M met about this time (cf. nos. 99–101).

96

Sì come secco legno in foco ardente
arder poss'io, s'i' non t'amo di core,
e l'alma perder, se null'altro sente.

E se d'altra beltà spirto d'amore
fuor de' tu' occhi è che m'infiammi o scaldi,
tolti sien quegli a chi sanz'essi muore.

S'io non t'amo e ador, ch'e' mie più baldi
pensier sien con la speme tanto tristi
quanto nel tuo amor son fermi e saldi.

Like dry wood in a burning fire
may I burn, if I don't love you from my heart,
and lose my soul, if it feels anything else.

And if a spirit of love heat and inflame me
with any beauty other than your eyes,
may they be taken from me, who'd die without them.

If I don't love and adore you, may my boldest
thoughts, along with their hope, become as sad
as they are firm and constant in love of you.

Three terza rima stanzas, apparently part of an incomplete *capitolo*; ca. 1534–8, probably for Tommaso de' Cavalieri. The theme and tone recall Petrarch's stanzas, "S' i' 'l dissi mai" (*Rime* no. 206).

1. *dry wood:* cf. nos. 97, 176.

3. *feels anything else:* feels love for anyone else.

Al cor di zolfo, a la carne di stoppa,
a l'ossa che di secco legno sièno;
a l'alma senza guida e senza freno
al desir pronto, a la vaghezza troppa;
*   a la cieca ragion debile e zoppa*   5
al vischio, a' lacci di che 'l mondo è pieno;
non è gran maraviglia, in un baleno
arder nel primo foco che s'intoppa.
*   A la bell'arte che, se dal ciel seco*
ciascun la porta, vince la natura,   10
quantunche sé ben prema in ogni loco;
*   s'i' nacqui a quella né sordo né cieco,*
proporzionato a chi 'l cor m'arde e fura,
colpa è di chi m'ha destinato al foco.

Having a heart of sulfur, and flesh of oakum,
and having bones that are made of dried wood;
having a soul with no guide and no rein,
quick to respond to desire and extreme beauty;
    with a brain that is blind and weak and lame   5
against the birdlime and snares the world is full of,
it's no great wonder if one bursts into flames
at the first fire that he comes upon.
    There's an art of beauty, which, if everyone
brings it with him from heaven, conquers nature,   10
even though nature imprints itself everywhere;
    if I was born neither deaf nor blind to that art,
and proportioned to him who burns and steals my heart,
it's the fault of him who destined me to the fire.

Sonnet for Tommaso de' Cavalieri, ca. 1534–6. There is a hint of astrological thinking in the conceit that M has received certain propensities from heaven at birth; cf. nos. 104, 119, 164, 173.

    1. *oakum:* loosely spun fibers soaked in tar, used for caulking and packing seams. *Stoppa* also means tow, that is, fibers without pitch, but the context here stresses flammability.

2. *dried wood:* cf. nos. 96, 176.

6. *birdlime:* a sticky substance derived from the holly plant, used to entrap small birds; figuratively, a trap or pitfall.

9. This line was cited by Varchi, in a slightly different version, in his *Lezzioni* on M's poetry. The topos of art's ability to conquer nature dates from antiquity; cf. no. 239.

13. *proportioned:* with a sensibility to beauty that matches his beauty (?).

14. *him:* God.

A che più debb'i' omai l'intensa voglia
sfogar con pianti o con parole meste,
se di tal sorte 'l ciel, che l'alma veste,
tard' o per tempo alcun mai non ne spoglia?

A che 'l cor lass' a più languir m'invoglia,   5
s'altri pur dee morir? Dunche per queste
luci l'ore del fin fian men moleste;
c'ogni altro ben val men c'ogni mia doglia.

Però se 'l colpo ch'io ne rub' e 'nvolo
schifar non posso, almen, s'è destinato   10
chi entrerà 'nfra la dolcezza e 'l duolo?

Se vint' e preso i' debb'esser beato,
maraviglia non è se nudo e solo
resto prigion d'un cavalier armato.

Why should I still pour out my intense desire
in weeping or in mournful words,
if heaven, which clothes all souls with such a fate,
strips no one of it, either early or late?

Why does my tired heart still make me long to languish   5
if others must also die? Therefore let my
final hours be made less wearisome for these eyes,
since all other good is worth less than all my pain.

Yet at least, if I cannot dodge the blow
I steal and rob from him—if it's ordained—   10
then who will win out between sweetness and sorrow?

If, to be happy, I must be conquered and chained,
it is no wonder that, naked and alone,
an armed cavalier's prisoner I remain.

Sonnet for Tommaso de' Cavalieri. The date is uncertain; the similarity of its images of binding and suffering to M's drawing for Cavalieri of the *Punishment of Tityos* (TC no. 345) suggests a date close to the drawing (1532–33), though Girardi placed it in 1534–35 and Frey as late as 1542–43. This poem and others for Cavalieri using metaphors of binding and capture are sometimes related to M's sculpture of *Victory* (Florence, Palazzo Vecchio), which shows an old warrior enslaved by a handsome young man; but the connection is only a general one, since that work was probably roughed out (and then abandoned) by 1530, before M met Cavalieri.

3. *such a fate:* i.e., to suffer for love. This poem is among M's most elliptical and obscure. The metaphorical protagonists are love and death, but it is ambiguous which of these M refers to in lines 10–11, *the blow I steal and rob from him.* The theme of the futility of love in the face of its universal end was familiar from Dante (*Purgatorio* 31:52–57, *Paradiso* 11:1–12) and Petrarch (*Trionfo della morte* 1:82–90).

13–15. *an armed cavalier:* a pun on the name of Cavalieri.

Ben mi dove' con sì felice sorte,
mentre che Febo il poggio tutto ardea,
levar da terra, allor quand'io potea,
con le suo penne, e far dolce la morte.

Or m'è sparito; e se 'l fuggir men forte   5
de' giorni lieti invan mi promettea,
ragione è ben c'all'alma ingrata e rea
pietà le mani e 'l ciel chiugga le porte.

Le penne mi furn'ale e 'l poggio scale,
Febo lucerna a' piè; né m'era allora   10
men salute il morir che maraviglia.

Morendo or senza, al ciel l'alma non sale,
né di lor la memoria il cor ristora:
ché tardi e doppo il danno, chi consiglia?

I should have seized on such a blessed fate,
while Phoebus was setting all the hill on fire,
to rise up from the earth, while I was able,
upon his feathers, and make death sweet for me.

Now he's vanished from me; and if the promise he held   5
to slow the flight of glad days was a vain hope,
it's right that to my ungrateful, guilty soul
mercy should shut its hands and heaven its gates.

His feathers were wings for me, his hill a stair,
Phoebus a lamp unto my feet; and death then seemed   10
as much a salvation as a miracle.

Now, dying without these, my soul can't rise to heaven,
nor the memory of them revive my heart;
for, so late and the damage done, who could guide me?

Sonnet, ca. 1535, for Febo di Poggio, a young Florentine with whom M seems to have been infatuated during his last year in that city. Their relationship was broken off, apparently somewhat unpleasantly, when M moved permanently to Rome late in 1534 (C. MXLI, CMXLII; R. 198). See also nos. 95, 100, 101, 117, 246.

2. *Phoebus*, i.e., Apollo, a pun on the first name of Febo; *hill* (*poggio*), on his surname,

meaning here the path of M's life (Apollo presided over the Muses on Mount Parnassus). Just as Petrarch made many plays on the name of his beloved Laura, M joins his frequent image of the lover's divine radiance to a specific reference to Phoebus Apollo, the Roman sun god (cf. no. 98, with its pun on "Cavalieri"). Petrarch mentions both Phoebus and Laura in his reply to a poem by Ser Dietisalvi di Siena (PD p. 591, no. 6).

3–4. *rise . . . upon his feathers:* M uses the same language in regard to Cavalieri, e.g., no. 59. Cf. the rising souls in the *Last Judgment,* begun about this time, and the upswept rapture of the eagle-borne youth in the *Ganymede* drawing of 1532/33 (TC no. 344).

4. *and make death sweet for me:* cf. the same phrase in no. 83.

9. *his hill a stair:* another pun on Febo's name, implying that this "hill" provides a means of ascent to heaven.

10. *a lamp unto my feet:* an allusion to Psalm 119:105, "Thy word is a lamp unto my feet, and a light unto my path."

Ben fu, temprando il ciel tuo vivo raggio,
solo a du' occhi, a me di pietà vòto,
allor che con veloce etterno moto
a noi dette la luce, a te 'l viaggio.

Felice uccello, che con tal vantaggio   5
da noi, t'è Febo e 'l suo bel volto noto,
e più c'al gran veder t'è ancora arroto
volare al poggio, ond'io rovino e caggio.

Heaven, in strengthening your living ray,
was merciful only to two eyes, not to me,
at the moment when, in its swift eternal course,
it gave us light and you mobility.

O happy bird, with such an advantage over us,   5
that Phoebus and his fair face are known to you;
and beyond that great sight, it's also granted to you
to fly to that hill from which I fall to my ruin.

Incomplete sonnet, ca. 1534–41, alluding to the name of Febo di Poggio in lines 6 and 8 (see nos. 99, 101, 117). Instead of imagining himself flying heavenward as in the earlier poems to Febo and Cavalieri, here M expresses envy of a bird who is free to fly to the radiant beloved while he is earthbound. The bird may be an eagle, which was believed to be able to look at the sun (cf. no. 80, "like an eagle in the sun") or M's oft-used phoenix, renewed in the flames of the sun (see no. 43, etc.).

1. Infusing divine light into your eyes.

8. The image of falling to ruin from the heights of Phoebus recalls M's drawing for Cavalieri (1532/33) of the *Fall of Phaethon* (TC nos. 340, 342, 343), who tried unsuccessfully to drive the sun-chariot of his father Phoebus Apollo and was thrown down from the sky and killed by Jupiter.

Perché Febo non torce e non distende
d'intorn' a questo globo freddo e molle
le braccia sua lucenti, el vulgo volle
notte chiamar quel sol che non comprende.

    E tant'è debol, che s'alcun accende   5
un picciol torchio, in quella parte tolle
la vita dalla notte, e tant'è folle
che l'esca col fucil la squarcia e fende.

    E s'egli è pur che qualche cosa sia,
cert'è figlia del sol e della terra;   10
ché l'un tien l'ombra, e l'altro sol la cria.

    Ma sia che vuol, che pur chi la loda erra,
vedova, scura, in tanta gelosia,
c'una lucciola sol gli può far guerra.

    Since Phoebus does not stretch out and curl
his luminous arms around this cold, moist globe,
the ordinary multitude desire
to call "night" that sun which they don't understand.

    She is so weak that, if anyone lights   5
even a small torch, at that spot he robs
the night of life; and she is so unstable
that a bit of tinder and flint can tear and split her.

    Yet if it's true that she is anything,
she's surely the daughter of the sun and the earth: 10
for the latter holds her shadow, the former alone creates it.

    But whatever she is, one who praises her is mistaken:
for she is a widow, gloomy, and so defensive
that a single firefly can wage war on her.

Sonnet, ca. 1535–41, considered to form a group with nos. 102–4, all of them praises of the
night. All four were probably sent to Tommaso de' Cavalieri, though the mention of Phoebus
in line 1 recalls the other poems for Febo di Poggio (nos. 99, 100, 117). Since M slept badly, he
often worked in darkness, inventing a headpiece that held a candle to illuminate his work (VM
7:276; see no. 299). Although these praises of night postdate the Medici Chapel, they offer a
sense of the personal meanings M would have read into his celebrated sculptures of Night and
the other times of day.

    13. *a widow:* that is, alone.

O notte, o dolce tempo, benché nero,
con pace ogn' opra sempr' al fin assalta;
ben vede e ben intende chi t'esalta,
e chi t'onor' ha l'intelletto intero.

Tu mozzi e tronchi ogni stanco pensiero   5
che l'umid' ombra e ogni quiet' appalta,
e dall'infima parte alla più alta
in sogno spesso porti, ov'ire spero.

O ombra del morir, per cui si ferma
ogni miseria a l'alma, al cor nemica,   10
ultimo delli afflitti e buon remedio;

tu rendi sana nostra carn' inferma,
rasciughi i pianti e posi ogni fatica,
e furi a chi ben vive ogn'ira e tedio.

O night, O time so sweet, even though black,
who infuses all labor with peace at the day's end,
whoever exalts you shows good judgment and vision
and whoever honors you has a sound mind.

You cut short and break off every tiring thought,   5
enfolding them in your moist shade and quiet,
and often in dreams you bear my soul from the lowest
to the highest sphere, to which I hope to journey.

O shadow of death, by whom is stilled
every misery hostile to the heart and soul,   10
last and effective remedy for the afflicted:

You restore our ailing flesh to health,
wipe dry our tears and put to rest all toil,
and take from him who lives rightly all wrath and weariness.

Sonnet of uncertain date, ca. 1535–41 (see no. 101). Among M's best-known poems; lines 3 and 4 were cited and discussed by Varchi in his *Lezzioni*. The lyrical description of peace at day's end recalls Petrarch, no. 50, although there the poet himself is excluded from this relief; cf. also Dante, *Inferno* 2:1–3.

7–8. Cf. Dante, *Paradiso* 33:22–24, "da l'infima lacuna"; and the sonnet by Lorenzo de' Medici, "O brevi e chiare notti" (LM no. cvi).

103

Ogni van chiuso, ogni coperto loco,
quantunche ogni materia circumscrive,
serba la notte, quando il giorno vive,
contro al solar suo luminoso gioco.
 E s'ella è vinta pur da fiamma o foco,   5
da lei dal sol son discacciate e prive
con più vil cosa ancor sue specie dive,
tal c'ogni verme assai ne rompe o poco.
 Quel che resta scoperto al sol, che ferve
per mille vari semi e mille piante,   10
il fier bifolco con l'aratro assale;
 ma l'ombra sol a piantar l'uomo serve.
Dunche, le notti più ch'e' dì son sante,
quanto l'uom più d'ogni altro frutto vale.

Every closed space and every covered place—
whatever is surrounded by any substance—
preserves the night, while the day is alive,
against the luminous play of its sunlight.
 And if it can be defeated by flame or fire,   5
its divine qualities can be driven off and stripped
by the sun, or even by something lowlier,
so that any worm can smash them a little or greatly.
 Whatever's left exposed to the sun, and heated
for a thousand different seeds and a thousand plants, 10
the fierce peasant attacks with his plow,
 but only shade will do for sowing mankind.
Therefore nights are more sacred than days,
as man is worth more than any other fruit.

Sonnet of uncertain date, ca. 1535–41 (see no. 101).

1–2. Cited by Varchi in his *Lezzioni*, 1547.

5. *it:* night (see note to no. 101:5).

8. *any worm:* cf. no. 101, "a single firefly can wage war on her." *them:* night's distinctive qualities, i.e., its shadows.

9–10. *and heated for:* heated by the sun, which thus causes the seeds to germinate.

12. *for sowing mankind:* for human procreation, which most often occurs at night. In a letter of 1547, M expressed the similar thought that the increased darkness that would result from Antonio da Sangallo's revised plan for Saint Peter's basilica in Rome would lead to "the raping of nuns and other rascalities" (C. MLXXI; R. 274).

Colui che fece, e non di cosa alcuna,
il tempo, che non era anzi a nessuno,
ne fe' d'un due e diè 'l sol alto all'uno,
all'altro assai più presso diè la luna.

Onde 'l caso, la sorte e la fortuna   5
in un momento nacquer di ciascuno;
e a me consegnaro il tempo bruno,
come a simil nel parto e nella cuna.

E come quel che contrafà se stesso,
quando è ben notte, più buio esser suole,   10
ond'io di far ben mal m'affliggo e lagno.

Pur mi consola assai l'esser concesso
far giorno chiar mia oscura notte al sole
che a voi fu dato al nascer per compagno.

He who created, out of nothingness,
time, which did not exist before anybody,
made two from its one, and gave the high sun to one,
and gave to the other the moon, which is much nearer.

From these in one moment there were born   5
the chance, destiny, and fortune of each of us;
and to me they allotted the dark time,
which I resembled at birth and in the cradle.

And now, just as one who imitates himself
grows darker as the night is well advanced,   10
so I'm troubled and grieved at doing so much wrong.

Yet I'm much comforted that the power to make
my night into day has been granted to the sun
that was given to you at birth as a companion.

Sonnet, ca. 1535–41 (see no. 101).

1, 5–6. Cited by Varchi in his *Lezzioni*, 1547. *out of nothingness:* literally, "not out of anything."

3. *made two from its one:* split time into day and night. M had painted God separating light from darkness and creating the sun and moon on the ceiling of the Sistine Chapel; at this

period he would have been seeing his own earlier work daily as he worked on the *Last Judgment* in the same room.

5–8, 14. The underlying metaphor is the astrological belief that the positions of the heavenly bodies at the time of one's birth influence character (cf. nos. 97, 119, 164, 173). Such notions are cited frequently by both Petrarch and Dante, e.g., Petrarch no. 50, "each has his destiny from the day he is born." Ficino had theorized that two people whose birth signs were respectively sun and moon would be mutually loving (*Sopra lo amore*, chap. 8).

9. *imitates:* literally "counterfeits," perhaps in the sense of reproducing and continuing M's lifelong evil tendencies.

12–13. Some editors propose an alternative reading of these lines: "I am comforted that my dark night can serve to make your sun seem brighter [by contrast]."

14. *you:* Cavalieri?

Non vider gli occhi miei cosa mortale
allor che ne' bei vostri intera pace
trovai, ma dentro, ov'ogni mal dispiace,
chi d'amor l'alma a sè simil m'assale;
e se creata a Dio non fusse equale, 5
altro che 'l bel di fuor, c'agli occhi piace,
più non vorria; ma perch'è sì fallace,
trascende nella forma universale.
Io dico ch'a chi vive quel che muore
quetar non può disir; né par s'aspetti 10
l'eterno al tempo, ove altri cangia il pelo.
Voglia sfrenata el senso è, non amore,
che l'alma uccide; e 'l nostro fa perfetti
gli amici qui, ma più per morte in cielo.

My eyes did not see any mortal object
when I found complete peace in your beautiful eyes,
but saw within them, where every evil's despised,
him who invests my soul, so like him, with love.
For if my soul weren't created equal to God, 5
it would wish for nothing more than outward beauty,
which pleases the eyes; but since that's so deceptive,
it rises beyond that, to the universal form.
I say that, for one who lives, whatever dies
cannot appease desire; nor can the eternal 10
be sought in time, where human flesh still alters.
Unbridled desire is merely the senses, not love,
and slays the soul; our love makes us perfect friends
down here, but even more, through death, in heaven.

Sonnet, ca. 1535–41, for Tommaso de' Cavalieri; known only from Varchi's transcription in his *Lezzioni*.

3. *where every evil's despised:* in the soul.

8. *universal form:* the unchanging ideal of beauty—a Platonic concept, as first noted by Varchi. Cf. the same expression in Dante, *Purgatorio* 33:91.

9. *one who lives:* one who lives righteously, hoping for eternal life in heaven.

9–10. Cf. Dante, *Purgatorio* 17:127–29: "Each one vaguely apprehends a good wherein the soul may find rest (*si quieti*), and desires it."

11. *in time:* in the world of transient earthly appearances, where everyone's body grows old.

12. The contrast between physical and spiritual love recalls Ficino, who insisted that there are "two Venuses in the soul, the one heavenly, the other earthly" (FJ p. 191). *Unbridled desire* and its consequences were the theme of M's drawing for Cavalieri of *The Punishment of Tityos*, 1532/33 (TC no. 345).

Per ritornar là donde venne fora,
l'immortal forma al tuo carcer terreno
venne com'angel di pietà sì pieno,
che sana ogn'intelletto e 'l mondo onora.

Questo sol m'arde e questo m'innamora, 5
non pur di fuora il tuo volto sereno:
c'amor non già di cosa che vien meno
tien ferma speme, in cui virtù dimora.

Nè altro avvien di cose altere e nuove
in cui si preme la natura, e 'l cielo, 10
è c'a' lor parti largo s'apparecchia;

né Dio, suo grazia, mi si mostra altrove
più che 'n alcun leggiadro e mortal velo;
e quel sol amo perch'in lui si specchia.

In order to return to where it came from,
the immortal form came down to your earthly prison
like an angel so full of compassion
that it heals every mind and honors the world.

This alone makes me burn and fall in love, 5
and not your mere external, tranquil face;
for surely a love in which virtue dwells
pins no strong hope on something that will fade.

For nought else happens to new and lofty things
over which nature labors, and at whose birth 10
heaven prepares its generosity;

nor does God, in his grace, show himself to me
anywhere more than in some fair mortal veil;
and that alone I love, since he's mirrored in it.

Sonnet, ca. 1536–46. In a letter of 1550 accompanying one of the numerous versions of this poem, M mentions that Tommaso de' Cavalieri had been very pleased by Varchi's mention of him in the recently published *Lezzioni* and had given back to M this sonnet, written for Cavalieri earlier, to send to Varchi (C. CXLIII; R. 343; see also TC no. 597r). The poem expresses the Neoplatonic ideal of anagogy, in which contemplation of earthly beauty leads to awareness of the divine source of all higher good.

2. *immortal form:* the soul, being the emanation of divinity. *earthly prison:* cf. Petrarch, no. 325: "The noble soul had not been long in the lovely prison from which it is now freed."

13. *mortal veil:* a physical body; cf. nos. 161, 188, 209, 215, 227. The belief expressed in these lines lies behind M's lifelong artistic interest in the human form. •

107

Gli occhi mie vaghi delle cose belle
e l'alma insieme della suo salute
non hanno altra virtute
c'ascenda al ciel, che mirar tutte quelle.
Dalle più alte stelle   5
discende uno splendore
che 'l desir tira a quelle,
e qui si chiama amore.
Né altro ha il gentil core
che l'innamori e arda, e che 'l consigli,   10
c'un volto che negli occhi lor somigli.

My eyes, desirous of beautiful things,
and my soul, likewise, of its salvation,
have no other means to rise
to heaven but to gaze at all such things.
For from the highest stars   5
descends a brilliant light
that pulls desire toward them,
and down here is called love.
Nor has the noble heart aught
that can make it burn and love, and that can guide it,   10
but a face that in its eyes resembles them.

Madrigal of uncertain date, ca. 1534–42, perhaps for Cavalieri; on the same sheet as no. 108. The theme has a long tradition in Italian lyric poetry, from Guinicelli onward, and also recalls Plato's theory of love and beauty descending from above and the mind ascending to them.

11. *resembles them:* resembles the stars in their brightness. A common image since the *dolce stil nuovo* of Dante (e.g., *Purgatorio* 12:90) and Petrarch (no. 72, "a sweet light that shows me the way that leads to heaven"). Cf. nos. 83, 89.

Last Judgment. Fresco. Vatican, Sistine Chapel, 1534–41.

Indarno spera, come 'l vulgo dice,
chi fa quel che non de' grazia o mercede.
Non fui, com'io credetti, in voi felice,
privandomi di me per troppa fede,
né spero com'al sol nuova fenice   5
ritornar più; ché 'l tempo nol concede.
Pur godo il mie gran danno sol perch'io
son più mie vostro, che s'i' fussi mio.

He who does what he should not do hopes in vain,
as the common people say, for grace or mercy.
Depriving me of myself out of excess faith
in you, I was not happy, as I thought I'd be;
nor do I hope to come back any more,   5
like the phoenix renewed in the sun, for time doesn't allow it.
Yet I delight in my great loss, just because
I'm more my own when yours than if I were mine.

A stanza from 1534–46, possibly for Tommaso de' Cavalieri; on the same sheet as no. 107.
Presumably complete in itself, since the rhyme scheme is that of an independent ottava rima,
and it was included among the poems for publication.

3. Cf. similar phrases in nos. 8, 161, 235.

6. *time:* M's advanced age. *phoenix:* cf. nos. 43, 52, 61, 62, 217.

8. *when yours:* when captivated by love for you. Giannotti records a similar remark:
Calling himself "the man most inclined to love people," M says that when he is attracted to a
man "I am no longer mine, but all his" (GD p. 68).

Non sempre a tutti è sì pregiato e caro
quel che 'l senso contenta,
c'un sol non sia che 'l senta,
se ben par dolce, pessimo e amaro.
Il buon gusto è si raro   5
c'al vulgo errante cede
in vista, allor che dentro di sé gode.
Così, perdendo, imparo
quel che di fuor non vede
chi l'alma ha trista, e ′ suo sospir non ode.   10
El mondo è cieco e di suo gradi o lode
più giova a chi più scarso esser ne vuole,
come sferza che 'nsegna e parte duole.

What satisfies the senses is not always
so valued and dear to all
that there's not one who feels
that, though it seems sweet, it is evil and bitter.
Good taste is so uncommon   5
that it appears to yield
to the misguided crowd, while delighting within itself.
Thus, in losing, I learn
what can't be seen from outside
by one with a sad soul, who can't hear its sighs.   10
The world is blind, and with its titles and praises
rewards most the one who wants to have them least,
like a whip that both teaches and hurts somewhat.

Madrigal, ca. 1536–44, probably for Tommaso de' Cavalieri; sent to Luigi del Riccio in 1545 (some time after it was written) with a brief letter (C. MXXIV; R. 258). The elaborate and scathing moral statement is somewhat obscured by the compression of the language. Threatened and disgusted by the base sensuality of most people, M dissembles and withdraws from society and scorns its rewards, learning from the pain of isolation to value his independence from common opinion.

4. *though it seems sweet:* to others, who are more earthly.

5–7. Good judgment is in such a powerless minority that those who have it, although privately convinced of their opinions, may pretend to concur with the ignorant majority.

8–10. In losing the freedom to act on my beliefs in the real world, I gain an inner awareness that is inaccessible to those who are insensitive to their own spiritual longing.

12. Some editors read: "benefits most those who deserve them least."

13. The world's unjust judgments are painful to bear but lead me to a desirable detachment from earthly vanities.

Io dico a voi c'al mondo avete dato
l'anima e 'l corpo e lo spirto 'nsïeme:
in questa cassa oscura è 'l vostro lato.

I say to you, who've given to the world
your soul, your body, and your spirit as well:
within this dark coffin is your destined place.

Epitaph, written after 1534. The Florentine architect and designer Bernardo Buontalenti (1531–1608) told Michelangelo the Younger that M painted a skeleton on the staircase wall of his house in Rome, holding a rough-hewn coffin on its shoulder on which this terza rima verse was inscribed (Guasti, 4). The leering skulls of the *Last Judgment* fresco may suggest something of the appearance of this lost sketch. The poem's macabre frankness recalls the grim carnival songs performed in Florence in M's youth, by processions of marchers dressed as skeletons (see Vasari, *Vita* of Piero de' Cosimo, and no. 21).

    1. *the world:* earthly concerns.

S'egli è, donna, che puoi
come cosa mortal, benché sia diva
di beltà, c'ancor viva
e mangi e dorma e parli qui fra noi,
a non seguirti poi,   5
cessato il dubbio, tuo grazia e mercede,
qual pena a tal peccato degna fora?
Ché alcun ne' pensier suoi,
co' l'occhio che non vede,
per virtù propia tardi s'innamora.   10
Disegna in me di fuora,
com'io fo in pietra od in candido foglio,
che nulla ha dentro, e èvvi ciò ch'io voglio.

If it's true, lady, that you,
although divine in beauty, can still live
like a mortal creature
and eat and sleep and speak among us here;
then not to follow you—   5
your grace and mercy having put an end to doubt—
what penalty fits such an outrageous sin?
A man lost in his own thoughts,
with an eye that does not see,
is slow to fall in love by his own powers;   10
so draw within me from outside,
as I do on a blank sheet or in stone
that has nothing within, and then what I want is there.

Madrigal, ca. 1536, among the first addressed to Vittoria Colonna, whom M met sometime in 1536 and remained close to until his death (see chapter 2). The bulk of his poetry in these years was addressed to her, and much of his production in the five years after her death consists of laments for his lost spiritual companion and artistic inspiration.

4. Cf. Dante, *Inferno* 33:140, where Branca Doria, not yet dead, still "eats and drinks and sleeps and puts on clothes."

6. *doubt:* about your divine nature, spiritual goodness.

11–13. M makes a revealing analogy between artistic shaping of a blank material and the spiritual reshaping of himself by Colonna's influence (cf. no. 162). As with Tommaso de' Cavalieri, M casts himself in a passive role, the *tabula rasa* in need of inspiring action by others. The term *disegno* (drawing, design) is central to Renaissance artistic theory, referring to the creative act of conceptualization that underlies all the arts. For M's comments on its importance, see Francisco de Hollanda, whose *Dialogues in Rome* record conversations between M and Colonna (esp. Dialogue 3; H p. 275).

Il mio refugio e 'l mio ultimo scampo
qual più sicuro è, che non sia men forte
che 'l pianger e 'l pregar? e non m'aita.
Amore e crudeltà m'han posto il campo:
l'un s'arma di pietà, l'altro di morte;   5
questa n'ancide, e l'altra tien in vita.
Così l'alma impedita
del mio morir, che sol poria giovarne,
più volte per andarne
s'è mossa là dov'esser sempre spera,   10
dov'è beltà sol fuor di donna altiera;
ma l'imagine vera,
della qual vivo, allor risorge al core,
perché da morte non sia vinto amore.

What ultimate refuge or escape for me
is there that's more secure, and no less strong
than weeping and prayer? Yet they're no help to me.
For love and cruelty have pitched camp against me:
the one is armed with mercy, the other with death;   5
the latter kills me, the other keeps me alive.
And thus my soul, prevented
from dying—which alone could benefit me—
has many times felt moved
to go up there where it hopes to be forever,   10
where beauty stands alone, outside any proud lady;
But then the true image
on which I live revives within my heart,
so that love might not be defeated by death.

Madrigal, ca. 1536–38. This is the first of the series of poems addressed to an unnamed "donna altera" or "donna bella e crudele," who spurns the poet's impassioned love, plunging him into grief. This woman, who is described in terms different from the spiritual sympathy M feels for Vittoria Colonna, has never been identified with a specific person and is probably a literary fiction (see chapter 2). As there is no external evidence to separate this sequence from the contemporaneous poems for Colonna, Girardi interweaves both groups, generally using the order in which M arranged his fair copies between 1542 and 1546, prior to their planned publication. This example is cited by Varchi in his *Lezzioni*.

10–11. *up there . . . beauty stands alone:* i.e., the abstract divine beauty that suffuses heaven, detached from any particular individual.

12. *the true image:* of the beloved lady.

113

Esser non può già ma' che gli occhi santi
prendin de' mie, com'io di lor, diletto,
rendendo al divo aspetto,
per dolci risi, amari e tristi pianti.
O fallace speranza degli amanti! 5
Com'esser può dissimile e dispari
l'infinita beltà, 'l superchio lume
da ogni mie costume,
che meco ardendo, non ardin del pari?
Fra duo volti diversi e sì contrari 10
s'adira e parte da l'un zoppo Amore;
né può far forza che di me gl'incresca,
quand'in un gentil core
entra di foco, e d'acqua par che n'esca.

It can never be that those blessed eyes
will take delight in mine, as I do in them,
repaying that godlike sight
for its sweet smiles with sad and bitter tears.
O illusory hope of lovers! 5
How can that infinite beauty and exceeding light
be so unequal and dissimilar
to all I've always been
that, though burning with me, they don't burn equally?
Between two faces, so different and opposed, 10
Love limps away from one of them, and gets angry;
yet he can't help but feel sorry for me,
since into a gentle heart
he enters as fire, and seems to leave as water.

Madrigal, on a Petrarchan theme, usually supposed among the early poems for Vittoria Colonna (ca. 1536–38), although the gender of the addressee is never specified.

10–11. Being forced to move back and forth between two people at two different speeds to match their opposite degrees of passion, Love becomes crippled, which angers him. Cf. no. 30:4.

14. *as water:* transformed into (or bathed in) my tears.

114

Ben vinci ogni durezza
cogli occhi tuo, com'ogni luce ancora;
ché, s'alcun d'allegrezza avvien che mora,
allor sarebbe l'ora
che gran pietà comanda a gran bellezza.   5
E se nel foco avvezza
non fusse l'alma, già morto sarei
alle promesse de' tuo primi sguardi,
ove non fur ma' tardi
gl'ingordi mie nimici, anz'occhi mei;   10
né doler mi potrei
di questo non poter, che non è teco.
Bellezza e grazia equalmente infinita,
dove più porge aita,
men puoi non tor la vita,   15
né puoi non far chiunche tu miri cieco.

You conquer every hardness
with your eyes, as you do likewise every light;
so, if it can happen that one can die of joy,
now would be the time,
when great beauty is inspired by great mercy.   5
Indeed, if my soul were not
used to the fire, I would have died already
at the promises held out by your first glances,
which my greedy enemies—
that is, my eyes—were never slow to seek;   10
and I cannot complain
of this inability, which isn't yours.
O beauty and grace, equally infinite,
the more you offer help
the less you can't take life,   15
nor can you not blind whomever you look at.

Madrigal, ca. 1536–46. Probably directed to either Vittoria Colonna or the *donna altera*, though the addressee's gender is unspecified. M is left dazzled and half-dead from the beauty and grace of his beloved but is too toughened by experience to die, to fully feel the joy these glances might bring.

1. *every hardness:* of heart. Cf. Petrarch, no. 213, "ch'ogni dur rompe ed ogni altezza inchina."

7. *the fire:* of love.

12. *this inability:* to die of love, to succumb to the beloved's glances. *which isn't yours,* which is not the fault of your weakness, but of my own resistance.

14. *you offer help:* by bestowing your loving glance.

15. The deliberately paradoxical double negatives might be rendered more idiomatically as "you can't help taking life," "you can't help blinding."

16. *whomever you look at:* alternatively, "whoever looks at you," as in one draft. The image of being blinded by the overpowering sight of a heavenly beauty parallels the blinding of Saul by God's light in M's fresco *The Conversion of St. Paul* in the Pauline Chapel of the Vatican (1542–45).

Lezi, vezzi, carezze, or, feste e perle,
chi potria ma' vederle,
cogli atti suo divin l'uman lavoro,
ove l'argento e l'oro
da le' riceve o duplica suo luce?   5
Ogni gemma più luce
dagli occhi suo che da propia virtute.

Wiles, ornaments, caresses, gold, feasts, and pearls:
who could ever notice
the human labor in her divine achievements,
since the silver and the gold
receive their light from her, or double it?   5
For every jewel shines more
by the power of her eyes than on its own.

Incomplete madrigal of uncertain date (ca. 1536–42), on the familiar theme of the heavenly power of the beloved woman's eyes (cf. no. 114).

4. *the silver and the gold:* with which she adorns herself.

  Non mi posso tener né voglio, Amore,
crescendo al tuo furore,
ch'i' nol te dica e giuri:
quante più inaspri e 'nduri,
a più virtù l'alma consigli e sproni;   5
e se talor perdoni
a la mie morte, agli angosciosi pianti,
com'a colui che muore,
dentro mi sento il core
mancar, mancando i mie tormenti tanti.   10
Occhi lucenti e santi,
mie poca grazia m'è ben dolce e cara,
c'assai acquista chi perdendo impara.

  I can't hold back, nor do I want to, Love
(faced with your mounting fury),
from saying and swearing to you:
the harsher and harder you grow,
the more you guide and spur my soul to virtue.   5
And if at times you take pity
upon my death, upon my anguished tears,
as you would on one who's dying,
then, as my many torments fade,
I feel my heart fading away within me.   10
O shining and blessed eyes,
my meager grace is sweet and dear to me,
for one who learns from loss gains a great deal.

Madrigal, ca. 1536–42, probably for Vittoria Colonna ("shining and blessed eyes," line 11).

  2. Or: as I am growing resistant to your fury.

  6. *take pity:* soften your attacks on me, relent.

  9. *my many torments:* of love, which keep me alive.

  9–10. Cf. Petrarch, no. 228: "Such do I find it [love] in my breast . . . a happy burden."

  13. *one who learns:* who is led to the path of virtue.

117

S'egli è che 'l buon desio
porti dal mondo a Dio
alcuna cosa bella,
sol la mie donna è quella,
a chi ha gli occhi fatti com'ho io.   5
Ogni altra cosa oblio
e sol di tant'ho cura.
Non è gran maraviglia,
s'io l'amo e bramo e chiamo a tutte l'ore;
né propio valor mio,   10
se l'alma per natura
s'appoggia a chi somiglia
ne gli occhi gli occhi, ond'ella scende fore.
Se sente il primo amore
come suo fin, per quel qua questa onora: 15
c'amar diè 'l servo chi 'l signore adora.

If it's true that a pure desire
for something beautiful
can bear us from earth to God,
my lady alone is that something
for one who has eyes fashioned as mine are;   5
I neglect everything else
and care only for that.
It's no great wonder, then,
if I love and desire and call her all the time,
nor due to my own worth   10
if my soul by its nature
leans on one who resembles
in her eyes those eyes out of which it descended.
If it feels the first love
is its goal, for that end it honors her here: 15
for one who adores the lord must love his servant.

Madrigal, ca. 1535–42. The theme and language echo Virgil's discourse on divine love in Dante, *Purgatorio* 17:91–111 (esp. line 14 here).

1–3. An expression of the Neoplatonic doctrine of anagogy, by which earthly beauty inspires the beholder to contemplate the higher divine beauty.

13–15. *those eyes . . . honors her:* Earlier copies read "honors Phoebus"; M changed *phebo* to *questa* in preparation for publication, suggesting the possibility that he originally wrote the poem for Febo di Poggio (see nos. 99–101), then altered the text to imply a female addressee, probably Vittoria Colonna. The evidence is not, however, conclusive: "Phoebus" was used by Petrarch simply to refer to the sun (e.g., PD, Excluded Poems, no. 5). Similarly, a sonnet written to Petrarch by Ser Dietisalvi Petri da Siena (ibid., 607) calls the sun "the beautiful eye of Apollo," a sense which fits M's metaphor here of the eye as a sign of the heavenly spirit.

14. *the first love:* God, the source of love.

16. *the lord: signore* means both "master" (or "sir") and "God," an ambiguity often played on in the Cavalieri poems.

Ancor che 'l cor già molte volte sia
d'amore acceso e da troppi anni spento,
l'ultimo mie tormento
sarie mortal senza la morte mia.
Onde l'alma desia   5
de' giorni mie, mentre c'amor m'avvampa,
l'ultimo, primo in più tranquilla corte.
Altro refugio o via
mie vita non iscampa
dal suo morir, c'un aspra e crudel morte;   10
né contr'a morte è forte
altro che morte, sì c'ogn'altra aita
è doppia morte a chi per morte ha vita.

Even though my heart has been many times already
enflamed by love and snuffed out by too great age,
this latest torment of mine
will be a deadly one without my death.
Therefore my soul desires,   5
while love sets me ablaze, to reach the last
of my days, the first in a more peaceful court.
No other path or refuge
is able to rescue my life
from its dying, except a harsh and cruel death,   10
and nothing other than death
has power against death; so any other help
gives a double death to one who gains life through death.

Madrigal, ca. 1536–42; two variant versions were apparently both prepared for publication. The theme is a common one in this period of M's life: only death can save him from the pains of love, which make life a living death.

3–4. This most recent amorous suffering will be deadly to my soul unless the death of my body frees me from it.

7. *first in a more peaceful court:* the beginning of an untroubled life in heaven.

11–12. Cf. Petrarch, no. 327: "I ask Death for help against Death."

Dal primo pianto all'ultimo sospiro,
al qual son già vicino,
chi contrasse già mai sì fier destino
com'io da sì lucente e fera stella?
Non dico iniqua o fella,   5
che 'l me' saria di fore,
s'aver disdegno ne troncasse amore;
ma più, se più la miro,
promette al mio martiro
dolce pietà, con dispietato core.   10
O desïato ardore!
ogni uom vil sol potria vincer con teco,
ond'io, s'io non fui cieco,
ne ringrazio le prime e l'ultime ore
ch'io la vidi; e l'errore   15
vincami; e d'ogni tempo sia con meco,
se sol forza e virtù perde con seco.

From my first cry until my final sigh,
which I'm already close to,
who ever received such a harsh destiny
as I have from such a bright and savage star?
I won't say unjust or wicked   5
—although that would be better,
if having her outward scorn would cut off my love—
but the more I look at her,
the more she promises
my anguish sweet mercy, with a merciless heart.   10
O longed-for heat of love!
only despicable men can win against you.
Thus I, not being blind,
am grateful to the first and the last hours
when I saw her; and may error   15
conquer me, and stay with me forever,
if strength and virtue can only lose against her.

Madrigal, ca. 1536–46, probably early 1540s, for the *donna altera*. Very similar to Petrarch no. 174, "It was a cruel star . . . under which I was born, and a cruel cradle where I lay" (cf. similar astrological imagery in nos. 97, 104, 164, 173). See also nos. 112, 114, 116, on the conflict between love and suffering or death; here, the poet resignedly prays that his moral scruples may be reduced so that he can succumb to the inevitable and desired love.

1. From birth to death.

4. *savage star:* cf. no. 123:9.

9–10. The more I delude myself that she might return my love, although I know she is devoid of love for me.

12. *only despicable men can win against you:* only those who lack both aesthetic sensibility (cf. line 13, *blind* to her beauty) and moral strength (cf. line 17) can resist the allure of passion.

Ben tempo saria omai
ritrarsi dal martire,
ché l'età col desir non ben s'accorda;
ma l'alma, cieca e sorda,
Amor, come tu sai,   5
del tempo e del morire
che, contro a morte ancor, me la ricorda;
e se l'arco e la corda
avvien che tronchi o spezzi
in mille e mille pezzi,   10
prega te sol non manchi un de' suoi guai:
ché mai non muor chi non guarisce mai.

Now surely should be the time
to withdraw from this anguish,
for old age is not compatible with desire.
But my soul, which, as you know,
O Love, is blind and deaf   5
to time and to dying,
and, even when faced with death, reminds me of her,
asks, even if you should cut
and shatter your bow and string
into a thousand pieces,   10
that you spare it not even one of its afflictions,
for one who never heals will never die.

Madrigal, ca. 1536–40. The repetition of "even" (implicit in the Italian text, though phrased differently in each case) emphasizes the poet's desperation to continue feeling love despite the many obstacles posed by failing health and thoughts of death.

1. Cf. Poliziano, "It surely would be time, Love, to have shaken off / your yoke from my neck . . . " (*Rispetti continuati*, no. 5; PO p. 181).

8–9. *cut and shatter your bow and string:* even if, from the effort of shooting so many arrows at me, you snap your bowstring and destroy your bow. The image, which recalls M's drawing of *Archers shooting at a herm* (TC no. 336, ca. 1530), is based on the traditional symbol of Cupid's bow and its enflaming love arrows.

12. For one who feels love's suffering at least knows that he is alive, still finds life worthwhile.

Come non puoi non esser cosa bella,
esser non puoi che pietosa non sia;
sendo po' tutta mia,
non può poter non mi distrugga e stempre.
Così durando sempre   5
mie pietà pari a tua beltà qui molto,
la fin del tuo bel volto
in un tempo con ella
fie del mie ardente core.
Ma poi che 'l spirto sciolto   10
ritorna alla suo stella,
a fruir quel signore
ch'e' corpi a chiunche muore
eterni rende o per quiete o per lutto;
priego 'l mie, benché brutto,   15
com'è qui teco, il voglia in paradiso:
c'un cor pietoso val quant'un bel viso.

As you cannot be anything but beautiful,
so may you fail to be anything but merciful,
so that, being all mine,
you cannot help destroying or melting me.
Then, since my mercy from you   5
remains always equal to your great beauty here,
the end of your fair face
at the same time as that
will end my burning heart.
But since the unbound soul   10
goes back up to its star,
to delight in that lord
who makes the bodies of those
who die eternal, either in peace or sorrow,
I pray you'll want mine, though ugly,   15
with you in paradise, as it is here:
for a pious heart's worth as much as a fair face.

Madrigal, late 1530s, probably for Vittoria Colonna; cf. no. 140.

7. *the end of your fair face:* the death of your earthly body.

8. *as that:* as your mercy to me here on earth, which will also end at your death.

10–11. *unbound soul:* released from the body. *its star:* M is conflating Christian ideas of the afterlife with Platonic and astrological images.

14. *either in peace or sorrow:* God gives the soul eternal life either in peaceful heaven or suffering hell.

15. *though ugly:* M was acutely conscious of his own physical imperfections, especially his misshapen nose, which had been broken in a youthful altercation with his fellow student, the sculptor Pietro Torrigiano (CW p. 108).

17. This line, working a variation on lines 5–6 about the lady's linked mercy and beauty, seems to refer to M's own soul, which he asserts is worthy of consideration for its moral qualities despite his ugly exterior.

Se 'l foco al tutto nuoce,
e me arde e non cuoce,
non è mia molta né sua men virtute,
ch'io sol trovi salute
qual salamandra, là dove altri muore.   5
Né so chi in pace a tal martir m'ha volto:
da te medesma il volto,
da me medesmo il core
fatto non fu, né sciolto
da noi fia mai il mio amore;   10
più alto è quel signore
che ne' tu' occhi la mia vita ha posta.
S'io t'amo, e non ti costa,
perdona a me, come io a tanta noia,
che fuor di chi m'uccide vuol ch'i' muoia.   15

If fire, which harms all things,
heats me yet does not sear me,
it's not through my greater or its lesser power
that I alone find safety,
like the salamander, there where others die;   5
and I don't know who's turned my peace into such torment.
Your face was not made by you,
nor my heart by myself,
nor will my bond of love
ever be untied by us;   10
for that lord's a higher power
who has placed all my life within your eyes.
If my love's no burden to you,
forgive me, as I do such a great tormentor
who, unlike her who kills me, wants me to die.   15

Madrigal, ca. 1536–46, probably for Vittoria Colonna.

    1–5. M similarly claims his difference from other people in nos. 73, 136.

    3. *my greater or its lesser power*: neither because of my increased power to resist the fire (of love) nor its decreasing intensity.

5. *salamander:* this lizardlike creature was believed to live and thrive in fire. Cf. Petrarch no. 207, "I feed on my death and live in flames, strange food and marvelous salamander!" M's drawing of a salamander (TC no. 304r) has been discussed in relation to this poem and M's desire to work for François I of France, who adopted the creature as his personal emblem (Charles de Tolnay, "La salamandra di Michelangelo," *Antichità viva* 12:2 [1973]: 3–5); cf. no. 73.

14–15. *such a great tormentor:* Love, who wishes me to die of my passion, although the woman I love does not wish that.

Quante più par che 'l mie mal maggior senta,
se col viso vel mostro,
più par s'aggiunga al vostro
bellezza, tal che 'l duol dolce diventa.
Ben fa chi mi tormenta, 5
se parte vi fa bella
della mie pena ria:
se 'l mie mal vi contenta,
mie cruda e fera stella,
che farie dunche con la morte mia? 10
Ma s'è pur ver che sia
vostra beltà dall'aspro mie martire,
e quel manchi al morire,
morend'io, morrà vostra leggiadria.
Però fate ch'i' stia 15
col mie duol vivo, per men vostro danno;
e se più bella al mie mal maggior siete,
l'alma n'ha ben più quiete:
c'un gran piacer sopporta un grande affanno.

The more I seem to feel my increased woe,
if my face shows it to you,
the more the beauty seems
to increase in yours, so that my pain grows sweet.
So he who torments me does good 5
if, from my cruel pain,
he also makes you beautiful.
If my woe pleases you,
my cruel and savage star,
how well would you do, then, if I were to die? 10
And yet, if it is true
that your beauty is derived from my harsh torment,
which ceases at my death,
then with my dying your loveliness will die too.
Therefore, keep me alive 15
along with my pain, to lessen your own harm.

And if you grow fairer at my increased woe,
my soul gains more peace from that:
for great joy makes great anguish bearable.

Madrigal, ca. 1536–46.

5. *he who torments me:* Love.

9. *my cruel and savage star:* cf. the similar phrase in no. 119.

19. My own pain is compensated by the benefit you reap from it, that is, the increase in your beauty that I can enjoy (literally, "a great joy endures a great anguish").

Questa mie donna è sì pronta e ardita,
c'allor che la m'ancide ogni mie bene
cogli occhi mi promette, e parte tiene
il crudel ferro dentro a la ferita.
E così morte e vita,   5
contrarie, insieme in un picciol momento
dentro a l'anima sento;
ma la grazia il tormento
da me discaccia per più lunga pruova:
c'assai più nuoce il mal che 'l ben non giova.   10

This lady of mine is so quick and bold
that even as she kills me, with her eyes
she promises me all my joys, while at the same time
she holds her cruel sword within my wound.
And thus, within my soul   5
I feel both death and life, though opposites,
together for a brief moment;
if her grace chases anguish
away from me, it's to set a longer ordeal:
for evil harms much more than good can help.   10

Madrigal, ca. 1536–46, probably early 1540s, full of Petrarchan oppositions.

10. The wound of love that she cruelly inflicts on me is too painful to be compensated by the joy of being near her and receiving her glances.

Tanto di sé promette
donna pietosa e bella,
c'ancor mirando quella
sarie qual fu' per tempo, or vecchio e tardi.
Ma perc'ognor si mette   5
morte invidiosa e fella
fra ' mie dolenti e ' suo pietosi sguardi,
solo convien ch'i' ardi
quel picciol tempo che 'l suo volto oblio.
Ma poi che 'l pensier rio   10
pur la ritorna al consueto loco,
dal suo fier ghiaccio è spento il dolce foco.

So much of herself she promises,
this merciful and fair lady,
that I, now old and slow,
could be again, looking at her, what I once was.
But since fierce, envious death   5
constantly places himself
between my sad glances and her merciful ones,
I'm only able to burn
in that brief time when I forget his face.
For when my dreadful thoughts   10
bring him back again to his accustomed place,
by his harsh ice is my sweet fire put out.

Madrigal, ca. 1536–42. The images are similar to no. 127, though with a different intent. Death is feminine in Italian but is here translated as masculine.

4. *old and slow:* cf. Dante, *Inferno* 26:106, "My companions and I were old and slow." M characterizes himself in this phrase several times, e.g., nos. 136, 175.

10–11. Whenever my mind returns to the sad thought of death, which so often preoccupies me.

Se l'alma è ver, dal suo corpo disciolta,
che 'n alcun altro torni
a' corti e brevi giorni,
per vivere e morire un'altra volta,
la donna mie, di molta 5
bellezza agli occhi miei,
fie allor com'or nel suo tornar sì cruda?
Se mie ragion s'ascolta,
attender la dovrei
di grazia piena e di durezza nuda. 10
Credo, s'avvien che chiuda
gli occhi suo begli, arà, come rinnuova,
pietà del mio morir, se morte pruova.

If it's true that the soul, freed from its body,
comes back in another one
to these brief and fleeting days
in order to live and die another time,
will my lady, who is 5
of great beauty to my eyes,
be then, on her return, as cruel as now?
If my thoughts are heeded,
I should expect to find her
full of grace and stripped of all her harshness. 10
I believe, if she should close
her beautiful eyes, that, when renewed, she'd take
pity on my dying, having experienced death.

Madrigal, ca. 1536–46, on the same theme as no. 230.

1–4. The belief in reincarnation (metempsychosis), which contradicts Christian doctrine, is taken from Plato, especially the *Phaedrus* and *Republic*.

8. *if my thoughts are heeded:* if heaven listens to my plea.

10. *full of grace:* M borrows the exact words used to characterize the Virgin Mary in the *Ave Maria* prayer.

127

Non pur la morte, ma 'l timor di quella
da donna iniqua e bella,
c'ognor m'ancide, mi difende e scampa;
e se talor m'avvampa
più che l'usato il foco in ch'io son corso,   5
non trovo altro soccorso
che l'immagin sua ferma in mezzo il core:
ché dove è morte non s'appressa Amore.

Not death itself, but the very fear of him
defends and rescues me
from a beautiful, unjust lady who constantly kills me.
And when at times the fire
I've fallen into burns me more than usually,   5
I find no other relief
than the image of him held firmly in my heart:
for where Death is found, Love does not come near.

Madrigal, probably early 1540s. The antithesis of love and death is similar to no. 125, but here M sees death as a savior from, rather than impediment to, earthly passion; cf. no. 128, which uses a similar opening line. In the first of Donato Giannotti's *Dialogues* (GD pp. 69–70), M is recorded discoursing on this very topic, saying that "it is marvelous, the effect of this thought of death, which, destroying all things by its very nature, preserves and maintains those who think of it, and defends against all human passions." He then recalls "having very suitably pointed [this] out in a little madrigal of mine," going on to recite the text of no. 127 (in a slightly variant version) to his friends.

Se 'l timor della morte
chi 'l fugge e scaccia sempre
lasciar là lo potessi onde ei si muove,
Amor crudele e forte
con più tenace tempre   5
d'un cor gentil faria spietate pruove.
Ma perché l'alma altrove
per morte e grazia al fin gioire spera,
chi non può non morir gli è 'l timor caro
al qual ogni altro cede.   10
Né contro all'alte e nuove
bellezze in donna altera
ha forza altro riparo
che schivi suo disdegno o suo mercede.
Io giuro a chi nol crede,   15
che da costei, che del mio pianger ride,
sol mi difende e scampa chi m'uccide.

If one who always flees
and drives away from himself the fear of death
could leave it behind there where it came from,
Love, being cruel and strong,
would make ruthless ordeals   5
for a gentle heart, with more unyielding vigor.
But since the soul does hope
to rejoice at last elsewhere through death and grace,
one who cannot help dying holds dear that fear
to which all others yield.   10
And against the lofty and novel
beauties of a proud woman,
no other shelter has power
to help me evade either her scorn or her mercy.
I swear to all nonbelievers   15
that from that woman who laughs at my weeping
only he who kills me can defend and save me.

Madrigal, ca. 1536–42; cf. no. 127.

1–3. If we on earth could ever fully free ourselves from the fear of death.

8. *at last elsewhere:* in heaven, after death.

10. *to which all others yield:* this phrase recalls, with an inversion of meaning, the well-known line from Virgil, *Eclogues* 10:69, "Love conquers all; let us, too, yield to Love" (cf. above, no. 29).

15. *nonbelievers:* those who do not believe my claim, because it seems incredible.

17. *he:* death, or more precisely in this context, the fear of it.

Da maggior luce e da più chiara stella
la notte il ciel le sue da lunge accende:
te sol presso a te rende
ognor più bella ogni cosa men bella.
Qual cor più questa o quella   5
a pietà muove o sprona,
c'ognor chi arde almen non s'agghiacc'egli?
Chi, senza aver, ti dona
vaga e gentil persona
e 'l volto e gli occhi e ' biondi e be' capegli.   10
Dunche, contr'a te quegli
ben fuggi e me con essi,
se 'l bello infra ' non begli
beltà cresce a se stessi.
Donna, ma s' tu rendessi   15
quel che t'ha dato il ciel, c'a noi l'ha tolto,
sarie più 'l nostro, e men bello il tuo volto.

With a greater light and by a clearer star
heaven, at night, lights its own from afar;
only you keep being made
more lovely by everything near you and less lovely.
Which one, this or that, can move   5
or spur your heart more to pity,
so that one who burns continually won't be frozen?
There's one who, lacking them, gives you
a kind and lovely form
and face and eyes and beautiful blond hair.   10
Thus, against your own interest
you flee them and me with them,
since beauty amidst nonbeauty
increases its own beauty.
But, lady, if you gave back   15
what heaven has given to you, and taken from us,
our face would be more beautiful, and yours less.

Madrigal, ca. 1536–42, a rather overelaborated version of the Petrarchan idea that the beloved's beauty is increased by contrast with something less beautiful.

2. *its own:* the moon (and, by poetic extension, the stars) which reflects the "greater light" of the sun.

5–7. Which of two reasons to stay close to me will convince you better to warm me with your love: the possibility to appear more beautiful by comparison with those who are less dazzling, or the grace to make others beautiful by letting them bask in your reflected beauty?

8–17. Because I am not beautiful, your beauty is enhanced by contrast with me; therefore you should not flee from me, since by so doing you lose that enhancement.

Non è senza periglio
il tuo volto divino
dell'alma a chi è vicino
com'io a morte, che la sento ognora;
ond'io m'armo e consiglio   5
per far da quel difesa anzi ch'i' mora.
Ma tuo mercede, ancora
che 'l mie fin sie da presso,
non mi rende a me stesso;
né danno alcun da tal pietà mi scioglie: 10
ché l'uso di molt'anni un dì non toglie.

It is not without danger,
this godlike face of yours,
to the soul of one who's close
to death, as am I, who feel it all the time.
Hence I arm and advise myself   5
to defend myself against it before I die.
But your own graciousness,
even though my end is near,
can't restore me to myself,
nor thought of any harm free me from such mercy;   10
for one day can't remove the habit of many years.

Madrigal, ca. 1534–42. On the same sheet as no. 131, which is a variation on the same theme. Both were sent to Luigi del Riccio in August or September 1542, with a note: "Messer Luigi: I pray you, who have the spirit of poetry, to shorten and revise for me one of these madrigals, whichever seems to you the less deplorable, as I have to give it to a friend of ours" (C. cmxcvii; R. 223). The gender of the poems' addressee is not specified; from the reference to "many years," the friend might be identified as Cavalieri.

10. Nor can the fear of punishment after death free me from the enchantment of your beauty.

Sotto duo belle ciglia
le forze Amor ripiglia
nella stagion che sprezza l'arco e l'ale.
Gli occhi mie, ghiotti d'ogni maraviglia
c'a questa s'assomiglia,   5
di lor fan pruova a più d'un fero strale.
E parte pur m'assale,
appresso al dolce, un pensier aspro e forte
di vergogna e di morte;
né perde Amor per maggior tema o danni: 10
c'un'or non vince l'uso di molt'anni.

Beneath two beautiful brows
Love recovers his strength
in the season that scorns his bow and wings.
My eyes, greedy for every marvelous thing
that resembles this one,   5
make themselves a test for more than one fierce dart.
Though there comes over me,
while I am close to sweetness, a strong, harsh thought
of shame and of death,
Love does not lose to fear of greater harm: 10
for an hour can't defeat the habit of many years.

Madrigal, ca. 1536–42; see no. 130. These two poems were sent to Luigi del Riccio about the same time as no. 91 (q.v.). Part of an early version of no. 131 is found on a sheet of anatomical studies probably made much earlier (TC no. 111v).

3. That is, old age, metaphorically the winter season of life, when love should be replaced with concern for the afterlife.

4. Cf. Dante, *Purgatory* 8:85, "My greedy eyes still went up to the sun."

6. *make themselves a test:* risk exposing themselves to Love's arrows. For other examples of arrows or darts, cf. nos. 22, 24, 27, 77, 137, 142, etc.

9. *shame and death:* shame at loving so passionately in old age and fear of dying in such sin.

10. My desire is not overcome by these premonitions of punishment.

11. Cf. similar expressions in nos. 130, 133, 161.

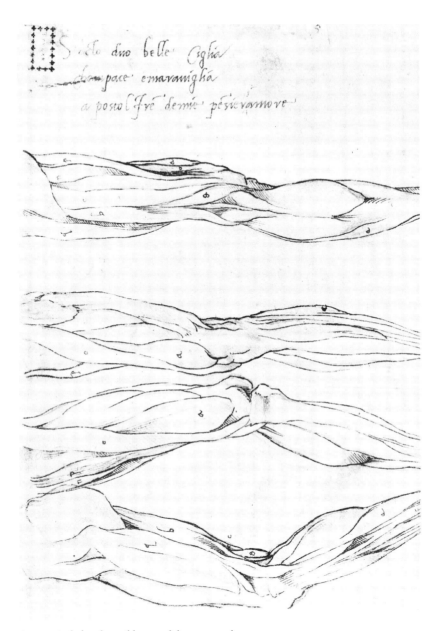

Anatomical sketches of legs and fragment of poem no. 131

132

Mentre che 'l mie passato m'è presente,
sì come ognor mi viene,
o mondo falso, allor conosco bene
l'errore e 'l danno dell'umana gente:
quel cor, c'alfin consente   5
a' tuo lusinghi e a' tuo van diletti,
procaccia all'alma dolorosi guai.
Ben lo sa chi lo sente,
come spesso prometti
altrui la pace e 'l ben che tu non hai   10
né debbi aver già mai.
Dunche ha men grazia chi più qua soggiorna:
ché chi men vive più lieve al ciel torna.

While all my past is present in front of me—
as happens constantly—
O false world, then do I well understand
the error and the loss of humankind:
that heart which yields at last   5
to your allurements and to your vain pleasures
acquires for the soul painful misfortunes.
One who feels it knows well
how you often promise to others
the peace and well-being that you do not have,   10
nor are you ever to have.
So one who stays here longer has less grace:
for one who lives less returns to heaven lighter.

Madrigal, ca. 1536–42. The theme is very similar to no. 133: it is better to die young, before the soul has given in to any sinful temptations (cf. also no. 226). Since the poem is addressed to "the false world" and does not specify the earthly person(s) who held out "vain pleasures," M could be referring to Cavalieri, Colonna, or the *donna altera*. At the bottom of the autograph, when sending it to Luigi del Riccio, M added a postscript: "To Messer Donato [Giannotti], mender of badly made things, I commend myself"—an indication of M's reliance on both men for help in polishing his verses.

1. Whenever the memory of my past comes back to my mind.

4. *the error and the loss:* sin and its punishment.

8. *feels:* experiences directly. Cf. Petrarch, no. 355, "now through experience I understand your frauds."

13. *lighter:* less burdened by sin. The image of returning to heaven recalls the resurrected souls rising to eternal peace in the *Last Judgment,* painted 1534–41.

Condotto da molt'anni all'ultim'ore,
tardi conosco, o mondo, i tuo diletti:
la pace che non hai altrui prometti
e quel riposo c'anzi al nascer muore.
La vergogna e 'l timore   5
degli anni, c'or prescrive
il ciel, non mi rinnuova
che 'l vecchio e dolce errore,
nel qual chi troppo vive
l'anima 'ncide e nulla al corpo giova.   10
Il dico e so per pruova
di me, che 'n ciel quel sol ha miglior sorte
ch'ebbe al suo parto più presso la morte.

Led by my many years to my final hours,
I understand too late, O world, your pleasures:
you promise to others the peace that you don't have
and that repose that dies prior to birth.
The shame and fear of age,   5
which heaven now ordains,
only bring back in me
that old and sweet error
through which one who lives too long
kills the soul and does no good for the body.   10
I say—and I know from
my own ordeal—that in heaven only he
has the better fate who, at his birth, had death nearer.

Madrigal, ca. 1536–42; see no. 132.

5. The shame for past actions and the fear of death that overtake us in old age; cf. no. 131, "thought of shame and of death."

8. *that old and sweet error:* the desire for passion and physical beauty; cf. nos. 130, 131, 161.

—*Beati voi che su nel ciel godete*
le lacrime che 'l mondo non ristora,
favvi amor forza ancora,
o pur per morte liberi ne siete?
   —*La nostra etterna quiete,*   5
fuor d'ogni tempo, è priva
d'invidia, amando, e d'angosciosi pianti.
   —*Dunche a mal pro' ch'i' viva*
convien, come vedete,
per amare e servire in dolor tanti.   10
Se 'l cielo è degli amanti
amico, e 'l mondo ingrato,
amando, a che son nato?
A viver molto? E questo mi spaventa:
ché 'l poco è troppo a chi ben serve e stenta.   15

   —O you blessed, up in heaven, who benefit
from the tears that this world cannot compensate,
does love still hold power over you,
or are you now, by death, set free from it?
   —Our eternal calm, outside   5
all time, is full of loving
but relieved of envy and of anguished tears.
   —Then it's a hard lot for me
to have to live, as you see,
to love and serve with so much suffering.   10
If heaven is a friend
to lovers, and the world thankless,
what was I, so loving, born to?
To live a long time? But this terrifies me:
for a little's too much for one who serves well and suffers.   15

Madrigal of uncertain date, ca. 1536–46. It is cast as a dialogue between M and the souls in heaven, which echoes Platonic theories of the afterlife and recalls the heavenly conversation in Dante's canzona *Donna ch'avete* (*Vita nuova*, no. 19). This fantasy of heavenly bliss follows logically from the poems in which M expresses his yearning to experience the bliss after earthly suffering, e.g., no. 161.

1–2. *who benefit from the tears:* enjoy the reward for the unhappiness experienced in worldly love, a consolation that can only come after departing from earthly life.

13. Since I am much given to love, what sad fate awaits me?

15. Even a short life is too much to bear for one who serves love well and receives only pain in return.

Mentre c'al tempo la mie vita fugge,
amor più mi distrugge,
né mi perdona un'ora,
com'i' credetti già dopo molt'anni.
L'alma, che trema e rugge,   5
com'uom c'a torto mora,
di me si duol, de' sua etterni danni.
Fra 'l timore e gl'inganni
d'amore e morte, allor tal dubbio sento,
ch'i' cerco in un momento   10
del me' di loro e di poi il peggio piglio;
sì dal mal uso è vinto il buon consiglio.

While with passing time my life is running out,
love consumes me even more,
giving not one hour's release,
as I thought he'd do now, after so many years.
My soul, which trembles and roars   5
like a man who's killed unjustly,
complains of me and its eternal loss.
Between the fear and the deceits
of love and death, I feel now such uncertainty
that at one moment I seek   10
the better of them, but then I seize the worse;
thus by bad habits is good counsel defeated.

Madrigal, ca. 1536–46, sent to Donato Giannotti with a brief note.

7. *eternal loss:* fear of damnation; the phrase *etterni danni* derives from Dante, *Inferno* 15:42.

8–9. *the fear and the deceits of love and death:* the fear of death and the deceptive attractions of love.

10–12. A variation on the final stanzas of Petrarch, no. 264, which lament that, because of "a pleasure so strong in me through habit . . . I seek new counsel for my life, and see the better but take hold of the worse."

L'alma, che sparge e versa
di fuor l'acque di drento,
il fa sol perché spento
non sie da loro il foco in ch'è conversa.
Ogni altra aita persa   5
saria, se 'l pianger sempre
mi resurge al tuo foco, vecchio e tardi.
Mie dura sorte e mie fortuna avversa
non ha sì dure tempre,
che non m'affligghin men, dove più m'ardi;   10
tal ch' e' tuo accesi sguardi,
di fuor piangendo, dentro circumscrivo,
e di quel c'altri muor sol godo e vivo.

The soul, which spills and pours
its inner waters out,
does so only so the fire
that it's been turned into won't be quenched by them.
Any other aid would be wasted,   5
since my continual weeping
revives me in your fire, though I'm old and slow.
But my harsh fate and my hostile fortune
have not so harsh a nature
that they don't afflict me less, when you burn me more;   10
so, while weeping out my tears,
I keep your burning glances enclosed within me,
and I alone enjoy and live on what kills others.

Madrigal, ca. 1542–46. The autograph is addressed to Luigi del Riccio. After including an alternative version for the last two lines, M adds, "Pick the one that is less deplorable in *messer* Donato's [Giannotti] judgment." The conception and imagery closely parallel Petrarch no. 55, "Quel foco ch' i' pensai che fosse spento," which also lies behind other poems of this period.

2. *its inner waters:* tears, weeping.

5–7. Any other attempt to help me live would be in vain, since only by weeping can I keep alive the energizing flame of your love.

7. *old and slow:* cf. the same phrase in nos. 125, 175.

13. *what kills others:* the fire of love. Cf. M's similar protestations of his difference from other people in nos. 73, 122.

Se per gioir pur brami affanni e pianti,
più crudo, Amor, m'è più caro ogni strale,
che fra la morte e 'l male
non dona tempo alcun, né brieve spazio:
tal c'a 'ncider gli amanti   5
i pianti perdi, e 'l nostro è meno strazio.
Ond'io sol ti ringrazio
della mie morte e non delle mie doglie,
c'ogni mal sana chi la vita toglie.

If to be happy, Love, you still crave trouble and tears,
then the crueler it is, the dearer to me is each dart
that leaves no time at all
between the wound and death, nor a short space;
so that, by killing lovers,   5
you lose our tears and make our torture less.
For this reason I thank you
only for my death, and not for my pains,
for he who takes away life cures every ill.

Madrigal, close in date and theme to no. 136.

2–4. I am grateful when your arrows become more intense, since the faster they kill me, the less time I will have to suffer. For other examples of arrows or darts, cf. nos. 22, 24, 27, 77, 131, 142, etc.

6. *you lose our tears:* you no longer enjoy the pleasure that the tears of a living lover offer you (as in line 1).

Porgo umilmente all'aspro giogo il collo,
il volto lieto a la fortuna ria,
e alla donna mia
nemica il cor di fede e foco pieno;
né dal martir mi crollo,   5
anz'ogni or temo non venga meno.
Ché se 'l volto sereno
cibo e vita mi fa d'un gran martire,
qual crudel doglia mi può far morire?

I humbly offer my neck to the harsh yoke,
my face to hostile fortune joyfully,
and, to my enemy lady,
my heart that's full of fire and faithfulness;
nor do I shrink from torture,   5
but rather fear constantly that it might diminish.
For if her tranquil face
makes food and life for me from my great torture,
what cruel pain could ever make me die?

Madrigal, ca. 1536–42, similar to no. 139.

    1. *the harsh yoke:* of love.

    8. *makes food . . . for me:* M also described Cavalieri as the food (*cibo*) on which he lived (C. CMXVI–CMXIXX; R. 193).

In più leggiadra e men pietosa spoglia
altr'anima non tiene
che la tuo, donna, il moto e 'l dolce anelo;
tal c'alla ingrata voglia
al don di tuo beltà perpetue pene   5
più si convien c'al mie soffrire 'l cielo.
I' nol dico e nol celo
s'i' bramo o no come 'l tuo 'l mie peccato,
ché, se non vivo, morto ove te sia,
o, te pietosa, che dove beato   10
mi fa 'l martir, si' etterna pace mia.
Se dolce mi saria
l'inferno teco, in ciel dunche che fora?
Beato a doppio allora
sare' a godere i' sol nel divin coro   15
quel Dio che 'n cielo e quel che 'n terra adoro.

No other soul contains sweet breath and motion,
my lady, in a mortal shell
more lovely and less merciful than yours,
so that your ingratitude
for the gift of your beauty deserves perpetual pains   5
even more than my suffering deserves heaven.
I don't say (but don't hide it)
whether I'd wish my sin to be like yours,
so I could be with you, if not while living, when dead;
or whether, if you grow kind, my eternal peace   10
might be where my suffering will make me blessed.
For if hell would be sweet
to me with you, what would it be like in heaven?
Then I alone would be
doubly blessed in the divine choir, to enjoy   15
the god I adore in heaven and the one I do on earth.

Madrigal, ca. 1536–46, similar to no. 138. The fantasy of a joyous life in heaven after earthly suffering parallels M's imagined dialogue with the heavenly souls in no. 134.

4. *your ingratitude:* toward me, by not returning my love for your beauty.

5. *perpetual pains:* in hell.

7. *but don't hide it:* but I am honest enough to admit both possibilities (in lines 8–11).

8–9. I might wish to sin (by loving you) as much as you do (by your cruel indifference to my love), so that we can be united in hell or, alternatively:

10–11. If you become more merciful to me, and hence worthy to go to heaven, perhaps I will have been made sufficiently worthy of joining you there by enduring the suffering of my love for you.

15. *in the divine choir:* having been transformed into an angel (cf. no. 134).

140

Se l'alma al fin ritorna
nella suo dolce e desïata spoglia,
o danni o salvi il ciel, come si crede,
ne l'inferno men doglia,
se tuo beltà l'adorna,   5
fie, parte c'altri ti contempla e vede.
S'al cielo ascende e riede,
com'io seco desio
e con tal cura e con sì caldo affetto,
fie men fruire Dio,   10
s'ogni altro piacer cede,
come di qua, al tuo divo e dolce aspetto.
Che me' d'amarti aspetto,
se più giova men doglia a chi è dannato,
che 'n ciel non nuoce l'esser men beato.   15

If in the end the soul
goes back into its sweet and longed-for shell,
and heaven either damns or saves it, as we believe,
then in hell, if your beauty adorns it,
there will be less suffering   5
as long as one can see and gaze at you.
But if it rises back to heaven,
where I wish to go with it
with such concern and such warm sentiments,
there will be less delight in God   10
if every other pleasure
yields there, as here, to your divine, sweet face.
So I hope to love you better
if it does more good for the damned to have less suffering
than it does harm in heaven to be less blessed.   15

Madrigal, ca. 1536–46, similar to no. 139 in imagining the poet's alternate fate, accompanied by his beautiful beloved (whose gender is in this case unspecified) in either heaven or hell. Cf. also similar ideas and phrases in no. 121.

1–3. The image of dead souls being reclothed in their earthly bodies parallels M's depiction of that moment in his *Last Judgment* fresco. Cf. nos. 186, 227.

6. *one:* the poet himself.

10–12. My enjoyment of the presence of God will be lessened by being overshadowed by your presence.

Perc'all'alta mie speme è breve e corta,
donna, tuo fé, se con san occhio il veggio,
goderò per non peggio
quante di fuor con gli occhi ne prometti;
ché dove è pietà morta,   5
non è che gran bellezza non diletti.
E se contrari effetti
agli occhi di mercé dentro a te sento,
la certezza non tento,
ma prego, ove 'l gioire è men che 'ntero,   10
sie dolce il dubbio a chi nuocer può 'l vero.

Since, compared to my high hopes, lady, your faith
is short and fleeting, if my eye sees soundly,
I'll content myself, to avoid worse,
with as much as you promise outwardly with your eyes;
for even where mercy's dead   5
it's not true that great beauty gives no delight.
And if I sense within you
feelings contrary to those of your merciful eyes,
I don't seek certainty,
but pray, although my joy is less than complete,   10
that doubt be sweet for one whom truth could hurt.

Madrigal, ca. 1536–46; cf. no. 174.

    1. *your faith:* your response to me, your sympathy to my desire.

    5–6. Even if you don't love me, I can still take delight in your beauty.

    7/8. *feelings contrary:* cf. nos. 47:11 and 141:7.

    11. Let me retain at least the hopefulness of not knowing your true feelings, since it would be painful to discover definitely that you don't love me.

Credo, perc'ancor forse
non sia la fiamma spenta
nel freddo tempo dell'età men verde,
l'arco subito torse
Amor, che si rammenta   5
che 'n gentil cor ma' suo colpo non perde;
e la stagion rinverde
per un bel volto; e peggio è al sezzo strale
mie ricaduta che 'l mio primo male.

I believe that Love, perhaps
so my flame wouldn't yet be quenched
in the cold weather of my less green age,
suddenly bent his bow
at me, remembering   5
that his blow's never wasted on a noble heart;
and he, with a beautiful face,
makes the season green again; and my relapse
under this last arrow is worse than my first illness.

Madrigal, ca. 1536–42, probably for Vittoria Colonna, whom M credited with reviving his capacity for love in old age.

3. *my less green age:* in my heart, chilled by old age like a tree in winter; cf. nos. 167, 253, 283.

5–6. This fundamental tenet of love in the *dolce stil nuovo* was similarly expressed by Guinizelli's canzone, "Al cor gentil repara sempre Amore" and in Dante's sonnet, "Amore e 'l cor gentil sono una cosa" (*Vita nuova,* no. 20).

7. *with a beautiful face:* by use of the face that he makes me fall in love with.

9. *this last arrow:* for similar images, cf. nos. 22, 24, 27, 77, 131, 137, etc. *my first illness:* my earlier love and its suffering; cf. nos. 175, 232.

Quant'ognor fugge il giorno che mi resta
del viver corto e poco,
tanto più serra il foco
in picciol tempo a mie più danno e strazio:
c'aita il ciel non presta   5
contr'al vecchio uso in così breve spazio.
Pur poi che non se' sazio
del foco circumscritto,
in cui pietra non serva suo natura
non c'un cor, ti ringrazio,   10
Amor, se 'l manco invitto
in chiuso foco alcun tempo non dura.
Mie peggio è mie ventura,
perché la vita all'arme che tu porti
cara non m'è, s'almen perdoni a' morti.   15

The more the days keep fleeing that remain to me
of my short and meager life,
the more the fire grips me
in the little time left, to my greater harm and torture;
for heaven can lend no aid   5
against old habit in so brief a span.
Yet, since you're not satisfied
by encircling me with fire
in which not even a stone can keep its form,
much less a heart, I thank you,   10
Love, since the less resistant,
enclosed by fire, will last no time at all.
My worst fate will be my good fortune,
for life under the weapons that you bear
is not dear to me, since at least you release the dead.   15

Madrigal, ca. 1536–44, beginning with a theme similar to no. 142. The autograph was sent to Luigi del Riccio, perhaps in 1544, with a light-hearted postscript: "For the melons and wine I thank you, and repay you with a *polizino*." This self-deprecating word, which may be translated as a "scrap of paper" or (hereinafter) a "scribble," is used in several of M's postscripts, e.g., no. 206, which may have been sent at about the same time as no. 143.

6. *old habit:* M often alludes to the power of his longstanding errors; cf. similar phrases in nos. 92, 130, 131.

9. *can keep its form:* i.e., would melt.

11. *the less resistant:* my heart, which lacks the strength of stone. The metaphor is drawn from the lime-kiln, in which stone is reduced to lime by heat (cf. nos. 63, 170).

13–15. The worst that could happen to me (death, brought on by the fire of love) would be fortunate, since the pain of a life subjected to your arrows will cease after death.

144

Passo inanzi a me stesso
con alto e buon concetto,
e 'l tempo gli prometto
c'aver non deggio. O pensier vano e stolto!
Ché con la morte appresso   5
perdo 'l presente, e l'avvenir m'è tolto;
e d'un leggiadro volto
ardo e spero sanar, che morto viva
negli anni ove la vita non arriva.

I get ahead of myself
with a lofty and fine conception,
and promise it the time
that I'm not to have. O vain and foolish thought!
For, with death near to me,   5
I lose the present, and the future's taken from me.
I burn for a lovely face
and hope to be cured of it, so I may live,
though dead, in the years that my life will not reach.

Madrigal, ca. 1536–44.

1–4. I have an idea for future work and promise myself to realize it, although I will probably be prevented from finishing by death, especially since, (lines 5–9) by daydreaming over my beloved, I waste what little time remains and imperil my future salvation and my reputation after death. For the artistic significance of the term *concetto*, see no. 151.

Se costei gode e tu solo, Amor, vivi
de' nostri pianti, e s'io, come te, soglio
di lacrime e cordoglio
e d'un ghiaccio nutrir la vita mia;
dunche, di vita privi   5
saremo da mercé di donna pia.
Meglio il peggio saria:
contrari cibi han sì contrari effetti
c'a lei il godere, a noi torrien la vita;
tal che 'nsieme prometti   10
più morte, là dove più porgi aita.
A l'alma sbigottita
viver molto più val con dura sorte
che grazia c'abbi a sé presso la morte.

If she enjoys and if you, Love, live only
on our tears, and if I am, like you, accustomed
to nourishing my life
on weeping and on anguish and on ice,
then we would be deprived   5
of life by her mercy, were the lady charitable.
The worse would be better:
opposite foods have such opposite effects
that they'd take away joy from her, and life from us.
Therefore, at the same time,   10
you threaten death more, the more you offer help;
for, to my terrified soul,
long life with a harsh fate is worth much more
than grace that carries death so near itself.

Madrigal, ca. 1536–44. A conflation of frequent themes: since Love, the beloved lady, and M himself all feed on the poet's lovesickness, any mutual consummation of that love would injure all three of them. On M's autograph is a note to the unknown recipient, "This is for the curd cheeses; the next one will be for the olives, if it's worth that much."

4. Both "feeding on tears" and ice (*ghiaccio* or *gelo*) are common Petrarchan figures of discomfort and love's pain (e.g., no. 93).

6. *charitable:* if the lady were to feel pity for me and hence give her affection more readily.

7–9. Although it might seem more desirable that the lady feed herself on pity rather than on her accustomed cruelty (and therefore return my love), it would actually be better if she continued to withhold her love, since if I receive it, she will no longer be able to enjoy my suffering, and Love and I will have no more of our habitual spiritual food. *Opposite effects:* cf. nos. 47:12 and 141:7.

Gli sguardi che tu strazi
a me tutti gli togli;
né furto è già quel che del tuo non doni;
ma se 'l vulgo ne sazi
e ' bruti, e me ne spogli,   5
omicidio è, c'a morte ognor mi sproni.
Amor, perché perdoni
tuo somma cortesia
sie di beltà qui tolta
a chi gusta e desia,   10
e data a gente stolta?
Deh, falla un'altra volta
pietosa dentro e sì brutta di fuori,
c'a me dispiaccia, e di me s'innamori.

All the glances with which you
torment others, you take from me;
it's not really theft, if you don't give what's yours,
but if you sate the crowd
and the beasts with them, and deprive me,   5
it's murder, since you keep driving me toward death.
Love, why do you permit
your highest favor, beauty,
to be taken away
from one who enjoys and wants it,   10
and given to foolish people?
Oh, remake her to be
inwardly merciful and so ugly outwardly
that she'll fall in love with me, and I'll dislike her.

Madrigal, ca. 1536–46 (TC no. 364r). Similar to no. 147 in its vengeful outcry against a
heartless woman (not, probably, Vittoria Colonna, who *was* responsive to him). The tone of
lines 12–14 recalls the close of Dante's canzone *Così nel mio parlar.*

—Deh dimmi, Amor, se l'alma di costei
fusse pietosa com'ha bell'il volto,
s'alcun saria sì stolto
ch'a sé non si togliessi e dessi a lei?
E io, che più potrei 5
servirla, amarla, se mi fuss'amica,
che, sendomi nemica,
l'amo più c'allor far non doverrei?
    —Io dico che fra voi, potenti dei,
convien c'ogni riverso si sopporti. 10
Poi che sarete morti,
di mille 'ngiurie e torti,
amando te com'or di lei tu ardi,
far ne potrai giustamente vendetta.
Ahimè, lasso chi pur tropp' aspetta 15
ch'i' gionga a' suoi conforti tanto tardi!
Ancor, se ben riguardi,
un generoso, alter e nobil core
perdon' e porta a chi l'offend' amore.

—Pray tell me, Love: If that woman's soul
were as merciful as her face is beautiful,
would anyone be so foolish
not to take himself from himself, to give to her?
Yet what more could I do 5
to serve and love her if she were my friend,
since now, while she's my enemy,
I love her more than I ever could do then?
    —O powerful gods! I tell you that, among you,
every adversity must be tolerated. 10
But after you are dead,
and she loves you as you now burn for her,
you will be able to take
your just revenge for her thousand wrongs and insults.
Alas, how weary is he who waits unhappily 15
for me to reach and comfort him so late!

And yet, if he sees rightly,
a generous and proud and noble heart
pardons and bears love for the one who hurts him.

Madrigal, ca. 1534–43; cf. no. 146. The two parts were often cited as if independent poems (GD p. 44; Varchi, *Lezzioni*) and were set to music separately by Jacob Arcadelt in 1542 (see no. 93). However, they were united for publication by Luigi del Riccio and thus form a dialogue between M and Love. Moreover, without the last line of part 1, the first line of part 2 would lack a corresponding rhyme. Thus combined, the interpretation of part 1 as a political allegory, which originated with Guasti, is discredited.

4. *take himself from himself:* deprive himself of liberty or emotional independence.

9. *among you:* among mortals. Some editors read *noi* (we) rather than *voi,* but "powerful gods" seems intended here as an interjection.

12–14. The line lengths have been interchanged for clarity.

Con più certa salute
men grazia, donna, mi terrie ancor vivo;
dall'uno e l'altro rivo
degli occhi il petto sarie manco molle.
Doppia mercé mie picciola virtute   5
di tanto vince che l'adombra e tolle;
né saggio alcun ma' volle,
se non sé innalza e sprona,
di quel gioir ch'esser non può capace.
Il troppo è vano e folle;   10
ché modesta persona
d'umil fortuna ha più tranquilla pace.
Quel c'a vo' lice, a me, donna, dispiace:
chi si dà altrui, c' altrui non si prometta,
d'un superchio piacer morte n'aspetta.   15

Less grace from you, my lady,
would keep me alive with more certainty of safety,
and my breast would be less wet
by the streams that flow from one eye and the other;
your double graciousness so overcomes   5
my little strength that it eclipses and robs it.
No wise man ever wished
(if he could rise no higher)
for any joy that he's not able to bear;
too much is foolish and useless,   10
for a moderate person
gains a more tranquil peace from modest fortune.
What's permitted to you, lady, is bad for me:
for one who gives others what they do not hope for
should expect their death from an excess of delight.   15

Madrigal, probably among the early poems for Vittoria Colonna, ca. 1536–38. There are several variants; on one ms., M added a note to Luigi del Riccio, restating the poem's theme: "When someone wants only half a loaf of bread, giving him a palace is not suitable." Cf. the similar themes in nos. 149, 150.

13. *what's permitted to you:* to shower me with your love.

149

Non posso non mancar d'ingegno e d'arte
a chi mi to' la vita
con tal superchia aita,
che d'assai men mercé più se ne prende.
D'allor l'alma mie parte   5
com'occhio offeso da chi troppo splende,
e sopra me trascende
a l'impossibil mie; per farmi pari
al minor don di donna alta e serena,
seco non m'alza; e qui convien ch'impari   10
che quel ch'i' posso ingrato a lei mi mena.
Questa, di grazia piena,
n'abonda e 'nfiamma altrui d'un certo foco,
che 'l troppo con men caldo arde che 'l poco.

I can't help seeming to lack talent and art
to her who takes my life
with such excessive help
that one would get more out of much less mercy.
Although my soul departs   5
like an eye hurt by one who shines too much,
and rises up above me
to what's out of my reach, it doesn't raise me with it
to make me equal to the smallest gift
of my lofty, calm lady; from which I should learn   10
that what I *can* do leaves me unworthy of her.
This lady, full of grace,
has so much that she lights others with a limited fire,
for too much burns with less heat than does a little.

Madrigal for Vittoria Colonna, ca. 1536–46. The sense of being overpowered and rendered
unworthy in comparison with the beloved's extreme goodness and beauty is common in
Petrarch, e.g., nos. 307, 339; cf. no. 148, and no. 150.

    1. *talent* (*ingegno*): on the meaning of this term, cf. nos. 44, 84, 151, 159, 284. Cf. Dante,
Purgatorio 27:130, where Virgil bids Dante farewell: "I have brought you here with *ingegno e*

con arte"; and Petrarch, no. 308 (on trying to describe Laura), "There fails my daring, my *ingegno* and my *arte*."

2–3. *to one:* compared to one who overcomes me with her gracious attention and talent; Colonna, too, wrote poetry, and M seems to be comparing his literary skills unfavorably to hers.

6. *one who shines too much:* comparing Colonna to the sun. The image recalls a line in her own poetry, "Qual occhio fu da troppo luce offeso" (CR p. 11), and the stunned, fallen figure of Saint Paul in M's fresco of *The Conversion of St. Paul* in the Pauline Chapel (1542–45).

12–13. The phrase "full of grace" recalls the wording of the Hail Mary prayer; cf. Petrarch, no. 366, on the Virgin Mary, "where sin abounded, grace abounds."

150

Non men gran grazia, donna, che gran doglia
ancide alcun, che 'l furto a morte mena,
privo di speme e ghiacciato ogni vena,
se vien subito scampo che 'l discioglia.
    Simil se tuo mercé, più che ma' soglia,   5
nella miseria mie d'affanni piena,
con superchia pietà mi rasserena,
par, più che 'l pianger, la vita mi toglia.
    Così n'avvien di novell'aspra o dolce:
ne' lor contrari è morte in un momento,   10
onde s'allarga o troppo stringe 'l core.
    Tal tuo beltà, c'Amore e 'l ciel qui folce,
se mi vuol vivo affreni il gran contento,
c'al don superchio debil virtù muore.

Great mercy, my lady, no less than great pain
can kill someone who's brought to death for theft,
if, devoid of hope and frozen in every vein,
a pardon that sets him free comes unexpectedly.
    Likewise, if your grace, greater than I'm used to   5
in my miserable life, so full of troubles,
should quiet me with an excessive mercy,
then it seems to take my life more than my tears do.
    The same happens to us from harsh or sweet news:
from both, though opposite, comes instant death,   10
since the heart either swells or contracts too much.
    So if your beauty, which Love and heaven sustain here,
wants me to live, let it curb its great pleasure,
for from excessive gifts frail strength dies.

Sonnet for Vittoria Colonna, similar to nos. 148 and 149; probably early in their friendship, ca. 1536–40.

    1. *great pain:* execution, death.

    3. *frozen in every vein:* by fear of death.

    11. Good news makes the heart burst with excitement; bad news crushes it with sadness.

    12. *here:* on earth.

    13. *its great pleasure:* the pleasure it gives me.

Non ha l'ottimo artista alcun concetto
c'un marmo solo in sé non circonscriva
col suo superchio, e solo a quello arriva
la man che ubbidisce all'intelletto.

   Il mal ch'io fuggo, e 'l ben ch'io mi prometto,   5
in te, donna leggiadra, altera e diva,
tal si nasconde; e perch'io più non viva,
contraria ho l'arte al disïato effetto.

   Amor dunque non ha, né tua beltate
o durezza o fortuna o gran disdegno   10
del mio mal colpa, o mio destino o sorte;

   se dentro del tuo cor morte e pietate
porti in un tempo, e che 'l mio basso ingegno
non sappia, ardendo, trarne altro che morte.

Not even the best of artists has any conception
that a single marble block does not contain
within its excess, and *that* is only attained
by the hand that obeys the intellect.

   The pain I flee from and the joy I hope for   5
are similarly hidden in you, lovely lady,
lofty and divine; but, to my mortal harm,
my art gives results the reverse of what I wish.

   Love, therefore, cannot be blamed for my pain,
nor can your beauty, your hardness, or your scorn,   10
nor fortune, nor my destiny, nor chance,

   if you hold both death and mercy in your heart
at the same time, and my lowly wits, though burning,
cannot draw from it anything but death.

Sonnet, ca. 1538–44, among M's best known and most important for his revelations of
Neoplatonic artistic theory. It was highly praised by Varchi, who made it the principal text of
his first *Lezzione* on M's poetry and artistic ideas, delivered to the Florentine Academy in
March 1547; M in turn thanked Varchi warmly for speaking so highly of this and other poems
(C. MCXLIII; R. 343). Vasari later printed part of the poem in his Life of M (VM 7:274; VB p.

422). The "lady" is undoubtedly Vittoria Colonna, although neither Varchi nor Vasari mentions her by name in this connection.

1–4. These lines express M's sculptural theory of subtraction, by which the artist physically removes excess outer mass in order to reveal the preexisting form-idea already present within; the term *concetto*, "conception," is complex and of central importance in Neoplatonic and Cinquecento art theory (see Introduction and Summers, 203–33). Several poems expound on the basic theme that this conception, or mental inspiration, precedes and guides the physical labor of carving: cf. nos. 38, 62, 144, 152, 236, 241, 275. Similarly, M wrote that "one paints with the head and not with the hands" (C. MI; R. 227), and expressed the same ideas to Francisco de Hollanda.

3. *that:* that conception.

8. That is, I lack the necessary degree of skill to bring out of you the joy I desire and instead can only find unhappiness.

13. *ingegno* (here "wits") is another term with subtle ramifications in contemporary art theory, combining both "skill" and "mind" (see Summers); cf. nos. 44, 84, 149, 159, 284.

Awakening Slave. Marble sculpture, ca. 1520–23. Florence, Galleria dell'Accademia.

152

Sì come per levar, donna, si pone
in pietra alpestra e dura
una viva figura,
che là più cresce u' più la pietra scema;
tal alcun'opre buone,   5
per l'alma che pur trema,
cela il superchio della propria carne
co' l'inculta sua cruda e dura scorza.
Tu pur dalle mie streme
parti puo' sol levarne,   10
ch'in me non è di me voler né forza.

Just as, by taking away, lady, one puts
into hard and alpine stone
a figure that's alive
and that grows larger wherever the stone decreases,
so too are any good deeds   5
of the soul that still trembles
concealed by the excess mass of its own flesh,
which forms a husk that's coarse and crude and hard.
You alone can still take them out
from within my outer shell,   10
for I haven't the will or strength within myself.

Madrigal, ca. 1538–44, for Vittoria Colonna. The sculpture metaphor is similar to no. 151, but the roles are reversed: there the sculptor chisels her; here he hopes she will cut through his physical limitations to reveal his inner goodness; cf. no. 46. In a well-known letter to Benedetto Varchi, M defined the art of sculpture as "that which is made by the action of taking away [levare]" (C. MLXXXII; R. 280).

2–3. Cf. nos. 239, 241.

6. *trembles:* fears for its future salvation, the motive for performing good deeds.

153

Non pur d'argento o d'oro
vinto dal foco esser po' piena aspetta,
vota d'opra prefetta,
la forma, che sol fratta il tragge fora;
tal io, col foco ancora   5
d'amor dentro ristoro
il desir voto di beltà infinita,
di coste' ch'i' adoro,
anima e cor della mie fragil vita.
Alta donna e gradita   10
in me discende per sì brevi spazi,
c'a trarla fuor convien mi rompa e strazi.

It's not only the mold
that, empty of finished work, waits to be filled
with fired silver or gold,
and which these can only be drawn from when it's shattered.
I, too, with the fire of love   5
refill the inner void
of my desire for infinite beauty,
for her whom I adore,
the soul and the heart of my fragile life.
But this noble and welcome lady   10
pours down into me through such narrow spaces
that to draw her out I must be torn and broken.

Madrigal for Vittoria Colonna, ca. 1536–42. Similar to nos. 151 and 152 in its sculptural metaphor, though here the image of the mold is taken not from marble carving but from bronze casting. Although M much preferred stone, he did cast a colossal bronze statue of Pope Julius II for Bologna in 1506 (later destroyed) and a bronze Hercules sent to France in 1508 (now lost).

3. *fired:* literally, "conquered by fire," i.e., molten.

11. *such narrow spaces:* the eyes, but also continuing the imagery of casting, in which molten metal is poured into the mold through narrow pipes.

154

Tanto sopra me stesso
mi fai, donna, salire,
che non ch'i' 'l possa dire,
nol so pensar, perch'io non son più desso.
Dunche, perché più spesso,   5
se l'alie tuo mi presti,
non m'alzo e volo al tuo leggiadro viso,
e che con teco resti,
se dal ciel n'è concesso
ascender col mortale in paradiso?   10
Se non ch'i' sia diviso
dall'alma per tuo grazia, e che quest'una
fugga teco suo morte, è mie fortuna.

You make me rise, my lady,
so far above myself
that I can't express, or even
imagine it, for I'm no longer myself.
Since you lend me your wings,   5
why, then, don't I lift up
and fly more often to your lovely face,
and why can't I stay with you,
if we're allowed by heaven
to ascend to paradise with our mortal part?   10
Nonetheless, it's my good fortune
that by your grace I'm separated from my soul,
and that it, remaining with you, can escape its death.

Madrigal for Vittoria Colonna, ca. 1536–40.

3–4. Cf. Dante, *Paradiso* 1:5–6.

9–10. Christian doctrine holds out the hope of bodily resurrection, but only at the Last Judgment (the fresco of which M was painting at this time). In the meantime, as M concludes, it is better to be spiritually uplifted by Colonna's example and, though necessarily leaving the earthly body behind, to find salvation for the soul.

155

Le grazie tua e la fortuna mia
hanno, donna, sì vari
gli effetti, perch'i' 'mpari
in fra 'l dolce e l'amar qual mezzo sia.
Mentre benigna e pia   5
dentro, e di fuor ti mostri
quante se' bella al mie 'rdente desire,
la fortun' aspra e ria,
nemica a' piacer nostri,
con mille oltraggi offende 'l mie gioire;   10
se per avverso po' di tal martire,
si piega alle mie voglie,
tuo pietà mi si toglie.
Fra 'l riso e 'l pianto, en sì contrari stremi,
mezzo non è c'una gran doglia scemi.   15

Your favors and my destiny, my lady,
have such shifting effects
that I must try to find
a middle way between sweetness and bitterness.
When you show my burning desire   5
how kind and merciful
you are within, and how beautiful without,
then harsh and wicked destiny,
the enemy of our pleasures,
attacks my joy with a thousand injuries;   10
if then, in a reversal of such suffering,
it gives in to my wishes,
your mercy's denied to me.
Between laughter and tears, such opposite extremes,
there's no middle way that can lessen my great pain.   15

Madrigal, often placed among those for Vittoria Colonna, but with little firm evidence for date or addressee; a second version, recasting the poem as an incomplete sonnet, was published separately by Guasti (pp. 73, 264). The emphasis on contrast of opposites is Petrarchan in inspiration. Cf. no. 157.

156

A l'alta tuo lucente dïadema
per la strada erta e lunga,
non è, donna, chi giunga,
s'umiltà non v'aggiugni e cortesia:
il montar cresce, e 'l mie valore scema,   5
e la lena mi manca a mezza via.
Che tuo beltà pur sia
superna, al cor par che diletto renda,
che d'ogni rara altezza è ghiotto e vago:
po' per gioir della tuo leggiadria   10
bramo pur che discenda
là dov'aggiungo. E 'n tal pensier m'appago,
se 'l tuo sdegno presago,
per basso amare e alto odiar tuo stato,
a te stessa perdona il mie peccato.   15

There is no one, my lady, who can reach
your lofty, shining diadem
over the long steep road,
if you don't add to it humility and kindness;
the ascent increases, and my strength grows weak,   5
and I'm short of breath halfway along the route.
That your beauty should still be
celestial, seems to give joy to my heart,
which greedily longs for all things rare and lofty;
but then, for me to enjoy your loveliness,   10
I still yearn for you to descend
to where I can reach you. And this thought consoles me
when I foresee your anger
for loving your state when low, hating it when high:
that you may pardon yourself for my sin.   15

Madrigal, probably for Vittoria Colonna, ca. 1538–42; at the bottom of the autograph M
wrote, "To be revised by day." The imagery of climbing toward a celestial lady recalls Dante's
ascent through Purgatory to Beatrice.

2. *diadem:* the crown of your beauty.

4. Unless you lower yourself within reach.

13–15. I imagine you will be angry at my inconsistency, since I love your beauty for being near me and resent it when it stays above me and out of reach; but I trust that in your understanding you will realize it is love for you that makes me commit this sin. Cf. Petrarch no. 236, "make her pardon herself for my sins."

157

Pietosa e dolce aita
tuo, donna, teco insieme,
per le mie parte streme
spargon dal cor gli spirti della vita,
onde l'alma, impedita   5
del suo natural corso
pel subito gioir, da me diparti.
Po' l'aspra tuo partita,
per mie mortal soccorso,
tornan superchi al cor gli spirti sparti.   10
S'a me veggio tornarti,
dal cor di nuovo dipartir gli sento;
onde d'equal tormento
e l'aita e l'offesa mortal veggio:
el mezzo, a chi troppo ama, è sempre il peggio.   15

Your merciful and sweet help,
together with you, lady,
spill the spirits of my life
out of my heart and through my outer shell,
so that my soul, obstructed   5
from its natural course
by unexpected joy, takes leave of me.
Then, at your harsh departure,
the dispersed spirits return
in excess to my heart, to my fatal relief;   10
if I see you return to me,
I feel them leaving my heart once again.
Therefore, with equal torture,
I look upon both help and hurt as fatal:
the middle, to one who loves too much, is worst.   15

Madrigal, ca. 1542–46, with a theme similar to no. 155. M sent one version to Luigi del Riccio with a note: "This is for the trout; the sonnet I told you about will be for the pepper, which is worth less; but I can't write." The sonnet in question may be no. 159.

1–4. When you are with me, the exaltation of your affection causes my spirits (in the sense of humors, bodily fluids) to flow outward toward you.

9–10. The return of my vital spirits is fatal because its suddenness and intensity overwhelms my heart.

15. *the middle:* the continual suspension between alternating joy and suffering, which is worse than the certainty of either love or indifference.

158

Amor, la morte a forza
del pensier par mi scacci,
e con tal grazia impacci
l'alma che, senza, sarie più contenta.
Caduto è 'l frutto e secca è già la scorza,   5
e quel, già dolce, amaro or par ch'i' senta;
anzi, sol mi tormenta,
nell'ultim'ore e corte,
infinito piacere in breve spazio.
Sì, tal mercé, spaventa   10
tuo pietà tardi e forte,
c'al corpo è morte, e al diletto strazio;
ond'io pur ti ringrazio
in questa età: ché s'i' muoio in tal sorte,
tu 'l fai più con mercé che con la morte.   15

Love, you seem to drive death
out of my thoughts by force,
and with such grace you hobble
my soul, which would be happier without it.
The fruit is fallen, and now its husk is dry,   5
and what once tasted sweet now seems bitter to me;
what's more, in my last, brief hours,
I can only feel tormented
by infinite pleasure in so short a time.
With such a gift, your mercy,   10
late and strong, terrifies me so
that it's death to my body, and torture to my joy.
And yet, I thank you for it
at this age: for if I die from such a fate,
you do it more with kindness than with death.   15

Madrigal of uncertain date, before 1542.

4. *without it:* i.e., my soul would be better off if it *could* meditate on death.

5. The fruit may symbolize both M's own aged body and the fruit of love.

6. *sweet . . . bitter:* cf. nos. 17, 76.

9. *so short a time:* the short time left to me of my life.

15. Understood: "at least it is some comfort to me that" you do it.

Per esser manco, alta signora, indegno
del don di vostra immensa cortesia,
prima, all'incontro a quella, usar la mia
con tutto il cor volse 'l mie basso ingegno.

Ma visto poi, c'ascendere a quel segno   5
propio valor non è c'apra la via,
perdon domanda la mie audacia ria,
e del fallir più saggio ognor divegno.

E veggio ben com'erra s'alcun crede
la grazia, che da voi divina piove,   10
pareggi l'opra mia caduca e frale.

L'ingegno, l'arte, la memoria cede:
c'un don celeste non con mille pruove
pagar del suo può già chi è mortale.

In order, lofty lady, to be less unworthy
of the gift of your immense graciousness,
on first encountering it, my lowly genius
wanted to use my own with all my heart.

But now that I've seen that my own worth can't open   5
a path for me to rise up to that standard,
my guilty audacity asks for your pardon,
and I'll grow ever wiser from my failure.

And I see clearly how anyone's mistaken
who believes the grace that rains down from divine you   10
could be equalled by my feeble and fleeting work.

Genius, and art, and memory give up:
for one who's mortal can't, from himself, repay
a heavenly gift, even with a thousand tries.

Sonnet for Vittoria Colonna, of uncertain date, ca. 1538–41; several variants passed between M and Giannotti for correction. Beneath M's autograph is a draft letter to Colonna (C. CMLXXXIII; R. 201) which parallels the theme of the poem. He alludes to unspecified gifts from the Marchesa and offers to expiate his sense of unworthiness to receive them by a return gift of his own art (cf. no. 161 and his similar sentiments about works given to Tommaso de'

Cavalieri, C. DCCCXCIX, R. 191, and poem no. 79). Three works for her are recorded, all on religious subjects appropriate to their spiritual relationship: a *Pietà* (generally considered to be the drawing in the Gardner Museum, Boston, TC no. 426r); a *Christ on the Cross* (generally considered to be the version in the British Museum, London, TC no. 411r); and a *Christ and the Woman of Samaria,* now lost but known through engravings (VM 7:275; see also Ramsden, appendix 26).

3–4. My unworthy mind wanted to reciprocate your graciousness with some product of my talents.

3, 12. *genius:* for the meaning of *ingegno,* see nos. 44, 84, 149, 151, 284.

11. *work:* presumably, given the context, his artwork, though the pair also exchanged poems.

12. Cf. Dante, *Paradiso* 33:56–57.

13. Cf. Dante, *Paradiso* 7:100–102, in which Beatrice explains how man was cut off by original sin from "being able to give satisfaction by himself."

S'alcun legato è pur dal piacer molto,
come da morte altrui tornare in vita,
qual cosa è che po' paghi tanta aita,
che renda il debitor libero e sciolto?

    E se pur fusse, ne sarebbe tolto   5
il soprastar d'una mercé infinita
al ben servito, onde sarie 'mpedita
da l'incontro servire, a quella volto.

    Dunche, per tener alta vostra grazia,
donna, sopra 'l mie stato, in me sol bramo   10
ingratitudin più che cortesia:

    ché dove l'un dell'altro al par si sazia,
non mi sare' signor quel che tant'amo:
ché 'n parità non cape signoria.

If one is truly bound by a great favor,
such as bringing someone back from death to life,
is there anything that could repay such help
and give the debtor freedom and release?

    And even if there were, the one well served   5
would be robbed of having hover over him
an infinite mercy, which thus would be deprived
of service in return, from one who turns to it.

    Therefore, lady, in order to keep your grace
high over my lowly state, I long to feel   10
only ingratitude rather than kindness.

    For if each satisfied the other equally,
the one I love so much would not be my lord:
for in equality there's no room for lordship.

Sonnet for Vittoria Colonna, ca. 1538–41, thematically related to no. 159: there he lamented his inferiority to her; here he goes further and wishes to retain it. M later used similar expressions to characterize his friendship with Luigi del Riccio, no. 252.

    2. M credits Colonna with restoring him to spiritual life.

    4–8. This quatrain is obscure; its central point is that to discharge his debt would be undesirable for both parties, since that would remove his inspiration to continue serving her.

    12–13. Although the addressee is clearly female, M switches here to referring to her as "lord" (*signor*); cf. his description of Colonna as "a man within a woman," no. 235, or his writing to her as an *amico* ("friend," masculine; C. MCXLVII; R. 347).

Per qual mordace lima
discresce e manca ognor tuo stanca spoglia,
anima inferma? or quando fie ti scioglia
da quella il tempo, e torni ov'eri, in cielo,
candida e lieta prima,   5
deposto il periglioso e mortal velo?
Ch'ancor ch'i' cangi 'l pelo
per gli ultim'anni e corti,
cangiar non posso il vecchio mie antico uso,
che con più giorni più mi sforza e preme.   10
Amore, a te nol celo,
ch'i' porto invidia a' morti,
sbigottito e confuso,
sì di sé meco l'alma trema e teme.
Signor, nell'ore streme,   15
stendi ver' me le tuo pietose braccia,
tomm'a me stesso e famm'un che ti piaccia.

From what sharp, biting file
does your tired skin keep growing thin and failing,
O ailing soul? When will time release you from it,
so you'll return to heaven, where you were
pure and joyful before,   5
your dangerous and mortal veil cast off?
For even if I change my hide
in my final brief years,
I cannot change my old established habits,
which, as more days pass, weigh down and compel me more.   10
Love, I won't hide it from you
that I envy the dead,
being so confused and terrified
that my soul, while with me, trembles and fears for itself.
O Lord, in my last hours,   15
stretch out toward me your merciful arms,
take me from myself and make me one who'll please you.

Madrigal, ca. 1538–41. The description of M's body as a deteriorating skin that must be sloughed off like a molting snake also appears in nos. 33, 51, and 94, though the metaphor is here complicated by the image of the sculptor's file. Alongside the autograph is the opening line of a letter to Vittoria Colonna, the full text of which is written next to no. 162 (C. CMLXVII; R. 202). This letter mentions M's *Crucifixion* (one of M's works for Colonna, which she apparently asked Cavalieri to return to him, to M's annoyance; see no. 159); lines 15–16 of the poem parallel the visual image of Christ stretching out his arms on the cross (cf. nos. 285, 290).

1–2. Cf. Dante, DC no. 103:22–26.

5. *before:* prior to descending to earth and taking on the burden of a mortal body.

6. *mortal veil:* cf. nos. 106, 188, 209, 215, 227.

9. A common lament of M's; cf. nos. 130, 131, 133.

11. *Love:* God, divine love.

12. Cf. Dante, *Vita nuova* 34:13, "I am envious of anyone who dies."

14. My soul, as long as it remains within my corrupt body, fears for its salvation.

17. Cf. Dante, *Paradiso* 31:88–90.

Ora in sul destro, ora in sul manco piede
variando, cerco della mie salute.
Fra 'l vizio e la virtute
il cor confuso mi travaglia e stanca,
come chi 'l ciel non vede,   5
che per ogni sentier si perde e manca.
Porgo la carta bianca
a' vostri sacri inchiostri,
c'amor mi sganni e pietà 'l ver ne scriva:
che l'alma, da sé franca,   10
non pieghi agli error nostri
mie breve resto, e che men cieco viva.
Chieggio a voi, alta e diva
donna, saper se 'n ciel men grado tiene
l'umil peccato che 'l superchio bene.   15

Now on the right foot and now on the left,
shifting back and forth, I search for my salvation.
Between virtue and vice,
my bewildered heart distresses and wearies me;
I'm like one who can't see heaven,   5
who gets lost on every path and misses his goal.
I offer my blank page
to your sacred ink, so that
love's deceptions may vanish and mercy may write the truth;
that my soul, freed from itself,   10
may not subject to our errors
the little that's left me, and I may live less blind.
I beg to know from you,
high and godly lady, whether humbled sin
holds a lower rank in heaven than sheer good.   15

Madrigal for Vittoria Colonna, ca. 1538–41; for the letter to her written alongside the draft of this poem, see no. 161.

1–3. *right, left*: symbolically, virtue and vice, as line 3 makes clear. *between virtue and vice* echoes the dilemma of Hercules, forced to choose at a crossroads between two allegorical figures representing the paths of virtue and vice. The parable, originating in Xenophon, was illustrated by Albrecht Dürer ca. 1496.

5. *one who can't see heaven:* one who does not have heaven to guide him, who has lost sight of spiritual comfort.

7–8. *your sacred ink:* M felt himself dependent on Colonna's inspirational poetry and letters for spiritual guidance; cf. the "blank sheet" of no. 111:12.

12. *the little that's left me:* the short time remaining to me in this life.

14–15. As in the biblical parable of the lost lamb, M hopes that heaven will look at least as kindly on a penitent sinner as on someone whose life has been entirely free from sin.

Quante più fuggo e odio ognor me stesso,
tanto a te, donna, con verace speme
ricorro; e manco teme
l'alma di me, quant'a te son più presso.
A quel che 'l ciel promesso   5
m'ha nel tuo volto aspiro
e ne' begli occhi, pien d'ogni salute:
e ben m'accorgo spesso,
in quel c'ogni altro miro,
che gli occhi senza 'l cor non han virtute.   10
Luci già mai vedute!
né da vederle è men che 'l gran desio;
ché 'l veder raro è prossimo a l'oblio.

The more I keep hating and fleeing from myself,
the more I run to you for help, my lady,
with honest hope; and my soul
fears for me less, the more I'm close to you.
What heaven has promised me,   5
I aspire to in your face,
and in you fair eyes, full of all salvation;
and often I realize clearly,
when I look at all the others,
that eyes, without the heart, possess no power. 10
O lights that are never seen,
or seen less than my great desire would wish!
For seldom seeing is the next thing to forgetting.

Madrigal for Vittoria Colonna, perhaps during one of her absences in Viterbo; written on the back of the final copy of no. 162. One of M's most elaborate glosses on the Dantesque-Petrarchan theme of the spiritual power of the beloved's eyes.

4. *fears for me:* for my salvation.

10. Beautiful eyes alone cannot captivate the viewer unless they embody the feelings of a noble soul.

13. Cf. A26, "for one who's not seen cannot be well loved."

Per fido esemplo alla mia vocazione
nel parto mi fu data la bellezza,
che d'ambo l'arti m'è lucerna e specchio.
S'altro si pensa, è falsa opinione.
Questo sol l'occhio porta a quella altezza   5
c'a pingere e scolpir qui m'apparecchio.
 S'e' giudizi temerari e sciocchi
al senso tiran la beltà, che muove
e porta al cielo ogni intelletto sano,
dal mortale al divin non vanno gli occhi   10
infermi, e fermi sempre pur là d'ove
ascender senza grazia è pensier vano.

As a trustworthy model for my vocation,
at birth I was given the ideal of beauty,
which is the lamp and mirror of both my arts.
If any think otherwise, that opinion's wrong:
for this alone can raise the eye to that height   5
which I am preparing here to paint and sculpt.
 Even though rash and foolish minds derive
beauty (which moves every sound mind
and carries it to heaven) from the senses,
unsound eyes can't move from the mortal to the divine,   10
and in fact are fixed forever in that place
from which to rise without grace is a vain thought.

Two *sestine* for Vittoria Colonna, ca. 1541–44, probably from the same period as no. 165, expounding the Neoplatonic theory of anagogy, through which one is led upward from earthly to divine beauty. For the quasi-astrological notion of receiving certain sensibilities at birth, cf. nos. 97, 104, 119, 173.

3. *both my arts:* painting and sculpture.

5. *that height:* to that lofty conception of beauty and grace that constitutes the ideal forms of Platonic thought.

10. *unsound eyes:* eyes trapped and misled by the merely physical aspect of beauty; *infermi* (sick) contrasts with *sano* (healthy, sound) in line 9.

Se 'l commodo degli occhi alcun constringe
con l'uso, parte insieme
la ragion perde, e teme;
ché più s'inganna quel c'a sé più crede:
onde nel cor dipinge 5
per bello quel c'a picciol beltà cede.
Ben vi fo, donna, fede
che 'l commodo né l'uso non m'ha preso,
sì di raro e' mie veggion gli occhi vostri
circonscritti ov' a pena il desir vola. 10
Un punto sol m'ha acceso,
né più vi vidi c'una volta sola.

If someone forces comfort on his eyes
by habit, he both loses
his judgment and fears for it,
for one's more deceived the more he trusts himself;
and thus, in his heart, he paints 5
as beautiful that which yields to a little beauty.
I swear to you, my lady,
that neither comfort nor habit has overcome me,
since so rarely do my eyes see yours,
confined where desire can fly only with effort. 10
A single moment enflamed me,
and I've not seen you more than just that once.

Madrigal, ca. 1541–44 (see no. 164).

1–2. If one accustoms himself to the pleasure of looking frequently upon his beloved.

6. *that which yields:* is, in reality, less beautiful than.

8. *neither comfort nor habit:* of seeing you.

9–10. A possible reference to the period when Colonna withdrew to a convent at Viterbo, 1541–44.

11. *A single moment:* Dante uses this expression several times to refer to the dramatic moment (or "point") at which one is overpowered by divine beauty or love, e.g., *Paradiso* 30:11, 33:94–96; and in *Inferno* 5:130–33, where Paolo and Francesca speak of the sudden overflowing of their passion.

Ben posson gli occhi mie presso e lontano
veder dov'apparisce il tuo bel volto;
ma dove loro, ai pie', donna, è ben tolto
portar le braccia e l'una e l'altra mano.

L'anima, l'intelletto intero e sano   5
per gli occhi ascende più libero e sciolto
a l'alta tuo beltà; ma l'ardor molto
non dà tal previlegio al corp' umano

grave e mortal, sì che mal segue poi,
senz'ali ancor, d'un'angioletta il volo,   10
e 'l veder sol pur se ne gloria e loda.

Deh, se tu puo' nel ciel quante tra noi,
fa' del mie corpo tutto un occhio solo;
né fie poi parte in me che non ti goda.

My eyes can easily see your beautiful face
wherever it appears, near or far away;
but my feet, lady, are prevented from bearing
my arms or either hand to that same place.

The soul, the intellect complete and sound,   5
more free and unfettered, can rise through the eyes
up to your lofty beauty; but great ardor
gives no such privilege to the human body,

which, weighed down and mortal, and still lacking wings,
can hardly follow the flight of a little angel;   10
so sight alone can take pride and pleasure in doing so.

If you have as much power in heaven as here among us,
make my whole body nothing but an eye:
let there be no part of me that can't enjoy you.

Sonnet for Vittoria Colonna, ca. 1541–44. Benedetto Varchi cited lines 1–2 (in an earlier version) and 5–8 in his *Lezzioni* and praised this as "one of his weightiest sonnets." The underlying Neoplatonic metaphor recalls Ficino's passage, "If the eye knows it, only the eye enjoys it; therefore only the eye enjoys bodily beauty" (*Sopra lo amore*, chap. 9).

4. *my arms or either hand:* i.e., so that I might embrace you.

11. That is, only the eyes can follow her.

167

La morte, Amor, del mie medesmo loco,
del qual, già nudo, trïonfar solevi
non che con l'arco e co' pungenti strali,
ti scaccia e sprezza, e col fier ghiaccio il foco
tuo dolce ammorza, c'ha dì corti e brevi.   5
In ogni cor veril men di le' vali;
e se ben porti l'ali,
con esse mi giugnesti, or fuggi e temi,
c'ogni età verde è schifa a' giorni stremi.

Death scorns you, Love, and chases you away
from that very place in me where you used to triumph,
not only with your bow and piercing arrows,
but even naked; and with its fierce ice damps
your sweet fire, which has but few and fleeting days.   5
In grown men's hearts you have less power than he;
and even though you have wings,
where you once reached me with them, now you flee in fear:
for all of green youth is hateful to our last days.

Madrigal, ca. 1541–44. Beneath the autograph sent to Luigi del Riccio is the dedicatory phrase, "For last night's duck."

 4–5. *ice . . . fire:* a common Petrarchan antithesis; cf. nos. 168, 171.

 9. Love, like everything associated with youth, "the green age" (for this expression cf. nos. 142, 253, 283), is found repugnant in extreme old age.

Perché 'l mezzo di me che dal ciel viene
a quel con gran desir ritorna e vola,
restando in una sola
di beltà donna, e ghiaccio ardendo in lei,
in duo parte mi tiene   5
contrarie sì, che l'una all'altra invola
il ben che non diviso aver devrei.
Ma se già ma' costei
cangia 'l suo stile, e c'a l'un mezzo manchi
il ciel, quel mentre c'a le' grato sia,   10
e' mie sì sparsi e stanchi
pensier fien tutti in quella donna mia;
e se 'lor che m'è pia,
l'alma il ciel caccia, almen quel tempo spero
non più mezz'esser, ma suo tutto intero.   15

Because the half of me that comes from heaven
wings its way back there with a great desire,
my staying in a single
woman of beauty, and burning in her ice,
keeps me split in two halves   5
so opposite that each one robs the other
of the good I should be having undivided.
But if she should ever change
her attitude, and one half of me lose
heaven as long as I am welcome to her,   10
my scattered, tired thoughts
would all be gathered in that lady of mine.
And if, when she's kind to me,
heaven drives away my soul, at least for that time
I hope to be hers, no longer halfway, but wholly.   15

Madrigal, ca. 1541–46. Three distinct versions survive, which M may have intended to publish as independent poems (see Frey, nos. 109:66, 69, 70; Girardi, no. 168n).

   1. That is, my soul.

   4. *burning in her ice:* or "burning like ice in her." Cf. nos. 167, 171.

   8–9. *changes her attitude:* begins to act more mercifully toward me.

Nel mie 'rdente desio,
coste' pur mi trastulla,
di fuor pietosa e nel cor aspra e fera.
Amor, non tel diss'io,
ch'e' no' ne sare' nulla   5
e che 'l suo perde chi 'n quel d'altri spera?
Or s'ella vuol ch'i' pèra,
mie colpa, e danno s'ha prestarle fede,
com'a chi poco manca a chi più crede.

  Even as I burn with desire
this woman toys with me,
outwardly kind but harsh and fierce of heart.
Didn't I tell you, Love,
that nothing would come of it,   5
that in hoping for something from others, one loses what's his?
So if now she wants me to die,
it's my fault, and harm, for having put faith in her,
since one who's believed too much is little to blame.

Madrigal, ca. 1542–6. In his postscript to Luigi del Riccio, M notes, "This is truly a scribble.
My best to you." See no. 170.

  5. *it:* my passion for her.
  9. That is, it's not her fault if I put more faith in her than I should have.

Spargendo gran bellezza ardente foco
per mille cori accesi,
come cosa è che pesi,
c'un solo ancide, a molti è lieve e poco.
Ma, chiuso in picciol loco,   5
s'il sasso dur calcina,
che l'acque poi il dissolvon 'n un momento,
come per pruova il sa chi 'l ver dicerne;
così d'una divina
de mille il foco ho drento   10
c'arso m'ha 'l cor nelle mie parte interne;
ma le lacrime etterne
se quel dissolvon già sì duro e forte,
fie me' null'esser c'arder senza morte.

Great beauty, strewing flaming fire over
a thousand kindled hearts,
is like a heavy weight
that, small and light on many, kills one alone.
But as, shut in a small space,   5
it turns hard rock to lime,
which water can then dissolve within an instant
(as those who can judge the truth know from experience),
so I have the fire of thousands
for this divine woman in me,   10
which, deep within me, has burned up my heart;
and if my eternal tears
dissolve that which was once so hard and strong,
it's better to be nothing than to burn without dying.

Madrigal, ca. 1542–46. Beneath the text, M appended the final version of the last line of no. 169, with the instruction to Luigi del Riccio, "Put this line at the bottom of the last scribble I sent you, because the one that's there is not suitable."

2–3. A heavy object will be fatal if it falls on a single person but not if its weight is shared by a large number of people.

5–7. The image is drawn from a limekiln, in which heat concentrated in an oven reduces hard marble to water-soluble lime for building. The metaphor derives from M's architectural interests; cf. nos. 63, 143.

Nella memoria delle cose belle
morte bisogna, per tor di costui
il volto a lei, com'a vo' tolto ha lui;
se 'l foco in ghiaccio e 'l riso volge in pianto,
con tale odio di quelle,   5
che del cor voto più non si dien vanto.
Ma se rimbotta alquanto
i suo begli occhi nell'usato loco,
fien legne secche in un ardente foco.

Into the memory of beautiful things
must come death, to take away that man's face
from your memory, as it has taken him from you,
since it turns fire to ice and laughter to tears
with such loathing of those things   5
that they may no longer strut over an empty heart.
If he put his lovely eyes,
even for a while, back in their usual place,
they'd be like dry tinder in a burning fire.

Madrigal, ca. 1542–46. Beneath the autograph is a letter to del Riccio, datable to Feb.–Mar. 1546 (C. MLVII; R. 250): "*Messer* Luigi, I beg you to send back to me the last madrigal, which you don't understand, so that I can revise it; because the bearer of my scribbles—that is, Urbino—was so eager that he didn't let me look it over. As to getting together tomorrow, I make my excuses to you with this, since the weather is bad and I have work to do at home. What we would have done tomorrow we'll do this coming Lent at Lunghezza, with a big tench [fish]."

M's compacted phrasing is difficult to translate clearly, since his distinction of overlapping references by pronoun gender cannot be matched in English. The poem is a prayer that death may compensate the dead man's loved ones for having taken him from them, by obliterating the intense memory of the man's beautiful face from the consciousness of the living, who are still readily tormented by its loss. The unspecified deceased might be Cecchino Bracci, del Riccio's nephew; see no. 179.

4. *fire to ice:* cf. nos. 167, 168.

5. By inspiring in the living a pious disdain for earthly beauty.

8. *their usual place:* in the memory of the living, where they have been for so long.

Costei pur si delibra,
indomit' e selvaggia,
ch'i' arda, mora e caggia
a quel c'a peso non sie pure un'oncia;
e 'l sangue a libra a libra   5
mi svena, e sfibra e 'l corpo all'alma sconcia.
La si gode e racconcia
nel suo fidato specchio,
ove sé vede equale al paradiso;
po', volta a me, mi concia   10
sì, c'oltr'all'esser vecchio,
in quel col mie fo più bello il suo viso,
ond'io vie più deriso
son d'esser brutto; e pur m'è gran ventura,
s'i' vinco, a farla bella, la natura.   15

   Surely she is determined,
this untamed, wild woman,
that I should burn, die, and shrink
into something that wouldn't even weigh an ounce;
she drains my blood pound by pound   5
and weakens my body, ruining it for my soul.
She enjoys herself and preens
before her trusted mirror,
where she sees herself equal to paradise;
then, turning to me, so mars me   10
that, besides being old,
my face makes hers more beautiful in there,
so that I'm mocked even more
for being ugly; yet it's my good fortune
if, by making her beautiful, I vanquish nature.   15

Madrigal, ca. 1542–46. At the end, M wrote, "I'm not setting this one down as a scribble, but as a dream [I had]." Some commentators read the poem as an allegory of art, or of the artist at work, attempting to surpass nature in the creation of beauty; but its unusually specific evocation of the "donna bella e crudele" and her actions, and the suggestion that it reports an actual dream, seem to argue for a more literal interpretation. The images of harsh and hurtful love recall Dante, e.g., DR nos. II, CXVI.

4. *into something:* alternatively, "for the sake of something" (i.e., her favor).

10–11. *so mars me that:* makes me so much uglier (by humiliating me with her scorn) that . . .

12. *in there:* in her mirror. For the image of a mirror betraying his ugliness, cf. no. 51.

15. *I vanquish nature:* similar to the theme of art's power to defeat nature; cf. nos. 97, 239.

Se dal cor lieto divien bello il volto,
dal tristo il brutto; e se donna aspra e bella
il fa, chi fie ma' quella
che non arda di me com'io di lei?
Po' c'a destinguer molto   5
dalla mie chiara stella
da bello a bel fur fatti gli occhi mei,
contr'a sé fa costei
non men crudel che spesso
dichi: —Dal cor mie smorto il volto viene.—   10
Che s'altri fa se stesso,
pingendo donna, in quella
che farà poi, se sconsolato il tiene?
Dunc'ambo n'arien bene
ritrarla col cor lieto e 'l viso asciutto   15
sé farie bella e me non farie brutto.

If the face grows beautiful from a happy heart,
and ugly from a sad one, what will become
of a harsh yet lovely woman
who will not burn for me as I do for her?
For, since my bright star made   5
my eyes quite capable
of distinguishing one beauty from another,
that woman is no less cruel
to herself when she often makes
me say, "On account of my heart my face grows dreary."   10
For if one portrays himself
in painting a woman, then what
will he make of her, if she keeps him unconsoled?
So we'd both do well if I
could draw her with my heart happy and my face dry: 15
she'd make herself lovely, and wouldn't make me ugly.

Madrigal, ca. 1542–46; the idea that an artist makes his subject reflect his own mood is repeated in no. 242, referring to sculpture rather than painting. The autograph is written on blue-gray paper; M added as a postscript, "Divine things are spoken of in a blue field" (i.e., the heavens).

    5. *bright star:* an astrological metaphor; cf. nos. 97, 104, 119, 164.

    15. *my face dry,* i.e., without crying for unrequited love.

174

Per quel che di vo', donna, di fuor veggio,
quantunche dentro al ver l'occhio non passi,
spero a' mie stanchi e lassi
pensier riposo a qualche tempo ancora;
e 'l più saperne il peggio,   5
del vostro interno, forse al mie mal fora.
Se crudeltà dimora
'n un cor che pietà vera
co' begli occhi prometta a' pianti nostri,
ben sarebb'ora l'ora,   10
c'altro già non si spera
d'onesto amor, che quel ch'è di fuor mostri.
Donna, s'agli occhi vostri
contraria è l'alma, e io, pur contro a quella,
godo gl'inganni d'una donna bella.   15

I hope that from what I see of you outwardly,
Lady (though my eye can't reach the truth within),
my weary and wretched thoughts
can draw rest for a little while longer,
since knowing more about   5
what's inside you might make my troubles worse.
If cruelty resides
in a heart that promises
true pity on my tears with its beautiful eyes,
now would surely be the time   10
—for virtuous love can hope
for nothing else—to show what appears outside.
If your soul is opposed
to your eyes, Lady, then I, in spite of it,
will enjoy the deceptions of a lovely lady.   15

Madrigal, ca. 1542–46, with numerous alternative versions. The theme and language are similar to no. 141.

12. *to show what appears outside:* to demonstrate the kindness that you seem to offer with your eyes.

14. *it:* your unfriendly soul.

175

No' salda, Amor, de' tuo dorati strali
fra le mie vecchie ancor la minor piaga,
che la mente, presaga
del mal passato, a peggio mi traporti.
Se ne' vecchi men vali,   5
campar dovria, se non fa' guerra a' morti.
S'a l'arco l'alie porti
contra me zoppo e nudo,
con gli occhi per insegna,
c'ancidon più ch'e' tuo più feri dardi,   10
chi fia che mi conforti?
Elmo non già né scudo,
ma sol quel che mi segna
d'onor, perdendo, e biasmo a te, se m'ardi.
Debile vecchio, è tardi   15
la fuga e lenta, ov'è posto 'l mie scampo;
e chi vince a fuggir, non resti in campo.

Not even the smallest among all my old wounds
has yet healed from your gilded arrows, Love,
and already my mind
moves me from past ills to foreseeing worse ones.
Since you've less power in the old,   5
I ought to escape, unless you fight the dead.
But if you join wings to bow
against me, hobbling and naked,
under the banner of those eyes
which have more power to kill than your fiercest darts,   10
whatever will relieve me?
Surely not helmet or shield,
but only what honors me
in my defeat and shames you if you burn me.
But I'm old and weak, and my flight,   15
in which I've put hope of escape, is late and slow;
and one who wins by fleeing shouldn't stay on the field.

Madrigal, ca. 1542–46, on the recto of a sheet bearing one version of no. 174; for similar themes, cf. nos. 142, 232.

5–6. Since you have less power over the aged, I should be able to avoid further suffering, unless you attack even after death.

7. *but if,* instead of accepting your diminished power over me, *you join* your *wings to* your *bow* to reinforce your attack.

7–11. For M's repeated use of arrow images and its relation to his drawing of *Archers shooting at a herm,* see nos. 3, 22–24, 27, 77, 90, 120, 131, 137, 142, 272; cf. Dante, DR no. 103:1–13, and Petrarch, no. 3. The power of the eyes to kill is also a Petrarchan standard that recurs throughout the *Rime.*

12. Cf. Petrarch no. 95, "that blow against which neither helmet nor shield availed."

15–16. M also calls himself *old* and *slow* in nos. 125, 136.

Mestier non era all'alma tuo beltate
legar me vinto con alcuna corda;
ché, se ben mi ricorda,
sol d'uno sguardo fui prigione e preda:
c'alle gran doglie usate   5
forz'è c'un debil cor subito ceda.
Ma chi fie ma' che 'l creda,
preso da' tuo begli occhi in brevi giorni,
un legno secco e arso verde torni?

It wasn't necessary for your blessed beauty
to bind me, once defeated, with any rope,
since, if I remember well,
by a single look I was made prey and prisoner;
for a feeble heart must yield   5
immediately to great and repeated torments.
But who will ever believe
that, captured by your fair eyes, in a few days
dry and charred wood could turn green again?

Madrigal; the fair copy is written on the back of a fragment of a letter from Luigi del Riccio dated 12 April 1543. The imagery of capture and binding parallels the poems for Cavalieri, e.g., no. 98. The idea of actual ropes being unnecessary to keep someone mentally enslaved recalls the numerous Slave figures M carved for the tomb of Julius II (ca. 1508–30), which have only nominal bonds or none at all.

    9. *dry . . . wood* is M's common image for himself as an old man; cf. nos. 96, 97.

In noi vive e qui giace la divina
beltà da morte anz'il suo tempo offesa.
Se con la dritta man face' difesa,
campava. Onde nol fe'? Ch'era mancina.

Here lies the heavenly beauty, attacked by death
before her time, who still lives on in us.
If she'd fought back with her right hand, she would have
escaped. Why didn't she? She was left-handed.

This epitaph, along with no. 178, was written on the death in 1543 of Faustina Mancini Attavanti, also known as "La Mancina." Her beloved, the Modenese poet Gandolfo Porrino, sent three sonnets to M, one praising his *Last Judgment* and two requesting a portrait of the deceased (see Papini, *La vita di Michelangiolo*, 428ff.). M, who disliked portraiture, probably composed these two verses as a substitute (as he did with Cecchino Bracci; see no. 179).

2. Cf. no. 193:7.

3–4. These lines pun on her name: *mancina* means "left-handed."

La nuova alta beltà che 'n ciel terrei
unica, non c'al mondo iniquo e fello
(suo nome dal sinistro braccio tiello
il vulgo, cieco a non adorar lei),
   per voi sol nacque; e far non la saprei   5
con ferri in pietra, in carte col pennello;
ma 'l vivo suo bel viso esser può quello
nel qual vostro sperar fermar dovrei.
   E se, come dal sole ogni altra stella
è vinta, vince l'intelletto nostro,   10
per voi non di men pregio esser dovea.
   Dunche, a quetarvi, è suo beltà novella
da Dio formata all'alto desir vostro;
e quel solo, e non io, far lo potea.

The new, lofty beauty that I'd deem unique
not just in this vile, wicked world, but in heaven
(the rabble, who must have been blind not to adore her,
called her by the name of her left arm)
   was born just for you; and I could not make her   5
with tools in stone, or on paper with a brush;
besides, her living face is the only thing
with which I could put an end to your hopeful longing.
   And if she still overpowers our minds,
as every other star's overpowered by the sun,   10
she must have been of no less worth to you.
   Therefore, in order to soothe you, her new beauty
is shaped by God to fit your lofty desire;
and he alone, and not I, could have made it.

Sonnet for Gandolfo Porrino, probably in 1543, replying to his sonnet requesting a portrait of "La Mancina" (see no. 177), whose name is again used for the pun in line 3/4. M's rhyme scheme repeats Porrino's, a common device when poems were formally exchanged; the autograph draft is headed, "Reply of *Messer* Michelangelo to *Messer* Gandolfo for the poems about La Mancina." Cf. M's similar pleas when declining to sculpt a posthumous portrait of Cecchino Bracci (no. 179).

9–11. She must have seemed even more precious to you when alive and present, if the mere memory of her can still exert such a powerful effect on us (who knew her less well).

Se qui son chiusi i begli occhi e sepolti
anzi tempo, sol questo ne conforta:
che pietà di lor vivi era qua morta;
or che son morti, di lor vive in molti.

If here his beautiful eyes are closed and buried
before their time, only this can comfort us:
that pity for them was dead here while they lived,
but now that they're dead, it lives for them in many.

Nos. 179–228 constitute a single group of poems—forty-eight epitaphs in quatrain form, one madrigal (no. 192) and one sonnet (no. 193)—written at the request of M's friend Luigi del Riccio to commemorate the death of Riccio's nephew, Cecchino (Francesco) Bracci (see also no. 171). Cecchino, who died at the age of fifteen on 8 January 1544, was beloved by del Riccio and his circle for his beauty and charm. Some scholars have maintained that M himself did not know Cecchino well. However, M refers to the boy as early as 1542 and even reports dreaming about him (C. CMLXIII, MVII; R. 215, 222); moreover, M's alternative draft of no. 197 seems to indicate some greater intimacy.

Other writers, including Donato Giannotti and Giovanni Aldobrandini, and del Riccio himself, responded to the tragedy with consolatory verses (see Clements, chap. 6). Del Riccio wanted M to execute a portrait for Cecchino's tomb, and M did go so far as to promise a drawing for a medallion portrait (C. MXXV, MXXVI; R. 239). However, M generally disliked portraiture (VM 7:271–72; VB 420) and in any case was preoccupied during 1544 with painting in the Pauline Chapel and with a serious illness (see Biographical Outline). As completed in 1545, the tomb (in Santa Maria in Araceli, Rome) was largely the work of M's assistant Urbino, though clearly indebted to M's ideas (C. MXLVI; R. 259; see also nos. 193, 206). The numerous poems were in part M's attempt to mollify del Riccio for not having sculpted the portrait himself.

The series, written between January and December 1544, recapitulates in miniature many of M's favorite themes: pessimistic ideas about the inevitability of death and laments for fleeting youth and beauty are balanced by his view of death and subsequent transcendence as preferable to earthly life. The sheer number of variations on these few Petrarchan themes, occasioned by del Riccio's exhortations (and repeated gifts), leads to some repetitious and labored examples. M's frequent postscripts as he sent batches of the poems to del Riccio are often facetious or exasperated in tone.

3. *pity:* implying, perhaps, pious love or appreciation, which has increased with absence. Cf. Petrarch, no. 338, "The world did not know her while it had her."

Deh serbi, s'è di me pietate alcuna
che qui son chiuso e dal mondo disciolto,
le lacrime a bagnarsi il petto e 'l volto
per chi resta suggetto alla fortuna.

If there is anyone who takes pity on me
who am enclosed here and cut loose from the world,
let him save his tears to bathe his breast and face
for whoever still remains subject to fortune.

Epitaph for Cecchino Bracci, 1544.

—*Perché ne' volti offesi non entrasti*
dagli anni, Morte, e c'anzi tempo i' mora?
    —*Perché nel ciel non sale e non dimora*
cosa che 'nvecchi e parte il mondo guasti.

"Why, Death, did you not pass into those faces
afflicted by the years, and why should I die too soon?"
    "Because nothing can rise to heaven or dwell there
that, as it grows old, is ruined by the world."

Epitaph for Cecchino Bracci, 1544.

Non volse Morte non ancider senza
l'arme degli anni e de' superchi giorni
la beltà che qui giace, acciò c'or torni
al ciel con la non persa sua presenza.

Death wished to kill the beauty that lies here
without using his weapons of the years
and excess days, so that it can now return
to heaven without having lost its appearance.

Epitaph for Cecchino Bracci, 1544.
   1. Literally, "death did not wish not to kill."

183

La beltà che qui giace al mondo vinse
di tanto ogni più bella creatura,
che morte, ch'era in odio alla natura,
per farsi amica a lei, l'ancise e stinse.

The beauty that lies here so overpowered
all the most beautiful creatures in the world
that Death, whom Nature looked upon with hatred,
to make friends with her, killed and extinguished it.

Epitaph for Cecchino Bracci, 1544.

184

Qui son de' Bracci, deboli a l'impresa
contr'a la morte mia per non morire;
meglio era esser de' piedi per fuggire
che de' Bracci e non far da lei difesa.

Here am I, one of the Arms, too weak for the task
of struggling against my death so as not to die;
better to have been one of the Feet, to flee,
than one of the Arms, and make no defense against it.

Epitaph for Cecchino Bracci, 1544.
  1. *Arms:* a pun on Cecchino's family name, which means "arms." Cf. nos. 212, 213, 217, 222.

Qui son sepulto, e poco innanzi nato
ero: e son quello al qual fu presta e cruda
la morte sì, che l'alma di me nuda
s'accorge a pena aver cangiato stato.

Here I am buried, yet I was only born
a short time ago; I'm one to whom death was
so quick and cruel that my soul, stripped of me,
has scarcely realized it has changed its state.

Epitaph for Cecchino Bracci, 1544.

Non può per morte già chi qui mi serra
la beltà, c'al mortal mie largir volse,
renderla agli altri tutti a chi la tolse,
s'alfin com'ero de' rifarmi in terra.

He who shuts me in here can't, through death, return
the beauty he was willing to lavish on my mortal self
to all the others whom he took it from,
if at last he must make me again as I was on earth.

Epitaph for Cecchino Bracci, 1544.

M wrote a note to Luigi del Riccio with this epitaph, providing his own paraphrase and commentary:

"Your dead friend speaks, saying: 'If heaven took every beauty away from all other men in the world to make me alone beautiful, as it did; and if, by divine law, on Judgment Day I must return to being the same as I was when alive, it follows that it cannot give the beauty that it gave me back to those from whom it took it, but that I must be more beautiful than others for eternity, and they ugly.' This is the opposite of the idea you gave me yesterday; one is a fiction, and the other is the truth" (C. MXIX; R. 235).

Del Riccio must have suggested the conceit that Cecchino, when resurrected, would himself become ugly. For other references to the belief that the risen dead would be reclothed in their earthly form, see nos. 140, 227.

187

L'alma di dentro di fuor non vedea,
come noi, il volto, chiuso in questo avello:
che se nel ciel non è albergo sì bello,
trarnela morte già ma' non potea.

The soul inside could not see on the outside,
as we did, the face enclosed within this sepulcher;
yet if there weren't as fair a dwelling in heaven,
death could never have drawn it out of there.

Epitaph for Cecchino Bracci, 1544.

Se dalla morte è vinta la natura
qui nel bel volto, ancor vendetta in cielo
ne fie pel mondo, a trar divo il suo velo
più che mai bel di questa sepoltura.

If down here nature is conquered by death
in this beautiful face, it will yet take revenge
for the world in heaven, by drawing his divine veil
out of this tomb more beautiful than ever.

Epitaph for Cecchino Bracci, 1544. The sequence of victories recalls Petrarch's *Trionfi,* with its successive allegorical triumphs of Death over Love and Divine Eternity over Death.

2. *it:* nature, which will reclothe Cecchino's soul after death (at the Resurrection). For *veil* as a Neoplatonic term for the body, cf. nos. 106, 161, 209, 215, 227.

189

Qui son chiusi i begli occhi, che aperti
facén men chiari i più lucenti e santi;
or perché, morte, rendon luce a tanti,
qual sie più 'l danno o l'util non siàn certi.

Here the beautiful eyes are shut that once, when open,
made the most shining and holy ones seem less bright;
since now, being dead, they restore light to so many,
we're not sure which is greater, the loss or the gain.

Epitaph for Cecchino Bracci, 1544.

Qui son morto creduto; e per conforto
del mondo vissi, e con mille alme in seno
di veri amanti; adunche a venir meno,
per tormen' una sola non son morto.

Here I am, believed dead; but I lived for the comfort
of the world, with the souls of a thousand true lovers
in my breast; therefore, although diminished
by taking just one of them from me, I'm not dead.

Epitaph for Cecchino Bracci, 1544. To this epitaph M appended the first of his postscripts referring to del Riccio's importunate gifts: "When you don't want any more of these, don't send me anything further."

3–4. Although I have been deprived of my own soul, I still live on in the souls of all those who loved and remember me.

Se l'alma vive del suo corpo fora,
la mie, che par che qui di sé mi privi,
il mostra col timor ch'i' rendo a' vivi:
che nol po far chi tutto avvien che mora.

That the soul can live outside its body, my own,
which here seems to deprive me of itself,
shows by the fear I inspire in the living:
for one who had fully died could not do that.

Epitaph for Cecchino Bracci, 1544; cf. no. 192, on a similar theme.

3. *the fear I inspire in the living:* that Cecchino's soul, or "ghost," might reappear to them.

S'è ver, com'è, che dopo il corpo viva,
da quel disciolta, c'a mal grado regge
sol per divina legge,
l'alma e non prima, allor sol è beata;
po' che per morte diva   5
è fatta sì, com'a morte era nata.
Dunche, sine peccata,
in riso ogni suo doglia
preschiver debbe alcun del suo defunto,
se da fragile spoglia   10
fuor di miseria in vera pace è giunto
de l'ultim'ora o punto.
Tant'esser de' dell'amico 'l desio,
quante men val fruir terra che Dio.

If it's true, as it is, that the soul lives after the body,
released from what it supports against its will
and only by divine law,
only then, and no earlier, is it blissful;
since it is made divine   5
by death, just as it was born to death.
Therefore, if anyone,
having left his fragile carcass,
is out of misery and has reached true peace
in his final hour or moment,   10
each of us could change his grief for his own deceased
into laughter, "without sin."
This should be as much the desire of a friend
as enjoying earth is worth less than enjoying God.

The sole madrigal among the poems for Cecchino Bracci, 1544; cf. no. 191. The Latin words *sine peccata* (without sin) in line 7 imply that to give up one's grief is not sinful but appropriate. M's postscript to del Riccio casts light on his reasons for including this phrase, whose spelling is grammatically wrong (probably altered to rhyme with *nata*):

"Not to speak sometimes in Latin, even if incorrectly, would make me ashamed, dealing so much with you. The sonnet of *Messer* Donato [Giannotti, who wrote three poems on the death of Cecchino] seems to me as beautiful as anything done in our time; but, since I have bad taste, I cannot value a new cloth, even if it's from Romagna [i.e., coarse and plain], less than used garments of silk and gold, which would make a tailor's mannequin look handsome. Write him about it, tell him about it, give it to him, and send him my best wishes."

The extent of M's knowledge of Latin is unclear. He was familiar with various Latin authors (though possibly through translations), but he usually signed the Italian version of contracts prepared in both languages. That he was familiar with only the rudiments of the language of scholarship is suggested by his comment to Giannotti in that author's *Dialogi* (GD p. 65): "You almost make me desire to study this book of his [Priscianese's Latin grammar, 1540] in order to learn Latin letters." Cf. no. 195.

A pena prima aperti gli vidd'io
i suo begli occhi in questa fragil vita,
che, chiusi el dì dell'ultima partita,
gli aperse in cielo a contemplare Dio.

    Conosco e piango, e non fu l'error mio,   5
col cor sì tardi a lor beltà gradita,
ma di morte anzi tempo, ond'è sparita
a voi non già, m'al mie 'rdente desio.

    Dunche, Luigi, a far l'unica forma
di Cecchin, di ch'i' parlo, in pietra viva   10
etterna, or ch'è già terra qui tra noi,

    se l'un nell'altro amante si trasforma,
po' che sanz'essa l'arte non v'arriva,
convien che per far lui ritragga voi.

Scarcely had I seen his beautiful eyes
opened for the first time in this fragile life
when, shut on the day of his last departure,
he opened them in heaven to gaze on God.

    I realize too late their welcome beauty, and mourn   5
for it in my heart; yet it was not my fault,
but premature death's, through which it has vanished
not so much from you, but from my burning desire.

    Therefore, Luigi, to make the unique form
of Cecchino, of whom I speak, eternal   10
in living stone, now that he's but dust down here:

    since without that form my art cannot succeed,
and since one lover's transformed into the other,
in order to make him, I should portray you.

The only sonnet among the poems for Cecchino Bracci, 1544; M sent a variant of lines 5–8 to
Luigi del Riccio with a note asking him to insert the improved version. The poem is a reply to
del Riccio's request that M carve an effigy of Cecchino for his tomb (see nos. 179, 206). An
extravagant compliment to del Riccio's feelings for the boy, which have made the grown man
resemble the beautiful youth.

1–4. Cf. Petrarch on Laura's death, "when I seemed to close my eyes, I opened them / in eternal light" (no. 279).

7. *it:* Cecchino's beauty.

9. *Luigi:* del Riccio.

12/13. This line is repeated in no. 194 and, in slightly different form, in no. 53; cf. Petrarch, nos. 51:5, 94:13.

Qui vuol mie sorte c'anzi tempo i' dorma,
né son già morto; e ben c'albergo cangi,
resto in te vivo, c'or mi vedi e piangi,
se l'un nell'altro amante si trasforma.

Here my fate wills that I should sleep too early,
but I'm not really dead; though I've changed homes,
I live on in you, who see and mourn me now,
since one lover is transformed into the other.

Epitaph for Cecchino Bracci, 1544. Accompanied by a note to Luigi del Riccio: "I didn't want to send this one to you, since it's very clumsy; but the trout and the truffles would compel heaven."

4. Cf. nos. 53, 193:13.

—*Se qui cent'anni t'han tolto due ore,*
un lustro è forza che l'etterno inganni.
    —*No: che 'n un giorno è vissuto cent'anni*
colui che 'n quello il tutto impara e muore.

"If two hours have robbed you of a hundred years here,
five years would have to deprive you of eternity."
    "No, for in one day he has lived a hundred years
who in that one learns everything and dies."

Epitaph for Cecchino Bracci, 1544. M's postscript identifies the speakers in this dialogue: "One who sees Cecchino dead and speaks to him, and Cecchino answers him."

2. *lustro* (a period of five years) derives from the Latin *lustrum,* the interval between certain ritual sacrifices and censuses. For M's desire to demonstrate what he knew of classical culture, see no. 192.

196

Gran ventura qui morto esser mi veggio:
tal dota ebbi dal cielo, anzi che veglio;
ché, non possendo al mondo darmi meglio,
ogni altro che la morte era 'l mie peggio.

It's my good fortune to see myself here dead;
instead of staying awake, I've a gift from heaven,
which had nothing better in the world to give me:
for everything other than death was worse for me.

Epitaph for Cecchino Bracci, 1544. M's postscript: "Now I have kept my promise of the fifteen scribbles; I'm not obligated to you for any more of them, if no others come down from paradise, where he is."
  2. *staying awake:* on earth, that is, growing old.

La carne terra, e qui l'ossa mie, prive
de' lor begli occhi e del leggiadro aspetto,
fan fede a quel ch'i' fu' grazia e diletto
in che carcer quaggiù l'anima vive.

My flesh, now earth, and my bones here, deprived
of their beautiful eyes and lovely countenance,
bear witness, for him whose grace and delight I was,
to what a prison the soul lives in down here.

Epitaph for Cecchino Bracci, 1544. In his postscript, M provided an alternative ending, with this cryptic explanation:

"Take these two lines below, which are a moral thing [*cosa morale*]; I send you this for the balance of the fifteen scribbles" [the first fifteen epitaphs; see no. 196]:

> fan fede a quel ch'i' fui grazia nel letto,
> che abbracciava e 'n che l'anima vive."

> bear witness for him whose grace I was in bed,
> who embraced me and in whom my soul lives on.

The unnamed person who "took delight" in Cecchino has been interpreted as del Riccio or as M himself, and the reference to embracing in bed is cited as evidence for either man's having had a sexual relationship with the youth. The passage certainly implies a great freedom of physical expression of affection, but cannot provide conclusive proof about the degree of sexual activity alluded to; Renaissance language regarding love is ambiguous, and many people shared beds without having intercourse. M's insistence that the variant lines are "moral" suggests that he knows they might be taken otherwise and that he is at pains to deny such an interpretation. While many of the surrounding poems have bantering postscripts, the alternative reading of this phrase as another lighthearted joke seems unlikely: it would be out of character for M to joke snidely about sexual transgression, either his own or that of a close friend.

Se fussin, perch'i' viva un'altra volta,
gli altru' pianti a quest'ossa carne e sangue,
sarie spietato per pietà chi langue
per rilegar lor l'alma in ciel disciolta.

If, so I could live once more, the tears of others
were to become flesh and blood for these bones here,
one who wept for me out of pity would be pitiless,
binding back to them the soul set free in heaven.

Epitaph for Cecchino Bracci, 1544. M's postscript: "For the salted mushrooms, since you don't want anything else."

199

Chi qui morto mi piange indarno spera,
bagnando l'ossa e 'l mie sepulcro, tutto
ritornarmi com'arbor secco al frutto;
c'uom morto non risurge a primavera.

One who weeps for me, who am dead here, hopes in vain,
by watering my bones and tomb, to restore me
completely, like a dry tree back to fruit;
for a dead man does not rise again in springtime.

Epitaph for Cecchino Bracci, 1544. M's postscript: "[I'm sending you] this clumsy one,
already said a thousand times, for the fennel." The theme of resurrection in springtime
inevitably calls to mind Botticelli's painting of *Primavera* (ca. 1476–78). M knew Botticelli
and probably also this picture, which was painted for Lorenzo di Pierfrancesco de' Medici,
later also a patron of M's.

3. *a dry tree:* cf. the same image in nos. 6, 22:37.

S'i' fu' già vivo, tu sol, pietra, il sai,
che qui mi serri, e s'alcun mi ricorda,
gli par sognar: sì morte è presta e 'ngorda,
che quel ch'è stato non par fusse mai.

If I was ever alive, only you, O stone,
who shut me here, know it, and if anyone recalls me,
he feels he's dreaming; for death is so quick and greedy
that what once was seems never to have been.

Epitaph for Cecchino Bracci, 1544. The image of life as a fleeting dream was used by M in his drawing of *The Dream of Human Life*, ca. 1530–35 (TC no. 333), possibly alluded to by Benedetto Varchi when he referred to Cavalieri as "that beautiful person or thing who sometimes awakens us from the dream of human life" (*Lezzioni*, ed. 1549, 50).

I' temo più, fuor degli anni e dell'ore
che m'han qui chiuso, il ritornare in vita,
s'esser può qua, ch'i' non fe' la partita;
po' c'allor nacqui ove la morte muore.

Having gotten beyond the power of the years and hours
that closed me in here, I fear the return to life,
if that were possible, more than I did leaving it;
for then I was born into the place where death dies.

Epitaph for Cecchino Bracci, 1544. M's postscript, alluding to a previous gift from Luigi del Riccio: "The trout say this, not I; so if you don't like the verses, don't marinate any more of them without pepper."

202

I' fu' de' Bracci, e se ritratto e privo
restai dell'alma, or m'è cara la morte,
po' che tal opra ha sì benigna sorte
d'entrar dipinto ov'io non pote' vivo.

I was one of the Bracci, and if I remain
a portrait, deprived of soul, then death is dear to me,
since that work of art has so fortunate a fate
as to enter, painted, where I could not while living.

Epitaph for Cecchino Bracci, 1544. Like many families in Rome's Florentine colony, the Bracci were *fuorusciti*, political exiles from the Medici regime. Whether any such painted portrait of Cecchino existed or was ever actually transported to Florence (line 4), remains conjectural. Cf. nos. 193, 215, which allude to the sculpted portrait of Cecchino. The concept that portraits are immortal has a long history in Renaissance art theory; see, e.g., Rosand, "The Portrait, The Courtier, and Death," 91–129.

De' Bracci nacqui, e dopo 'l primo pianto,
picciol tempo il sol vider gli occhi mei.
Qui son per sempre; né per men vorrei,
s'i' resto vivo in quel che m'amò tanto.

I was born a Bracci, and after my first cry
my eyes saw the sun for only a short time.
I'm here forever, and would not wish for less,
if I remain living in him who loved me so.

Epitaph for Cecchino Bracci, 1544.

Più che vivo non ero, morto sono
vivo e caro a chi morte oggi m'ha tolto;
se più c'averne copia or m'ama molto,
chi cresce per mancar, gli è 'l morir buono.

Dead, I'm more alive and dear today to him
from whom death's robbed me, than I was alive;
if he loves me more now than when he had plenty of me,
then death is good for one who grows by decreasing.

Epitaph for Cecchino Bracci, 1544.

205

Se morte ha di virtù qui 'l primo fiore
del mondo e di beltà, non bene aperto,
anzi tempo sepulto, i' son ben certo
che più non si dorrà chi vecchio muore.

If death has buried here before its time
the world's finest flower of virtue and of beauty,
not fully opened, then I am quite certain
that he who dies old won't be lamented more.

Epitaph for Cecchino Bracci, 1544.
    4. Cf. M's similar line on the death of his aged father, no. 86:18.

Dal ciel fu la beltà mie diva 'n intera,
e 'l corpo sol mortal dal padre mio.
Se morte è meco quel che ebbi d'Iddio
che dunche il mortal sol da morte spera?

My divine and perfect beauty came from heaven,
and only my mortal body from my father.
If what I got from God is dead with me,
what can my mere mortal part hope for from death?

Epitaph for Cecchino Bracci, 1544; see also nos. 179, 193. M sent a first draft to Luigi del Riccio, who sent it back with some melons and wine and a request for a drawing M had promised to make for the tomb of Cecchino (for del Riccio's letter, see *Carteggio*, MXXV). In a letter accompanying the revised version of the poem (C. MXXVI; R. 239), M wrote: "I'm paying you back for the melons with a scribble, but not yet the drawing; but I'll certainly do it, since I can draw better. Remember me to Baccio, and tell him that if I could have here those delicious dishes he gave me over there, today I'd be another Gratian; and thank him on my behalf" (see also no. 143, which alludes to a similar gift and thus may have been sent to del Riccio close in time to no. 206). In June and July of 1544, M fell very ill and was cared for in del Riccio's home; Baccio Rontini was his physician. The Roman emperor Gratian (r. 375–83) was famous for gluttony.

Per sempre a morte, e prima a voi fu' dato
sol per un'ora; e con diletto tanto
porta' bellezza, e po' lasciai tal pianto
che 'l me' sarebbe non esser ma' nato.

First I was given to you for just an hour,
and then to death forever; I brought so much
beauty and joy, then left behind such tears
that it would have been better never to have been born.

Epitaph for Cecchino Bracci, 1544. M's postscript: "For the turtledove [*la tortola*, alternatively "turtle"]; Urbino will pay you back for the fish, since he gorged himself on them."

Qui chiuso è 'l sol di c'ancor piangi e ardi:
l'alma suo luce fu corta ventura.
Men grazia e men ricchezza assai più dura;
c'a' miseri la morte è pigra e tardi.

Shut here is the sun for which you still weep and burn;
its blessed light favored us only briefly.
Less bounty and less grace endure much longer,
for death is sluggish and late for the wretched.

Epitaph for Cecchino Bracci, 1544. M's postscript: "Refine it as you wish." Cf. Petrarch no.
248: "since death steals the best first and lets the wicked be."

209

Qui sol per tempo convien posi e dorma
per render bello el mie terrestre velo;
ché più grazia o beltà non have 'l cielo,
c'alla natura fussi esempro e norma.

Here must I lie down and sleep too early,
in order to return my fair earthly veil;
for heaven has no greater grace or beauty
that could serve as a standard and a model to nature.

Epitaph for Cecchino Bracci, 1544.

2. *return:* to God (or: "to make my mortal veil beautiful," i.e., by having it immortalized in the tomb sculpture). *earthly veil:* my physical, mortal body; a common Neoplatonic image, cf. nos. 106, 161, 188, 209, 215, 227.

Se gli occhi aperti mie fur vita e pace
d'alcun, qui chiusi, or chi gli è pace e vita?
Beltà non già, che del mond'è sparita,
ma morte sol, s'ogni suo ben qui giace.

If my eyes, when open, gave life and peace to someone,
who, now they're closed here, gives peace and life to him?
Surely not Beauty, who has vanished from the earth,
but Death alone, since all his good lies here.

Epitaph for Cecchino Bracci, 1544.

Se, vivo al mondo, d'alcun vita fui
che gli è qui terra or la bellezza mia,
mort'è non sol, ma crudel gelosia
c'alcun per me non mora innanzi a lui.

If, while alive, I was the life of someone
for whom my beauty is now, here, nought but dust,
not only death's cruel to him, but the jealous fear
that someone else might die for me before him.

Epitaph for Cecchino Bracci, 1544. M's postscript betrays increasing irritation with both himself and Luigi del Riccio: "Clumsy things! The spring [*fonte*, i.e., the well of inspiration] is dry; we'll have to wait for rain, and you're in too much of a hurry."

212

Perc'all'altru' ferir non ave' pari
col suo bel volto il Braccio che qui serro,
morte vel tolse e fecel, s'io non erro,
perc'a lei ancider toccava i men chiari.

Because the Braccio I enclose here had no equal
in wounding others with his beautiful face,
death took him from you; he did so, if I'm not wrong,
since all *he* was getting to kill were the lesser lights.

Epitaph for Cecchino Bracci, 1544.

1/2. *Braccio:* here, as in nos. 184, 213, 217, 222, the possibility exists of a pun on Cecchino's name, meaning "arm," though it is not essential to the conceit of the epitaph.

Sepulto è qui quel Braccio, che Dio volse
corregger col suo volto la natura;
ma perché perso è 'l ben, c'altri non cura,
lo mostrò al mondo e presto sel ritolse.

Entombed here is that Braccio with whose face
God had intended to make nature better;
but since a good thing that others don't heed is wasted,
God showed him to the world and quickly took him back.

Epitaph for Cecchino Bracci, 1544.

    1. *Braccio:* cf. nos. 184, 212, 217, 222.

    4. Cf. the similar thought in no. 265:8–10. Both parallel a line in Vittoria Colonna's poetry, "Che sol ne mostrò il ciel, poi se 'l ritolse" (CR p. 58).

Era la vita vostra il suo splendore:
di Cecchin Bracci, che qui morto giace.
Chi nol vide nol perde e vive in pace:
la vita perde chi 'l vide e non muore.

The splendor of him was your very life:
of Cecchino Bracci, who lies here dead.
Those who didn't see him, don't lose him, and live in peace;
those who saw him, and do not die, lose their lives.

Epitaph for Cecchino Bracci, 1544. M's postscript explains: "The tomb speaks to whoever reads these verses. They're awkward, but if you want me to make a thousand of these, there will necessarily be all kinds." The completed tomb in Santa Maria in Araceli (see no. 179) does have an inscription tablet below the sarcophagus, but it does not bear any of M's verses (see also nos. 216, 219).

215

A la terra la terra e l'alma al cielo
qui reso ha morte; a chi morto ancor m'ama
ha dato in guardia mie bellezza e fama,
ch'etterni in pietra il mie terrestre velo.

Death has here returned earth to the earth,
the soul to heaven, and to him who still loves me dead
has given custody of my beauty and fame,
to immortalize in stone my earthly veil.

Epitaph for Cecchino Bracci, 1544.

2. *dead:* although I am dead; even now, after my death.

4. *my earthly veil:* my transient physical beauty; cf. nos. 106, 161, 188, 209, 215, 227. M did not, in fact, carve the monument to Cecchino, though he did provide the drawing for his assistant Urbino to execute (on the history of the tomb project see nos. 179, 193, 206).

Qui serro il Braccio e suo beltà divina,
e come l'alma al corpo è forma e vita,
è quello a me dell'opra alta e gradita;
c'un bel coltello insegna tal vagina.

Here I enclose Bracci and his divine beauty,
and, as the soul is form and life to the body,
so is he to my noble and prized work;
for such a scabbard signals a beautiful knife.

Epitaph for Cecchino Bracci, 1544. At the head of the autograph M wrote, "Above the vault," i.e., representing the tomb's own thoughts; cf. no. 214.

3. Bracci is the soul that has animated the tomb itself, since it was his beauty that inspired the sculptor to create a masterful work of art that will be much admired. Once again, M conveniently overlooks the fact that Cecchino's tomb was actually carried out by an undistinguished assistant (see no. 179).

4. The Italian *vagina,* here "scabbard" or "sheath," also refers to the female genitalia; cf. no. 54:23.

S'avvien come fenice mai rinnuovi
qui 'l bel volto de' Bracci di più stima,
fie ben che 'l ben chi nol conosce prima
per alcun tempo il perda e po' 'l ritruovi.

If, like the phoenix, Bracci's fair face here
should ever be reborn to greater esteem,
it will do him good who didn't prize its goodness
before, to have lost it a while and then refound it.

Epitaph for Cecchino Bracci, 1544.
   1. *phoenix:* cf. nos. 43, 52, 61, 62, 108. *here:* sculpted on the tomb.
   1/2. For other puns on *Bracci,* "arm," cf. nos. 184, 212, 213, 222.

Col sol de' Bracci il sol della natura,
per sempre estinto, qui lo chiudo e serro:
morte l'ancise senza spada o ferro,
c'un fior di verno picciol vento il fura.

With the sun of Bracci I shut and lock in here
the sun of nature, now put out forever;
death killed him without any sword or steel,
for a slight wind can carry off a winter flower.

Epitaph for Cecchino Bracci, 1544. M's postscript to del Riccio: "For the fig-bread."

219

I' fui de' Bracci, e qui mie vita è morte.
Sendo oggi 'l ciel dalla terra diviso,
toccando i' sol del mondo al paradiso,
anzi per sempre serri le suo porte.

I was one of the Bracci, and here my life is death.
If heaven were cut off from earth today,
and I alone, of all the world, reached paradise,
even so, let it close its gates forever.

Epitaph for Cecchino Bracci, 1544. At the beginning of the text M wrote, "Below the head, that it may speak"—again referring to Cecchino's portrait bust and the inscription tablet below it (cf. no. 214). His postscript reads, "We'll see each other next St. Martin's Day, if it doesn't rain."

Deposto ha qui Cecchin sì nobil salma
per morte, che 'l sol ma' simil non vide.
Roma ne piange, e 'l ciel si gloria e ride,
che scarca del mortal si gode l'alma.

In dying, Cecchino has here laid down a corpse
so noble that the sun has never seen its equal.
Rome weeps for him, but heaven smiles with pride
that his soul, unburdened of mortal load, rejoices.

Epitaph for Cecchino Bracci, 1544. Nos. 220–223 were sent together, on the same sheet (see no. 223).

3. *Rome weeps:* Luigi del Riccio had used this phrase in a letter to Donato Giannotti shortly after Cecchino's death.

Qui giace il Braccio, e men no si desìa
sepulcro al corpo, a l'alma il sacro ufizio.
Se più che vivo, morto ha degno ospizio
in terra e 'n ciel, morte gli è dolce e pia.

Here lies Bracci; one could not wish for more
of a tomb for his body, or prayers for his soul.
Since he has a more worthy home dead than alive,
in earth and heaven, death is sweet and kind to him.

Epitaph for Cecchino Bracci, 1544 (see no. 223).

1. Other editors read, more literally, "one could not wish for less," but this reading seems inconsistent with the sense of lines 3–4.

2. *prayers:* literally "holy office," the liturgical term.

Qui stese il Braccio e colse acerbo il frutto
morte, anz'il fior, c'a quindici anni cede.
Sol questo sasso il gode che 'l possiede,
e 'l resto po' del mondo il piange tutto.

Here death stretched out his Arm and plucked the unripe
fruit—or rather, the flower, which yields at age fifteen.
Only this rock, which possesses him, enjoys him,
while all the rest of the world now weeps for him.

Epitaph for Cecchino Bracci, 1544 (see no. 223).

1. *Arm:* another pun on Cecchino's family name; cf. nos. 184, 212, 213, 217, 221. The
phrase could also be read, "Here death laid out Bracci" himself.

2. *fifteen:* Cecchino's age at his death (see no. 179).

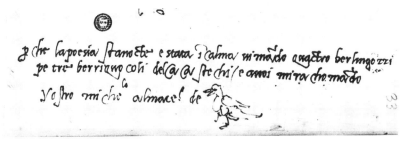

Drafts of Bracci epitaphs and Michelangelo's drawing of a crow (TC no. 367r)

223

I' fu' Cecchin mortale e or son divo:
poco ebbi 'l mondo e per sempre il ciel godo.
Di sì bel cambio e di morte mi lodo,
che molti morti, e me partorì vivo.

I was Cecchino when mortal, and now I'm divine;
I had little of the world and now enjoy heaven forever.
I rejoice in such a fine change and in death,
who gave birth to many others dead, but to me alive.

Epitaph for Cecchino Bracci, 1544, sent to Luigi del Riccio on the same sheet with nos. 220, 221, and 222 (TC no. 367r). M's postscript, after no. 223: "Since poetry has been becalmed tonight, I'm sending you four *berlingozzi* for the miser's three *berriquocoli*. My best to you. Your Michelangelo, in Macel de'. . . . " After the last word M sketched a crow; the name of his street in Rome, Macel de' Corvi, means "Slaughterhouse of the Crows."

Berlingozzi are puff pastries, a term used by Vasari to refer disparagingly to his own art works; *berriquocoli* are a type of fine pasta. The implication, couched as so often in terms of food, is that M's literary production is unworthy of del Riccio's frequent gifts (or, perhaps, of comparison with someone else's literary encomiums on Cecchino).

4. Death can "give birth," i.e., deliver a soul up to, a subsequent period of spiritual suffering (hell) or, as in Cecchino's case, of spiritual rejoicing (everlasting life in heaven).

Chiusi ha qui gli occhi e 'l corpo, e l'alma sciolta
di Cecchin Bracci morte, e la partita
fu 'nanz' al tempo per cangiar suo vita
a quella c'a molt'anni spesso è tolta.

Death has enclosed here Cecchino Bracci's eyes
and body, and released his soul; his departure
came so early to change his life into the one
that is often taken away after many years.

Epitaph for Cecchino Bracci, 1544.

I' fu' de' Bracci, e qui dell'alma privo
per esser da beltà fatt'ossa e terra:
prego il sasso non s'apra, che mi serra,
per restar bello in chi m'amò già vivo.

I was a Bracci, and here, deprived of my soul
to be turned from beauty into bones and earth,
I beg the rock that encloses me not to open
so I may stay fair to him who once loved me alive.

Epitaph for Cecchino Bracci, 1544.
   4. *to:* in the memory of.

Che l'alma viva, i' che qui morto sono
or ne son certo e che, vivo, ero morto.
I' fu' de' Bracci, e se 'l tempo ebbi corto,
chi manco vive più speri perdono.

That the soul lives on, I who am dead here
am sure, and that while still living, I was dead.
I was a Bracci; if I had but a short time,
one who lives less may hope for more forgiveness.

Epitaph for Cecchino Bracci, 1544.

    3. *if I had but a short time:* (understood) it does not displease me, since . . .

    4. Because of having had less time to sin; cf. nos. 132, 133.

Ripreso ha 'l divin Braccio il suo bel velo:
non è più qui, c'anz'al gran dì l'ha tolto
pietà di terra; che s'allor sepolto
fussi, lu' sol sarie degno del cielo.

The divine Bracci has taken back his fair veil.
It's no longer here; pity's taken it from earth
before the great day, for if it were still
buried then, it alone would be worthy of heaven.

Epitaph for Cecchino Bracci, 1544. A variation on the belief that dead souls will take back their earthly bodies at the Last Judgment ("the great day"), as depicted by M in his Vatican fresco. Cf. nos. 140, 186.

1. *veil:* his mortal body; cf. nos. 106, 161, 188, 209, 215.

2. *pity:* God, in his divine mercy toward others (so they will not suffer by comparison—see line 4).

Conversion of Paul. Fresco. Vatican, Pauline Chapel.

228

Se 'l mondo il corpo, e l'alma il ciel ne presta
per lungo tempo, il morto qui de' Bracci
qual salute fie mai che 'l soddisfacci?
Di tanti anni e beltà creditor resta.

Since earth lends us the body for a long time,
and heaven the soul, what treasure ever could
discharge their debt to the dead Bracci here?
He's still owed so many years and so much beauty.

Epitaph for Cecchino Bracci, 1544. At the end, M wrote, "For the fun of it, not for the tally," suggesting that this poem was written last and actually made one more than the fifty agreed upon (for the possible missing poem, see Clements, 140, n. 2).

229

Occhi mie, siate certi
che 'l tempo passa e l'ora s'avvicina,
c'a le lacrime triste il passo serra.
Pietà vi tenga aperti,
mentre la mie divina   5
donna si degna d'abitare in terra.
Se grazia il ciel disserra,
com'a' beati suole,
questo mie vivo sole
se lassù torna e partesi da noi,   10
che cosa arete qui da veder poi?

O my eyes, you may be sure
that time passes and the hour is drawing near
that will close down the path of your sad tears.
May mercy keep you open
as long as my divine   5
lady shall condescend to dwell on earth.
And if grace should unlock heaven,
as it usually does for the blessed,
so that this living sun
of mine takes leave of us and goes back up there,   10
what then will you have to look at down here?

Madrigal, ca. 1544–46, probably referring to Vittoria Colonna. The imagery is Dantesque; cf., e.g., *Vita nuova* 23:34–36.

3. That is, through death, you will no longer be able to weep over your love for her.

7. Or: if heaven should unlock its grace [for her].

Perché tuo gran bellezze al mondo sièno
in donna più cortese e manco dura,
prego se ne ripigli la natura
tutte quelle c'ognor ti vengon meno,
   e serbi a riformar del tuo sereno   5
e divin volto una gentil figura
del ciel, e sia d'amor perpetua cura
rifarne un cor di grazia e pietà pieno.
   E serbi poi i mie sospiri ancora,
e le lacrime sparte insieme accoglia   10
e doni a chi quella ami un'altra volta.
   Forse a pietà chi nascerà in quell'ora
la moverà co' la mie propia doglia,
né fie persa la grazia c'or m'è tolta.

So that your great charms may remain on earth
in a woman who is kinder and less stubborn,
I pray that Nature will take back to itself
all the ones that are fading from you day by day,
   and store them up to refashion from your divine   5
and serene face another tender, heavenly form,
and that Love will take continual care to make
a new heart for it, full of grace and mercy.
   And let it store up all my sighs as well,
gather them together with the tears I've shed,   10
and give them to someone who'll love her once again.
   Perhaps he who will be born on that day
will move her to pity with my own misery,
and won't lose the grace that's now denied to me.

Sonnet, on the same theme as no. 126. A first draft, ca. 1542, was addressed to a man (possibly Cavalieri); this final version, ca. 1544–46, was changed to a female addressee, perhaps with an eye toward the planned publication. Varchi cited the first line of the original version in his *Lezzioni*.

   9. *it:* nature.

231

Non è più tempo, Amor, che 'l cor m'infiammi,
né che beltà mortal più goda o tema:
giunta è già l'ora strema
che 'l tempo perso, a chi men n'ha, più duole.
Quante 'l tuo braccio dammi,   5
morte i gran colpi scema,
e ' sua accresce più che far non suole.
Gl'ingegni e le parole,
da te di foco a mio mal pro passati,
in acqua son conversi;   10
e Die 'l voglia c'or versi
con essa insieme tutti e' mie peccati.

There's no more time, Love, for you to enflame my heart
or for me to enjoy or fear earthly beauty:
now the final hour's been reached,
when time wasted most grieves one who has least of it.
Whatever your arm deals me,   5
Death lessens your great blows
and strengthens his own beyond what they used to be.
The thoughts and the words
that issued from you like fire, to my misfortune,
have been turned into water;   10
and now, God willing, let me
pour out all of my sins along with it.

Madrigal, ca. 1544–45; the postscript to Luigi del Riccio reads, "For Lent; your Michelangelo sends you his best."

4. Cf. Dante, *Purgatorio* 3:78, "For wasting time most displeases one who's most wise."

10. *water:* my tears (of repentance or regret). For a similar pairing of fire and water, cf. no. 235.

Non altrimenti contro a sé cammina
ch'i' mi facci alla morte,
chi è da giusta corte
tirato là dove l'alma il cor lassa;
tal m'è morte vicina,   5
salvo più lento el mie resto trapassa.
Né per questo mi lassa
Amor viver un'ora
fra duo perigli, ond'io mi dormo e veglio:
la speme umile e bassa   10
nell'un forte m'accora,
e l'altro parte m'arde, stanco e veglio.
Né so il men danno o 'l meglio:
ma pur più temo, Amor, che co' tuo sguardi
più presto ancide quante vien più tardi.   15

One who's led from a court of justice to the place
where the soul leaves the heart
walks no less unwillingly
than I do toward death;
death is just as close to me,   5
except that what's left to me runs out more slowly.
Even so, Love doesn't let me
live even one hour in peace
between two dangers, whether I sleep or wake:
on one side, lowered hope   10
greatly distresses me,
while the other side burns me, though I'm old and weary.
I don't know which hurts less,
yet I fear you more, Love, for with your glances
you kill more quickly the later you arrive.   15

Madrigal of uncertain date, perhaps 1544–45 by its thematic relation to no. 231.

    1–2. *the place where the soul leaves the heart:* the scaffold or gallows, place of execution.

    6. *what's left to me:* the time I have remaining in life.

    9. *between two dangers:* between approaching death and the continuing power of love.

    10. *lowered hope:* my hope for the future, humbled and made fearful by the thought of impending death.

    15. A familiar theme; cf. nos. 142, 175.

233

Se da' prim'anni aperto un lento e poco
ardor distrugge in breve un verde core,
che farà, chiuso po' da l'ultim'ore,
d'un più volte arso un insaziabil foco?

Se 'l corso di più tempo dà men loco   5
a la vita, a le forze e al valore,
che farà a quel che per natura muore
l'incendio arroto d'amoroso gioco?

Farà quel che di me s'aspetta farsi:
cenere al vento sì pietoso e fero,   10
c'a' fastidiosi vermi il corpo furi.

Se, verde, in picciol foco i' piansi e arsi,
che, più secco ora in un sì grande, spero
che l'alma al corpo lungo tempo duri?

If a little, slow heat of passion quickly destroys
a green heart, open since its early years,
what then will a voracious fire make
of one burned many times and shut by its final hours?

If, as more time passes, it provides less space   5
for life and for one's powers and for courage,
what will the increased blaze of the amorous game
make of one who by his nature is dying?

It will make what I expect it to make of me:
ashes in a wind so fierce yet merciful   10
that it robs the body from the besetting worms.

For if I, when green, wept and burned in a small fire,
how can I, now drier and in such a large one,
hope that my soul will stay in my body much longer?

Sonnet of uncertain date, ca. 1544–45; cf. no. 253. M's postscript, probably to Luigi del Riccio: "For one of the mullet eggs" (a type of caviar).

2. *open:* to love.

9. Cf. Petrarch, *Triumph of Death* 1:72.

13. *large one:* the more vehement fire of passion in old age.

Tanto non è, quante da te non viene,
agli occhi specchio, a che 'l cor lasso cede;
che s'altra beltà vede,
gli è morte, donna, se te non somiglia,
qual vetro che non bene   5
senz'altra scorza ogni su' obbietto piglia.
Esempro e maraviglia
ben fie a chi si dispera
della tuo grazia al suo 'nfelice stato,
s'e' begli occhi e le ciglia   10
con la tuo pietà vera
volgi a far me sì tardi ancor beato:
a la miseria nato,
s'al fier destin preval grazia e ventura,
da te fie vinto il cielo e la natura.   15

Whatever does not come from you can't be
a mirror to my eyes, to which my tired heart yields;
for it's death to the heart, Lady,
if it sees other beauty that, not resembling you,
is like glass with no further skin   5
that cannot capture any object well.
It would certainly be
a marvelous example for one who despairs
of your graciousness toward his unhappy state,
if you turned, with your true mercy,   10
your fair eyes and brows
to make me blessed, even though it's so late.
Since I was born to misery,
if grace and luck prevail over my harsh fate
both heaven and nature will have been conquered by you.   15

Madrigal, perhaps ca. 1545, for Vittoria Colonna.

5–6. *like glass with no further skin* (literally, "no other bark"): any other beautiful person whose appearance does not mirror your own is as useless (for easing my heart's pain and the longing of my eyes) as a pane of glass that, lacking the necessary film of metal applied to the back to make a mirror, cannot reflect the objects placed in front of it; cf. Dante, *Paradiso* 2:89–90. For other examples of mirror imagery, see nos. 51, 172, 253, 269.

10–12. If you turned your gaze toward me, bringing me bliss despite my old age. The exchange of loving glances is central to *dolce stil nuovo* and Neoplatonic ideas of love.

Un uomo in una donna, anzi uno dio
per la sua bocca parla,
ond'io per ascoltarla
son fatto tal, che ma' più sarò mio.
I' credo ben, po' ch'io   5
a me da lei fu' tolto,
fuor di me stesso aver di me pietate;
sì sopra 'l van desio
mi sprona il suo bel volto,
ch'i' veggio morte in ogni altra beltate.   10
O donna che passate
per acqua e foco l'alme a' lieti giorni,
deh, fate c'a me stesso più non torni.

A man within a woman, or rather a god
speaks through her mouth, so that I,
by having listened to her,
have been made such that I'll never be my own again.
I do believe, since I've been   5
taken from myself by her,
that, being outside myself, I'll take pity on myself;
her beautiful face spurs me
so far above vain desire
that I see death in every other beauty.   10
O lady who pass souls
through fire and water on to days of joy:
Pray, make me never turn back to myself again.

Madrigal in two versions, 1544–46, for Vittoria Colonna; the theme is a realization of the wish expressed in no. 234. This poem and no. 236 were later sent by M to his Florentine friend, the cleric Giovan Francesco Fattucci, in a letter of 1 August 1550 (C. MCXLVII; R. 347; TC no. 597v), in which he describes the late Colonna as "a very great friend," using the masculine form *amico*, corresponding to his description of her here as "a man within a woman."

    4. *I'll never be my own again:* i.e., will no longer have control over myself or my emotions. Cf. similar phrases in nos. 8, 108, and in Giannotti's account of M's words in the *Dialogi,*

"Whenever I see someone who has some virtue . . . I am compelled to fall in love with him . . . so utterly that I am no longer mine [non sono più mio]" (GD p. 68).

5–7. Cf. expressions of being "taken from myself" in nos. 8, 108, 161, and M's comment to Giannotti, following the remark cited above, in which he declined a dinner invitation out of fear that each of the persons present "would take away a part of me" to the extent that "I would be destroyed and lost" (GD pp. 68–69). The idea of being removed from his own body recalls his self-portrait in the flayed skin of Saint Bartholomew in the *Last Judgment*. (For a psychoanalytic reading of M's "sense of fragile ego boundaries," see Liebert, 171–76, 270–311.)

11–12. You lead souls to a blessed life by causing the transformative pain of love (fire) and its resultant tears (water); cf. no. 231:9–10.

Se ben concetto ha la divina parte
il volto e gli atti d'alcun, po' di quello
doppio valor con breve e vil modello
dà vita a' sassi, e non è forza d'arte.

Né altrimenti in più rustiche carte, 5
anz'una pronta man prenda 'l pennello,
fra ' dotti ingegni il più accorto e bello
pruova e rivede, e suo storie comparte.

Simil di me model di poca istima
mie parto fu, per cosa alta e prefetta 10
da voi rinascer po', donna alta e degna.

Se 'l poco accresce, e 'l mie superchio lima
vostra mercé, qual penitenzia aspetta
mie fiero ardor, se mi gastiga e 'nsegna?

If the portion that's divine has well conceived
the face and gestures of someone, then through that
double power, and with a short-lived, lowly model,
he can give life to stone, which is beyond craft's power.

And it's no different with the roughest sketch: 5
before one's eager hand takes up the brush,
he checks and reworks the most beautiful and clever
of his learned ideas, and lays out his subjects.

It's the same with me: at birth I was a model
of little worth, to be reborn through you, 10
noble and worthy lady, as a noble and perfect thing.

If your grace builds up what I lack, and files down
my excess, what penitence should my fierce ardor
expect, if it is to chastise and teach me?

Sonnet, ca. 1545–56, reworked and sent to Giovan Francesco Fattucci in 1550 with the indication it was written for Vittoria Colonna (see no. 235). This is the first of a group of poems (nos. 237, 239, 240, 242) concerned with the Neoplatonic theory of art. On the superiority of *concetto,* or the ideating function of the artist, which is inspired by God, over the manual aspects of art, cf. no. 151.

1. *the portion that's divine:* the (artist's) mind or intellect. *concetto:* here used as a past participle ("conceived"), but also important in art theory as the noun for the artist's preliminary mental "conception" of the subject.

3, 9. *model:* in the sense of a small-scale preliminary study in clay or wax (hence fragile and cheap) for a permanent sculpture. The metaphor is extended to painting (the "rough sketch" of line 5) in lines 4–8.

3–4. *double power . . . beyond craft's power:* by using the skills of both the mind and the hand, the end product will be raised above the level of mere craft to true art.

10. *reborn through you:* through your work of moral inspiration, which amounts to "artistic" revision of my original, lowly form.

12. Cf. Dante, *Purgatorio* 15:15, "che del soverchio visibile lima."

14. *it:* the penitence exacted by the lady in the name of "correcting" M's defective "model."

Molto diletta al gusto intero e sano
l'opra della prim'arte, che n'assembra
i volti e gli atti, e con più vive membra,
di cera o terra o pietra un corp' umano.

Se po' 'l tempo ingiurioso, aspro e villano   5
la rompe o storce o del tutto dismembra,
la beltà che prim'era si rimembra,
e serba a miglior loco il piacer vano.

Those whose taste is whole and sound draw much delight
from works of the first art, which reproduces for us
the faces and gestures of the human body
in wax, clay, or stone, with limbs even more alive.

If harsh, coarse, and offensive time should then   5
disfigure, or break, or dismember it completely,
the beauty that once existed is remembered,
and preserves our vain pleasure for a better place.

Two quatrains, ca. 1545; probably an unfinished sonnet, on the same sheet as no. 238. See no. 236.

2. *the first art:* sculpture, which M regarded as the highest art form (he frequently signed himself "Michelangelo scultore"). It was also considered chronologically first, since God had "sculpted" Adam from the earth. In his first *Lezzione* on M's poetry and art, Benedetto Varchi expressed the same opinion on the superiority of this medium, basing himself on M's poem no. 151. Later, Varchi inquired further through the Florentine academician Luca Martini as to M's opinions (C. MLXXXII, MLXXVII; R. 280, 281; see Ramsden, appendix 37).

4. *even more alive* than they seem on the actual person portrayed.

5–8. This quatrain depends on Neoplatonic notions of art, in which the *concetto* (see no. 151), or divinely inspired idea underlying the work, preexists the physical object and can survive it in the mind. There it continues to point toward our eventual reunion in heaven (*a better place*) with the source of all pure ideas, which will be superior to any delight we may take in transient and imperfect earthly embodiments of them (*vain pleasure*).

Non è non degna l'alma che n'attende
etterna vita, in cui si posa e quieta,
per arricchir dell'unica moneta
che 'l ciel ne stampa, e qui natura spende.

The soul is not unworthy to expect
eternal life, where it will find rest and calm,
for having grown rich in that unique currency
that heaven mints for us and nature spends here.

Quatrain, ca. 1545, on the same sheet as no. 237. Although somewhat ambiguous, the text makes a distinction between material wealth, which might render a person unworthy of salvation (if achieved through usury or other immoral means), and spiritual wealth, which consists of virtue (*that unique currency*) expressed ("spent") through good deeds on earth. Cf. Dante, *Paradiso* 23:130–35.

Com'esser, donna, può quel c'alcun vede
per lunga sperïenza, che più dura
l'immagin viva in pietra alpestra e dura
che 'l suo fattor, che gli anni in cener riede?
   La causa a l'effetto inclina e cede,   5
onde dall'arte è vinta la natura.
I' 'l so, che 'l pruovo in la bella scultura,
c'all'opra il tempo e morte non tien fede.
   Dunche, posso ambo noi dar lunga vita
in qual sie modo, o di colore o sasso,   10
di noi sembrando l'uno e l'altro volto;
   sì che mill'anni dopo la partita,
quante voi bella fusti e quant'io lasso
si veggia, e com'amarvi i' non fu' stolto.

How can it be, Lady, as one can see
from long experience, that the live image
sculpted in hard alpine stone lasts longer
than its maker, whom the years return to ashes?
   The cause bows down and yields to the effect,   5
from which it's clear that nature's defeated by art;
and I know, for I prove it true in beautiful sculpture,
that time and death can't keep their threat to the work.
   Therefore, I can give both of us long life
in any medium, whether colors or stone,   10
by depicting each of these faces of ours;
   so that a thousand years after our departure
may be seen how lovely you were, and how wretched I,
and how, in loving you, I was no fool.

Sonnet in several versions, ca. 1538–46, for Vittoria Colonna; one of M's best-known poems, expressing his belief in the power of art to triumph over time (see no. 236; cf. nos. 97, 277). The poem parallels a remark by Colonna reported in Francisco de Hollanda's First Dialogue: "To one who dies it [painting] gives many years of life" (H p. 246). M's imagining of himself and Colonna as a potentially immortal couple is poignant in light of the fact that her own comment was in part a reference to her deceased husband.

3. Cf. similar expressions in nos. 152:2–3 and 241.

5. *cause . . . effect:* the sculptor is outlived by his creation.

6. The power of art to overcome nature's process of decay and death is a classic topos of art theory, dating back to Pliny.

12–14. M's sentiment here is in marked contrast to his deliberate departure from the actual features of the two dukes he sculpted for the Medici Chapel in the 1520s; in 1544, Niccolò Martelli recalled the sculptor defending the idealized lack of verisimilitude of the two figures by "saying that a thousand years from now no one would be able to know that they looked otherwise" (see de Tolnay, *Medici Chapel*, 68).

Sol d'una pietra viva
l'arte vuol che qui viva
al par degli anni il volto di costei.
Che dovria il ciel di lei,
sendo mie questa, e quella suo fattura,   5
non già mortal, ma diva,
non solo agli occhi mei?
E pur si parte e picciol tempo dura.
Dal lato destro è zoppa suo ventura,
s'un sasso resta e pur lei morte affretta.   10
Chi ne farà vendetta?
Natura sol, se de' suo nati sola
l'opra qui dura, e la suo 'l tempo invola.

Art wills this lady's face
to live down here as long
as years go by, if only in living stone.
Then what should God do for her,
this being my handiwork, and she being his,   5
not merely mortal but godly,
and not only in my eyes?
And yet she'll last but a short time and must leave;
and her fortune will be hobbled on its right side
if a rock remains and death still hurries her on.   10
Who'll take revenge for her?
Nature alone, since only her children's works
last here below, and time carries off her own.

Madrigal of uncertain date, perhaps ca. 1544–45, for Vittoria Colonna; related in theme to no. 239, though in a more pessimistic key (cf. also nos. 236, 241). Although earlier editors supposed that the poem refers to an actual portrait bust of Colonna, since lost, there is no evidence that any such work was ever made.

5. *this:* my sculpture.

9–10. She will be crippled or impeded on her path to a heavenly destiny (the "right" or better side of her fate) if the heavy statue weighs down her left (inferior, earthly) side. Cf. Petrarch, no. 88: "and I flee, even though so weak and hobbled / on the side where desire has twisted me."

12. *her children's works:* the art works created by Nature's human children, which outlast on earth their mortal makers (*her* [Nature's] *own* works), who succumb to the passing of time.

   Negli anni molti e nelle molte pruove,
cercando, il saggio al buon concetto arriva
d'un'immagine viva,
vicino a morte, in pietra alpestra e dura;
c'all'alte cose nuove   5
tardi si viene, e poco poi si dura.
Similmente natura,
di tempo in tempo, d'uno in altro volto,
s'al sommo, errando, di bellezza è giunta
nel tuo divino, è vecchia, e de' perire: 10
onde la tema, molto
con la beltà congiunta,
di stranio cibo pasce il gran desire;
né so pensar né dire
qual nuoca o giovi più, visto 'l tuo 'spetto,   15
o 'l fin dell'universo o 'l gran diletto.

   After many years of seeking and many attempts,
the wise artist only attains a living image
faithful to his fine conception,
in hard and alpine stone, when he's near death;
for at novel and lofty things   5
one arrives late, and then lasts but a short time.
Likewise, if nature, straying
from one face to another, and from age to age,
has reached the peak of beauty in yours, which
is divine, then she is old, and must soon perish.   10
And consequently terror,
closely linked to beauty,
feeds my great desire with a strange food;
and I can't decide or say,
having seen your face, which is greater, the hurt or the joy: 15
the end of the universe, or my great pleasure.

Madrigal, ca. 1542–44, comparing Nature's creation of Vittoria Colonna with the artist's achievement of perfect beauty, both of which, he fears, must signal impending death; cf. no.

240. In a postscript to Luigi del Riccio, M wrote: "Since you want some scribbles, I can't send you anything but the ones I have. It's your bad luck, but your Michelangelo sends you his greetings."

1–4. M felt keenly the disparity between his ideal mental *concetti* and his often imperfect realizations of them in physical form (on *concetto*, see no. 151). It was partly for this reason that he destroyed many works or left them unfinished, as noted by Condivi (CW p. 107) and Vasari (VM 7:243; VB p. 404). Cf. A35.

4. *hard and alpine stone:* cf. nos. 152, 239.

5. Cf. no. 178, "new and lofty beauty."

7. *straying:* the Italian *errando* can mean both "wandering" and "erring" (i.e., experimenting unsuccessfully).

S'egli è che 'n dura pietra alcun somigli
talor l'immagin d'ogni altri a se stesso,
squalido e smorto spesso
il fo, com'i' son fatto da costei.
E par ch'esempro pigli   5
ognor da me, ch'i' penso di far lei.
Ben la pietra potrei,
per l'aspra suo durezza,
in ch'io l'esempro, dir c'a lei s'assembra;
del resto non saprei,   10
mentre mi strugge e sprezza,
altro sculpir che le mie afflitte membra.
Ma se l'arte rimembra
agli anni la beltà per durare ella,
farà me lieto, ond'io le' farò bella.   15

Since it's true that, in hard stone, one will at times
make the image of someone else look like himself,
I often make her dreary
and ashen, just as I'm made by this woman;
and I seem to keep taking myself   5
as a model, whenever I think of depicting her.
I could well say that the stone
in which I model her
resembles her in its harsh hardness; but
in any case I could not,   10
while she scorns and destroys me,
sculpt anything but my own tormented features.
So, since art preserves the memory
of beauty through the years, if she wants to last,
she will make me glad, so that I'll make her beautiful.   15

Madrigal, ca. 1540–44, to which M added a brief postcript—"For sculptors"—indicating that he is writing about a tendency to self-identification with one's work that will be understood by others in his profession (see no. 236). Savonarola preached that "every painter paints himself" in his Lenten sermons of 1497, no. 26 (*Prediche sopra Ezechiel*, Venice, 1517, f. 71v). M himself later said the same, with an uncomplimentary twist, regarding a fine depiction of an ox by an otherwise mediocre artist: "Every painter paints himself well [*ritrae se medesimo bene*]" (VM 7:280; VB 427 [alternate translation]).

1–2. In no. 173, M expresses the same thought in terms of the art of painting.

1. Dante also compared his hard lady to hard stone (e.g., DR nos. 102, 103).

7. *I could well say:* in defense of my tendency to depict her unflatteringly.

14–15. Cf. no. 240.

Ognor che l'idol mio si rappresenta
agli occhi del mie cor debile e forte,
fra l'uno e l'altro obbietto entra la morte,
e più 'l discaccia, se più mi spaventa.

L'alma di tale oltraggio esser contenta   5
più spera che gioir d'ogni altra sorte;
l'invitto Amor, con suo più chiare scorte,
a suo difesa s'arma e s'argomenta;

Morir, dice, si può sol una volta,
né più si nasce; e chi col mie 'mor muore,   10
che fie po', s'anzi morte in quel soggiorna?

L'acceso amor, donde vien l'alma sciolta,
s'è calamita al suo simile ardore,
com'or purgata in foco, a Dio si torna.

Every time that my idol appears again
in the eyes of my heart, which is faint yet strong,
Death comes between one object and the other,
and the more he scares me, the more he drives it away.

My soul hopes to draw more happiness from this trouble   5
than it could delight from any other fate;
but Love, unbeaten, arms for his own defense
with his sharpest equipment, and reasoning, he says:

"One can only die once, and is not born again;
and if one stays with my love before death,   10
then what will become of him, dying with it?

Since flaming love, by which the soul's released,
draws it, like a magnet, to a similar heat,
the soul, cleansed in fire like gold, will return to God."

Sonnet, ca. 1545, written on a sheet bearing sketches of windows from ca. 1533 (TC no. 552v). See no. 244.

1–2. *idol:* the mental image of his beloved, which keeps appearing *in the eyes of my heart:* in my mind's eye.

2. *faint yet strong:* susceptible to fear, yet given to passionate intensity.

3. Between my heart and the image of my beloved.

4. *it:* the image or thought of my beloved.

8. *his sharpest equipment:* normally, Love's arrows, but here also implying his subtlest logical arguments.

10–14. Love, defending himself against the fear of death which might drive the speaker away from thoughts of his beloved, asserts that one should not fear death from love. Rather, Love argues, exquisite joy and salvation await one who, after living all his life "with me"— that is, nourishing earthly love—succeeds in dying while still loving someone earthly; for that earthly love will draw the soul higher to the kindred love of God and assure the soul entry to heaven (in Neoplatonic thought).

Se 'l duol fa pur, com'alcun dice, bello,
privo piangendo d'un bel volto umano,
l'essere infermo è sano,
fa vita e grazia la disgrazia mia:
ché 'l dolce amaro è quello   5
che, contr'a l'alma, il van pensier desia.
Né può fortuna ria
contr'a chi basso vola,
girando, trïonfar d'alta ruina;
ché mie benigna e pia   10
povertà nuda e sola,
m'è nuova ferza e dolce disciplina:
c'a l'alma pellegrina
è più salute, o per guerra o per gioco,
saper perdere assai che vincer poco.   15

If grief can make one beautiful, as they say,
then for me, deprived of a lovely face, and weeping,
being sick is healthy,
and my misfortune brings new life and fortune.
For that sweetness which our vain thoughts   5
desire, against the soul's best interests, is bitter;
and evil Fortune, turning,
can't triumph by throwing down
from the heights to his ruin one who is flying low.
My naked and lonely poverty,   10
benign and merciful,
is a new spur and sweet discipline to me:
since to the pilgrim soul
it's a greater salvation, either in war or love,
to know how to lose a lot than to gain a little.   15

Madrigal, ca. 1545, on the same sheet as part of no. 243.

   5. *our vain thoughts:* our earthly appetites.

   7–9. M is alluding (incompletely) to the traditional image of Fortune's wheel, which in its perpetual rotation raises people up to happiness and success and then casts them down. *one who is flying low:* one whose condition is already continually unhappy (cf. English "flying high").

12. *discipline:* source of moral education or improvement.

14. *love:* literally, "the game" (of love).

13–15. For our souls, which wander through life as pilgrims seeking salvation (cf. no. 258:5), it is of more value in the long run to lose the greatest earthly pleasures and become resigned to that loss, than to attain even a few of those tempting delights, which are meager, transitory, and threatening to the achievement of eternal life.

—*Se 'l volto di ch'i' parlo, di costei,*
no' m'avessi negati gli occhi suoi,
Amor, di me qual poi
pruova faresti di più ardente foco,
s'a non veder me' lei   5
co' suo begli occhi tu m'ardi e non poco?
   —*La men parte del gioco*
ha chi nulla ne perde,
se nel gioir vaneggia ogni desire:
nel sazio non ha loco   10
la speme e non rinverde
nel dolce che preschive ogni martire—.
Anzi di lei vo' dire:
s'a quel c'aspiro suo gran copia cede,
l'alto desir non quieta tuo mercede.   15

"If the face of which I speak, that face of hers,
had not denied its eyes to me, O Love,
then how much more scorching
a fire you would make me undergo,
since even when I can't see her very well   5
you burn me with her eyes to no small degree!"
   "He who loses nothing in the game
gets the least out of it,
since every desire dissipates in fulfillment;
in fullness there's no room   10
for hope, and it doesn't revive
in the sweetness that banishes all torment."
   "Even so, I'd say of her that,
even if she grants what I aim for in abundance,
your reward won't slake my lofty desire."   15

Madrigal, ca. 1545–47, on the verso of a sheet that contains no. 265 on the recto. A dialogue between M and Love: The poet imagines that satisfaction of his desire for his lady's eyes would be more intense than his present yearning, to which Love replies that, on the contrary, it is preferable to retain some element of hopeful longing than to lose all desire in the bliss of fulfillment. The poet then counters with a proposal that aims to reconcile both points of view: his desire is so infinite that even receiving all her attentions would not eliminate all his yearning.

7–9. One who never suffers deprivation in *the game* of love (cf. no. 244:14) can't be said to have profited from the activity (or even, alternatively, to have participated: "takes the least part in it"), since desire ceases to exist once it is fulfilled.

9. Cf. no. 249:11–13.

11. *it:* hope.

15. *your reward:* the results of merciful intercession by Love, who will have convinced her to be more generous with her affections and glances.

Te sola del mie mal contenta veggio,
né d'altro ti richieggio amarti tanto;
non è la pace tua senza il mio pianto,
e la mia morte a te non è 'l mie peggio.
Che s'io colmo e pareggio   5
il cor di doglia alla tua voglia altera,
per fuggir questa vita,
qual dispietata aita
m'ancide e strazia e non vuol poi ch'io pera?
Perché 'l morir è corto   10
al lungo andar di tua crudeltà fera.
Ma chi patisce a torto
non men pietà che gran iustizia spera.
Così l'alma sincera
serve e sopporta e, quando che sia poi,   15
spera non quel che puoi:
ché 'l premio del martir non è tra noi.

Only you do I see delighted at my woe,
yet I ask for nothing but to love you greatly;
there is no peace for you unless I'm weeping,
and you don't think death is the worst that I could get.
For if, to flee this life,   5
I flood my heart with grief up to a level
that matches your haughty will,
what pitiless kind of help
will torture and kill me, then not wish me to die?
For dying is short, compared   10
to the long span of your fierce cruelty.
But one who suffers unfairly
hopes for great justice no less than for mercy:
therefore my faithful soul
serves and endures and hopes someday to have,   15
not what is in your power,
but the martyr's reward, which is not found among us.

This poem began ca. 1524 as a *capitolo* in terza rima addressed to a woman. M revised it ca. 1534 to refer to a man; this version is found on a letter to Febo di Poggio (C. CMXLI; R. 198), who may thus have been the addressee; see no. 99. The final version printed here, now in madrigal form, was prepared for the planned publication of 1546, and the addressee changed back to a woman.

4. Since you like to see me suffer and my death would put an end to that misery, you would prefer to keep me alive and unhappy.

5. *to flee this life:* if I tried to kill myself.

7. The comparison between how high his "cup of suffering" is filled and the lady's high degree of disdain for him is somewhat more forcefully implied in Italian, where *altera* (haughty) is closer to *altezza* (height) than are the corresponding English terms.

8–9. How cruel you could be by seeming to offer help, that is, by giving me just enough attention to prevent me from dying but not enough to relieve the misery of my longing (cf. no. 245).

13. This reading, reversing the literal meaning of the Italian, accords better with the sense of what follows.

15–17. My soul does not hope for that (limited) joy which you are able to to give here, but rather for the greater spiritual reward which is given only in heaven to those who have borne suffering on earth.

247

Caro m'è 'l sonno, e più l'esser di sasso,
mentre che 'l danno e la vergogna dura;
non veder, non sentir m'è gran ventura;
però non mi destar, deh, parla basso.

Sleep is dear to me, and being of stone is dearer,
as long as injury and shame endure;
not to see or hear is a great boon to me;
therefore, do not wake me—pray, speak softly.

Epigram, composed in 1545–46 in response to a quatrain by the Florentine academician Giovanni di Carlo Strozzi that praised M's sculpture of Night in the Medici Chapel (begun in 1524); both were copied and printed together, with M's epigram headed, "Buonarroti's Reply." Strozzi's text, which puns on the artist's name, reads:

> The Night that you see sleeping in such a
> graceful attitude, was sculpted by an Angel
> in this stone, and since she sleeps, she must have life;
> wake her, if you don't believe it, and she'll speak to you.

M had imagined the words of both Night and Day many years before (no. 14), but in light of the changed situation in Florence since 1530, this later poem has a clear political content. The final establishment of the Medici dynasty, which led to the exile of many of M's Florentine friends in Rome and his own refusal to return to the city, was deplored by M. In several nearly contemporaneous poems, M alluded to the wickedness and ingratitude of his native city (see nos. 248–250), just as his sculptured bust of Brutus, the Roman who assassinated Julius Caesar, was reportedly commissioned by the *fuorusciti* Donato Giannotti and Cardinal Ridolfi sometime after the murder of Duke Alessandro de' Medici in 1537 to commemorate what to them was a parallel tyrannicide (VM 7:262; VB 413). In Giannotti's *Dialogi*, the speakers discuss Strozzi's epigram and M's reply, which one calls "very relevant to our times" (GD pp. 44–45); the continuing "injury and shame" in line 2 would have been understood as a criticism of Alessandro's successor Duke Cosimo and his regime, which the statue, "trapped" in Florence, prefers not to see.

Night. Marble sculpture. Florence, Medici Chapel, San Lorenzo.

Dal ciel discese, e col mortal suo, poi
che visto ebbe l'inferno giusto e 'l pio,
ritornò vivo a contemplare Dio,
per dar di tutto il vero lume a noi.

Lucente stella, che co' raggi suoi   5
fe' chiaro a torto el nido ove nacqu'io,
né sare' 'l premio tutto 'l mondo rio;
tu sol, che la creasti, esser quel puoi.

Di Dante dico, che mal conosciute
fur l'opre suo da quel popolo ingrato   10
che solo a' iusti manca di salute.

Fuss'io pur lui! c'a tal fortuna nato,
per l'aspro esilio suo, co' la virtute,
dare' del mondo il più felice stato.

He came down from heaven, and once he had seen
the just hell and the merciful one, he went
back up, with his body alive, to contemplate God,
in order to give us the true light of it all.

For such a shining star, who with his rays   5
undeservedly brightened the nest where I was born,
the whole wicked world would not be enough reward;
only you, who created him, could ever be that.

I speak of Dante, for his deeds were poorly
appreciated by that ungrateful people   10
who fail to welcome only righteous men.

If only I were he! To be born to such good fortune,
to have his harsh exile along with his virtue,
I would give up the happiest state in the world.

One of two sonnets in praise of Dante (see also no. 250), 1545–46. M knew Dante's work
intimately, as attested by his detailed discussions in Donato Giannotti's *Dialogi*, whose subject
is, broadly, the question of how long Dante spent in Hell and Purgatory. At the conclusion of
the book, the participants prevail on M to recite this poem, which is printed in full in one of
several earlier versions (GD p. 98). M here identifies personally with the great poet, since
both were forced into exile from Florence. For related poems, see nos. 247, 249.

2. *the just hell:* cf. *Inferno* 3:4, an inscription over the portal of Hell declaring, "Justice moved my high maker." *and the merciful one:* Purgatory (cf. no. 63).

2–3. *he went back up:* to Heaven, to observe the events described in his third volume, *Paradiso.*

4. Cf. *Paradiso* 17:128, where Virgil bids Dante "make manifest all that you have seen."

5–6. i.e., whose glory made Florence (the birthplace of both M and Dante) far more famous than the city deserved (see line 10).

8. *you:* God.

10. *that ungrateful people:* the Florentines, as M explicitly stated in an earlier draft; see also no. 250. In 1512, M had written to his father that "I have never encountered a more arrogant or ungrateful people than the Florentines" (C. cvii; R. 82). Cf. Dante, *Inferno* 15:61–62, referring to the Florentines as "that ungrateful, spiteful people / who came down from Fiesole in ancient times"; M had similarly echoed Dante's criticisms of the citizens of Pistoia (no. 71).

14. *give up:* in exchange. *the happiest state:* as in English, *stato* may here refer either to a state of being (condition of happiness) or a geographical-political state (implicitly, Florence); cf. M's earlier use of this ambiguity in no. 10:13.

—Per molti, donna, anzi per mille amanti
creata fusti, e d'angelica forma;
or par che 'n ciel si dorma,
s'un sol s'appropia quel ch'è dato a tanti.
Ritorna a' nostri pianti   5
il sol degli occhi tuo, che par che schivi
chi del suo dono in tal miseria è nato.
    —Deh, non turbate i vostri desir santi,
ché chi di me par che vi spogli e privi,
col gran timor non gode il gran peccato;   10
ché degli amanti è men felice stato
quello, ove 'l gran desir gran copia affrena,
c'una miseria di speranza piena.

"For many, even a thousand lovers, Lady,
were you created, with an angelic form;
now heaven must be sleeping,
if one can take for himself what was given to many.
Give back to our weeping eyes   5
the sun of your eyes, which seems to be avoiding
those born in such misery without its gifts."
    "Pray, do not let your righteous desires be troubled,
since the one who seems to have deprived you of me,
living in great terror, can't enjoy his great sin;   10
for, of lovers' conditions, that one is less happy
in which great abundance reins in great desire,
than a misery still full of hope."

Madrigal, 1545–46; a political allegory in the form of a dialogue between the frustrated lover
and his beloved lady, who is selfishly held captive by another. In explanation, Luigi del Riccio
wrote above the autograph, "By Michelangelo, meaning by the lady, Florence." Cf. the
related poems, nos. 247, 248, 250.

4. *one:* probably Cosimo de' Medici, then duke of Florence, whose family had taken
absolute control of the city, previously a republic ("given to many").

7. That is, those who are destined to feel sad as long as they remain deprived of the light of
your eyes.

10. A tyrant, who must always live in fear of revenge from those he has forcibly sup-
pressed, cannot afford to relax in the enjoyment of the fruits of his violent seizure.

12–13. Complete satisfaction in love reduces its passion, whereas at least one who is still
unsatisfied can hope for future fulfillment of his desire. Cf. no. 245:9–12.

250

Quante dirne si de' non si può dire,
ché troppo agli orbi il suo splendor s'accese;
biasmar si può più 'l popol che l'offese,
c'al suo men pregio ogni maggior salire.

Questo discese a' merti del fallire 5
per l'util nostro, e poi a Dio ascese;
e le porte, che 'l ciel non gli contese,
la patria chiuse al suo giusto desire.

Ingrata, dico, e della suo fortuna
a suo danno nutrice; ond'è ben segno 10
c'a' più perfetti abonda di più guai.

Fra mille altre ragion sol ha quest'una:
se par non ebbe il suo exilio indegno,
simil uom né maggior non nacque mai.

All that should be said of him cannot be said,
for his splendor flamed too brightly for our eyes;
it's easier to blame the people who hurt him
than for all our greatest to rise to his least virtue.

This man descended to the just deserts of error 5
for our benefit, and then ascended to God;
and the gates that heaven did not block for him
his homeland shut to his righteous desire.

I call her ungrateful, and nurse of her fortune
to her own detriment, which is a clear sign 10
that she lavishes the most woes on the most perfect.

Among a thousand proofs this one suffices:
no exile was ever as undeserved as his,
and no man equal or greater was ever born.

The second sonnet on Dante, 1545–46; cf. no. 248. Beneath the autograph, M wrote, "*Messer Donato* [Giannotti], you ask me for something I don't have." The recipient, like his fellow Florentine *fuorusciti*, would have understood the lament over Dante's unjust exile in contemporary political terms (cf. also nos. 247, 249).

3. *the people who hurt him:* the Florentine citizenry (see line 7).

424

4. *all our greatest*: every one of the great figures of the city, past and present.

5. *to the just deserts of error*: to the place where sin receives its appropriate punishments, i.e., Hell and Purgatory.

7–8. Although even God welcomed him to heaven, his own compatriots (the Florentines) refused to allow him to return to his city of birth.

9. *her*: the city of Florence.

Nel dolce d'una immensa cortesia,
dell'onor, della vita alcuna offesa
s'asconde e cela spesso, e tanto pesa
che fa men cara la salute mia.
    Chi gli omer' altru' 'mpenna e po' tra via   5
a lungo andar la rete occulta ha tesa,
l'ardente carità d'amore accesa
là più l'ammorza ov'arder più desia.
    Però, Luigi mio, tenete chiara
la prima grazia, ond'io la vita porto,   10
che non si turbi per tempesta o vento.
    L'isdegno ogni mercé vincere impara,
e s'i' son ben del vero amico accorto,
mille piacer non vaglion un tormento.

Within the sweetness of an enormous kindness
there is often disguised and hidden some offense
to my honor and life, and it weighs so heavily
that it makes my health seem less precious to me.
    One who gives wings to another's shoulders, and then,   5
as time passes, spreads a concealed net in his path,
damps the flame of gratitude that's lit by love
just when it would like to burn most warmly.
    Therefore, my Luigi, keep clearly shining
your original grace, to which I owe my life,   10
so it won't be blotted out by storm or wind.
    Anger can manage to overcome every mercy,
and, if I rightly understand true friendship,
a thousand pleasures are not worth one torment.

Sonnet, early 1545, related in theme and origin to no. 252. The reference to Luigi's (del Riccio) "original grace" probably alludes to M's gratitude for the first of two periods when he fell seriously ill and was taken into del Riccio's apartments in the Strozzi palace and nursed back to health (in late 1544 and 1545–46). The unspecified "offense" that soon provoked M's anger is unclear, but seems related to a complaint in a letter he wrote to del Riccio in January

1545: "It is still within the power of one who delivered me from death to insult me. . . . I therefore beg and entreat you by the true friendship which exists between us to have that plate which I do not like destroyed, and the impressions that have been printed burned" (C. MLVI; R. 244). Various theories interpret this unauthorized "printing" to refer to some of M's poems, to reproductions of his art works, or to a portrait of M poorly engraved by Giulio Bonasone (see Ramsden, 2:244–50, appendix 27). Despite his deep hurt, M ends the poem with a plea to del Riccio to preserve what is most valued in their friendship.

4. *my health:* which I owe to you (cf. line 10).

5–6. One who raises the spirits (or expectations) of a friend but subsequently deceives him.

11. *storm or wind:* of anger (line 12).

12. *overcome every mercy:* make one forget every impulse to gratitude for past kindnesses.

14. All the previous proofs of your affection are insufficient to compensate for this one pain you are causing me. The line is a quotation from Petrarch, no. 231:4.

Perch'è troppo molesta,
ancor che dolce sia,
quella mercé che l'alma legar suole,
mie libertà di questa
vostr'alta cortesia   5
più che d'un furto si lamenta e duole.
E com'occhio nel sole
disgrega suo virtù ch'esser dovrebbe
di maggior luce, s'a veder ne sprona,
così 'l desir non vuole   10
zoppa la grazia in me, che da vo' crebbe.
Ché 'l poco al troppo spesso s'abbandona,
né questo a quel perdona:
c'amor vuol sol gli amici, onde son rari,
di fortuna e virtù simili e pari.   15

Because it is too burdensome,
even though it is sweet,
my freedom suffers and mourns
over this high kindness of yours,
this mercy which usually binds the soul,   5
more than it would over a robbery.
And, as the power of an eye
fixed on the sun dissolves, though it should be capable
of seeing more light, since the sun enables sight,
so I do not desire   10
the grace in me, which grew from you, to be lame.
For little often surrenders to too much,
nor does the latter tolerate the former:
for love only wants as friends (that's why they're rare)
those of similar character and equal virtue.   15

Madrigal, ca. 1545, surviving in several versions; see nos. 160, 251. Luigi del Riccio responded with another madrigal, using similar rhymes, assuring M of his reciprocal affection.

    5–6. Although your kindness is of the sort that would normally bind the soul of the recipient to the giver in gratitude, it seems more like a theft to me, since I am indebted by it in a way that I can never repay.

7–11. I am afraid that the feelings of gratitude engendered in me by your graciousness will be diminished to inadequacy by the superiority of your kindness, just as the visual power of the eye is overwhelmed by direct experience of the sun's light, rather than being increased.

12–15. And this may happen because a small amount of good qualities cannot make fair repayment for another person's magnanimity, and therefore the more generous partner loses interest in the inferior one.

14–15. Cf. no. 255:15–17.

S'i' fussi stati ne' prim'anni accorto
del fuoco, allor di fuor, che m'arde or drento,
per men mal, non che spento,
ma privo are' dell'alma il debil core
o del colpo, or ch'è morto;   5
ma sol n'ha colpa il nostro prim'errore.
Alma infelice, se nelle prim'ore
alcun s'è mal difeso,
nell'ultim' arde e muore
del primo foco acceso: 10
ché chi non può non esser arso e preso
nell'età verde, c'or c'è lume e specchio,
men foco assai 'l distrugge stanco e vecchio.

If in my early years I had been wary
of the fire that then burned me from without,
now from within, then to suffer less, I'd not only
have put it out, but deprived my fragile heart
of its soul, and thus of the blow that now has killed it;   5
but my first mistake bears all the blame for it.
Unhappy soul, for if one defended himself
poorly in his early days,
in his last he'll burn and die
from the fire lit that first time: 10
For one who couldn't avoid being captured and burned
in his green years, which are now our light and mirror,
can now, old and tired, be destroyed by far less fire.

Madrigal, perhaps 1546, similar in theme and language to Petrarch no. 65 ("Alas, I was not wary enough in the beginning"); cf. no. 233. M wrote two explanatory lines below the first draft—"O song, born at night in the midst of my bed, you are to be revised tomorrow evening"—which closely parallel Petrarch no. 237:38–39 ("O song born at night in the midst of the woods, you will see a rich shore tomorrow evening"). A further postcript declared that "it [the poem?] would be as sweet as Adam's apples, but I have no apples in my body."

6. My early failure to eliminate the power of love over me is alone to blame for my fatal susceptibility to love now. Literally, *"our* first mistake," which may also allude to Adam's original sin (as in the postscript regarding the apple of Eden).

12. *which are now our light and mirror:* the sad example of the poet's foolish youth (*his green years;* cf. nos. 142, 167, 283) now serves to enlighten him and provide an example of wiser behavior. For the mirror as a symbol of self-reflection, cf. nos. 51, 172.

Donn', a me vecchio e grave,
ov'io torno e rientro
e come a peso il centro,
che fuor di quel riposo alcun non have,
il ciel porge le chiave. 5
Amor le volge e gira
e apre a' iusti il petto di costei;
le voglie inique e prave
mi vieta, e là mi tira,
già stanco e vil, fra ' rari e semidei. 10
Grazie vengon da lei
strane e dolce e d'un certo valore,
che per sé vive chiunche per le' muore.

To me, weighed down with age,
heaven offers the keys
to the lady I keep coming back to
as a weight does to its center,
away from which it can have no rest. 5
Love turns and rotates them
and opens to the righteous that woman's breast;
my wicked, depraved desires
she blocks, and draws me,
once tired and worthless, up among the godlike few. 10
From her come gracious gifts
so singular and sweet and of such power
that whoever dies for her lives for himself.

Madrigal, possibly early 1546. M's postscript to Luigi del Riccio reads: "Old love has produced offspring, or at least a sprout."

1–5. These lines, grammatically unclear, are usually read as addressing the "lady" directly about a gift of "the keys to heaven," but that would be inconsistent with the use of the third person in lines 6–13.

4. *weight:* a hanging weight, or pendulum, which if set in motion will tend to return to the stable center point of its swing.

5–7. Cf. Dante, DC 104:87.

13. Cf. Christ's words, "He who loses his life for my sake shall find it" (Matthew 10:39).

Mentre i begli occhi giri,
donna, ver' me da presso,
tanto veggio me stesso
in lor, quante ne' mie te stessa miri.
Dagli anni e da' martiri   5
qual io son, quegli a me rendono in tutto,
e ' mie lor te più che lucente stella.
Ben par che 'l ciel s'adiri
che 'n sì begli occhi i' mi veggia sì brutto,
e ne' mie brutti ti veggia sì bella;   10
né men crudel e fella
dentro è ragion, c'al core
per lor mi passi, e quella
de' tuo mi serri fore.
Perché 'l tuo gran valore   15
d'ogni men grado accresce suo durezza,
c'amor vuol pari stato e giovanezza.

As you turn your lovely eyes
toward me, Lady, from close by,
the more I see myself
in them, the more you see yourself in mine.
Yours fully reflect to me   5
what I've become from all these years and torments,
while mine reflect you to them, brighter than a star.
Heaven surely must be angry
that in such lovely eyes I see myself so ugly,
and in my ugly ones you see yourself so lovely;   10
and the thoughts behind them are
no less cruel and unjust,
since through mine you reach my heart
while those of yours shut me out.
And the reason why your great worth   15
grows harder toward all those of lesser rank
is that love desires equal status and youth.

Madrigal in several versions, two of them written on part of a sheet of sketches for the *Last Judgment* (TC nos. 353v, 356v). Thus M may have set down his original idea as early as 1535–40, though the final revision was made for the planned publication of 1546.

7. *to them:* to your eyes.

11–14. The inner sentiments that control the differing actions of our eyes are cruelly unbalanced, since my desire for you allows you to penetrate my soul through my eyes, while your indifference toward me prevents me from entering your affections through gazing at you.

15–17. The metaphor of rank, though couched in terms of social standing, refers to degrees of beauty or moral goodness. Cf. no. 252:14–15.

256

S'alcuna parte in donna è che sie bella,
benché l'altre sien brutte,
debb'io amarle tutte
pel gran piacer ch'i' prendo sol di quella?
La parte che s'appella,   5
mentre il gioir n'attrista,
a la ragion, pur vuole
che l'innocente error si scusi e ami.
Amor, che mi favella
della noiosa vista,   10
com'irato dir suole
che nel suo regno non s'attenda o chiami.
E 'l ciel pur vuol ch'i' brami,
a quel che spiace non sie pietà vana:
ché l'uso agli occhi ogni malfatto sana.   15

If there's some part of a woman that is beautiful,
although the others are ugly,
must I love all of them
for the sake of the great joy I take in that one alone?
And while that part of her   5
saddens my joy, it appeals
to my reason, wishing me
to excuse and even love its guiltless fault.
But Love, who addresses me
about this distasteful sight,   10
keeps telling me angrily
that in his realm such pleas are never heeded.
Yet heaven wants me to yearn,
and not to lack pity for the unpleasant part:
for habit heals every defect to our eyes.   15

Madrigal, which went through numerous drafts. The earliest version is written over a sketch possibly for M's plan to fortify the Vatican Borgo (TC no. 607v) and would thus date 1545–46 or later. The theme of a painfully unattractive woman is unique, since M habitually idealizes those he loves. The sentiments expressed here would fit Vittoria Colonna—who was known to be quite plain, in contrast to her spiritual beauty—but it seems unlikely M would have addressed such a frank critique to her.

8. *guiltless fault:* the woman's defects of appearance, over which she has no control.

Perché sì tardi e perché non più spesso
con ferma fede quell'interno ardore
che mi lieva di terra e porta 'l core
dove per suo virtù non gli è concesso?
   Forse c'ogn' intervallo n'è promesso   5
da l'uno a l'altro tuo messo d'amore,
perc'ogni raro ha più forz'e valore
quant'è più desïato e meno appresso.
   La notte è l'intervallo, e 'l dì la luce:
l'una m'aghiaccia 'l cor, l'altro l'infiamma   10
d'amor, di fede e d'un celeste foco.

Why does it come so slowly, and why not more often,
that inner ardor, full of steady faith,
that lifts me from the earth and transports my heart
up there where it's not admitted on its own merit?
   Perhaps you've set for us such a long interval   5
between one dispatch of your love and the next
because every rare thing has more power and value
the more desired it is and the less near.
   The interval is night, and your light the day:
one freezes my heart, the other sets it on fire   10
with love, with faith, and with a heavenly flame.

Incomplete sonnet of uncertain date, perhaps 1546–47; possibly addressed to Vittoria Colonna. Cf. the similar language in no. 258.

   4. *up there:* heaven, state of spiritual bliss.

   9. *your light:* the radiance of your inspiring message of love.

   10. For the typically Petrarchan antithesis of burning and freezing, cf. nos. 19, 87, 89, 261, 281, etc.

Quantunche sie che la beltà divina
qui manifesti il tuo bel volto umano,
donna, il piacer lontano
m'è corto sì, che del tuo non mi parto,
c'a l'alma pellegrina   5
gli è duro ogni altro sentiero erto o arto.
Ond' il tempo comparto:
per gli occhi il giorno e per la notte il core,
senza intervallo alcun c'al cielo aspiri.
Sì 'l destinato parto   10
mi ferm'al tuo splendore,
c'alzar non lassa i mie ardenti desiri,
s'altro non è che tiri
la mente al ciel per grazia o per mercede:
tardi ama il cor quel che l'occhio non vede.   15

Although it is true that your human face
makes divine beauty manifest down here,
Lady, that distant pleasure
is so fleeting that I can't move away from yours;
for to my pilgrim soul   5
every other steep and narrow path is hard.
Thus I allot my time:
the day for your eyes and the night for your heart,
with no intervals in which to aspire to heaven.
My fate, ordained at birth,   10
keeps me so fixed on your brilliance
that it doesn't permit my burning desires to rise,
unless there's someone else
to draw my mind toward heaven through grace or mercy:
for the heart is slow to love what the eye can't see.   15

Madrigal of uncertain date, probably among the last for Vittoria Colonna, 1546–47; cf. similar images in no. 257.

1–6. Unfortunately, the joy of divine presence (*that distant pleasure*) can be experienced only fitfully and faintly (*fleeting*) by *my pilgrim soul* (cf. no. 244:14), forced to wander through a difficult earthly life (*down here*) away from spiritual fulfillment. Consequently, I cannot move from the pleasure of your physical beauty (*yours,* line 4) toward contemplating the less accessible spiritual delight to which it bears witness.

6. Cf. Dante, *Purgatorio* 27:132, "You are beyond the steep roads and the narrow ones."

8. I spend my days gazing at you, and my nights thinking about you.

10. An astrological metaphor.

15. Cf. nos. 163:13, A26.

Ben può talor col mie 'rdente desio
salir la speme e non esser fallace,
ché s'ogni nostro affetto al ciel dispiace,
a che fin fatto arebbe il mondo Iddio?

Qual più giusta cagion dell'amart'io   5
è, che dar gloria a quella eterna pace
onde pende il divin che di te piace,
e c'ogni cor gentil fa casto e pio?

Fallace speme ha sol l'amor che muore
con la beltà, c'ogni momento scema,   10
ond'è suggetta al variar d'un bel viso.

Dolce è ben quella in un pudico core,
che per cangiar di scorza o d'ora strema
non manca, e qui caparra il paradiso.

Surely there are some times when my hope can mount
along with my burning desire, and not prove false,
for if every feeling of ours displeased heaven,
to what end would God have made the world?

What better reason for my loving you   5
can there be, than to glorify that eternal peace
from which descends the divine I love through you,
and which makes every tender heart pure and pious?

Only false hope can be held by the love that dies
with beauty, which decreases with every hour,   10
so that hope is subject to changing of a fair face.

But sweet is that hope found in a chaste heart,
which is not reduced by changes in the flesh
or the final hour, and is our pledge of paradise.

The first three versions of this sonnet address a "signor mio," probably Tommaso de' Cavalieri; the fourth and final version, given here, eliminates any specific reference to the addressee. Version 1 is superimposed on architectural sketches for Saint Peter's in Rome, where M was appointed principal architect in 1547 (TC no. 591v; see no. 260, on the same sheet).

6. *eternal peace:* God, the eternal source of peace.

9–11. Any love that derives merely from physical attraction can never hope for true satisfaction, since the beauty that inspires it is mortal and doomed to continual decline.

12–14. By contrast, a love based on spiritual sympathy is unaffected by physical decline (*scorza,* literally "bark," expresses contempt for the body's mere external covering) or by death and provides some assurance to those here on earth that heavenly bliss is to follow.

14. *pledge of paradise:* cf. no. 263:10.

Non è sempre di colpa aspra e mortale
d'una immensa bellezza un fero ardore,
se poi sì lascia liquefatto il core,
che 'n breve il penetri un divino strale.

Amore isveglia e desta e 'mpenna l'ale,   5
né l'alto vol preschive al van furore;
qual primo grado c'al suo creatore,
di quel non sazia, l'alma ascende e sale.

L'amor di quel ch'i' parlo in alto aspira;
donna è dissimil troppo; e mal conviensi   10
arder di quella al cor saggio e verile.

L'un tira al cielo, e l'altro in terra tira;
nell'alma l'un, l'altr'abita ne' sensi,
e l'arco tira a cose basse e vile.

A violent burning for prodigious beauty
is not always a source of harsh and deadly sin,
if then the heart is left so melted by it
that a divine dart can penetrate it quickly.

Far from hindering empty passion from flying higher,   5
love stirs and wakes us, and feathers our wings;
and from that first step, with which it's not satisfied,
the soul can mount up and rise to its creator.

The love I speak of aspires to the heights;
woman is too different from that, and it's not worthy   10
of a wise and manly heart to burn for her.

One love draws toward heaven, the other draws down to earth;
one dwells in the soul, the other in the senses,
and draws its bow at base and vile things.

Sonnet, written on the back of no. 259, ca. 1546–47 (TC no. 591r). M here celebrates in misogynistic terms the classical-Neoplatonic ideal of ennobling *amicitia,* or spiritual friendship between men, a theme that recalls many of his poems for Cavalieri; cf. nos. 39, 62, 83. As in his earlier poems, the conceit is drawn from Ficino's commentary on Plato's *Symposium,* with its distinction between "two Venuses in the soul, the one heavenly, the other earthly" (FJ p. 191); cf. no. 276.

7. *that first step:* earthly, physical love.

9–14. The love of men, conceived as spiritual, encourages the soul to rise toward thoughts of God, while the love of women, being more sensual, holds the lover's attention on ignoble, earthly matters.

Se 'l troppo indugio ha più grazia e ventura
che per tempo al desir pietà non suole,
la mie, negli anni assai, m'affligge e duole,
ché 'l gioir vecchio picciol tempo dura.

Contrario ha 'l ciel, se di no' sente o cura,   5
arder nel tempo che ghiacciar si vuole,
com'io per donna; onde mie triste e sole
lacrime peso con l'età matura.

Ma forse, ancor c'al fin del giorno sia,
col sol già quasi oltr'a l'occaso spento,   10
fra le tenebre folte e 'l freddo rezzo,

s'amor c'infiamma solo a mezza via,
né altrimenti è, s'io vecchio ardo drento,
donna è che del mie fin farà 'l mie mezzo.

Though long delay yields more grace and good fortune
than desire usually gains from early mercy,
mine, coming after many years, grieves and pains me,
for joy in old age lasts but a short time.

Heaven, if it cares for us, must be opposed   5
to burning at a time when we should freeze,
as I do for a lady; therefore my sad
and lonely tears equal my great age in weight.

But perhaps, though I am at the end of my day—
with my sun nearly gone out below the horizon,   10
already amid the dense shadows and cold darkness—

since love only inflames us in the middle of our path,
yet I, an old man, am burning inside, she is
the lady who'll turn my end into my middle.

Sonnet, on the same sheet as no. 264, probably ca. 1546.

1–4. By waiting until old age for satisfaction, the lover ought to gain greater happiness than is enjoyed by a youthful love that is achieved without suffering. Paradoxically, however, my own late-arriving happiness is a source of misery, because I know I have little time left to enjoy it.

6. For other examples of the Petrarchan antithesis of freezing and burning, cf. nos. 19, 87, 89, 257, 281, etc.

7–8. The older I get, the heavier flow my tears (literally, "I weigh my tears with my age").

11. Cf. no. 2.

12–14. Since love is characteristic of the middle years and not the late ones, I hope that the love inspired by this lady will rejuvenate me in my old age by making me feel middle-aged again. The expression *middle of our path* recalls Dante, *Inferno* 1:1, "midway in the journey of our life," referring to age 35.

Amor, se tu se' dio,
non puo' ciò che tu vuoi?
Deh fa' per me, se puoi,
quel ch'i' fare' per te, s'Amor fuss'io.
Sconviensi al gran desio　　　　　　　　　　　　5
d'alta beltà la speme,
vie più l'effetto a chi è press'al morire.
Pon nel tuo grado il mio:
dolce gli fie chi 'l preme?
Ché grazia per poc'or doppia 'l martire.　　　　　10
Ben ti voglio ancor dire:
che sarie morte, s'a' miseri è dura,
a chi muor giunto a l'alta suo ventura?

Love, since you are a god,
can't you do whatever you want?
Then do for me, if you can,
what I would do for you if I were Love.
For one who's close to death,　　　　　　　　　　5
it's not even fitting to hope
for the beauty he so desires, much less to attain it.
So please grant what I wish:
Can that which crushes him ever turn sweet,
when grace that lasts only hours is double torment?　10
And I want to ask you further:
If death's hard for the unhappy, how might it be
for one who dies at the height of his good fortune?

Madrigal, of which six alternative versions survive. The earliest draft is written on a sheet containing a sketch for the knee of Saint Lawrence in the *Last Judgment* (TC no. 356), and thus dates from 1534 or after, the other versions between 1541 and 1547. M alternates between first-person pleas or questions addressed to Love and descriptions of his own present and hypothetical plight, cast in the third person. Cf. no. 263:16–17.

3–4, 8. Free me from my passionate desire and/or assure that it will never be satisfied, because:

9–10. Even if he (the man close to death, that is, M himself) were to gain the love he seeks, it could not satisfy him at this age, since the knowledge that he could enjoy it only for a short time would make it painful.

12–13. Moreover, if his desire were satisfied and did provide some measure of happiness, then he would find it even more painful to give up this life than do people with little to lose.

263

La nuova beltà d'una
mi sprona, sfrena e sferza;
né sol passato è terza,
ma nona e vespro, e prossim'è la sera.
Mie parto e mie fortuna,   5
l'un co' la morte scherza,
né l'altra dar mi può qui pace intera.
I' c'accordato m'era
col capo bianco e co' molt'anni insieme,
già l'arra in man tene' dell'altra vita,   10
qual ne promette un ben contrito core.
Più perde chi men teme
nell'ultima partita,
fidando sé nel suo propio valore
contr'a l'usato ardore: 15
s'a la memoria sol resta l'orecchio,
non giova, senza grazia, l'esser vecchio.

Once again a woman's beauty
cuts me loose, and spurs and lashes me;
not only has Terce gone by,
but None and Vespers too, and evening is near.
Between my birth and fortune,   5
the one dallies with death,
and the other can't give me real peace down here.
I, who had come to terms
with both my white head and my many years,
already held in my hand the pledge of the next life   10
for which a truly penitent heart hopes.
One who fears less loses more
at his final departure,
by entrusting himself to his own power to fight
against his longstanding passion: 15
even if only an echo remains in memory,
just being old won't help him, without grace.

Madrigal, on the same sheet as fragments of two letters from 1547 (C. MLXXIII, MLXXXII; R. 276, 280; TC no. 424r); the poem was probably written slightly before the letters. In the second letter, M thanks Benedetto Varchi for sending the manuscript of his *Lezzioni* (see Introduction and no. 151) and notes, in a tone similar to the poem, "I am not only an old man, but almost numbered among the dead."

2. Cf. Dante, *Rime* 111:3, and the verses by Girolamo Benivieni, "Amor mi sferza, Amor mi sprona" (*Opere*, Venice, 1522, f. 101r).

3–4. *Terce, None, Vespers:* In the ecclesiastical ordering of the day, these prayers are recited respectively at morning, afternoon, and dusk.

5–7. Both my physical life (*birth*, i.e., the path of life begun then) and my spiritual destiny are causing me pain in old age; the former because it is heading toward death, the latter because I am so susceptible to earthly love, which cannot bring happiness during life.

10–11. I had already begun to anticipate life in heaven and felt that I had earned it. Cf. no. 259, "pledge of paradise."

12–15. One who does not fear God's wrath and the power of temptation sufficiently will believe that he can overcome temptation by himself, but it is so powerful that he will be overcome and, when death comes, will find himself condemned for his sins.

16–17. Even a faint memory of old passion suffices to overcome the resistance of age, unless God's grace intervenes. The sentiment is similar to no. 262, where M appeals to the classical god Amor for rescue.

Come portato ho già più tempo in seno
l'immagin, donna, del tuo volto impressa,
or che morte s'appressa,
con previlegio Amor ne stampi l'alma,
che del carcer terreno   5
felice sie 'l dipor suo grieve salma.
Per procella o per calma
con tal segno sicura,
sie come croce contro a' suo avversari;
e donde in ciel ti rubò la natura,   10
ritorni, norma agli angeli alti e chiari,
c'a rinnovar s'impari
là sù pel mondo un spirto in carne involto,
che dopo te gli resti il tuo bel volto.

Lady, as I've already carried the image
of your face pressed into my breast for a long time,
now that death is approaching,
let Love print it on my soul exclusively,
so that it may happily   5
shed the heavy corpse of its earthly prison.
May it, through storm or calm,
be safe with such a sign
to act like a cross against its enemies;
and return to heaven, from which nature stole you,   10
as a model for the lofty, shining angels
to learn to make, up there,
another spirit wrapped in flesh for the world,
so your fair face may stay in it after you.

Madrigal, 1547. Unlike Raphael and other contemporaries, M had little interest in reproducing his creations in engravings, and the imagery here, taken from printmaking, is rare; cf. no. 90, where he also describes himself marked by the imprint of his beloved as a source of power and safety. The word *mandato* (sent) written above this poem has led some editors to suppose that it was sent to Colonna during her final illness, but it is doubtful whether the poem's acknowledgment of death and the sentiments expressed would be comforting to a dying person. In any case, it is the speaker who is near death, not the lady addressed.

4. *exclusively:* M's phrase is an Italian equivalent of the Latin *cum privilegio (ad imprimendum solum),* "with the privilege of sole printing," customarily applied to prints issued under the protection of a ruler as a statement of copyright.

5. *it:* my soul.

6. *heavy corpse:* cf. no. 290:1. *earthly prison:* the body, proleptically a "corpse."

8–9. The cross was believed to frighten away devils and was also credited with miraculous powers to intimidate worldly enemies, as in the legend of Emperor Constantine (frescoed at San Francesco in Arezzo by Piero della Francesca in the 1450s). In a dream, Constantine saw the cross and heard the prophecy, "In this sign you shall conquer."

13. Cf. Dante, *Paradiso* 11:8, "nel diletto de la carne involto."

14. *it:* the earthly world.

Per non s'avere a ripigliar da tanti
quell'insieme beltà che più non era,
in donna alta e sincera
prestata fu sott'un candido velo,
c'a riscuoter da quanti   5
al mondo son, mal si rimborsa il cielo.
Ora in un breve anelo,
anzi in un punto, Iddio
dal mondo poco accorto
se l'ha ripresa, e tolta agli occhi nostri.   10
Né metter può in oblio,
benché 'l corpo sie morto,
i suo dolci, leggiadri e sacri inchiostri.
Crudel pietà, qui mostri,
se quanto a questa il ciel prestava a' brutti,   15
s'or per morte il rivuol, morremo or tutti.

So as not to have to recover from great numbers
that unified beauty that was no longer on earth,
heaven lent it all in the form of the white veil
of one noble and pure lady,
for it would be poorly repaid   5
if it had to collect from everyone in the world.
And now, in one short breath,
nay, in an instant, God
has taken her back from an unwary world
and robbed our eyes of her.   10
But, though her body is dead,
he can't make us forget
her sweet, her lovely and her sacred writings.
Cruel mercy, you've shown us here
that if heaven had lent to the ugly as much as to her,   15
and now willed its return through death, then we'd all die.

This madrigal (on the same sheet as no. 245) and no. 266 were inspired by the death of
Vittoria Colonna in February 1547, which affected M deeply (C. MLXXVIII; R. 281). The basic

metaphors derive from Petrarch's mourning for Laura, e.g., nos. 337, 350; the images of lending, calling in loans, and repayment echo the frequent concern for financial matters in M's letters around this time (e.g., C. MXCII; R. 291). On art's power to preserve memory, cf. nos. 85:25–27, 277.

1. *great numbers:* of individuals (line 4).

1–6, 15–16. A similar metaphor of reapportioning a finite amount of beauty was used for Cecchino Bracci (no. 186).

3/4. *white veil:* a chaste body.

5. *it:* heaven.

7. *one short breath:* Colonna's last breath.

8. Cf. the similar thought in no. 213.

13. *sacred writings:* literally, "inks." Colonna wrote some 215 poems of a lofty religious character, many of which she exchanged with M. Cf. no. 277.

14. *cruel mercy:* of God, whose merciful relief of Colonna's suffering nevertheless pains her survivors. *here:* on earth.

Qual meraviglia è, se prossim'al foco
mi strussi e arsi, se or ch'egli è spento
di fuor, m'affligge e mi consuma drento,
e 'n cener mi riduce a poco a poco?

Vedea ardendo sì lucente il loco   5
onde pendea il mio greve tormento,
che sol la vista mi facea contento,
e morte e strazi m'eran feste e gioco.

Ma po' che del gran foco lo splendore
che m'ardeva e nutriva, il ciel m'invola,   10
un carbon resto acceso e ricoperto.

E s'altre legne non mi porge amore
che lievin fiamma, una favilla sola
non fie di me, sì 'n cener mi converto.

Is it any wonder, since, when near the fire,
I was melted and burned, if now that it's extinguished
outside me, it besets and consumes me inside,
and bit by bit reduces me to ashes?

While it still burned, the source of my great burden   5
of suffering seemed so luminous to me
that the mere sight of it could make me happy,
and anguish and death were for me a joyful feast.

But now that heaven has robbed me of the radiance
of that great fire which burned and nourished me,   10
I'm left an ember, lit but nearly smothered.

And if Love does not supply fresh firewood
to revive my flame, then not a single spark
will be left of me, I'm turning so quickly to ashes.

Sonnet, 1547, on the death of Vittoria Colonna (see no. 265), who is personified as a flame gone out, which in turn leads to the waning of the poet's own passionate heat. M follows closely Petrarch's poem on the departed Laura, no. 270:16–19, 31–32; cf. similar language and metaphors in Lorenzo de' Medici (LM nos. XII, XIII, CXXII).

4, 11: *ashes . . . ember:* cf. nos. 92, 272:14.

8. *joyful feast:* cf. no. 281:4.

267

I' sto rinchiuso come la midolla
da la sua scorza, qua pover e solo,
come spirto legato in un'ampolla:
    e la mia scura tomba è picciol volo,
dov'è Aragn' e mill'opre e lavoranti,   5
e fan di lor filando fusaiuolo.
    D'intorn'a l'uscio ho mete di giganti,
ché chi mangi'uva o ha presa medicina
non vanno altrove a cacar tutti quanti.
    I' ho 'mparato a conoscer l'orina   10
e la cannella ond'esce, per quei fessi
che 'nanzi dì mi chiamon la mattina.
    Gatti, carogne, canterelli o cessi,
chi n'ha per masserizi' o men vïaggio
non vïen a mutarmi mai senz'essi.   15
    L'anima mia dal corpo ha tal vantaggio,
che se stasat' allentasse l'odore,
seco non la terre' 'l pan e 'l formaggio.
    La toss' e 'l freddo il tien sol che non more;
se la non esce per l'uscio di sotto,   20
per bocca il fiato a pen' uscir può fore.
    Dilombato, crepato, infranto e rotto
son già per le fatiche, e l'osteria
è morte, dov'io viv' e mangio a scotto.
    La mia allegrezz' è la maninconia,   25
e 'l mio riposo son questi disagi:
che chi cerca il malanno, Dio gliel dia.
    Chi mi vedess' a la festa de' Magi
sarebbe buono; e più, se la mia casa
vedessi qua fra sì ricchi palagi.   30
    Fiamma d'amor nel cor non m'è rimasa;
se 'l maggior caccia sempre il minor duolo,
di penne l'alma ho ben tarpata e rasa.
    Io tengo un calabron in un orciuolo,
in un sacco di cuoio ossa e capresti,   35
tre pilole di pece in un bocciuolo.

Gli occhi di biffa macinati e pesti,
i denti come tasti di stormento
c'al moto lor la voce suoni e resti.

   La faccia mia ha forma di spavento;   40
i panni da cacciar, senz'altro telo,
dal seme senza pioggia i corbi al vento.

   Mi cova in un orecchio un ragnatelo,
ne l'altro canta un grillo tutta notte;
né dormo e russ' al catarroso anelo.   45

   Amor, le muse e le fiorite grotte,
mie scombiccheri, a' cemboli, a' cartocci,
agli osti, a' cessi, a' chiassi son condotte.

   Che giova voler far tanti bambocci,
se m'han condotto al fin, come colui   50
che passò 'l mar e poi affogò ne' mocci?

   L'arte pregiata, ov'alcun tempo fui
di tant'opiniön, mi rec'a questo,
povero, vecchio e servo in forz'altrui,
   ch'i' son disfatto, s'i' non muoio presto.   55

   I am shut up here, all alone and poor,
as is the pulp of a fruit by its husk,
like a genie bound up in a bottle;
   and there's little room to fly in my dark tomb
where Arachne and a thousand of her workers,   5
spinning, make little bobbins of themselves.
   Around my doorway I find gigantic dung-heaps,
as if nobody who eats grapes, or has taken
a physic, ever goes anywhere else to shit.
   I myself have gotten to know urine   10
and the little tube it comes out of, through that slit
that calls me every morning before daybreak.
   No one ever comes to clean here without leaving
the carcasses of cats, or chamberpots,
either to furnish my house or to save a trip.   15
   My soul is so much better off than my body
that if, once unstopped, my body let out its stink,
not even bread and cheese could hold the soul in.

Only my cough and cold keep the soul from dying,
for it cannot get out by the lower exit,   20
and even my breath can scarcely get out of my mouth.
   I have been weakened, ruptured, crushed and broken
by all my labors, and I already live
and eat my meals on credit at death's inn.
   From melancholy I get my happiness,   25
and these discomforts are my source of rest:
may God give such misfortune to him who seeks it.
   Whoever saw me would say I'm right for a part
on the Magi's Feast, especially if he saw
my house among such splendid palaces here.   30
   Not a spark of love is left within my heart;
since a greater pain always drives out a lesser,
my soul's wings have been fully clipped and plucked.
   I've got a bumblebee inside my jug,
some bones and strings inside my leather bag,   35
and three pills of pitch inside my little vial;
   eyes of a bluish color, ground and crushed,
and teeth like the keys on a wind instrument,
at whose movements my voice may sound or cease.
   My face has a shape that's enough to terrify;   40
my clothes could chase crows, with no further rags,
away from fresh, dry seed and into the wind.
   In one of my ears a spiderweb is nestled,
and in the other a cricket sings all night;
my raspy breath keeps me from sleeping or snoring.   45
   Love, the Muses, and the flowery grottoes:
my scribbles are only good for tambourines
and wrapping, for innkeepers, latrines, and brothels.
   What good was my wish to make so many playthings;
if they've brought me to the same end as that man   50
who crossed the sea only to drown in snot?
   That esteemed art in which I, for some time,
enjoyed such renown, has brought me to this state:
poor, and old, and a servant in the power of others,
so that I'm done for, if I don't die soon.   55

Capitolo of uncertain date, ca. 1546–50. Lines 10–12 and 36 may refer to M's problems with urination due to kidney stones, about which he wrote in numerous letters between May 1548 and December 1549. The poem is full of self-mocking and even bitter denunciations of the trials and infirmities of old age, intensifying his early, occasional comic vein (e.g., nos. 5, 20, 54) into scatological and grotesque images. The underlying metaphor is the soul shut up in an increasingly decrepit and recalcitrant body; cf. M's desire to shed this corpselike earthly burden, no. 264:6. See also A16 for a similar catalogue of his ills and problems in old age.

4. *tomb:* my house, where I live as if already dead.

5. *Arachne* challenged Athena to a weaving contest and was punished for her presumption by being transformed into a spider. M means that his house is full of cobwebs.

10–12. Condivi also reports that in his later years M had great difficulty urinating (CW p. 108).

13–15. The passage is obscure but seems to suggest that those who come to clean M's house (or, alternatively, to visit him) leave behind filthy things, either because they think he wants to furnish his disorderly house with them, or because the visitors don't want to carry them any farther.

16–18. Another obscure passage, apparently claiming that his body is so inhospitable to his soul that not even eating good food could induce the soul to stay in the body, and if his constipation were to be relieved by breaking wind, the soul would seek to escape along with the body's unpleasant gases.

19–21. Besides the constipation that blocks one path of escape from the body (*the lower exit*, i.e., the anus; cf. lines 16–18), the other condition that keeps my soul from leaving the body is my respiratory congestion, which prevents even ordinary breath from escaping normally.

23–24. *I already live . . . at death's inn:* I'm "one foot in the grave." Cf. no. 263.

27–30. M claims self-mockingly that he would be suitable to represent Befana, the ugly old woman believed to come down the chimney bringing presents on the Feast of the Magi (6 January, called Epiphany or Twelfth Night in English, *Epifania* in Italian). Moreover, his house is so meager compared to those of his neighbors that it is like the biblical stable of Christ's birth, i.e., M feels himself old and ugly and poor. Many years earlier, M had written somewhat defensively of this same dwelling that "it is true that I live simply in my own house, and intend to do so" (C. cxvii; R. 89). Bernardo Buontalenti later recalled that M had painted a skeleton in the stairwell of the house, further evidence of his somber and austere home life (see no. 110). The sentiment of line 27 and the Epiphany metaphor recall Francesco Berni's "Sopra la mula d'Alcionio": ". . . il dì di Befania / anunzio il malan, che Dio gli dia."

31. Cf. no. 266:13–14: The image of his spiritual wings now plucked of their feathers (cf. line 4) contrasts poignantly with his earlier images of ecstatic flight, e.g., nos. 59, 61, 89.

34. That is, a buzzing sound inside my head or ears: cf. line 44.

35. My bones and muscles seem to rattle around in my sagging skin. Condivi noted that M's "body tends more to nerves and bones than to flesh and fat" (CW p. 108).

36. Pitch derived from pine trees was often used medicinally. This image has been variously interpreted as an allusion to constipation (material trapped in the intestine) or to M's kidney stones (trapped in these organs).

37. Condivi describes M's eyes as "horn colored. . . . with little flecks of yellow and blue" (CW p. 108).

38–39. My teeth are so loose in my jaw that they move up and down and, like the valves on a musical instrument that permit or impede passage of air, they alternately permit or prevent speech.

40. Cf. the terrifying, grotesque portrait of M's face in the flayed skin of Saint Bartholomew in the *Last Judgment*.

41–42. My clothes are as worn and unkempt as those of a scarecrow and would suffice by themselves to frighten off crows even from a field of newly sown seed that has not yet been soaked by rain. M's house was located in the street called *Macel de' Corvi*, "slaughterhouse of the crows."

43–44. I can't hear at all in one ear, and the other one rings constantly. M had noted a ringing in his ear as early as a letter of 1518 (C. CCLXXXVI; R. 119).

46–55. This final renunciation of artistic activity, both literary and visual, persists through the rest of the *Rime*, e.g., nos. 282, 285, 288.

46–48. The poems I wrote on romantic subjects are of no use now, except that the paper on which I wrote them (and perhaps, by extension, my drawings) might serve to cover tambourines, to wrap packages (especially for innkeepers), or for cleaning toilets and brothels (literally "alleys"). M's dismissal of traditional, hackneyed subjects is formulaic, since he himself never did write about muses or grottoes. He wrote in regard to his poetry in February 1550 that "I contend with death and that my mind is on other things" (C. MCXLIII; R. 343).

52. *that esteemed art:* sculpture.

54. *a servant in the power of others:* subject to the whims of his patrons. M's difficulties with the heirs of Julius II over his contract for the pope's tomb, which he compared to slavery, lasted into the 1540s. After 1547 he had to work closely with the officers of the *fabbrica* of Saint Peter's, to whom he also referred to himself as a servant (C. MCXLII; R. 342).

Perché l'età ne 'nvola
il desir cieco e sordo,
con la morte m'accordo,
stanco e vicino all'ultima parola.
L'alma che teme e cola   5
quel che l'occhio non vede,
come da cosa perigliosa e vaga,
dal tuo bel volto, donna, m'allontana.
Amor, c'al ver non cede,
di nuovo il cor m'appaga   10
di foco e speme; e non già cosa umana
mi par, mi dice, amar . . .

Because old age robs us
of blind and deaf desire,
I'm making my peace with death,
now that I'm tired and nearing my last word.
My soul, which fears and adores   5
what the eye cannot see,
is distancing me from your fair face, Lady,
as if from something dangerously seductive.
But Love, who won't yield to truth,
delights my heart anew   10
with fire and hope, and seems to say to me
that love's not merely human . . .

Unfinished madrigal, on the recto of same sheet as nos. 269 and 270 (TC no. 353). The sheet contains sketches for the *Last Judgment* (ca. 1535), including one for the leg of Christ (on the verso, next to no. 269). The poems are later than the drawings; while most editors date the poems after the death of Vittoria Colonna in 1547, the continuing presence of her temptation in no. 268 suggests she was still alive when it was written, perhaps 1545–46.

2. *blind and deaf*: to the demands of virtue.

6. *what the eye cannot see*: God.

11–12. Love tries to make his temptation acceptable by insinuating that the feeling being induced is not mere mortal attraction but something spiritual.

Or d'un fier ghiaccio, or d'un ardente foco,
or d'anni o guai, or di vergogna armato,
l'avvenir nel passato
specchio con trista e dolorosa speme;
e 'l ben, per durar poco,   5
sento non men che 'l mal m'affligge e preme.
Alla buona, alla rie fortuna insieme,
di me già stanche, ognor chieggio perdono:
e veggio ben che della vita sono
ventura e grazia l'ore brieve e corte,   10
se la miseria medica la morte.

Once armed with cruel ice and the fire of passion,
now with old age and troubles, and with shame,
I see my future reflected in my past
with sad and aching hope;
and joy, being short-lived,   5
distresses and burdens me no less than pain.
I keep asking pardon from both good and bad
fortune, who are already tired of me;
and I see clearly that the short, fleeting hours
of life are a lucky blessing,   10
since only death can cure our misery.

Madrigal, on the same sheet as nos. 268 and 270, over a sketch for the *Last Judgment*.

1–4. Reflecting on my past, I see that my future will be no better, for the tortures of youthful love have been replaced by the ills and remorse of old age, and my only hope for respite is the longing for death (line 11).

270

Tu mi da' di quel c'ognor t'avanza
e vuo' da me le cose che non sono.

You only give me what you have left over,
and you want things from me that I do not have.

Fragment, on the same sheet as nos. 268 and 269, addressed to Love.

Di te con teco, Amor, molt'anni sono
nutrito ho l'alma e, se non tutto, in parte
il corpo ancora; e con mirabil arte
con la speme il desir m'ha fatto buono.
    Or, lasso, alzo il pensier con l'alie e sprono   5
me stesso in più sicura e nobil parte.
Le tuo promesse indarno delle carte
e del tuo onor, di che piango e ragiono . . .

On you and with you, Love, for many years
I fed my soul, and—in part, though not entirely—
my body, too; and desire, nourished by hope,
made me strong with its miraculous skill.
    But now, weary, I raise my thoughts on wings, and spur   5
myself toward a more secure and noble place.
In vain do the promises you made on paper
and on your honor, which I speak of and lament . . .

Two quatrains, probably the beginning of an unfinished sonnet, written at the top of a sheet containing a sketch for the plan of Saint Peter's from late 1546 (TC no. 592r); the poem probably dates 1546–50. Translation of the last sentence, which is incomplete, is conjectural.

    6. *a more secure and noble place:* heaven, spiritual goals.

Tornami al tempo, allor che lenta e sciolta
al cieco ardor m'era la briglia e 'l freno;
rendimi il volto angelico e sereno
onde fu seco ogni virtù sepolta,

    e' passi spessi e con fatica molta,   5
che son sì lenti a chi è d'anni pieno;
tornami l'acqua e 'l foco in mezzo 'l seno,
se vuo' di me saziarti un'altra volta.

    E s'egli è pur, Amor, che tu sol viva
de' dolci amari pianti de' mortali,   10
d'un vecchio stanco oma' puo' goder poco;

    ché l'alma, quasi giunta a l'altra riva,
fa scudo a' tuo di più pietosi strali:
e d'un legn'arso fa vil pruova il foco.

Bring back to me the time when bridle and bit
were slack, and scarcely reined in my blind desire;
give back to me that face, angelic and calm,
along with which every virtue has been buried.

    My shuffling steps, taken with so much effort,   5
are so slow in one so loaded down with years;
bring back the water and fire to my breast
if you would gorge yourself on me once more.

    For if it's really true, O Love, that you
live only on the bittersweet tears of mortals,   10
you won't enjoy many of those from a tired old man.

    For my soul, which has almost reached the other shore,
shields me from your arrows with far more merciful ones,
and fire can do little to charred wood.

Sonnet on the death of Vittoria Colonna, 1547 or after, of which several drafts survive. One draft is written on the back of a sheet containing no. 273 (TC no. 396); another on TC no. 424v; and part of the near-final version is written on a sheet of drawings, dating from about 1540, showing the bases of architectural columns for the Campidoglio in Rome (TC no. 607r). The repeated plea to bring back evidence of lost love recalls no. 95, inspired by Tommaso de' Cavalieri, now with the added poignancy of lost youth as well.

7. *water and fire:* the passion and tears of love.

9–10. Cf. Petrarch, no. 93:14, where Love declares, "I feed on tears."

12. *other shore:* M's fresco of the *Last Judgment* in the Sistine Chapel (1535–41) depicts the classical image, familiar from Dante, of the river Styx, across which dead souls are ferried to the shores of the afterlife.

13. *more merciful ones:* arrows of divine, rather than earthly, love, which cause pangs of remorse that are a spur to salvation.

14. *charred wood,* i.e., already burned by love. Cf. nos. 92, 266.

Se sempre è solo e un quel che sol muove
il tutto per altezza e per traverso,
non sempre a no' si mostra per un verso,
ma più e men quante suo grazia piove.

A me d'un modo e d'altri in ogni altrove: 5
più e men chiaro o più lucente e terso,
secondo l'egritudin, che disperso
ha l'intelletto a le divine pruove.

Nel cor ch'è più capace più s'appiglia,
se dir si può, 'l suo volto e 'l suo valore;   10
e di quel fassi sol guida e lucerna.

. . . .

. . . . . .

truova conforme a la suo parte interna.

While he who alone moves everything, both high
and wide, remains always one and the same,
he doesn't always show himself the same way,
but showers his grace on us in different amounts.

He appears in one way to me, but in other ways   5
to everyone else: more or less clear and radiant
in proportion to how much one's sickness has dulled
one's mind to the evidence of divinity.

In a heart that is more capable, one might say,
his face and worth are grasped more readily,   10
and only to such does he make himself guide and light.

. . . .

. . . .

he finds consistent with his inner part.

Unfinished sonnet, ca. 1547, writtten on the recto of a sheet whose verso contains a version of no. 272 (TC no. 396). Between lines 11 and 14 is a sketch of a hand holding a book, which apparently predates the poem.

1–4. Cf. Dante, *Paradiso* 1:1–9.

1–2. *both high and wide:* literally, "vertically and horizontally," i.e., God controls all things everywhere, up to the heavens and across the entire earth.

7. *sickness:* moral infirmity or weakness.

9. *more capable:* possessing a greater sensitivity toward the divine (because not tainted or distracted by sin).

274

Deh fammiti vedere in ogni loco!
Se da mortal bellezza arder mi sento,
appresso al tuo mi sarà foco ispento,
e io nel tuo sarò, com'ero, in foco.

Signor mie caro, i' te sol chiamo e 'nvoco   5
contr'a l'inutil mie cieco tormento:
tu sol puo' rinnovarmi fuora e drento
le voglie e 'l senno e 'l valor lento e poco.

Tu desti al tempo, Amor, quest'alma diva
e 'n questa spoglia ancor fragil e stanca   10
l'incarcerasti, e con fiero destino.

Che poss'io altro che così non viva?
Ogni ben senza te, Signor, mi manca;
il cangiar sorte è sol poter divino.

I pray you, make me see you everywhere!
Then, if I feel I'm burning from mortal beauty,
my fire will be extinguished next to yours,
and I'll be aflame in yours as I was before.

My dear Lord, I call and appeal to you alone   5
against my tormenting passion, blind and futile:
you alone can renew, within and without,
my will, my judgment, and my meager strength.

You, Love, gave my divine soul over to Time,
and imprisoned it, with a harsh destiny,   10
within this mortal carcass now frail and tired.

What else can I do so as not to live this way?
Without you, Lord, I'm deprived of every blessing,
and the power to change fate is God's alone.

Sonnet from mid-1547. Written on the same sheet as a version of no. 272, which also bears a fragment of a letter to Benedetto Varchi and (on the verso) M's letter to Varchi regarding his lecture on M's poetry (C. MLXXXII; R. 280; see no. 151); see also TC no. 424v. Girardi (*Studi*, 124) transcribes a prayer with similarly beseeching religious sentiments written on the autograph ms. of the *Rime* (*Ricordi* CCXLVII), though it is not known whether M himself composed it.

4. *as I was before*: before birth, when the soul was still in heaven, enraptured by the presence of God (cf. lines 9–11).

9–10. You, O loving God, took my soul from heaven and consigned it to the earthly world, where its fate is to be subject to the passage of time and to death.

Dagli alti monti e d'una gran ruina,
ascoso e circunscritto d'un gran sasso,
discesi a discoprirmi in questo basso,
contr'a mie voglia, in tal lapedicina.
   Quand'el sol nacqui, e da chi il ciel destina   5

· · · · · · · · · · ·

Once hidden and enclosed in a great rock,
I came down, against my will, from a great ravine
in the high mountains to this lower place,
to be revealed within this little stone.
   When the sun was born, by one whom heaven destines   5

· · · · · · · · · · ·

Fragment of a sonnet, of uncertain date. Frey placed it ca. 1547–50, during M's first years working on the construction of Saint Peter's, when he would often have been surrounded by "great rocks." The fragment is obscure; it seems that a statue is speaking and lamenting that the block of stone from which it was carved was brought down from the mountain quarries only to be reduced to a pitiful condition in the course of carving. This reading is consistent with M's Neoplatonic idea that the sculpture is already present but "hidden and enclosed" within the superfluous material of the raw stone block; cf. nos. 151, 152, and Charles de Tolnay, *The Art and Thought of Michelangelo*, 83–108.

Passa per gli occhi al core in un momento
qualunque obbietto di beltà lor sia,
e per sì larga e sì capace via
c'a mille non si chiude, non c'a cento,
    d'ogni età, d'ogni sesso; ond'io pavento,   5
carco d'affanni, e più di gelosia;
né fra sì vari volti so qual sia
c'anzi morte mi die 'ntero contento.
    S'un ardente desir mortal bellezza
ferma del tutto, non discese insieme   10
dal ciel con l'alma; è dunche umana voglia.
    Ma se pass'oltre, Amor, tuo nome sprezza,
c'altro die cerca; e di quel più non teme
c'a lato vien contr'a sì bassa spoglia.

Anything that seems beautiful to my eyes
passes through them instantly into my heart,
along a path that is so broad and spacious
that it's wide open to hundreds, even thousands
    of all ages and all sexes. Thus I'm fearful,   5
burdened with worries, and even more with suspicions:
for among such varied faces, I can't tell
which could make me completely happy before I die.
    If a burning desire stops short entirely
at mortal beauty, then it did not descend   10
from heaven along with the soul, and must be earthly.
    But if it goes further, Love, it scorns your name,
for it seeks another god, and no longer fears
that you'll come near to attack so wretched a carcass.

Sonnet, ca. 1547–50; a draft of no. 235 is written on the same side of this sheet and part of no. 236 on the recto. The theme is the familiar Neoplatonic and Dantesque-Petrarchan concern of differentiating between heavenly and earthly love; cf. no. 260. On M's extreme susceptibility to visual charms (lines 1–5), Condivi noted that "he has loved not only human beauty but everything beautiful in general" (CW p. 105).

4. *wide open:* literally, "not closed."

9. (Understood): This, then, is the rule to follow in distinguishing between all these seductive faces:

10. *it:* my desire, which is proved not to be divine.

12–14. On the other hand, if my desire looks beyond the mere physical beauty of someone and views that beauty as a manifestation of the divine, then it transcends the definition of mere earthly love (Amor or Cupid, addressed here by his name) and no longer fears that carnal impulses will tempt my frail body into sin. Some editors read *die* (line 13) as another "day," i.e., eternal life.

Se con lo stile o coi colori avete
alla natura pareggiato l'arte,
anzi a quella scemato il pregio in parte,
che 'l bel di lei più bello a noi rendete,
   poi che con dotta man posto vi sete   5
a più degno lavoro, a vergar carte,
quel che vi manca, a lei di pregio in parte,
nel dar vita ad altrui, tutta togliete.
   Che se secolo alcuno omai contese
in far bell'opre, almen cedale, poi   10
che convien c'al prescritto fine arrive.
   Or le memorie altrui, già spente, accese
tornando, fate or che fien quelle e voi,
malgrado d'esse, etternalmente vive.

While, with your pencil and with your colors,
you had already made art the equal of nature,
and had, in fact, diminished her glory in part,
since you gave her beauties back to us more beautiful,
   now that you've set yourself, with your learned hand,   5
to the worthier task of putting pen to paper,
you've taken from her, by giving life to others,
even that part of her glory that you still lacked.
   For any age that ever vied with her
in making beautiful works, had to yield to her,   10
since all things must come to their ordained end.
   But now, by rekindling memories of others,
long extinguished, you make both them and yourself
live for eternity, despite their fate.

Sonnet sent to Giorgio Vasari in 1550, in gratitude for Vasari's account of M in the first edition of his *Lives of the most eminent painters, sculptors, and architects,* published early in that year. The poem was reprinted and discussed by Vasari in his second edition, 1568 (VM 7:229; VB p. 394). In a slightly later letter to Vasari of August 1550, M thanked him for several letters that had praised him, saying, "Since you revive the dead, I'm not surprised that you should prolong the life of the living" (C. MCXLVIII; R. 348). M expressed similar thoughts on the power of poetry by Francesco Berni (no. 85:25–27) and Vittoria Colonna (no. 265) to keep memory alive. No. 299 may also have been written for Vasari; nos. 285 and 288 were sent to him.

1. *pencil and . . . colors:* drawing and painting. M had seen (and drily criticized) Vasari's frescoes of Pope Paul III in the Palazzo della Cancelleria in Rome, painted in 1546.

9–11. The attempts of artists in every past age to rival nature were doomed to fail, since both the art works and their mortal makers are destined to decay with time; cf. no. 239.

Chi non vuol delle foglie
non ci venga di maggio.

One who does not want leaves
should not come here in May.

Late fragment, in the form of a proverb or epigram. It is written on a plaque within the entablature of an elaborate window frame on a drawing of uncertain date, perhaps for the Campidoglio in Rome (TC no. 605r). The import of the verses is similar to the biblical passage, "To everything there is a season" (Ecclesiastes), and recalls, with an ironic reversal, Poliziano's hymn to spring greenery, "Ben venga maggio" (PO p. 143, no. XIII).

La forza d'un bel viso a che mi sprona?
C'altro non è c'al mondo mi diletti:
ascender vivo fra gli spirti eletti
per grazia tal, c'ogni altra par men buona.
    Se ben col fattor l'opra suo consuona,   5
che colpa vuol giustizia ch'io n'aspetti,
s'i' amo, anz'ardo, e per divin concetti
onoro e stimo ogni gentil persona?

To what does the power of a fair face spur me?
There's nothing on earth that gives me joy, except
to rise, still alive, among the blessed spirits
through a grace so great no other can compare.
    Since all his works harmonize with their Creator,   5
how can justice expect me to feel any guilt
if I love, nay burn, and I honor and esteem
every noble person for his divine conception?

Two late quatrains, probably an unfinished sonnet though expressing a complete thought. Uncertain date, ca. 1547–50; written on the verso of the sheet containing no. 280. The conceit of the face or eyes of the beloved inspiring the lover to heavenly thoughts is familiar from both Dante (e.g., *Purgatorio* 31:22–24; *Paradiso* 1:46–72, 18:7–21) and Petrarch (e.g., nos. 72, 264:37–54).

5–8. Since all mortals are made in the image of God, and thus reflect and point to his creative power and spiritual perfection, divine judgment (justice) must find my passionate admiration of especially beautiful individuals ultimately spiritual and praiseworthy, not carnal or evil. (On M's complex understanding of the term *concetto*, "conception," see no. 151.)

7. *love, nay burn:* cf. no. 39:7.

L'alma inquieta e confusa in sé non truova
altra cagion c'alcun grave peccato
mal conosciuto, onde non è celato
all'immensa pietà c'a' miser giova.

    I' parlo a te, Signor, c'ogni mie pruova   5
fuor del tuo sangue non fa l'uom beato:
miserere di me, da ch'io son nato
a la tuo legge; e non fie cosa nuova.

My soul, troubled and perplexed, finds within itself
no other reason for this than some grave sin
scarcely known to me, although it's not concealed
from the boundless pity that relieves the wretched.
    I'm speaking to you, Lord, since all my efforts   5
can't make a man blessed without your blood:
Have mercy on me, seeing I was born
subject to your law; that won't be anything new.

Two quatrains, probably an incomplete sonnet, on the recto of the sheet containing no. 279. Uncertain date, ca. 1547–50.

    2–3. Cf. no. 291:1–2.

    3–4. God, who is merciful, knows me better than I do myself.

    5–6. *my efforts . . . your blood:* an allusion to the belief in the superiority of faith or grace (symbolized by the blood of Christ's passion) over good works as the path to salvation. From this point on, M's poetry appeals frequently to the blood of Christ's sacrifice, e.g., nos. 289, 290, 294, 298, 302. During the years 1548–54, he was working on the Florence *Pietà*, intended for his own tomb, in which he depicted himself in the guise of Nicodemus, looking down mournfully on the crucified Christ.

    8. *that won't be anything new:* it would not be the first time you have responded to my prayers for mercy; cf. no. 286.

Arder sole' nel freddo ghiaccio il foco;
or m'è l'ardente foco un freddo ghiaccio,
disciolto, Amor, quello insolubil laccio,
e morte or m'è, che m'era festa e gioco.

   Quel primo amor che ne diè tempo e loco,   5
nella strema miseria è grave impaccio
a l'alma stanca . . .

My fire once used to burn even in cold ice,
but that burning fire is cold ice to me, Love,
now that the unbreakable knot has been untied,
and what was a joyful feast is now death to me.
   The love that once opened to us all time and space   5
is, to the tired soul in its final distress,
a burdensome weight . . .

Fragment of a sonnet, ca. 1552–54; on the same sheet as a draft of no. 285.

   1–2. *fire . . . ice:* a common Petrarchan antithesis throughout the *Rime,* e.g., nos. 19, 87, 89, 257, 261, 269, etc.

   3. That is, now that I no longer feel the heat of passion that in earlier times never left me.

   4. *joyful feast:* cf. no. 266:8.

282

Con tanta servitù, con tanto tedio
e con falsi concetti e gran periglio
dell'alma, a sculpir qui cose divine.

In such slavery, and with so much boredom,
and with false conceptions and great peril
to my soul, to be here sculpting divine things.

Three lines, perhaps for the sestet of a sonnet, written on a draft of a letter from October 1552; the same sheet contains nos. 283, 284, and one version of no. 285 (TC no. 423r). The only "divine thing" M was sculpting at this time was the Florence *Pietà* for his own tomb, which he never finished and partly destroyed, perhaps out of frustration that its execution did not live up to his *concetto* (see no. 151) or that his initial idea for the composition had turned out, as he says here, to be a "false conception" (a bad idea) (VM 7:242; VB p. 404). Though incomplete, this fragment seems intended as an ironic rejection of his achievements in art: "divine things" was a term of praise applied to M's works by Vasari and others, but here the sculptor emphasizes the troubles of his profession and his sense of inadequacy.

283

Non può, Signor mie car, la fresca e verde
età sentir, quant'a l'ultimo passo
si cangia gusto, amor, voglie e pensieri.
    Più l'alma acquista ove più 'l mondo perde;
l'arte e la morte non va bene insieme: 5
che convien più che di me dunche speri?

The fresh green years cannot imagine how much
one's tastes and loves, desires and thoughts all change,
my dear Lord, as the final steps approach.
    The soul gains more, the more it loses the world,
and art and death do not go well together;   5
in which, then, should I place my further hope?

Probably the sestet of an incomplete sonnet, though lines 2 and 5 do not rhyme. Written in late 1552, on the same sheet as nos. 282 and 285 (284 and part of 285 are on the verso).

1. *the fresh green years:* youth; cf. nos. 142, 167, 253.

2. Cf. no. 293:6.

3. *the final steps:* old age and death, the end of life's path.

4–5. The pursuit of art, and by extension of earthly beauty, distracts us from the spiritual thoughts appropriate to impending death.

284

S'a tuo nome ho concetto alcuno immago,
non è senza del par seco la morte,
onde l'arte e l'ingegno si dilegua.
    Ma se, quel c'alcun crede, i' pur m'appago
che si ritorni a viver, a tal sorte   5
ti servirò, s'avvien che l'arte segua.

When I conceive some image in your name,
it's never without its equal attendant, death,
at which my art and genius melt away.
    But if, as some believe, I can still console myself
that one returns to life, with such a fate   5
I'll serve you again, if my art comes back with me.

Sestet of an incomplete sonnet, 1552. Written on the verso of the sheet bearing nos. 282 and 283. On the same side as no. 284 is part of a draft of no. 285; underlying the text are two sketches, perhaps for a crucified Christ (TC no. 423v). The fragment, addressed to God as the source of creative intelligence, seems to flirt with the officially heretical idea of reincarnation.

    2. *death:* the premonition of death.

    3. *genius:* for M's use of *ingegno* and its meanings, see nos. 44, 84, 149, 151, 159.

Giunto è già 'l corso della vita mia,
con tempestoso mar, per fragil barca,
al comun porto, ov'a render si varca
conto e ragion d'ogni opra trista e pia.
    Onde l'affettüosa fantasia   5
che l'arte mi fece idol e monarca
conosco or ben com'era d'error carca
e quel c'a mal suo grado ogn'uom desia.
    Gli amorosi pensier, già vani e lieti,
che fien or, s'a duo morte m'avvicino?   10
D'una so 'l certo, e l'altra mi minaccia.
    Né pinger né scolpir fie più che quieti
l'anima, volta a quell'amor divino
c'aperse, a prender noi, 'n croce le braccia.

The voyage of my life at last has reached,
across a stormy sea, in a fragile boat,
the common port all must pass through, to give
an accounting for every evil and pious deed.
    So now I recognize how laden with error   5
was the affectionate fantasy
that made art an idol and sovereign to me,
like all things men want in spite of their best interests.
    What will become of all my thoughts of love,
once gay and foolish, now that I'm nearing two deaths?   10
I'm certain of one, and the other looms over me.
    Neither painting nor sculpture will be able any longer
to calm my soul, now turned toward that divine love
that opened his arms on the cross to take us in.

Sonnet, among M's best-known poems, which underwent numerous drafts between October 1552 and September 1554. One version is written on a draft of a letter to his nephew Lionardo from April 1554 (C. MCXCIV; R. 388), another on TC no. 423v (see nos. 281–84). The final version was sent to Giorgio Vasari in a letter of September 1554 (C. MCXCVII; R. 390); Vasari replied with a sonnet in matching rhymes and later reprinted and discussed the poem in the second edition of his *Lives* (VM 7:246; VB p. 406). The contrast in theme with M's earlier sonnet no. 277, dedicated to Vasari, is marked; cf. no. 288, also sent to Vasari.

1–3. The image of life as a storm-tossed boat seeking port recalls Petrarch, no. 189, "My ship laden with forgetfulness," and (more generally) his no. 80. Cf. similar boat images in nos. 45:13–15, 299:5–8.

3. *common port:* death, the final harbor shared by all souls and the time for divine judgment.

5–8. It was my own lack of understanding (fantasy)—which was, however, well intentioned and impassioned—that made me exalt art, as all men pursue some worldly desire even though it is sinful or distracting (cf. no. 284).

5. *laden with error:* cf. Petrarch, no. 132:12.

10–11. *two deaths:* that of the body, which is certain, and that of the soul in damnation, which seems imminent. Cf. nos. 43:12, 293:3.

14. This line parallels the fantasy of heavenly embrace in a poem by Girolamo Benivieni, "Already, in thought / I seem to be welcomed into his arms" (*Opere,* Venice, 1522, f. 100v); cf. also Petrarch, no. 264:14–15. Visually, it recalls M's series of late Crucifixion drawings showing Christ with his arms outstretched (TC nos. 410–422). For similar images of arms, cf. nos. 161, 290.

Christ on the Cross (TC no. 411r)

Gl'infiniti pensier mie d'error pieni,
negli ultim'anni della vita mia,
ristringer si dovrien 'n un sol che sia
guida agli etterni suo giorni sereni.
   Ma che poss'io, Signor, s'a me non vieni   5
coll'usata ineffabil cortesia?

My innumerable thoughts, all full of error,
ought to be, in the last years of my life,
reduced to a single one, which then may act
as a guide toward its serene, eternal days.
   But how can I do that, Lord, if you don't come to me   5
with your usual ineffable graciousness?

Fragment of a sonnet, of uncertain date, ca. 1552–54; on the same theme as no. 287.
   4. *its serene, eternal days:* my life's (i.e., the life of my soul) everlasting peace in heaven.
   6. Cf. no. 280:7–8.

287

Di giorno in giorno insin da' mie prim'anni,
Signor, soccorso tu mi fusti e guida,
onde l'anima mia ancor si fida
di doppia aita ne' mie doppi affanni.

Day after day, ever since my early years,
Lord, you have been my helper and my guide;
therefore my soul is even now confident
of doubled support in my doubled sufferings.

Fragment of a sonnet, of uncertain date, ca. 1552–54. Written on the verso of a sheet whose recto bears a draft of no. 288. The theme recalls Psalm 46, "God is our refuge and strength, a very present help in trouble"; cf. no. 286.

Le favole del mondo m'hanno tolto
il tempo dato a contemplare Iddio,
né sol le grazie suo poste in oblio,
ma con lor, più che senza, a peccar volto.

Quel c'altri saggio, me fa cieco e stolto   5
e tardi a riconoscer l'error mio;
manca la speme, e pur cresce il desio
che da te sia dal propio amor disciolto.

Ammezzami la strada c'al ciel sale,
Signor mie caro, e a quel mezzo solo   10
salir m'è di bisogno la tuo 'ita.

Mettimi in odio quante 'l mondo vale
e quante suo bellezze onoro e colo,
c'anzi morte caparri eterna vita.

The fables of the world have robbed from me
the time allotted for contemplating God,
and not only have I disregarded his graces,
but have turned to sin more with them than without them.

What makes others wise makes me blind and foolish   5
and slow to recognize my own errors;
though hope is dimming, yet my desire increases
to be set free by you from my self-love.

Shorten by half the road that ascends to heaven,
my dear Lord, and I still will need your help   10
even to ascend just the remaining half.

Make me despise whatever the world treasures,
and all its beauties I honor and adore,
that I may, before death, secure eternal life.

Sonnet, 1555, similar in theme and expression to Petrarch's renunciation of his lifelong love for Laura (no. 364). Copies were sent to two correspondents, first in March 1555 to Monsignor Ludovico Beccadelli, archbishop of Ragusa, who replied with a sonnet in matching rhymes. M had known Beccadelli, who was at this time one of the overseers of construction at Saint Peter's, since his service to the reformist Cardinal Reginald Pole, a close spiritual friend of Vittoria Colonna (see also no. 300). M then sent this sonnet and no. 289 to Vasari in a letter of May 1555 (C. MCCVI; R. 399), asking Vasari to deliver the sonnets to his old friend the cleric Giovan Francesco Fattucci at Florence Cathedral.

1. *fables*: the Italian *favole*, as in English, means both "alluring fantasy" and "untruth, fabrication." Thus it expresses the same attitude toward his earlier commitment to art as the term *fantasia* in no. 285, also sent to Vasari.

4. Notwithstanding the abundance of God's grace toward me, I have sinned more than I would have if I were deprived of all grace.

6. Cf. similar phrases about acknowledging error in nos. 132, 133.

9. Cf. no. 293:13.

Non è più bassa o vil cosa terrena
che quel che, senza te, mi sento e sono,
onde a l'alto desir chiede perdono
la debile mie propia e stanca lena.

Deh, porgi, Signor mio, quella catena   5
che seco annoda ogni celeste dono:
la fede, dico, a che mi stringo e sprono;
né, mie colpa, n'ho grazia intiera e piena.

Tanto mi fie maggior, quante più raro
il don de' doni, e maggior fia se, senza,   10
pace e contento il mondo in sé non have.

Po' che non fusti del tuo sangue avaro,
che sarà di tal don la tuo clemenza,
se 'l ciel non s'apre a noi con altra chiave?

There is no earthly thing more lowly or worthless
than what I feel I am, and am, without you;
and therefore my own weak and tired breath
asks pardon of you, who are the highest desire.

I pray you, my Lord, stretch out to me that chain   5
which brings, bound with it, every heavenly gift:
I mean faith, which I strive to embrace,
but whose full grace, through my own guilt, I lack.

This gift of gifts will seem the greater to me
for being so rare, and also since, without it,   10
the world by itself has neither peace nor joy.

Although you were not miserly with your blood,
what use will be such a merciful gift from you
if heaven's not opened for us with another key?

Sonnet, of which numerous drafts survive, sent to Giovan Francesco Fattucci through Vasari in 1555 (see no. 288).

8. *through my own guilt:* the Italian, *mie colpa,* echoes the Latin phrase of penitence *mea culpa;* cf. no. 23.

12–14. God's sacrifice on the cross is of no avail unless we also receive the gift of faith that will enable us to believe and trust in that gesture of salvation. For other examples of blood imagery at this time, see no. 280.

Scarco d'un'importuna e greve salma,
Signor mie caro, e dal mondo disciolto,
qual fragil legno a te stanco rivolto
da l'orribil procella in dolce calma.

Le spini e ' chiodi e l'una e l'altra palma 5
col tuo benigno umil pietoso volto
prometton grazia di pentirsi molto,
e speme di salute a la trist'alma.

Non mirin co' iustizia i tuo sant'occhi
il mie passato, e 'l gastigato orecchio; 10
non tenda a quello il tuo braccio severo.

Tuo sangue sol mie colpe lavi e tocchi,
e più abondi, quant'i' son più vecchio,
di pronta aita e di perdono intero.

Relieved of a troublesome and heavy corpse,
and set free from the world, I turn to you,
my dear Lord, as a tired and fragile boat
heads from the frightful tempest toward sweet calm.

Your thorns and your nails and both of your palms, 5
and your benign, humble, and merciful face,
promise to my unhappy soul the grace
of deep repentance and hope of salvation.

May your holy eyes not look upon my past
with justice alone, nor likewise your pure ear, 10
and may your stern arm not stretch out to it.

May your blood suffice to wash and cleanse my sins,
and the older I grow, the more may it overflow
with ever-ready aid and full forgiveness.

Sonnet, ca. 1555 or later. There are two drafts, one on the recto of a sheet whose verso bears a sketch for a *Christ in the Garden*, ca. 1556 (TC no. 406), the other on the recto of a sheet whose verso bears no. 291 (TC no. 490). This poem and no. 294 were published shortly after M's death by Dionigi Atanagi, in his *De le rime di diversi nobili poeti toscani* (Venice, 1565), vol. 2, 38.

1. *heavy corpse:* proleptically, the earthly body and its burden of sin; cf. the same phrase in no. 264:6.

3–4. For similar images of life as a ship weathering storms and seeking port, cf. nos. 264:7, 285:1–4 and Petrarch, no. 80.

5. The images refer to the instruments of Christ's passion; the nails pinning him to the cross are visible in M's drawing of the *Crucifixion* for Vittoria Colonna (TC no. 411r). *both of your palms:* the same phrase occurs in Dante, *Paradiso* 9:123, with a different meaning.

10. *with justice alone:* i.e., may your judgment be tempered with mercy. *your pure ear:* may you hear my prayers for mercy.

11. *your stern arm:* the image recalls M's figure of Christ in the Sistine *Last Judgment*, with his arm raised to condemn the sinners. Cf. similar images of Christ's arms in nos. 161, 285.

12. For other blood images, see no. 280.

Penso e ben so c'alcuna colpa preme,
occulta a me, lo spirto in gran martire;
privo dal senso e dal suo propio ardire
il cor di pace, e 'l desir d'ogni speme.
　　Ma chi è teco, Amor, che cosa teme 5
che grazia allenti inanzi al suo partire?

I think, indeed I know, that my spirit is crushed
by some sin, concealed from me, into great torment;
my senses and their own burning have deprived
my heart of peace and my desire of all hope.
　　But one who's with you, Love, need he fear that anything 5
could make your grace diminish before he leaves?

Incomplete sonnet, ca. 1555 or later. Written over a sketch of a candlestick for the tomb of Pope Julius II from about 1543 (TC no. 490v). On the recto of this sheet is a draft of no. 290.

　　2. Cf. no. 280, "some grave sin scarcely known to me."

　　4. *desire:* yearning for salvation.

　　5. *one who's with you, Love:* one who keeps God (divine love) spiritually close to him.

　　6. *before he leaves:* before death, i.e., during this life.

Ben sarien dolce le preghiere mie,
se virtù mi prestassi da pregarte:
nel mio fragil terren non è già parte
da frutto buon, che da sé nato sie.
    Tu sol se' seme d'opre caste e pie,   5
che là germuglian, dove ne fa' parte;
nessun propio valor può seguitarte,
se non gli mostri le tuo sante vie.

The prayers I'd make would certainly be sweet
if you granted me the strength to pray to you;
for in my feeble soil there's not one part
good for fruit, that was born by itself.
    You alone are the seed of pure and pious deeds,   5
which sprout up wherever you strew yourself;
no one can follow you by his own power
unless you show him the path of your holiness.

Incomplete sonnet of uncertain date, after 1555, written on the other side of the sheet bearing no. 293. The metaphors of seed, fruit, and path recall Beatrice's speech to Dante, *Purgatorio* 30:109–138, and, more closely, Petrarch, no. 71:101–05, "If any good fruit is born from me . . . "

   3. Whatever small part of me (*my feeble soil,* my weak earthly being) has attained a state of spiritual "fertility" has done so only through your aid.

293

Carico d'anni e di peccati pieno
e col trist'uso radicato e forte,
vicin mi veggio a l'una e l'altra morte,
e parte 'l cor nutrisco di veleno.

Né propie forze ho, c'al bisogno sièno   5
per cangiar vita, amor, costume o sorte,
senza le tuo divine e chiare scorte,
d'ogni fallace corso guida e freno.

Signor mie car, non basta che m'invogli
c'aspiri al ciel sol perché l'alma sia,   10
non come prima, di nulla, creata.

Anzi che del mortal la privi e spogli,
prego m'ammezzi l'alta e erta via,
e fie più chiara e certa la tornata.

Loaded down with years and filled with sins
and with bad habits, strong and deeply rooted,
I see that I am close to both of my deaths,
and yet I still nourish my heart with poison.

And I haven't, on my own, the strength that's needed   5
to change my life, love, habits or destiny,
without your divine and shining companionship,
my guide and rein on every treacherous route.

It's not enough, dear Lord, just to make me yearn
for heaven, for my soul to be remade,   10
and not as it was the first time, out of nothing:

Before you strip it of its mortal flesh,
I pray you, shorten by half the high, steep road,
so my way back may be more clear and certain.

Sonnet of uncertain date, 1555 or later; on the recto of the same sheet whose verso bears no. 292, on a similar theme.

   2. *bad habits:* of sin. Cf. Petrarch, no. 81:1–2.

   3. *both of my deaths:* of the body and the soul; cf. nos. 43:12, 285:10.

   4. *poison:* earthly passions.

   6. Cf. no. 274:7–8,14, and no. 283:3.

   12. *it:* my soul.

   13. Cf. no. 288:9.

   14. *my way back:* my return to heaven.

Mentre m'attrista e duol, parte m'è caro
ciascun pensier c'a memoria mi riede
il tempo andato, e che ragion mi chiede
de' giorni persi, onde non è riparo.

Caro m'è sol, perc'anzi morte imparo   5
quant'ogni uman diletto ha corta fede;
tristo m'è, c'a trovar grazi' e mercede
negli ultim'anni a molte colpe è raro.

Ché ben c'alle promesse tua s'attenda,
sperar forse, Signore, è troppo ardire   10
c'ogni superchio indugio amor perdoni.

Ma pur par nel tuo sangue si comprenda,
se per noi par non ebbe il tuo martire,
senza misura sien tuo cari doni.

While it saddens and pains me, I hold dear in part
each thought that brings back to my memory
times gone by, and asks for an accounting
of the days whose loss cannot be remedied.

Each is dear to me only since, before death, it teaches   5
how short a promise has every human joy;
and it's painful to me, since rarely can we find
grace and mercy in our last years, with so many sins.

For even though we're counting on your promises,
perhaps it is too daring, Lord, to hope   10
that love may pardon every excess delay.

And yet your blood seems to give us understanding
that, just as there was no equal to your suffering,
so, too, there's no limit to your precious gifts.

Late sonnet, probably after 1555. Published by Dionigi Atanagi shortly after M's death (see no. 290). On the verso is a sketch related to the drawing for *Christ in the Garden* that accompanies no. 290 (TC no. 407r).

5. *it teaches:* literally, "I learn" (from it).

11. That God's merciful love may still forgive those who have waited too long to repent of their sins.

12. For other blood images, see no. 280.

Di morte certo, ma non già dell'ora,
la vita è breve e poco me n'avanza;
diletta al senso, è non però la stanza
a l'alma, che mi prega pur ch'i' mora.

Il mondo è cieco e 'l tristo esempro ancora   5
vince e sommerge ogni prefetta usanza;
spent'è la luce e seco ogni baldanza,
trionfa il falso e 'l ver non surge fora.

Deh, quando fie, Signor, quel che s'aspetta
per chi ti crede? c'ogni troppo indugio   10
tronca la speme e l'alma fa mortale.

Che val che tanto lume altrui prometta,
s'anzi vien morte, e senza alcun refugio
ferma per sempre in che stato altri assale?

Certain of death, though not yet of its hour,
life is short and little of it is left for me;
it delights my senses, but is no fit home
for my soul, which is begging me to die.

The world is blind, and bad example goes on   5
overcoming and drowning even the best of habits.
The light is extinguished, and with it all valor;
error triumphs, and truth cannot sally forth.

Lord, when will come what is awaited by those
who believe in you? For every excess delay   10
shortens hope and puts the soul in mortal danger.

What good is your promise of great light to all,
if death attacks first, and fixes them forever
in the state he finds them in, with no escape?

Late sonnet, after 1555.

5. *the world is blind:* cf. Dante, *Purgatorio* 16:66.

7. *the light:* of divine grace. Cf. no. 87:11, "the sun of your light, extinguished in this world."

10. *delay:* cf. no. 294:11.

11. Increases the risk of damnation, by allowing more time for temptation.

12–14. The longer you put off the fulfillment of your promise of salvation, the greater the chance that death will overtake me and, finding me still in a state of sinfulness, will consign me irredeemably to hell. Cf. no. 296:14.

S'avvien che spesso il gran desir prometta
a' mie tant'anni di molt'anni ancora,
non fa che morte non s'appressi ognora,
o là dove men duol manco s'affretta.
   A che più vita per gioir s'aspetta,   5
se sol nella miseria Iddio s'adora?
Lieta fortuna, e con lunga dimora,
tanto più nuoce quante più diletta.
   E se talor, tuo grazia, il cor m'assale,
Signor mie caro, quell'ardente zelo   10
che l'anima conforta e rassicura,
   da che 'l propio valor nulla mi vale,
subito allor sarie da girne al cielo:
ché con più tempo il buon voler men dura.

If my great desire often gives false hope
to my many years, of many more years to come,
that doesn't keep death from drawing ever nearer—
though he comes less quickly to those who suffer less.
   Why expect that longer life will bring more joy,   5
since we adore God only in distress?
A happy lot that lasts for a long time
harms us more, the more that it delights us.
   And if at times, my dear Lord, through your grace
my heart is stricken by that burning fervor   10
that comforts and encourages my soul,
   then that would be the moment to rise to heaven,
since my own powers are no use at all:
for the longer the time, the less good intentions last.

Sonnet from 1555, surviving in numerous drafts. Some of the versions are written on sheets containing drawings for architectural elements of Saint Peter's (TC no. 602r and v) and for the entrance hall of the Library of San Lorenzo in Florence or the Campidoglio in Rome (TC no. 606v). M sent suggestions for the completion of the library to Florence, for execution by Bartolommeo Ammannati, in September 1555 (C. MCCXIV, MCCXV; R. 405, 406); for this project, see also no. 299.

1. *my great desire:* to live, my love of life.

4. The more one suffers, the faster death approaches (hence, if I am deluded into thinking death is still far away, it will in fact come more slowly).

5–6. But why should we hope that the comfort of a prolonged life will bring greater happiness, since only when we are unhappy (in the fear of death) do we turn to God, the source of salvation (the greatest happiness).

10. *burning fervor:* of faith.

14. *the longer the time:* on earth.

Se lungo spazio del trist'uso e folle
più temp'il suo contrario a purgar chiede,
la morte già vicina nol concede,
né freno il mal voler da quel ch'e' volle.

Although a long span of mad and wicked habits
asks for even more time of its opposite, to be cleansed,
Death, already near, will not grant this to me,
nor can I rein in my evil desire's old wishes.

Quatrain, ca. 1555, written on the verso of a late version of no. 296.

1–2. Since I have lived for so long in habitual sin, I would need to live at least as long again in a state of repentant virtue in order to purify myself of all those past transgressions.

Non fur men lieti che turbati e tristi
che tu patissi, e non già lor, la morte,
gli spirti eletti, onde le chiuse porte
del ciel, di terra a l'uom col sangue apristi.

Lieti, poiché, creato, il redemisti   5
dal primo error di sua misera sorte;
tristi, a sentir c'a la pena aspra e forte,
servo de' servi in croce divenisti.

Onde e chi fusti, il ciel ne diè tal segno
che scurò gli occhi suoi, la terra aperse,   10
tremorno i monti e torbide fur l'acque.

Tolse i gran Padri al tenebroso regno,
gli angeli brutti in più doglia sommerse;
godé sol l'uom, c'al battesmo rinacque.

No less delighted than disturbed and sad
were the blessed spirits, that you, and not they,
suffered death, through which you opened for man on earth
the closed gates of heaven with your blood.

Delighted, because you redeemed what you'd created   5
from that first sin that led to his wretched fate;
sad, from feeling how, in harsh and intense pain,
you made yourself, on the cross, the slave of slaves.

Heaven signaled who you were and where you came from
by darkening its eyes; the earth fell open,   10
the mountains trembled, and the seas grew stormy.

He freed the Patriarchs from the realm of shadows,
and sank the fallen angels in greater pain;
only man rejoiced, to gain rebirth through baptism.

Late sonnet, of uncertain date. M describes the events of the crucifixion in the three realms of earth, heaven, and hell; his language closely parallels a poem by Vittoria Colonna, "Gli angeli eletti" (ed. Venice, 1540, 36). The theme of the crucified Christ also occupied him sculpturally during these final years; his Rondanini *Pietà* was begun ca. 1556 (left unfinished at his death), as was the Palestrina *Pietà*, probably worked largely by assistants.

4. For other examples of blood imagery, see no. 280.

6. *that first sin:* original sin, the fall of Adam and Eve.

8. *slave of slaves:* or "servant of servants," as in the Latin title for the Pope, *servus servorum Dei,* "servant of the servants of God."

10. *by darkening its eyes:* blotting out the heavenly bodies. The eclipse of the sun and the earthquake that occurred at the moment of the crucifixion are recounted by Matthew 27:45–54, Mark 15:33. The same events are recalled by Dante, *Paradiso* 7:46–48, 29:97–102.

12. After the crucifixion, Christ descended to the underworld and released the Old Testament patriarchs (Adam, Noah, Moses, et al.) from Limbo; cf. Dante, *Inferno* 4:46–63.

Al zucchero, a la mula, a le candele,
aggiuntovi un fiascon di malvagia,
resta sì vinta ogni fortuna mia,
ch'i' rendo le bilance a san Michele.

Troppa bonaccia sgonfia sì le vele,   5
che senza vento in mar perde la via
la debile mie barca, e par che sia
una festuca in mar rozz'e crudele.

A rispetto a la grazia e al gran dono,
al cib', al poto e a l'andar sovente   10
c'a ogni mi' bisogno è caro e buono,

Signor mie car, ben vi sare' nïente
per merto a darvi tutto quel ch'i' sono:
ché 'l debito pagar non è presente.

By the sugar, by the mule, and by the candles,
and a large flask of malmsey on top of that,
all my resources are so far outweighed
that I must give the scales back to Saint Michael.

Too much calm weather so deflates my sails   5
that my frail boat, with no wind, loses its way
over the water, and it seems to be
a wisp of straw on a rough and cruel sea.

Compared with your great kindness and your gifts—
the food, the drink, and the means of frequent travel,   10
which are apt and welcome for all of my needs—

my dear lord, even to give you all I am
would be nothing at all like what you deserve:
for repayment of a debt is not a gift.

Sonnet, ca. 1555–59, addressed to someone who had sent M the various gifts enumerated in lines 1–2. The recipient is often assumed to be Giorgio Vasari, who mentions having sent a gift of candles to M (VM 7:276; VB p. 423), but there is no firm proof. On the verso is a draft of a letter to the sculptor and architect Bartolommeo Ammannati and a sketch of the staircase for the entrance hall of the Library at San Lorenzo in Florence, whose completion M directed by correspondence between 1555 and 1559 (TC no. 526r; VM 7:236ff.; C. MCCXIV, MCCXV, MCCLXXXIV; R. 405, 406, 448, and Draft 11). See also nos. 101, 296.

2. *malmsey*: a sweet wine.

4. *Saint Michael*: the heavenly archangel, whose attribute is the scales of justice in which the worth of souls is weighed after death. That is, M gives up hope of repaying the gifts in this world. He expressed similar sentiments about the impossibility of earthly recompense in a letter to Vasari of 1551: "I can never hope to settle my account in this world, but only in the next" (VM 7:235–6; VB p. 399; C. MCLXIV; R. 364).

5–8. Having received so much good makes me feel lost in my own inadequacy to reciprocate. The metaphor is a reversal of the opening lines of *Purgatorio* 1:1–3, where Dante compares his imagination to a small boat filling its sails to leave a cruel sea. The self-portrayal as a "frail boat" also recalls nos. 43, 285.

300

Per croce e per grazia e per diverse pene
son certo, monsignor, trovarci in cielo;
ma prima c'a l'estremo ultimo anelo,
goderci in terra mi parria pur bene.

Se l'aspra via coi monti e co 'l mar tiene   5
l'un da l'altro lontan, lo spirto e 'l zelo
non cura intoppi o di neve o di gelo,
né l'alia del pensier lacci o catene.

Ond'io con esso son sempre con voi,
e piango e parlo del mio morto Urbino,   10
che vivo or forse saria costà meco,

com'ebbi già in pensier. Sua morte poi
m'affretta e tira per altro cammino,
dove m'aspetta ad albergar con seco.

Thanks to the cross, and grace, and our various sufferings,
I'm sure, Monsignor, that we'll meet in heaven;
but before our final breath, I would still like
for us to enjoy each other here on earth.

Though a rough road, with mountains and sea, may keep us   5
far from each other, yet the spirit and feelings
pay no heed to obstacles, either of snow or frost,
nor the wings of thought to snares or impediments.

Thus I am with you always in my thoughts,
and I weep, and speak about my dead Urbino   10
who, were he alive, might have been there with me,

as I once had in mind. But now his death
urges and draws me down another path,
to where he waits for me to lodge with him.

Sonnet, 1556, written in reply to one sent to M by his friend Archbishop Ludovico Beccadelli (see no. 288) in February of that year. Beccadelli, who was to be transferred from Ragusa to Dalmatia, lamented that distance was keeping the two men apart and expressed the hope of residing with M in heaven. M's reply echoes the complaint about the physical barriers to their meeting but goes on to explain that his intention to visit the prelate has been interrupted by the death of his servant Urbino, which has caused him to think only of going to heaven.

1–2. These lines echo Beccadelli's, "seize this new cross as a ladder to heaven."

5. *mountains and sea:* Beccadelli's new post lay across the Adriatic from Italy.

10. *Urbino:* Francesco d'Amadore, known as Urbino, who had been M's devoted servant and companion for twenty-six years, died after a long illness on 3 December 1555. M's great sense of loss is attested by several letters (C. MCCXVI–MCCXIX; R. 407–10), the last of which was reprinted by Vasari (VM 7:240; VB pp. 402–3); the letter to Vasari echoes the present poem: "nothing is left to me but the hope of seeing him again in Paradise." See also A41.

11. *there:* with Beccadelli.

Di più cose s'attristan gli occhi mei,
e 'l cor di tante quant'al mondo sono;
se 'l tuo di te cortese e caro dono
non fussi, della vita che farei?
Del mie tristo uso e dagli esempli rei,   5
fra le tenebre folte, dov'i' sono,
spero aita trovar non che perdono,
c'a chi ti mostri, tal prometter dei.

My eyes are saddened by so many things,
and my heart by as many as there are on earth,
that if it weren't for the gracious and dear gift
you make of yourself, what would I do with life?
For my evil habits, and against the bad examples   5
among the dense shadows where I find myself,
I hope not only for pardon, but for help:
you must promise those you reveal yourself to this much.

Unfinished sonnet, ca. 1560, written on the same sheet as no. 302. Both are on the back of an undated letter to an unnamed cardinal, in which M alludes to changes made in his design for Saint Peter's (C. MCCLXVI; R. 358). This letter has traditionally been assumed to be addressed to Ridolfo Pio da Carpi and dated to 1560, when Cardinal Pio was involved with the *fabbrica* of Saint Peter's. Ramsden dates the letter to 1550, before Pio was supervising the basilica, but the handwriting of the poems is closer to the late style of ca. 1560. In any case, the mood of disillusionment with worldly matters accords with M's request to Pio, in a letter of September 1560, to be relieved of his architectural duties (C. MCCCXXXVIII; R. 462). The theme of no. 301 is similar to that of A32.

5–8. I hope to receive from you both forgiveness for my own past sins and assistance in continuing to resist the temptations that surround me in this evil world. *evil habits:* cf. nos. 293:2, 297:1. *bad examples:* cf. no. 295:5.

Non più per altro da me stesso togli
l'amor, gli affetti perigliosi e vani,
che per fortuna avversa o casi strani,
ond'e' tuo amici dal mondo disciogli,
   Signor mie car, tu sol che vesti e spogli,   5
e col tuo sangue l'alme purghi e sani
da l'infinite colpe e moti umani,

.   .   .   .

You've no longer any other way to rid me
of love, that dangerous and futile passion,
than by misfortune or those fateful blows
by which you set your friends free from this world,
   my dear Lord, you who alone can clothe and strip   5
our souls, and with your blood purify and heal them
of their countless sins and human impulses,

.   .   .   .

Incomplete sonnet, ca. 1560, written on the same sheet as no. 301.

  4. *your friends:* those who believe in you.

  5–6. *clothe and strip our souls:* of the body, at birth and death. Cf. no. 98:3–4.

  6. For other examples of blood imagery, see no. 280.

Appendix

A 1

La morte è 'l fin d'una prigione scura.

Death is the end of a dark prison.

Written, along with A2, on a sheet from May 1501, also bearing some figure sketches (TC no. 15v). This fragment is a line from Petrarch, *Trionfo della Morte*, 2:34, indicating that already at the age of twenty-six Michelangelo was familiar with the poet who would be such a lifelong influence on his work.

A 2

La voglia invoglia e ella ha poi la doglia.

Desire creates desire and then feels pain.

On the same sheet as A1, 1501.

Sketches for bronze *David* with text of A3 (TC no. 19r)

A 3

Davitte colla fromba e io coll'arco.
                          Michelagnolo.

David with his sling, and I with my bow.
                          Michelangelo.

Written along with A4 and A5, on a sheet containing sketches of M's lost bronze *David* and his marble *David* in Florence, 1501–02 (TC no. 19). M's colossal marble *David*, originally intended for the Duomo, was commissioned in 1501 and finished in 1504. The fragment draws a parallel between the powers and weapons of the sculptor and of his subject; "bow" may refer to M's powers of intellect (as against David's physical force) or to his sculptor's tools, as first suggested by Charles Seymour, *Michelangelo's David: A Search for Identity.*

A 4

Rott'è l'alta colonna e 'l verde lauro.

Broken are the tall column and the green laurel.

On the same sheet as A3 and A5, 1501–02. The line is a quote from Petrarch, 269:1, where he punningly lamented the deaths of Cardinal Giovanni Colonna and Petrarch's own beloved Laura.

A 5

Al dolce mormorar d'un fiumicello
c'aduggia di verd'ombra un chiaro fonte
c'a star il cor [?] . . .

At the sweet murmuring of a little brook
which a clear spring covers with green shadows,
for the heart to remain . . .

Written on the verso of the sheet containing A3 and A4, 1501–02.

A 6

Vidi donna bella
ch'i'. . . la sorte mia . . .
io mi senti' consolato

.   .   .   .   .

I saw a beautiful lady
whom I . . . my fate . . .
I felt consoled . . .

Fragment from the early period of M's poetic activity, ca. 1505, written on the verso of a drawing of figures and costumes (Paris, Louvre, cat. Reiset, no. 116).

A 7

. . . dolce stanza nell'inferno.

. . . a sweet abode in hell.

A7–9 are written on a sheet of drawings also containing the draft for no. 1, datable ca. 1503–06 (TC no. 36r).

A 8

. . . Dio devotamente.

. . . God devotedly.

See A7.

A 9

Deus in nomine tuo salvum me fac.

In your name, O God, keep me well.

A short Latin prayer; see A7.

A 10

. . . che Febo alle . . . nora
. . .ti del suo vago e bel soggiorno
. . .do all'ombra mi refugi' el giorno
del suo lume le campagne indora [?]
. . . dove sie d'una [?] mi addolora
. . .mo . . . . discolora.

. . . that Phoebus in the . . .
. . . of his beautiful and pleasant stay
. . . I take refuge in the shade during the day
with his light he gilds the fields
. . . where one hurts me
. . . bleaches out.

On the same sheet as no. 2 (TC no. 46v); much of it is nearly illegible. Although probably written before M met Febo di Poggio, it shows him already developing the kind of sun imagery he later used to describe the young man.

A 11

Raccoglietele al piè del tristo cesto.

Gather them up at the foot of the wretched bush.

A quotation from Dante, *Inferno* 13:142, referring to the leaves shaken from the human trees in the wood of the suicides. This fragment and A12 are written on a sheet of figure studies, including sketches for the sculptures of Saint Matthew and for the Moses of the tomb of Julius II, ca. 1505–06 (TC no. 21v).

A 12

In omo Dio tu se'.
In pensier . . .

God, you are in man.
In thought . . .

See A11.

A 13

    L'ardente nodo ov'io fu' d'ora in ora,
contando anni ventuno ardendo preso,
morte disciolse; né già mai tal peso
provai, né credo c'uom . . .

    The fiery knot I was caught in, hour by hour,
burning for a count of twenty-one years,
death has untied; I never felt such a weight,
nor do I believe that man . . .

A quotation from Petrarch, 271:1–4, slightly altered. Written below several sketches for the tomb of Julius II, ca. 1505–06 (TC no. 20v).

A 14

Di pensier . . .
Chi dire' ch'ella f. . .
di mie mano
Di pensier in pensier . . .

From thought . . .
Who would say that she . . .
by my hand
From thought to thought . . .

Written, along with A15, on a drawing of Saint Anne with the Virgin and the infant Christ, ca. 1505–06 (TC no. 26r), analyzed by Alexander Perrig in *Authentication in the Visual Arts: A Multi-Disciplinary Symposium* (Amsterdam, 1977), 27–56. "Di pensier in pensier" recalls a line from Petrarch, 129:1.

A 15

Laudate parvoli,
el Signore nostro,
laudate sempre.

Praise our Lord,
little ones,
praise him always.

An exhortation to children to pray to God. See A14.

A 16

Febbre, fianchi, dolor, morbi, occhi e denti.

Fevers, flanks, aches, diseases, eyes and teeth.

A string of complaining nouns, similar in form to the series created by Petrarch, 303:5. The date is uncertain; though written on a strip of paper attached to M's draft of the Bracci epitaphs from 1544 (nos. 179–228), it is not related to them. Some editors suggest it might be a continuation of the physical complaints of no. 267, but it seems to predate that poem.

A 17

La m'arde e lega e temmi e parm'un zucchero.

She burns and binds and holds me, and seems like sugar.

On the same sheet as no. 4, dated 1507, and similar in theme.

A 18

Però amando m'affatico
che la vittoria fie quant'è 'l nemico.

Thus I struggle hard in love,
for victory is like an enemy.

A18–20 are written on a sheet of various sketches of figures and ornament, ca. 1520–24 (TC no. 198r).

A 19

Agli occhi, alla virtù, al tuo valore

.   .   .   .

To your eyes, your virtue, and your worthiness . . .

See A18.

A 20

c'altro piacer non hanno,
ove se vivo [?] . . . ove morto io defunto,
e di niente so' fatto appunto appunto.

for they have no other pleasure,
whether I am alive, or dead and gone,
and I am made of absolutely nothing.

See A18.

A 21

Dentr'a me giugne al cor, già fatto tale.

It pierces to my heart, already so made . . .

On the same sheet as nos. 15 and 16 (ca. 1521–24) and probably related to the thought of no. 16, with which it shares a rhyme.

A 22

Valle locus clausa toto mihi nullus in orbe.

Vaucluse, a place like no other in all the world to me.

A quotation of the first line of Petrarch's Latin elegy to his longtime residence of Vaucluse, in France. Written on a sheet bearing a sketch of a putto urinating, variously dated ca. 1517–32 (TC no. 70r). Beneath the verse, M wrote, "I beg you not to make me draw this evening, since Perino [Gherardo Perini?] is not here."

A 23

L'una di par sen va con la mia sorte,
l'altra mirando pur mi porge aita.

One of the pair goes away with my fate,
the other, still looking at me, offers me help.

Written on the back of a letter to Giovan Francesco Fattucci dated April 1523 (C. DLXXI; R. 152).

A 24

Non altrimenti Dedal si riscosse,
non altrimenti el sol l'ombra discaccia.

No differently did Daedalus rouse himself,
no differently does the sun chase away the shadow.

Written on a letter to Giovan Francesco Fattucci from January 1524 (C. DCII; R. 159). The first line is a variation on Dante, *Purgatorio* 9:34, replacing Dante's Achilles with Daedalus, the ill-fated mythical inventor who flew by attaching wax wings to himself.

    1, 2. *no differently:* in the same way.

    2. *chase away the shadow:* compare A25:5.

A 25

...o e stanco anelo
...o el tempo rio
... luce al gioir mio
... in tenebre e gelo
... ombra discaccia   5
... e l'altra penna
...terno porta
... el ciel conforta.

... and tired breath
... evil time
... light to my joy
... in shadows and frost
... chases away the shadow   5
... and the other wing
... bears forever
... comforts heaven.

Written, probably in the 1520s, on a sheet that was later torn in half.
  5. *chases away the shadow*: compare A24:2.

A 26

Che mal si può amar ben chi non si vede.

For one who's not seen cannot be well loved.

Written on the same sheet as nos. 28 and 29, with which it shares the theme of seeking the sight of the beloved; compare nos. 163:13, 258:15.

A 27

. . .*ser può che d'ogni angoscia e tedio*
. . .*sie sol rimedio*
. . . *fra noi non è già cosa umana*
. . .*r po' el cor, la mente l'alma sana*
. . . *mal d'ogni errore*   5
. . . *sdegno e furore*
. . . *discaccia e l'una e l'altra morte*
. . . *nella mi' sorte.*

. . . it may be that for all anguish and boredom
. . . might be the only cure
. . . among us there is nothing human at all
. . . then the soul heals the heart and mind
. . . the evil of all error   5
. . . anger and fury
. . . drives away both deaths
. . . in my fate.

Written on the same sheet, later cut, as no. 31 (TC no. 267v).

A 28

. . .*va e fera*
. . . *al fiore s'appressa amore*
. . . *donna altiera*
passar per li occhi al core.

. . . and savage
. . . love comes near the flower
. . . haughty lady
to pass through my eyes to my heart.

Written on the same sheet containing no. 33 (TC no. 390r), next to a sketch of the Madonna and Child.

A 29

Fatto arsicciato e cotto dal sole e da maggior caldi.

Scorched and baked by the sun and by even greater heat.

Written on one of the drafts of no. 81 (ca. 1526–34).

A 30

Così dentro o di fuor da' raggi suoi,
nel foco son, che m'arde 'l corpo debile,
e so. . .
  Così colmo di grazia e d'amar pieno,
un occulto pensier mi mostra e dice: 5
A veder lei t'aspetto un'altra volta:
quel che fie rivedella in tristo aspetto.

Thus, whether in or outside of her rays,
I'm in the fire that burns my feeble body,
and I . . .
  Thus, overflowing with grace and filled with love,
a hidden thought shows itself to me, and says: 5
I wait for you to see her another time,
which will make you see her again with a sad face.

Fragments of unrhymed lines, on a sheet with sketches of one of the slaves for the tomb of Julius II and a seated male figure, ca. 1532 (TC no. 101v).

A 31

Signore, io fallo e veggio el mio fallire,
ma fo com'uom che arde e 'l foco ha 'n seno,
ché 'l duol pur cresce, e la ragion vien meno
ed è già quasi vinta dal martire.
Sole' spronare el mio caldo desire   5
per non turbare el bel viso sereno:
non posso più; di man m'ha' tolto 'l freno,
e l'alma disperando ha preso ardire.

Lord, I transgress, and I see my transgression,
but I act like a man whose breast is on fire,
for my pain keeps increasing, and my reason falters,
and already is nearly overcome by my suffering.
I used to rein in my heated desire   5
so as not to trouble that calm and lovely face;
I no longer can, for you've taken the reins from my hand,
and my soul, in despair, has grown more bold.

M's transcription of the octave of Petrarch's sonnet, no. 236, with several small variations. On
the verso of a sheet containing architectural sketches and an eagle with outstretched wings
(TC no. 626v); uncertain date, perhaps ca. 1534.

   5. *rein in:* M wrote *spronare*, "to spur on," but Petrarch's original was *frenare,* which alone
makes sense in this context; perhaps a memory lapse while transcribing.

A 32

Du' occhi asciutti, e' mie, fan tristi el mondo.

Two dry eyes—my own—make the world sad.

Written, along with A33, on a sheet containing a drawing of a crucified Christ (TC no. 421r).
Similar in theme to no. 301.

A 33

.   .   .   .

un'altra sera, ché stasera piove,
e mal può dir chi è 'spettato altrove.

.   .   .   .

some other evening, for this evening it's raining,
and one who's expected elsewhere can't speak well.

On the same sheet as A32.

A 34

Nulla già valsi

.   .   .   .

il tuo volto nel mio
ben può veder, tuo grazia e tuo mercede,
chi per superchia luce te non vede.

I was worth nothing

.   .   .   .

your face can well be seen
in mine, thanks to your mercy and your grace,
by one who, through excess light, cannot see you.

A34–39 are fragments of poems by M that were cited and discussed by Benedetto Varchi in his *Lezzioni* of 1547 (published 1550) but are otherwise lost today.

A 35

Non ha l'abito intero
prima alcun, c'a l'estremo
dell'arte e della vita.

No one has full mastery
before reaching the end
of his art and his life.

See A34. Thematically similar to no. 241.

A 36

In tal misero stato, il vostro viso
ne presta, come 'l sol, tenebre e luce.

When I'm in such a wretched state, your face
offers me, like the sun, both light and shadows.

See A34.

A 37

Se ben talor tuo gran pietà m'assale,
non men che tuo durezza curo o temo,
ché l'uno e l'altro stremo
è ne' colpi d'amor piaga mortale.

Though sometimes your great mercy falls upon me,
I mind and fear it no less than your harshness,
for, with the blows of love,
either extreme can give a mortal wound.

See no. A34.

A 38

Né so se d'altro stral già mai s'avviene,

.　　.　　.　　.　　.　　.　　.　　.

ma mie fortuna vinse il suo costume.

I don't know if it ever happens with other darts,

.　　.　　.　　.　　.　　.　　.　　.　　.

but my good fortune defeated his usual ways.

See A34.

A 39

Che posso o debbo o vuoi ch'io pruovi ancora,
Amore, anzi ch'io mora?

　　.　　.　　.　　.　　.

.　　.　　.　　.　　.

Dille che sempre ognora
suo pietà vinta da tuo fera stella,

.　　.　　.　　.　　.　　.　　.

What more can or should I feel at your wish,
O Love, before I die?

　　.　　.　　.　　.　　.

.　　.　　.　　.　　.

Tell her that her mercy,
defeated by your wild star, will always

.　　.　　.　　.　　.　　.　　.

See A34.

Pietà, pencil drawing (TC no. 426r)

A 40

Non vi si pensa quanto sangue costa.

No one thinks of how much blood it costs.

A line from Dante, *Paradiso* 29:91, which M inscribed vertically on the upright of the cross in a *Pietà* drawn for Vittoria Colonna, ca. 1546 (TC no. 426r; CW, 103). The verse is a reference by Beatrice to the difficulties of propagating the true faith in the world.

A 41

Mal fa chi tanta fé sì tosto oblia.

One does wrong who so soon forgets such faithfulness.

A line from Petrarch, 206:45, written at the head of a letter to the widow of his servant Urbino, dated 28 April 1557 (C. MCCXLVI; R. 431; TC no. 425v). As in the letter itself, M is referring to his enduring memory of Urbino, who had then been dead just over a year. M had quoted the same line as early as 1539, in a letter to Vittoria Colonna (C. CMLXVII; R. 202).

Bibliography

The bibliography of Michelangelo scholarship is vast. Only works consulted for the present edition or of specific relevance to his poetry have been cited below. Editions and translations of Michelangelo's poems (in chronological order) and other writings are grouped first by title. For the bibliographical abbreviations used in the poem annotations, see page 63.

EDITIONS OF MICHELANGELO'S POETRY

Rime di Michelangelo Buonarroti. Ed. Michelangelo Buonarroti il Giovane. Florence, 1623.

Le rime di Michelangelo Buonarroti. Ed. Cesare Guasti. Florence, 1863.

The Sonnets of Michel Angelo and Tommaso Campanella. Trans. John Addington Symonds. London, 1878.

Die Dichtungen des Michelagniolo Buonarroti. Ed. Carl Frey. Berlin, 1897.

Sonnets of Michelangelo. Trans. S. Elizabeth Hall. London: Routledge and Kegan Paul, 1905.

Le rime. Ed. Valentino Piccoli. Turin: Einaudi, 1930.

Michelangelo Buonarroti: Le rime. Ed. Ausonio Dobelli. Milan: Signorelli, 1933.

Rime di Michelangelo. Ed. G. R. Ceriello. Milan: Rizzoli, 1954.

The Complete Poems of Michelangelo. Trans. Joseph Tusiani. London: Peter Owen, 1960.

Michelangelo Buonarroti: Rime. Ed. Enzo Noè Girardi. *Scrittori d'Italia,* 217. Bari: Laterza, 1960.

Complete Poems and Selected Letters of Michelangelo. 1964. Reprint. Trans. Creighton Gilbert and ed. Robert N. Linscott. Princeton: Princeton University Press, 1980.

Michelangelo Buonarroti: Rime. Ed. Ettore Barelli. Milan: Rizzoli, 1975.

OTHER WRITINGS BY MICHELANGELO

Il carteggio di Michelangelo. Ed. Giovanni Poggi, Paola Barocchi, and Renzo Ristori. 5 vols. Florence: Sansoni, 1965–79.

The Letters of Michelangelo. Trans. and ed. E. H. Ramsden. 2 vols. London: Owen, 1963.

I ricordi di Michelangelo. Ed. Lucilla Bardeschi Ciulich and Paola Barocchi. Florence: Sansoni, 1970.

SECONDARY SOURCES

Akrigg, G. P., ed. *Letters of King James VI and I*. Berkeley: University of California Press, 1984.

Aretino, Pietro. *Lettere sull'arte di Pietro Aretino*. Ed. Ettore Camesasca and Fidenzio Pertile. 3 vols. Milan: Edizioni del milione, 1957–60.

Barocchi, Paola, ed. *Trattati d'arte del Cinquecento*. 3 vols. Bari: Laterza, 1960.

Binni, Walter. *Michelangelo scrittore*. Turin: Einaudi, 1975.

Boswell, John. *Christianity, Social Tolerance, and Homosexuality*. Chicago: University of Chicago Press, 1980.

Cambon, Glauco. *Michelangelo's Poetry: Fury of Form*. Princeton: Princeton University Press, 1985.

Cellini, Benvenuto. *Autobiography*. Trans. George Bull. Harmondsworth: Penguin, 1956.

Clements, Robert. *Michelangelo's Theory of Art*. New York: New York University Press, 1961.

———. *The Poetry of Michelangelo*. New York: New York University Press, 1965.

Colonna, Vittoria. *Le rime di Vittoria Colonna*. Rome, 1840.

Condivi, Ascanio. *Life of Michelangelo*. 1553. Trans. Alice Sedgwick Wohl and ed. Hellmut Wohl. Baton Rouge: University of Louisiana Press, 1976.

Croce, Benedetto. *Poesia popolare e poesia d'arte*. Bari: Laterza, 1946.

Dante Alighieri. *The Divine Comedy*. Trans. and ed. Charles Singleton. Princeton: Princeton University Press, 1977.

———. *Vita nuova; Rime*. Ed. Fredi Chiappelli. Milan: Mursia, 1983.

Dollimore, Jonathan. "Subjectivity, Sexuality, and Transgression: The Jacobean Connection." *Renaissance Drama*, n.s. 17 (1986): 53–81.

Eissler, Kurt R. *Leonardo da Vinci: Psychoanalytical Notes on the Enigma*. New York: International Universities Press, 1961.

Ferguson, Margaret, Maureen Quilligan, and Nancy Vickers, eds. *Rewriting the Renaissance: The Discourses of Sexual Difference in Early Modern Europe*. Chicago: University of Chicago Press, 1986.

Ficino, Marsilio. *Commentarium in Convivio Platonis*. 1474. Trans. and ed. Sears R. Jayne. Columbia: University of Missouri Press, 1943.

Foscolo, Ugo. "Poems of Michel Angelo." 1826. Reprinted in *Edizione nazionale delle opere di Ugo Foscolo*, vol. 10, 468–91. Florence, 1953.

Foucault, Michel. *The History of Sexuality*. Trans. Robert Hurley. Harmondsworth: Penguin, 1978.

Freadman, Anne. "Of Cats, and Companions, and the Name of George Sand." In

Grafts: Feminist Cultural Criticism, ed. Susan Sheridan. New York: Routledge, Chapman and Hall, 1988.

Freud, Sigmund. "The Moses of Michelangelo." 1914. Reprinted in *Standard Edition of the Works of Sigmund Freud* 13:211–36.

Frommel, Christoph L. *Michelangelo und Tommaso de' Cavalieri*. Amsterdam: Castrum Peregrini, 1979.

Giannotti, Donato. *Dialoghi di Donato Giannotti*. Ed. Dioclecio Redig de Campos. Florence: Sansoni, 1939.

Gibaldi, Joseph. "Vittoria Colonna: Child, Woman, and Poet." In *Women Writers of the Renaissance and Reformation*, ed. Katharina M. Wilson, 22–46. Athens: University of Georgia Press, 1987.

Girardi, Enzo Noè. *Studi sulle rime di Michelangiolo*. Milan: L'Eroica, 1964.

———. *Studi su Michelangiolo scrittore*. Florence: Olschki, 1974.

Hallock, Anne. *Michelangelo the Poet*. Pacific Grove, Cal.: Page-Ficklin Publications, 1978.

Hartt, Frederick. *Michelangelo: The Complete Sculpture*. New York: Abrams, 1968.

Hibbard, Howard. *Michelangelo*. New York: Harper and Row, 1974.

Hirst, Michael. *Michelangelo and His Drawings*. New Haven: Yale University Press, 1988.

Hollanda, Francisco de. *Four Dialogues on Painting*. Trans. A. F. G. Bell. 1928. Reprint. London: Oxford University Press, 1979.

Holroyd, Charles. *Michael Angelo Buonarroti*. London: Duckworth; New York: Scribner's, 1911.

Kamenetz, Rodger. "Daniele da Volterra, the Breeches-Maker, on Michelangelo's Last Judgment Poems." *The New Republic* 197:40.

LaBalme, Patricia, ed. *Beyond Their Sex: Learned Women of the European Past*. New York: New York University Press, 1980.

Leites, Nathan. *Art and Life: Aspects of Michelangelo*. New York: New York University Press, 1986.

Liebert, Robert S. *Michelangelo: A Psychoanalytic Study of His Life and Images*. New Haven: Yale University Press, 1983.

Lucente, Gregory. "Absence and Desire in Michelangelo's Poetry: Literary Traditions and the Lesson(s) of the Manuscript." *Quaderni d'italianistica* 8 (1987): 216–26.

———. "Lyric Tradition and the Desires of Absence: Rudel, Dante, and Michelangelo ('Vorrei voler')." *Canadian Review of Comparative Literature*, September 1983:305–32.

Manuzzi, Giuseppe, ed. *Vocabolario della lingua italiana, già compilato dagli Accademici della Crusca*. 4 vols. 2d ed., revised. Florence, 1863.

Medici, Lorenzo de'. *Canzoniere*. Ed. Paolo Orvieto. Milan: Mondadori, 1984.

Mirollo, James. *Mannerism and Renaissance Poetry*. New Haven: Yale University Press, 1984.

Montale, Eugenio. *Michelangelo poeta*. Ed. Armando Brissoni. Bologna: Boni, 1976.

Nelson, John Charles. *Renaissance Theory of Love*. New York: Columbia University Press, 1958.

Oremland, Jerome. *Michelangelo's Sistine Ceiling: A Psychoanalytic Study of Creativity*. Madison, Conn.: International Universities Press, 1989.

Panofsky, Erwin. *Studies in Iconology: Humanistic Themes in the Art of the Renaissance*. New York: Oxford University Press, 1939.

Papini, Giovanni. *La vita di Michelangiolo nella vita del suo tempo*. Milan: Garzanti, 1949.

Perrig, Alexander. "Bemerkungen zur Freundschaft zwischen Michelangelo und Tommaso de' Cavalieri." In *Stil und Uberlieferung in der Kunst des Abendlandes* 2:164–71. Acts of the Twenty-first International Congress of the History of Art, Bonn, 1964. Berlin: Mann, 1967.

Petrarch (Francesco Petrarca). *Petrarch's Lyric Poems: The "Rime Sparse" and Other Lyrics*. Trans. and ed. Robert M. Durling. Cambridge: Harvard University Press, 1976.

Poliziano, Angelo. *Poesie italiane*. Ed. Saverio Orlando. Milan: Rizzoli, 1976.

———. *Stanze per la Giostra, Orfeo, Rime*. Ed. Bruno Maier. Novara: Istituto geografico de Agostini, 1968.

Popham, A. E., and Wilde, Johannes. *The Italian Drawings of the Fifteenth and Sixteenth Centuries in the Collection of His Majesty the King at Windsor Castle*. London: Phaidon, 1949.

Robb, Nesca. *Neoplatonism of the Italian Renaissance*. London: Allen and Unwin, 1935.

Rosand, David, and Robert Hanning, eds. *Castiglione: The Ideal and the Real in Renaissance Culture*. New Haven: Yale University Press, 1983.

Salmi, Mario, ed. *Michelangelo artista, pensatore, scrittore*. Novara: Istituto geografico de Agostini, 1965.

Saslow, James M. *Ganymede in the Renaissance: Homosexuality in Art and Society*. New Haven: Yale University Press, 1986.

———. " 'A Veil of Ice between My Heart and the Fire': Michelangelo's Sexual Identity and Early Modern Constructs of Homosexuality." *Genders* 2 (1988): 77–90.

Seymour, Charles. *Michelangelo's David: A Search for Identity*. Pittsburgh: University of Pittsburgh Press, 1967.

Steinberg, Leo. "The Metaphors of Love and Birth in Michelangelo's *Pietàs*." In *Studies in Erotic Art*, ed. Theodore Bowie and Cornelia V. Christensen, 231–338. New York: Basic Books, 1970.

———. *Michelangelo's Last Paintings: The "Conversion of Saint Paul" and "The Crucifixion of Saint Peter" in the Cappella Paolina, Vatican Palace*. New York: Oxford University Press, 1975.

Summers, David. *Michelangelo and the Language of Art*. Princeton: Princeton University Press, 1981.

Symonds, John Addington, ed. *The Life of Michelangelo Buonarroti*. 3d ed. 2 vols. London, 1899.

Tolnay, Charles de. *The Art and Thought of Michelangelo*. New York: Pantheon, 1964.

———. *Corpus dei disegni di Michelangelo*. 4 vols. Novara: Istituto geografico de Agostini, 1975–80. Citations are to drawing numbers.

————. *Michelangelo*. 5 vols. Princeton: Princeton University Press, 1943–60.

Varchi, Benedetto. *Due lezzioni*. Florence, 1549. Reprinted in *Trattati d'arte del Cinquecento*, ed. Paola Barocchi. 3 vols. Bari: Laterza, 1960. Trans. John Addington Symonds in his *Renaissance in Italy*, vol. 2. New York, 1893.

Vasari, Giorgio. *Le vite de' più eccellenti pittori scultori ed architettori*. 1568. Ed. Gaetano Milanesi. 9 vols. Florence, 1865–79.

————. *Lives of the Artists*. Vol. 1. Trans. George Bull. Harmondsworth: Penguin, 1971.

Wallace, William. "Studies in Michelangelo's Finished Drawings, 1520–34." Ph.D. diss., Columbia University, 1983.

Weeks, Jeffrey. *Sex, Politics and Society: The Regulation of Sexuality since 1800*. London: Longman, 1981.

————. *Sexuality and Its Discontents: Meanings, Myths and Modern Sexuality*. London: Routledge and Kegan Paul, 1985.

Wilde, Johannes. *Italian Drawings in the Department of Prints and Drawings in the British Museum: Michelangelo and His Studio*. London: British Museum, 1953.

Concordance to Editions and Translations of Michelangelo's Poetry

Girardi (Poem Number)	Guasti (Page Number)	Symonds (Sonnet Number)	Frey Ceriello Tusiani (Poem Number)	Dobelli (Poem Number)	Gilbert (Poem Number)
1	—	—	166.9/167	—	1
2	279	—	22	183	2
3	—	—	2	38	3
4	178	20	7	39	4
5	158	5	9	1	5
6	156	3	3	179	6
7	90	—	5	—	7
8	50	—	6	43	8
9	280	—	4	44	9
10	157	4	10	180	10
11	106	—	13	41	11
12	49	—	11	46	12
13	—	—	18	181	—
14	—	—	17	181	—
15	92	—	19	165	13
16	281	—	21	42	14
17	260	—	12	55	15
18	281	—	14	—	16
19	146	—	15	45	17
20	338	—	37, 167	6	18
21	350	—	136	187	19
22	343	—	110	192	20
23	257	—	111	99	21
24	269	—	112	153	22
25	206	45	113	195	23

Girardi (Poem Number)	Guasti (Page Number)	Symonds (Sonnet Number)	Frey Ceriello Tusiani (Poem Number)	Dobelli (Poem Number)	Gilbert (Poem Number)
26	276	—	23	48	24
27	249	—	24	47	25
28	147	—	26	49	26
29	281	—	27	196	27
30	96	—	29	124	28
31	—	—	166.3	—	29
32	259	—	25	201	30
33	—	—	—	—	31
34	186	28	92	139	32
35	312	—	93	172	33
36	252	—	35	14	34
37	273	—	59	225	35
38	272	—	60	160	36
39	248	—	61	149	37
40	266	—	130	—	38
41	182	24	31	76	39
42	183	25	32	168	40
43	198	39	33	71	41
44	254	—	34	73	42
45	310	—	99	154	43
46	226	61	101	157	44
47	227	62	100	158	45
48	280	—	105	197	46
49	280	—	62	149	47
50	279	—	131	—	48
51	347	App. 3	49	203	49
52	267	—	38	183	50
53	271	—	39	186	51
54	329	—	36	5	52
55	336	—	56	5	53
56	278	—	41	162	54
57	278	—	42	162	55
58	195	36	43	24	56
59	190	32	44	21	57
60	217	55	45	22	58
61	211	50	46	20	59
62	223	59	109.87	145	60
63	193	34	109.88	146	61

Girardi (Poem Number)	Guasti (Page Number)	Symonds (Sonnet Number)	Frey Ceriello Tusiani (Poem Number)	Dobelli (Poem Number)	Gilbert (Poem Number)
64	279	—	132	209	62
65	277	—	47	—	63
66	239	71	48	212	64
67	317	—	163	7	65
68	325	—	69	7	66
69	93	—	70	61	67
70	—	—	71	—	68
71	160	6	68	2	69
72	180	22	50	25	70
73	278	—	51	26	71
74	263	—	52	26	72
75	276	—	53	—	73
76	199	40	75	32	74
77	208	47	55	27	75
78	210	49	106	74	76
79	168	12	88	122	77
80	187	29	89	107	78
81	84	—	109.10	111	79
82	185	27	63	35	80
83	216	54	64	37	81
84	174	16	65	23	82
85	287	—	57	3	83
86	297	—	58	4	84
87	244	75	140	217	85
88	194	35	109.18	167	86
89	188	30	109.19	29	87
90	177	19	109.95	30	88
91	51	—	109.30–31	28	89
92	142	—	109.33	191	90
93	82	—	109.40	33	91
94	179	21	66	40	92
95	197	38	109.91	110	93
96	313	—	72	62	94
97	176	18	109.94	109	95
98	189	31	76	31	96
99	228	63	103	16	97
100	262	—	104	17	98
101	204	43	77	174	99

Girardi (Poem Number)	Guasti (Page Number)	Symonds (Sonnet Number)	Frey Ceriello Tusiani (Poem Number)	Dobelli (Poem Number)	Gilbert (Poem Number)
102	205	44	78	173	100
103	203	42	109.20	175	101
104	202	41	109.21	176	102
105	214	52	79	36	103
106	218	56	109.105	150	104
107	33	—	109.99	138	105
108	337	—	109.42	51	106
109	27	—	109.51–52	161	107
110	4	—	137	209	108
111	145	—	107	133	109
112	45	—	109.1	70	110
113	65	—	109.2	123	111
114	78	—	109.3	60	112
115	149	—	114	169	113
116	99	—	109.4	115	114
117	43	—	109.5	147	115
118	120, 121	—	109.6, 41	104	116
119	113	—	109.9	92	117
120	122	—	109.11	91	118
121	83	—	109.12	143	119
122	79	—	109.13	119	120
123	97	—	109.14	58	121
124	68	—	109.15	57	122
125	143	—	109.22	101	123
126	81	—	109.24	81	124
127	41	—	109.25	102	125
128	64	—	109.26	103	126
129	47	—	109.27	63	127
130	129	—	109.28	89	128
131	130	—	109.29	90	129
132	124	—	109.32	189	130
133	123	—	109.34	190	131
134	40	—	109.35	223	132
135	131	—	109.36	72	133
136	132	—	109.38	88	134
137	63	—	109.39	105	135
138	61	—	109.54	78	136
139	71	—	109.55	80	137

Girardi (Poem Number)	Guasti (Page Number)	Symonds (Sonnet Number)	Frey Ceriello Tusiani (Poem Number)	Dobelli (Poem Number)	Gilbert (Poem Number)
140	103	—	109.96	79	138
141	56	—	109.56	52	139
142	72	—	109.57	83	140
143	134	—	109.58	106	141
144	126	—	109.59	163	142
145	60	—	109.60	77	143
146	69–70	—	109.63	59	144
147	48, 107	—	109.64	68, 185	145
148	58–59	—	109.84	128	146
149	80	—	109.85	130	147
150	184	26	109.100	126	148
151	173	15	83	166	149
152	37	—	84	144	150
153	39	—	109.61	114	151
154	62	—	109.62	116	152
155	73, 264	—	109.44	65	153
156	46	—	109.76	121	154
157	66–67	—	109.80	66	155
158	119	—	109.81	93	156
159	169	13	109.82	129	157
160	196	37	90	127	158
161	144	—	87	210	159
162	30	—	109.97	134	160
163	57	—	109.98	137	161
164	32	—	94	159	162
165	91	—	95	136	163
166	181	23	109.8	50	164
167	125	—	109.65	95	165
168	75–77	—	109.66.69,70	69	166
169	54	—	109.73	54	167
170	55	—	109.74	67	168
171	42	—	109.75	10	169
172	137	—	109.77	164	170
173	34	—	109.89	64	171
174	105	—	109.90	53	172
175	135	—	124	96	173
176	115	—	109.43	87	174
177	4	—	109.67	15	175

Girardi (Poem Number)	Guasti (Page Number)	Symonds (Sonnet Number)	Frey Ceriello Tusiani (Poem Number)	Dobelli (Poem Number)	Gilbert (Poem Number)
178	165	10	109.68	15	176
179	5	—	73.1	9.3	177
180	5	—	73.2	9.4	178
181	6	—	73.3	9.5	179
182	6	—	73.4	9.6	180
183	6	—	73.5	9.7	181
184	7	—	73.6	9.8	182
185	7	—	73.7	9.9	183
186	7	—	73.8	—	184
187	8	—	73.9	—	185
188	8	—	73.10	9.10	186
189	8	—	73.11	9.11	187
190	9	—	73.12	9.12	188
191	9	—	73.13	—	189
192	26	—	73.14	9.2	190
193	162	8	73.15	9.1	191
194	9	—	73.16	9.13	192
195	10	—	73.17	9.14	193
196	10	—	73.18	—	194
197	10	—	73.19	—	195
198	11	—	73.20	9.15	196
199	11	—	73.21	9.16	197
200	11	—	73.22	9.17	198
201	12	—	73.23	9.18	199
202	12	—	73.24	—	200
203	12	—	73.25	—	201
204	13	—	73.26	9.19	202
205	13	—	73.27	9.20	203
206	13	—	73.28	—	204
207	14	—	73.29	9.21	205
208	14	—	73.30	9.22	206
209	14	—	73.31	9.23	207
210	15	—	73.32	9.24	208
211	15	—	73.33	—	209
212	15	—	73.34	9.25	210
213	16	—	73.35	9.26	211
214	16	—	73.36	9.27	212
215	16	—	73.37	9.28	213

Girardi (Poem Number)	Guasti (Page Number)	Symonds (Sonnet Number)	Frey Ceriello Tusiani (Poem Number)	Dobelli (Poem Number)	Gilbert (Poem Number)
216	17	—	73.38	9.29	214
217	17	—	73.39	—	215
218	17	—	73.40	9.30	216
219	18	—	73.41	—	217
220	18	—	73.42	9.31	218
221	18	—	73.43	9.32	219
222	19	—	73.44	9.33	220
223	19	—	73.45	—	221
224	20	—	73.46	9.34	222
225	20	—	73.47	9.35	223
226	20	—	73.48	9.36	224
227	21	—	73.49	—	225
228	21	—	73.50	9.37	226
229	74	—	109.23	151	227
230	191, 192	33	109.46	82	228
231	114	—	109.47	205	229
232	141	—	109.83	94	230
233	207	46	109.86	84	231
234	118	—	96	140	232
235	94, 95	—	135	120	233
236	171, 172	14	134	131	234
237	253	—	85	171	235
238	277	—	86	204	236
239	175	17	109.92	113	237
240	38	—	109.45	170	238
241	36	—	109.50	118	239
242	35	—	109.53	112	240
243	222	58	126	142	241
244	102	—	127	198	242
245	104	—	129	132	243
246	100, 303, 307	—	109.7	56	244
247	3	App. 3	109.17	—	245
248	153	1	109.37	177	246
249	25	App. 3	109.48	184	247
250	155	2	109.49	178	248
251	161	7	74	13	249
252	28	—	109.71–72	12	250

Girardi (Poem Number)	Guasti (Page Number)	Symonds (Sonnet Number)	Frey Ceriello Tusiani (Poem Number)	Dobelli (Poem Number)	Gilbert (Poem Number)
253	133	—	109.78	86	251
254	127	—	109.79	117	252
255	116	—	109.93	125	253
256	108–12	—	121	75	254
257	256	—	97	—	255
258	44	—	109.104	108	256
259	224	60	109.101	34	257
260	215	53	91	193	258
261	209	48	109.102	135	259
262	138	—	118	85	260
263	136	—	122	97	261
264	101	—	109.103	141	262
265	31	—	98	156	263
266	229	64	102	155	264
267	294–96	—	81	8	265
268	128	—	115	—	266
269	148	—	116	188	267
270	281	—	117	—	268
271	251	—	139	—	269
272	212, 213	51	119	100	270
273	247	—	120	226	271
274	240	72	123	216	272
275	277	—	125	—	273
276	220, 221	57	128	194	274
277	167	11	133	18	275
278	4	—	138	—	276
279	250	—	141	148	277
280	265	—	142	206	278
281	255	—	143	202	279
282	280	—	144	208	280
283	274	—	145	202	281
284	275	—	146	206	282
285	230	65	147	208	283
286	279	—	148	213	284
287	277	—	149	—	285
288	232	66	150	219	286
289	234	67	151	218	287
290	241	73	152	211	288

Girardi (Poem Number)	Guasti (Page Number)	Symonds (Sonnet Number)	Frey Ceriello Tusiani (Poem Number)	Dobelli (Poem Number)	Gilbert (Poem Number)
291	270	—	153	207	289
292	258	—	154	222	290
293	238	70	155	220	291
294	246	77	156	215	292
295	237	69	157	221	293
296	242	74	158	199	294
297	278	—	159	—	295
298	245	76	160	224	296
299	164	9	161	11	297
300	235	68	162	19	298
301	261	—	164	214	299
302	268	—	165	200	300
A1	—	—	—	—	—
A2	—	—	—	—	301
A3	—	—	1	—	—
A4	—	—	1	—	—
A5	—	—	166.1	—	302
A6	—	—	166.2	—	303
A7	—	—	—	—	304
A8	—	—	—	—	305
A9	—	—	—	—	—
A10	—	—	—	—	306
A11	—	—	—	—	—
A12	—	—	—	—	307
A13	—	—	—	—	—
A14	—	—	—	—	—
A15	—	—	—	—	—
A16	—	—	82	—	308
A17	—	—	8	—	309
A18	—	—	—	—	310
A19	—	—	—	—	311
A20	—	—	—	—	312
A21	281	—	20	—	14
A22	—	—	—	—	—
A23	—	—	166.5	—	313
A24	—	—	166.6	—	314
A25	—	—	166.7	—	315

Girardi (Poem Number)	Guasti (Page Number)	Symonds (Sonnet Number)	Frey Ceriello Tusiani (Poem Number)	Dobelli (Poem Number)	Gilbert (Poem Number)
A26	—	—	28	—	—
A27	—	—	166.4	—	316
A28	—	—	—	—	317
A29	—	—	54	—	318
A30	—	—	—	—	319
A31	—	—	67	—	—
A32	—	—	—	—	320
A33	—	—	—	—	321
A34	282	—	80.1	—	322
A35	282	—	80.2	—	323
A36	282	—	80.3	—	327
A37	282	—	80.4	—	324
A38	283	—	80.5	—	326
A39	283	—	80.6	—	325
A40	—	—	—	—	—
A41	—	—	—	—	—

Concordance to Michelangelo's Drawings Catalogued by Charles de Tolnay (1975–80)

Tolnay Drawing Number	Michelangelo Poem Number	Tolnay Drawing Number	Michelangelo Poem Number
15v	A1, A2	336	65, 74, 90, 120,
19	A3, A4, A5	340	100
20v	A13	342	100
21v	A11, A12	343	100
25v	20	344	79, 84, 89, 99
26r	A14, A15	345	41, 79, 98, 105
36r	A7, A8, A9	353r	268, 270
36v	1	353v	255, 269
46	2, A10	356	255, 262
70r	A22	364r	146
96v	35	366r	84
101v	A30	367r	220, 221, 222, 223
102v	3, 6, 7, 8, 9	390r	33, A28
111v	131	396r	273
174r	5	396v	272
181v	27	406	290
185v	15, 16, A21	407	294
189r	13	410–422	285
198r	A18, A19, A20	411r	159, 161, 290
201r	14	421r	A32, A33
207bis	43, 44	423r	282, 283
225r	45	423v	284, 285
237v	51	424r	263
267v	31, A27	424v	272, 274
304r	122	425v	A41
306r	27	426r	159, A40
312	47	485	83
333	200	490r	290

Tolnay Drawing Number	Michelangelo Poem Number	Tolnay Drawing Number	Michelangelo Poem Number
490v	291	597r	106
526	299	597v	235
531r	36	602	296
536r	50	605r	278
538r	76	606v	296
552v	243, 244	607r	272
557r	81	607v	256
591r	260	626v	A31
591v	259	627r	68
592r	271	627v	71

Index of First Lines

ENGLISH TEXT

General Index